NATO ASI Series

Advanced Science Institutes Series

A series presenting the results of activities sponsored by the NATO Science Committee, which aims at the dissemination of advanced scientific and technological knowledge, with a view to strengthening links between scientific communities.

The Series is published by an international board of publishers in conjunction with the NATO Scientific Affairs Division

A Life Sciences **B Physics**	Plenum Publishing Corporation London and New York
C Mathematical and Physical Sciences **D Behavioural and Social Sciences** **E Applied Sciences**	Kluwer Academic Publishers Dordrecht, Boston and London
F Computer and Systems Sciences **G Ecological Sciences** **H Cell Biology** **I Global Environmental Change**	Springer-Verlag Berlin Heidelberg New York London Paris Tokyo Hong Kong Barcelona Budapest

NATO-PCO DATABASE

The electronic index to the NATO ASI Series provides full bibliographical references (with keywords and/or abstracts) to more than 30000 contributions from international scientists published in all sections of the NATO ASI Series. Access to the NATO-PCO DATABASE compiled by the NATO Publication Coordination Office is possible in two ways:

- via online FILE 128 (NATO-PCO DATABASE) hosted by ESRIN, Via Galileo Galilei, I-00044 Frascati, Italy.
- via CD-ROM "NATO-PCO DATABASE" with user-friendly retrieval software in English, French and German (© WTV GmbH and DATAWARE Technologies Inc. 1989).

The CD-ROM can be ordered through any member of the Board of Publishers or through NATO-PCO, Overijse, Belgium.

Series F: Computer and Systems Sciences Vol. 96

The ASI Series Books Published as a Result of Activities of the Special Programme on ADVANCED EDUCATIONAL TECHNOLOGY

This book contains the proceedings of a NATO Advanced Research Workshop held within the activities of the NATO Special Programme on Advanced Educational Technology, running from 1988 to 1993 under the auspices of the NATO Science Committee.

The books published so far as a result of the activities of the Special Programme are:

Vol. F 67: Designing Hypermedia for Learning. Edited by D. H. Jonassen and H. Mandl. 1990.

Vol. F 76: Multimedia Interface Design in Education. Edited by A. D. N. Edwards and S. Holland. 1992.

Vol. F 78: Integrating Advanced Technology into Technology Education. Edited by M. Hacker, A. Gordon, and M. de Vries. 1991.

Vol. F 80: Intelligent Tutoring Systems for Foreign Language Learning. The Bridge to International Communication. Edited by M. L Swartz and M. Yazdani. 1992.

Vol. F 81: Cognitive Tools for Learning. Edited by P.A.M. Kommers, D.H. Jonassen, and J.T. Mayes. 1992.

Vol. F 84: Computer-Based Learning Environments and Problem Solving. Edited by E. De Corte, M. C. Linn, H. Mandl, and L. Verschaffel. 1992.

Vol. F 85: Adaptive Learning Environments. Foundations and Frontiers. Edited by M. Jones and P. H. Winne. 1992.

Vol. F 86: Intelligent Learning Environments and Knowledge Acquisition in Physics. Edited by A. Tiberghien and H. Mandl. 1992.

Vol. F 87: Cognitive Modelling and Interactive Environments in Language Learning. Edited by F. L. Engel, D. G. Bouwhuis, T. Bösser, and G. d'Ydewalle. 1992.

Vol. F 89: Mathematical Problem Solving and New Information Technologies. Edited by J. P. Ponte, J. F. Matos, J. M. Matos, and D. Fernandes. 1992.

Vol. F 90: Collaborative Learning Through Computer Conferencing. Edited by A. R. Kaye. 1992.

Vol. F 91: New Directions for Intelligent Tutoring Systems. Edited by E. Costa. 1992.

Vol. F 92: Hypermedia Courseware: Structures of Communication and Intelligent Help. Edited by A. Oliveira. 1992.

Vol. F 93: Interactive Multimedia Learning Environments. Human Factors and Technical Considerations on Design Issues. Edited by M. Giardina. 1992.

Vol. F 95: Comprehensive System Design: A New Educational Technology. Edited by C. M. Reigeluth, B. H. Banathy, and J. R. Olson. 1992.

Vol. F 96: New Directions in Educational Technology. Edited by E. Scanlon and T. O'Shea. 1992.

Vol. F 97: Advanced Models of Cognition for Medical Training and Practice. Edited by D. A. Evans and V. L. Patel. 1992.

New Directions in Educational Technology

Edited by

Eileen Scanlon
Tim O'Shea

Institute of Educational Technology
The Open University
Walton Hall
Milton Keynes MK7 6AA, U. K.

Springer-Verlag
Berlin Heidelberg New York London Paris Tokyo
Hong Kong Barcelona Budapest
Published in cooperation with NATO Scientific Affairs Division

Proceedings of the NATO Advanced Research Workshop on New Directions in Advanced Educational Technology, held in Milton Keynes, UK, 10–13 November, 1988

CR Subject Classification (1991): K.3.1, K.4, I.2.1, I.2.6

Additional material to this book can be downloaded from http://extra.springer.com

ISBN-13:978-3-642-77752-3 e-ISBN-13:978-3-642-77750-9
DOI: 10.1007/978-3-642-77750-9

Library of Congress Cataloging-in-Publication Data New directions in educational technology / edited by Eileen Scanlon, Tim O'Shea p cm – (NATO ASI series. Series F, Computer and system sciences ; vol. 96) "Published in cooperation with NATO Scientific Affairs Division." Includes bibliographical references. ISBN-13:978-3-642-77752-3
1. Educational Technology. I. Scanlon, Eileen. II O'Shea, Tim, 1949- . III. North Atlantic Treaty Organization. Scientific Affairs Division. IV. Series NATO ASI series. Series F, Computer and system sciences ; vol. 96.
LB1028.3.N5544 1992 371.3'078–dc20 92-31544

Softcover reprint of the hardcover 1st edition 1992

Typesetting: Camera ready by authors
45/3140 - 5 4 3 2 1 0 - Printed on acid-free paper

Preface

This book is based on the workshop that kickstarted the NATO Science Committee Special Programme on Advanced Educational Technology. We invited the leaders in the field to attend this inaugural meeting and were delighted by the quality of the attendance, the papers delivered at the workshop and this book. Many of the authors have subsequently run other meetings funded by the Special Programme and have, or are in the process of, editing books which focus on particular topics. This book covers all the major themes in the area ranging from fundamental theoretical work to empirical studies of state of the art technological innovations. Tim O'Shea chaired the NATO Survey Group which planned the Programme and the subsequent Panel which disbursed funds in the first two years of the Programme. He would like to thank the other group and panel members, namely, Professor N Balacheff, Professor D Bjorner, Professor H Bouma, Professor P C Duchastel, Professor A Dias de Figueiredo, Dr D Jonassen and Professor T Liao. He would like to offer his special thanks to Dr L V da Cunha the NATO Programme Director for his unfailing support and patience. Eileen Scanlon was the Director of the Workshop which is the basis of this book. She offers heartfelt thanks to the contributors and to the following who provided practical help with the meeting or the production of this book: Mrs Pauline Adams, Dr Mike Baker, Mrs Kathy Evans, Mrs Patricia Roe, Mr Dave Perry and Ms Fiona Spensley.

Special thanks were due to Mrs Olwyn Wilson our Institute Secretary for help in planning the meeting and the control of financial systems. Finally we offer our thanks and admiration to Mr Dave Perry who has worked tirelessly and with great effect to ensure that the camera ready manuscript meets the publisher's guidelines and is an attractive text object.

July 1992

Eileen Scanlon
Tim O'Shea
Institute of Education Technology
Open University

Table of Contents

1 Instructional Systems Need Instructional Theory: Comments on a Truism 1
M. Jones

2 Toward a Design Science of Education 15
A. Collins

3 A Workbench for Discovering Task Specific Theories of Learning 23
K. VanLehn

4 Computers in Teaching and Learning: An Interpretation of Current Practices and Suggestions for Future Directions 33
D. L. Ferguson

5 New Directions for Educational Technology 51
C. M. Reigeluth

6 Formative Experiments on the Coevolution of Technology and the Educational Environment 61
D. Newman

7 Towards Intelligent Tutoring Systems that Teach Knowledge Rather than Skills: Five Research Questions 71
S. Ohlsson

8 The Present and Future of Intelligent Tutoring Systems 97
E. Costa

9 Intelligent Tutoring Systems: Navigating the Rocky Road to Success 107
G. I. McCalla

10 Designing Hypertext for Learning 123
D. H. Jonassen

11 A Prototype Futuristic Technology for Distance Education 131
R. B. Smith

12 Tools for Scientific Thinking: Learning Physical Concepts with Real-Time Laboratory Measurement Tools 139
R. K. Thornton

13 Constructing Student Knowledge in Science 153
R. F. Tinker, R. K. Thornton

14 Technology for All Pupils: An English School System Context 171
A.T. Gordon, G. Job

15 Research in Advanced Educational Technology: Two Methods 177
M. Vivet

16 Towards More Versatile Tutors for Programming 191
B. du Boulay

17 Problem Solving and Explanation in Intelligent Tutoring Systems: Issues for Future Research 199
B. J. Reiser

18 Mental Models and Understanding: A Problem for Science Education 211
J. R. Frederiksen, B. Y. White

19 A Microworld-Based Approach to Science Education 227
B.Y. White

Biographies 243

Subject Index 249

1

Instructional Systems Need Instructional Theory: Comments on a Truism

Marlene Jones
Advanced Technologies
Alberta Research Council
Calgary, Alberta, CANADA

Abstract: Developers of Artificial Intelligence (AI) -based instructional software have not yet paid a sufficient amount of attention to the instructional capabilities of such systems. In this paper, we briefly discuss candidate theories of instructional design with the goal of convincing the reader that there do exist instructional theories with which developers of AI-based instructional software should be familiar. We also investigate what additional information is required to supplement such theories, and suggest directions for future research and development.

Keywords: ACT*, cognitive diagnosis, cognitive processes, cognitive skills, component display theory, design theory, expert system, goal lattice, inquiry teaching, instructional design, instructional theory, intelligent computer-assisted instruction, intelligent tutoring Systems, ITS, knowledge elicitation techniques, learning hierarchies, learning outcome, motivation, PEDAGOGUE,routines, schemata, sequencing, sequencing strategy, snowball method, Structured Learning Theory, subject matter analysis, tacit knowledge, task analysis, think-aloud protocol

1. Introduction

Many a student has been frustrated by a professor who simply did not know how to teach. I recall a certain mathematics professor, immensely knowledgeable regarding the subject matter, but unable to alter his instructional strategies when faced with obvious failure; rather he continued to mutter into the blackboard, assuming that the students would eventually utter "eureka". Unfortunately, in North America, professors are typically expected to undertake the role of instructor with little instructional knowledge, let alone expertise. Are AI-based instructional systems suffering from the same shortcoming? Neither theories of knowing (expertise in subject matter) nor theories of learning (expertise regarding how learners acquire knowledge), "nor both together, provide a fully adequate foundation upon which to design effective AI courseware...." [47 p.5].

We have not yet paid a sufficient amount of attention to the instructional capabilities of instructional software. The literature of the past decade (for example, see [33 p.14]) has contained many criticisms of Computer-Assisted Instruction (CAI) and Computer-Based Training (CBT) systems, including such comments as:

— inability to alter the teaching strategy to meet a learner's needs
— inability to accept unanticipated responses, such as 'four' instead of '4'.

After a conference presentation in which Alan Lesgold had apparently made remarks similar to those above, David Merrill in the question period stated that he preferred the old-fashion CAI systems to the current AI-based instructional systems, such as Intelligent Tutoring Systems (ITSs) [30]. There is cause for alarm when a world-renowned instructional designer who is generally progressive towards the use of instructional software takes such a stand. The reason for Merrill's position: traditional CAI and CBT systems typically contain explicit, albeit shallow, representations of instructional goals and expertise. Such information is usually lacking within an ITS. The argument is perhaps best put forward by Lesgold himself:

> "Intelligent computer-assisted instruction attempts to represent all the knowledge that constitutes the expertise that is to be taught. Interestingly, though, it generally does not possess an explicit curriculum based on a theory of learning and instruction. Where conventional instruction has an explicit curriculum but fails to have an explicit and complete representation of the knowledge that is to be taught, intelligent instructional systems have tended to represent the target knowledge explicitly but not to represent explicitly that body of knowledge that specifies the goal structure for instruction, the curriculum." [21. p.117].

Instructional design represents a large and complex area of educational research. Embedded within this area is a wealth of information regarding how to design instruction from broad goals governing topic selection down to niggling details of what displays to present to the learner, under what conditions, what responses to anticipate, how to alter instruction to meet the learner's needs, etc. "Instructional design is concerned with understanding, improving, and applying methods of instruction. [It is a] process of deciding what methods of instruction are best for bringing about desired changes in student knowledge and skills for a specific course content and a specific student population." [35 p.7]. Given these goals, it would appear that this is just the knowledge that the developers of instructional software should be seeking. Yet, the AI/Education research community has not embraced instructional design theory for several reasons.

There is "a miscomprehension within the ITS community about the nature and extent of educational theory" [15 p.291]. There is uncertainty as to what instructional design theory can offer. Researchers within the area are, themselves, not in agreement, making it difficult for an outsider to decipher what is worth pursuing and what is not. As yet, there are no "off the shelf" models ready to be applied; rather developers must be encouraged to select what is relevant to their needs, possibly choosing aspects of several different theories. There are also common misconceptions regarding instructional design. For example, some researchers mistakenly believe that by explicitly stating objectives which a learner is expected to master, instruction is reduced to regurgitation of facts. This misconception can be dispelled by the fact that one can state objectives for high-level cognitive skills such as forming judgements, as well as for the affective and psycho-motor domains.

During the past decade, we have made substantial progress in many areas regarding the development of AI-based instructional systems: representation of domain knowledge, student modelling, diagnosis of misconceptions, interface design. It is time to increase our efforts with regard to the instructional component. We need to assess what instructional design, as well as other aspects of instructional research, can offer; determine what additional knowledge must still be gleaned; and undertake the necessary research and development projects. In this paper, we briefly discuss candidate theories of instructional design, what additional information is required to supplement such theories, and directions for future research and development.

2. Models of Instructional Design

Instructional design can be viewed as a process of developing a blueprint as to what the instruction should be like; it is a prescription as to what methods of instruction should be employed for that particular content and student. There are two issues here: what is to be included within the blueprint and the process by which the blueprint is developed. It is important to note the distinction between *instructional* theory (just discussed) and *learning* theory; the latter deals with conditions of learning, for which the designer would then need to develop methods of instruction. For an excellent overview of instructional design and the description of several such theories, the reader should consult [35]; for the application of such theories, see [37].

It is not our intent here to describe any of the various instructional theories in detail, but rather convince the reader that there do exist instructional theories with which a developer of instructional software should be familiar. The theories discussed herein have been selected because they deal with the cognitive domain, the territory of most instructional systems, and they provide some worthwhile guidelines that can be incorporated into a system's instructional component. For some of these theories, developers are already pursuing computational models based upon the theory.

2.1 Components of Instructional Design

The process of instructional design can be broken roughly into *selection* and *production*. The former includes the selection and sequencing of content. (Note we are not addressing issues of curriculum development here, which also concerns the tasks of selecting and sequencing content but in a broader setting; the interested reader should consult [43,42].) Production concerns developing a lesson plan to teach an idea, the specification as to how the content will be delivered. This division of selection vs delivery can also be adapted within an AI-based instructional system; see the recent work of Brecht [5]. Ohlsson also describes this separation between content and form as a principle for ITS development:

> "The Principle of Generative Inferences: In order to provide adaptive instruction, a tutor must distinguish between the subject matter and the formats in which it can be presented, and be able to generate different presentations of each subject matter unit as needed, at each moment in time choosing the form which is most beneficial for the learner at the moment." [32 p.217].

2.2 Selection and Sequencing of Content

Both Scandura's Structured Learning Theory (SLT) (see [39] and the references therein) and Landa's Algo-Heuristic Theory of Instruction (see [18] and the references therein) present techniques for selecting and sequencing content, and the theories possess certain similarities. In Scandura's theory, the selection process is implemented via rules; in Landa's via algorithms. Both decompose rules or algorithms into elementary constituents, termed *atomic components* or *elementary operations*, respectively. The first step is to determine the content to be taught; within SLT this requires a structural analysis of the content to determine what rules must be learned in order to master a set of lesson objectives. The rules are now the content to be taught and are refined into their atomic components. Where possible, rules are replaced by *higher-order rules* (in Landa's theory, *general algorithms* play a similar role). For each prescribed instructional objective, one is seeking a *path* of atomic components which satisfy that objective. One SLT sequencing strategy is that less complex paths are taught first in a lesson. In contrast to the similarity of Scandura's and Landa's two theories in regards to selection, the theories do differ with regard to sequencing strategies.

One sequencing strategy employed by Landa is the *snowball method*: when teaching a chain of cognitive operations, the first elementary operation is taught and practised alone, then the second is introduced, practised alone and then practised with the first, the third is now introduced, and so on. The snowball approach need not be applied solely in the context of Landa's theory. A system developer may choose to select particular sequencing strategies from either theory, rather than adopting whole-heartedly one particular theory.

Scandura claims that his instructional theory is particularly useful in designing individualized instruction, especially in a computer environment. Further, Stevens and Scandura claim [139 p.165] that the strength of SLT-based lessons is the precision of content selection and sequencing, and their match to learner needs. SLT appears to be particularly suited to the instruction of algorithmic tasks. It does involve a thorough analysis as to which paths each learner has and has not mastered, and then teaches only those paths that the learner has not mastered. In other words, it is tailored to the individual. The approach does, however, require a substantial amount of up-front analysis, as well as repeated assessment of the individual. Reigeluth raises a concern regarding the cost-effectiveness of this approach [35 p.215].

2.3 Delivery or Production of Instruction

Gagné's theory of instruction concerns both the selection of content and the delivery of instruction. For a discussion of task analysis, including analyzing tasks for prerequisites, refining objectives into enabling objectives, deriving external conditions of learning, the reader should consult [14 Ch. 13]. Gagné's theory of delivery or production of instruction centres around the notion of instructional events.

> "The province of an instructional theory is to propose a rationally based relationship between instructional events, their effects on learning processes, and the learning outcomes that are produced as a result of these processes." [14 p.244].

Gagné views learning as a set of internal processes which allow one to attend to, encode and respond to information in one's environment. He classifies candidate learning outcomes into five categories: intellectual skills, cognitive strategies, verbal information, attitudes, and motor skills. For each type of learning outcome, Gagné posits different instructional events. In [14 Ch. 12], he outlines a typical sequence of nine internal processes of learning and the corresponding instructional events. For example, given the internal process "expectancy" the corresponding instructional event is "informing learners of the objective". The internal process "retrieval to working memory" has the corresponding instructional event "stimulating recall of prior learning". For each instructional event, the model provides different instructional techniques for each of the five possible learning outcomes. For example, if the instructional event is "inform the learner of the objective" and the learning outcome is "verbal information" the suggested instructional technique is "describe what the learner will be expected to state"; if the learning outcome is "motor skill" the suggested technique is "demonstrate the expected performance" Gagné's model of instruction can be employed as a guiding framework; it alone does not, however, provide a sufficient amount of detail. For example, if an instructional technique is "recall prerequisite rules and concepts" the designer must still determine whether a verbal reminder suffices, whether review exercises are necessary, etc.

Unlike Gagné's theory, Merrill's Component Display Theory (CDT) is quite specific, providing details that are lacking in other theories (see [26,29] and the references therein). The theory is, however, quite restricted addressing only the cognitive domain and solely the micro level of instruction: teaching of a single idea.

"CDT attempts to indicate what set of method components... is most likely to optimize achievement of the desired outcomes under the specified conditions" [35 p.281].

The term *display* is used to mean all information needed to present an idea. Merrill claims there are, in fact, only a few primitive displays, and that every cognitive presentation is a sequence of displays. As indicated above, the theory is based upon the belief that there is a correlation between the content to be taught and suitable sequences of displays. Factors taken into account within CDT are the type of content (fact, concept, procedure, principle) and the desired level of performance (remember, use, find). Based upon limited information such as this, CDT provides a read-the-chart approach to developing an appropriately written objective, and information regarding presentation forms (initial presentation, practice and performance/evaluation). For example if the learner is expected to use a concept, it is important that two or more examples initially be presented to the learner, and that the learner practice on new examples or generalities. Similarly, in order to evaluate whether the learner has mastered the concept, previous examples cannot be employed as test items. This is only a simple example of principles that one can apply from CDT. The theory also supplies guidelines regarding the development of appropriate test items and testing conditions. Although overall it is very appealing, one frustration with CDT is the cryptic notation.

It is important to note that Merrill's theory is still evolving [28,29]. Recently Merrill has been extending CDT so that it is more appropriate for handling interactive instruction, as required within instructional systems. Consequently, he has been concentrating on the use of *transactions* rather than displays, and has extended content types to content structures. This recent work has also included the development of a set of "cardinal" principles of instruction; for example, the Cognitive Structure Principle states that "The purpose of instruction is to promote the development of that cognitive structure which is most consistent with the desired learned performance." [28 p.24]. It is important to note that Merrill's instructional theory is not in juxtaposition to Gagné's, but rather incorporates and extends much of Gagné's work.

2.4 Other Instructional Issues

There are other aspects of instruction which must be addressed within any instructional environment, computer-based or otherwise; a few examples are systematic review (see Reigeluth-Merrill's Elaboration Theory [36]), motivation (see [17] [1] and the references therein), cueing the learner [47], and selection of media or presentation form [14 Ch. 14. 26].

As can be concluded from the above descriptions of the various theories, they are not "off the shelf" models that can instantly be applied within a computational setting. They are, for the most part, valuable frameworks, some providing more detail than others. There is nothing to prevent an instructor or developer from mixing and matching theories or models to meet the needs of the instructional environment at hand. Current instructional theories do not provide all the necessary answers. Although the theories discussed herein are applicable to the development of instructional systems, for the most part, instructional designers have not yet specified their theories at a sufficient level of detail for use within an ITS. For an excellent discussion of issues such as this and directions for future research, see the chapter by Reigeluth in this volume.

3. Other Sources of Instructional Knowledge

Theories of instructional design do not suffice; they must be supplemented with knowledge from other sources, such as studies concerning the implementation and evaluation of instruction. The knowledge of human experts, including experienced teachers, must be tapped. Consider the development of an expert system to do oil-well analysis; although there exist models upon which the system can be based, the models are not sufficiently detailed to map out all situations, possible variations, etc. Input from human experts is also required. The task of developing an instructional system is no less complicated. Instruction is a complex domain, in which it is difficult to determine the relevant factors, let alone assess them.

Elicitation of the expertise needed for the development of an expert system is recognized to be a difficult task. Goodyear [15] provides an excellent discussion of the difficulties of eliciting knowledge from teachers. In particular, asking the instructor to verbalize what he/she is doing, introduces justification information; the instructor feels compelled to justify his/her actions to the observer. Goodyear also points out that concurrent verbalization methods will not be able to access procedural or tacit knowledge. He concludes that:

> "The consequence for data collecting methods is simply that we must supplement the elicitation and analysis of think-aloud protocols with observation and analysis of action. ... We need to develop techniques more suited to a cognitive mediational than a behavioural model of teachers' action-techniques which enable the linking of observational data to data derived from verbal protocols." [15 p.295].

Of course, we are not the only group of developers who encounter these difficulties; it is pervasive throughout expert system development. For discussions of candidate knowledge elicitation techniques, see [3,4,44].

3.1 Learning From Instructors

Although elicitation from instructors is difficult, there have been some excellent studies in this regard, providing developers with further insight. It is not our intent to provide a comprehensive survey nor a detailed analysis of such studies here. Rather we intend to highlight the type of results gleaned from such research and later suggest what additional research is required. Goodyear [15] provides a succinct discussion of relevant studies; a slightly more detailed survey is contained in [5]. Relevant work includes that of Collins and Stevens [41], Douglas [13], Leinhardt and Greeno [19], Littman and Soloway [22], Littman, Pinto and Soloway [23,24], McKendree, Reiser and Anderson [25], Ohlsson [32], Woolf and McDonald [51], among others.

Much of this work concerns specialized experiments focussing on restricted aspects of tutoring, typically within narrow domains of expertise (such as tutoring LISP or PASCAL programming). Via these studies, researchers hope to capture the fine-grained detail, which is typically lacking within instructional models. The work of Littman, Pinto and Soloway can be employed as an illustration here.

In their 1985 study, Littman, Pinto and Soloway analyzed the techniques of experienced tutors within the context of introductory PASCAL programming classes. They assessed the priorities employed by the tutors; for example, did the tutor concentrate on fixing mistakes within the student's program or did the tutor attempt to clear up the underlying causes of the mistakes. Littman, Pinto and Soloway examined why the tutors grouped certain bugs together and concluded that grouping appears to be related to the tutor's process of constructing an explanation for why the bugs occurred. More recent work of Littman, Pinto and Soloway [24] has extended these finding; they have identified five considerations (criticality, bug category, cause, tutorial goals, tutorial interventions) that tutors employ when assessing appropriate interventions for students' programming bugs. Moreover, their data indicates that tutors are consistent in the use of particular knowledge in order to reason about the five considerations.

It would be incorrect to assume that the human tutor, even an expert tutor, is infallible. In fact, Douglas [13] concludes that human tutors spend approximately 20% of their time repairing their tutoring failures. Douglas examined the interaction between human tutors and their students within the context of teaching a second (natural) language. Her observations highlight the complex process of interaction failure and subsequent repair. Tutor performance failure includes both *slips* which are unintended actions and *bugs*, the remaining failures which result from failure in formation of intention. Bugs include the failure to diagnose properly the student's knowledge and hence selecting an inappropriate instructional goal, selection of an inappropriate teaching strategy, misjudging the difficulty of the curricular content, sequencing the content in an inappropriate manner, and a failure to coordinate what is said with the current context. Although certain types of tutoring failures can be reduced by employing an ITS, others, termed *model failures*, are an inherent part of the teaching of complex knowledge.

Douglas' study of the mechanisms of failure detection and repair that are employed by human tutors provides some illuminating information for developers of ITSs.

Much of the research concerning studies of human teachers has resulted in sets of heuristics for tutoring within specific domains and for a restricted set of tasks. In some cases, it is reasonable to believe that these results can be generalized to tutoring within a broader context. Alternatively, some of the aforementioned research, particularly that of Collins and Stevens [11] and Leinhardt and Greeno [19], has tried to address a somewhat broader context.

Through a variety of studies, Collins and Stevens' have analyzed the goals and strategies employed by human teachers. Based upon their findings, Collins and Stevens [12] have developed a particular instructional theory concerning inquiry teaching, which is particularly suited to the instruction of experimental science reasoning skills. The theory consists of the instructor's goals, strategies by which to realize the goals, and a control structure for selecting and pursuing different goals. A candidate goal might be "teach a general rule or theory" Possible techniques or strategies by which to realize the various goals include: selecting positive and negative models or examples, varying cases systematically, selecting counter-examples, generating hypothetical cases, etc. Given a set of top-level goals, the teacher selects cases that optimize the ability of the student to master those goals. Collins and Stevens identify a few overall strategies that instructors apply when selecting cases. Two such strategies are: select cases that illustrate more important factors before less important factors; select cases to move from concrete to abstract factors. Like Scandura's theory of instruction, Collins and Stevens' theory calls for the selection and sequencing of content based upon a learner's current misconceptions.

Leinhardt and Greeno [19] examined the instruction of elementary mathematics with the ambitious goal of understanding the skill of successful teachers. Based upon their studies of both expert and novice teachers, they have developed a formal model of the process of instruction in elementary mathematics.

It is Leinhardt and Greeno's belief that teaching is a complex cognitive skill and hence amenable to analysis in a manner similar to other cognitive skills. They purport that teaching skill rests on two fundamental knowledge systems: lesson structures and subject matter. They propose that a skilled teacher has a complex knowledge structure composed of inter-related sets of organized actions, termed *schemata*, which are applied with little cognitive effort within the classroom context. Skilled teachers also possess a large repertoire of activities, termed *routines*, that they perform fluently. These routines have simple, transparent objectives such as: increase the amount of time that students are directly engaged in learning or practising mathematics; to reduce the cognitive load for the instructor; to establish a frame that permits easy transmission of information in mutually known and recognized settings. A major difference between the expert and novice teachers was in the experts' use of well-practised routines. Leinhardt and Greeno's observations highlighted that both instructors and students benefited significantly by the use of familiar routines. Such routines allow students to concentrate on the content of the lesson rather than interpretation of the instructions, and instructors on the progress of the students. For additional discussion regarding the instructional use of routines, as well as further differences between expert and novice teachers, the reader should consult [19,20] and the references therein.

Inspired by Leinhardt and Greeno's analysis of the skill of teaching, Ohlsson [32] reflected upon what teaching tactics and strategies are needed by a tutor, human or computer, in order to provide instruction which is adaptive to the learner. Ohlsson claims that the main promise of computer tutors "lies in their potential for moment-by-moment adaptation of instructional content and form to the changing cognitive needs of the individual learner, and our task, as I see it, is to find principles which can guide the construction of tutors which fulfil that promise." [32 p.204]. In an attempt to determine these underlying principles, Ohlsson examines the areas of cognitive diagnosis and subject matter analysis, as well as teaching tactics and strategies.

With regard to teaching tactics, Ohlsson breaks these into six categories: tactics for presenting the target procedure, tactics for presenting precursors, tactics for presenting purposes, tactics for presenting justifications, tactics related to errors, and tactics related to student's solutions. Within tactics for presenting the target procedure, the possibilities include: defining necessary terms in order to discuss the procedure, describing the procedure, prompting recall, demonstrating the procedure, applying the procedure, and practising the procedure. Candidate tactics for presenting precursors are priming, in which the tutor reminds the student of the precursor such as by naming it, reviewing the precursor, and marking those steps in a presentation with which the student should be familiar. Ohlsson's teaching tactics are similar to the instructional events proposed within Gagné's theory of instruction. Ohlsson does not address the circumstances under which each tactic is most appropriately applied, nor does he claim that the included tactics are anything more than an initial attempt to list the various actions needed in the repertoire of an intelligent tutor.

Ohlsson's tactics and principles are best interpreted as a guiding framework, rather than an operational model. To illustrate the nature of the included principles, consider the previously stated Principle of Generative Interfaces, as well as the following:

> "The Principle of Versatile Output. In order to provide adaptive instruction, a tutor must have a wide range of instructional actions to choose from" [32 p.220].

> "The Principle of Teaching Plans. A tutor needs to be able to generate a teaching plan on the basis of its representation of the student, its knowledge of the subject matter, and its current tutorial goal; furthermore, it should be able [to] revise its plan if it discovers that the plan does not fit the student." [32 p.232].

Although Ohlsson has generally restricted his attention to the teaching of cognitive skills, such as skills within elementary mathematics, he has tackled a broader range of instruction than most of the other studies cited earlier within this section. He has also taken the important step of pulling together several different strands of research, most notably cognitive psychology and ITS.

3.2 Additional Studies and Aids Required

Studying the instructional behaviour of teachers is not sufficient. As noted earlier, Goodyear [15] raised concerns regarding the ability to tap procedural or tacit knowledge. This concern stems from the work of Calderhead [8] and others.

> "In a Primary (elementary) school classroom a teacher will typically engage in 200 to 300 distinguishable interactions per hour (8 11). In this time they are unlikely to make more than six teaching decisions, in the sense of considered choices between alternative courses of action." [15 p.295].

Instructors' plans also significantly influence both student's participation and learning during instruction [10], and hence need to be examined. Based upon Clark and Peterson's data, Winne concludes that:

> "Topics that a teacher considers in planning for lessons do not consume the teacher's attention during teaching. Topics that a teacher ignores in planning require frequent attention during teaching" [48 p.4].

In addition to the information gleaned from studies of experienced teachers, it is possible to gain insight through studies of less effective instructors such as novice teachers; for example, see [19]. Based upon such studies, it would be helpful to develop a set of heuristics regarding what not to do under certain conditions.

The role of the student in the learning process cannot be understated. Recent research has demonstrated the importance of the learner's cognitive processing; for example, see [34,47]. Cognitive processes are unobservable mental actions used to manipulate information. Possible examples within the context of instruction are reciting the conjugation of an irregular French verb over and over to oneself, or relating two concepts to one another. A student's cognitive processing is not simply a response to events within the instructional environment, nor is it a complete internal determinant of a student's performance. It is important to realize that during the learning process, students cannot be passive recipients of teaching; hence, an instructor's behaviour is not the sole factor in determining the student's achievements.

> "Teachers need information about students' cognitive mediations of instruction to design instructional environments which optimize students' cognitive participation in learning from teaching." [48 p.11].

There exist models of cognitive processing which provide some insight: Gagné's nine internal processes [14 Ch. 12], Winne's five primitive processes (SMART) [46,47], and Anderson's ACT* (Adaptive Control of Thought) [2]. The five fundamental cognitive processes identified by Winne are: stimulating (S) or activating, the involuntary process that transfers information dormant in long-term memory to an active state in working memory; monitoring (M), a process of determining the match between a prototype of information and the current nature of information; assembling or associating (A), taking two currently unconnected items of information and joining them; rehearsing (R); translating (T), taking information in one form and outputting the same information but in a different code. Students apply these fundamental cognitive processes to concepts, propositions, etc., as guided by the student's individual *plan* for accomplishing the task at hand. How students apply these processes accounts for variations in their performances.

Van Lehn, in the chapter in this volume on "Task-Specific Theories of Learning" raises a concern regarding cognitive theories which attempt to be universal. He points out that such theories are limited because they do not account for the fact that cognitive behaviours are at least partially determined by one's current knowledge and one's environment. For example, students, when faced with an impasse due to incomplete or mistaken knowledge, solve the dilemma in different ways; they invoke different plans. This leads Van Lehn to consider means of generating domain-specific theories.

As with models of instructional design, there is a need to supplement models of cognitive processing with information drawn from studies of learners. For example, evidence from various studies demonstrates that it is advantageous if an instructor assists a student in choosing, adapting and executing plans [6,46,47]. One means of doing so is by providing appropriate instructional cues regarding the instructional goal to be achieved, and about how curricular information can be cognitively processed to reach this goal. There is evidence that information in instructional cues enables students to learn the curriculum more effectively and efficiently than if the instructional cues were absent; for example, see [34,40].

It is only recently that researchers have begun to explore students' cognitive processing during teaching and to describe the ways in which their cognitive processing relates to what they learn. It is important that we study the cognitive processes of the learner, not just for short durations, but throughout lengthy learning activities. The strategies employed by a learner during the initial few minutes of a task may differ from those employed after an extended amount of on-task time. For a discussion of one such study by Chi and colleagues [9], see Van Lehn's chapter on "Task-Specific Theories of Learning".

> "Theories of instruction must step beyond description to prescribe how instruction should unfold in order to meet pre-specified objectives (7). Thus, one recommendation for designing AI courseware is this: Operationalize a theory of instruction which extends theories of knowing and theories of learning:
>
> (1) in order to account for the interactive participation of instructor and learner and
>
> (2) to prescribe how that interaction would unfold so that instruction is effective."

[47 p.5].

Existing theories of instructional design are appropriate starting points; however, they alone do not suffice.

4. What Has Been Achieved

Several of the instructional design models discussed earlier are, in fact, the bases of implementations. Instructional systems have been developed based upon Scandura's SLT (for example, see the references in [39]). One project particularly worthy of note is the expert system being developed based upon Merrill's CDT [27,31]. The Instructional System Design (ISD) Expert assists with instructional design decisions, excluding the front-end task analysis, and culminates in a set of specifications upon which implementation can then be based. One criticism of the initial prototype was the extent of the proposed dialogues by which the expert system would elicit the necessary knowledge from the developer [50]. However, in a second implementation, using Nexpert and HyperCard on a Macintosh, some of the overwhelming detail exhibited within the first has disappeared. Merrill is also developing a simple authoring tool that takes the specifications produced by ISD Expert and develops a corresponding lesson. In the process of creating a lesson, the authoring system can seek additional input from the user, although it already knows the concepts to be taught and certain attributes thereof. The current domain of operation is extremely limited; the system can generate only one type of lesson, with corresponding restrictions on screen layout and menus. Nevertheless, this research represents a step in the right direction. Two other relevant projects are the Instructional Design Environment (IDE) which is a framework for specification of instructional design decisions [38] and "Expert" CML which includes environments for curriculum and course development [50]. All three of these projects represent instructional knowledge, to varying degrees, and hence have implications for developers of ITSs.

In a recent paper, Lesgold [21] tackles the issue of what knowledge must be represented within an ITS. In particular, he is concerned with representing the goal structure of instruction, *the curriculum*, or as he aptly describes it, *the glue* which connects the content of related lessons. Hence, he proposes an architecture for ITSs that represents both content and curriculum. Lesgold suggests there are, in fact, three types of knowledge that an intelligent tutor must possess: the knowledge to be taught, the curriculum knowledge, and various meta-issues. Embedded within the knowledge layer, termed the *goal lattice*, are a number of goal hierarchies, each corresponding to a viewpoint of teaching the course content. The second layer, the curriculum knowledge, is a subgoal lattice of lessons which are connected by prerequisite relations. Each subgoal can either be viewed as a single unit, i.e. a lesson, or it can be further refined into sub-subgoals. The subgoal lattice is in fact a means of representing what Gagné termed *learning hierarchies*. The third layer is a representation of certain student characteristics to which instruction should be sensitive; candidate characteristics are aptitude, reading ability, and verbal facility. Whether Lesgold's framework is sufficient to incorporate the various issues we have discussed herein is yet to be determined; although the work is preliminary, it represents a step towards addressing the lack of representation of instructional knowledge within current ITS architectures.

Progress is also being made in another direction. Due to accumulating evidence that teachers, particularly novice teachers, are inadequately prepared, Winne launched an ambitious project called DOCENT. His goal is to make instructional expertise available to instructors, and ultimately instructional systems, in a digestible format [49]. DOCENT's main components are SYLLABUS, PEDAGOGUE, and PLANNER. SYLLABUS is charged with the selection and sequencing tasks; PEDAGOGUE is a model of reasoning about instruction, and PLANNER is responsible for developing plans for teaching and evaluating them in a hypothetical instructional world. To accomplish all this, DOCENT accesses several knowledge bases: LIBRARY (published research studies about instruction and experienced teachers), INSTRUCTIONAL EFFECTS (information regarding discrepancies between plans and actual classroom events), STUDENT (data regarding students' accumulating achievements and information regarding their actual participation in lessons), CONTENT KNOWLEDGE (curricular information), and PLANS (a repository for information derived from research on teaching such as lesson agendas). DOCENT is an enormous undertaking; the LIBRARY alone represents an immense but needed contribution.

4.1 Summary Remarks

There has been some excellent work undertaken by researchers within the AI/Education community in an attempt to tap the expertise of accomplished teachers. There is a strong need to continue with such studies as a means of fleshing out the frameworks provided by instructional design researchers. Such studies need to be systematically undertaken, perhaps employing Goodyear's expertise model as a means of selecting participants [15], and initially restricted to certain types of instructional strategies. The difficulties with regard to knowledge elicitation must be addressed; a variety of techniques are required to tap the required expertise. At the same time, a more concerted effort must be made to learn from the studies already undertaken by education researchers. In particular, additional information is required with regard to the impact of instructors' plans, students' cognitive processes, and motivational issues, and how to exploit these factors to advantage within an AI-based instructional system. A means of cataloguing the information accumulated from various studies is required; hence, the appeal of a project such as DOCENT. We must continue our efforts to develop working prototypes based upon this accumulated information; this entails the iterative development of models and implementations in a variety of problem-solving domains.

Acknowledgements

Financial support from both the Natural Sciences and Engineering Research Council of Canada and the Alberta Research Council is gratefully acknowledged. I would like to thank Julia Driver, Jim Greer and Kevin Wipond for their comments on an earlier draft of this paper, and Phil Winne for several interesting discussions.

References

1. Ames, R., and Ames, C., (eds), *Research on Motivation,* Vol. 3, New York: Academic Press, 1988.
2. Anderson, J.R., *The Architecture of Cognition,* Cambridge: Harvard University Press, 1983.
3. Boose, J., *Expertise Transfer for Expert System Design,* Elsevier, 1986.
4. Boose, J., and Gaines, B., (eds), *Proceedings of the 2nd AAAI Workshop on Knowledge Acquisition for Knowledge-Based Systems,* Banff, 1987.
5. Brecht, B., *Deciding What Needs to be Said: Instructional Planning for Intelligent Tutoring* Technical Report 88-6, ARIES Laboratory, Dept. of Computational Science, University of Saskatchewan, 1988.
6. Brown, A.L., Knowing When, Where, and How to Remember: A Problem of Metacognition in: R. Glaser, (ed), *Advanced in Instructional Psychology,* Vol. 1, Lawrence Erlbaum Associates, Hillsdale, NJ, 1978.
7. Bruner, J.S., *Toward a Theory of Instruction,* W.W. Norton, New York, NY, 1966.
8. Calderhead, J., *Teachers' Classroom Decision Making,* Holt, London, 1984.
9. Chi, M.T.H., Bassok, M., Lewis, M., Reimann, P., and Glaser, R., Learning Problem Solving Skills from Studying Examples *Cognitive Science,* 13, p.145-182 1989.
10. Clark, and Peterson, Teachers' Thought Processes. in: M.C. Wittrock (ed), *Handbook of Research on Teaching,* 3rd edition, Macmillan, New York, p.255-296, 1986.
11. Collins, A., and Stevens, A.L., Goals and Strategies of Enquiry Teachers. in: R. Glaser (ed), *Advances in Instructional Psychology,* Vol. 2, Lawrence Erlbaum Associates, Hillsdale, NJ, p.65-119, 1982.
12. Collins, A., and Stevens, A.L., A Cognitive Theory of Inquiry Teaching. in: C.M. Reigeluth (ed), *Instructional Design Theories and Models: An Overview of their Current Status,* Lawrence Erlbaum Associates, Hillsdale, NJ, p.247-278, 1983.
13. Douglas, S.A., Detecting and Repairing Tutoring Failures, Technical Report CIS-TR-88-09, Dept. of Computer and Information Science, University of Oregon, 1988.

14. Gagné, R.M., *The Conditions of Learning and Theory of Instruction*, 4th edition, Holt, Rinehart and Winston, New York, NY, 1985.
15. Goodyear, P., Approaches to the Empirical Derivation of Teaching Knowledge for Intelligent Tutoring Systems. *Proceedings of Intelligent Tutoring Systems (ITS-88)*, Montreal, p.291-298, 1988.
16. Jones, M., and Wipond, K., *Intelligent Environments for Curriculum and Course Development.* (in press).
17. Keller, J.M., Motivational Design of Instruction. in: C.M. Reigeluth (ed), *Instructional-Design Theories and Models: An Overview of their Current Status,* Lawrence Erlbaum Associates, Hillsdale, NJ, p.383-434, 1983.
18. Landa, L.N., Descriptive and Prescriptive Theories of Learning and Instruction: An Analysis of Their Relationships and Interactions. in: C.M. Reigeluth (ed), *Instructional-Design Theories and Models: An Overview of their Current Status,* Lawrence Erlbaum Associates, Hillsdale, NJ, p.163-211, 1983.
19. Leinhardt, G., and Greeno, J.G., The Cognitive Skill of Teaching. *Journal of Educational Psychology,* Vol. 78. No. 2, p.75-79, 1986.
20. Leinhardt, G., and Weidman, C., and Hammond, K.M., Introduction and Integration of Classroom Routines by Expert Teachers. *Curriculum Inquiry*, Vol. 17, No. 2, p.135-176, 1987.
21. Lesgold, A., Toward a Theory of Curriculum for Use in Designing Intelligent Instructional Systems. in: H. Mandl and A. Lesgold (eds), *Learning Issues for Intelligent Tutoring Systems,* Springer-Verlag, p.114-137, 1988.
22. Littman, D., and Soloway, E., Toward an Empirically-Based Process Model for a Machine Programming Tutor. *Proceedings of the IEEE International Conference on Systems, Man and Cybernetics,* Atlanta, 1986.
23. Littman, D., Pinto, J., and Soloway, E., Observations on Tutorial Expertise. *Proceedings of IEEE Conference on Expert Systems in Government,* Washington D.C., 1985.
24. Littman, D., Pinto, J., and Soloway, E., An Analysis of Tutorial Reasoning about Programming Bugs. *Proceedings of the Annual Conference of the American Association for Artificial Intelligence (AAAI)-86,* Philadelphia, p.320-326, 1986.
25. McKendree, J., Reiser, B., and Anderson, J., Tutorial Goals and Strategies in the Instruction of Programming Skills. *Proceedings of the Sixth Annual Conference of the Cognitive Society,* p.252-254, 1984.
26. Merrill, D., Component Display Theory. in: C.M. Reigeluth (ed), *Instructional Design Theories and Models: An Overview of their Current Status,* Lawrence Erlbaum Associates, Hillsdale, NJ, p.279-333, 1983.
27. Merrill, D., An Expert System for Instructional Design. *IEEE Expert*, Vol. 2 No. 2, p.25-37, 1987a.
28. Merrill, D., The New Component Design Theory: Instructional Design for Courseware Authoring. *Instructional Science,* Vol. 16, p.19-34, 1987b.
29. Merrill, D., *Micro-level Design Strategies and Expert Systems as Instructional Design Tools*. Symposium on Instruction, Canadian Centre for Learning Systems, Calgary, 1988a.
30. Merrill, D., *Personal Communication,* 1988b.
31. Merrill, D., and Li, Z., An Instructional Design Expert System, manuscript in course notes: *Micro-level Design Strategies and Expert Systems as Instructional Design Tools* Symposium on Instruction, Canadian Centre for Learning Systems, Calgary, 1988.
32. Ohlsson, S., Some Principles for Intelligent Tutoring. in: R. Lawler and M. Yazdani (eds), *AI and Education: Learning Environments and Intelligent Tutoring Systems.,* Ablex Publishing, NJ, p.203-237, 1987.
33. O'Shea, T., *Self-Improving Teaching Systems,* Birkhauser Verlag, Basel, 1979.

34. Peterson, P.L., and Swing, S.R., Beyond Time on Task: Students' Reports of Their Thought Processes During Direct Instruction. *Elementary School Journal,* Vol. 82, p.481-491, 1982.
35. Reigeluth, C.M. (ed), *Instructional Design Theories and Models: An Overview of their Current Status,* Lawrence Erlbaum Associates, Hillsdale, NJ, 1983.
36. Reigeluth, C.M., and Stein, F.E., The Elaboration Theory of Instruction. in: C.M. Reigeluth (ed), *Instructional Design Theories and Models: An Overview of their Current Status,* Lawrence Erlbaum Associates, Hillsdale, NJ, p.335-381, 1983.
37. Reigeluth, C.M. (ed), *Instructional Theories in Action: Lessons Illustrating Selected Theories and Models,* Lawrence Erlbaum Associates, Hillsdale, NJ, 1987.
38. Russell, D.M., Moran, T.P., and Jordan, D.S., The Instructional Design Environment. in: J. Psotka, L.D. Massey and S.A. Mutter (eds), *Intelligent Tutoring Systems: Lessons Learned,* Lawrence Erlbaum Associates, Hillsdale, NJ, 1988.
39. Scandura, J.M., Instructional Strategies Based on the Structural Learning Theory. in: C.M. Reigeluth (ed), *Instructional Theories in Action: Lessons Illustrating Selected Theories and Models,* Lawrence Erlbaum Associates, Hillsdale, NJ, p.213-246, 1987.
40. Stayrook, N.G., Corno, L., Winne P.H., Path Analyses Relating Student Perceptions of Teacher Behavior to Student Achievement. *Journal of Teacher Education,* Vol. 24, No. 2, p.51, 1978.
41. Stevens, G.H., and Scandura, J.M., A Lesson Design Based on Instructional Prescriptions from the Structural Learning Theory. in: C.M. Reigeluth (ed), *Instructional Theories in Action: Lessons Illustrating Selected Theories and Models,* Lawrence Erlbaum Associates, Hillsdale, NJ, p.161-199, 1987.
42. Tanner, D., and Tanner, L., *Curriculum Development: Theory into Practice,* Macmillan, New York, NY, 1975.
43. Tyler, R.W., *Basic Principles of Curriculum and Instruction,* University of Chicago Press, Chicago, IL, 1949.
44. Welbank, M., *A Review of Knowledge Acquisition Techniques for Expert Systems.* Technical Report, British Telecom Research Laboratories, 1983.
45. Winne, P.H., Steps Toward Promoting Cognitive Achievements. *Elementary School Journal,* Vol. 85, p.673-693, 1985a.
46. Winne, P.H., Cognitive Processing in the Classroom. in: T. Husen and T.N. Postlethwaite (eds), *International Encyclopaedia of Education,* Pergamon, Oxford, p.795-808, 1985b.
47. Winne, P.H., *Theories of Instruction and of Intelligence for Designing Artificially Intelligent Courseware.* manuscript, 1988a.
48. Winne, P.H., *Project DOCENT-Phase II: Artificially Intelligent Systems for Teaching and Learning.* manuscript, 1988b.
49. Winne, P.H., and Kramer, L.L, Representing and Inferencing with Knowledge About Teaching: DOCENT - An Artificially Intelligent Planning System for Teachers. *Proceedings of Intelligent Tutoring Systems (ITS-88),* Montreal, p.7-15, 1988.
50. Wipond, K., and Jones, M., Curriculum and Knowledge Representation in a Knowledge-Based System for Curriculum Development. *Proceedings of Intelligent Tutoring Systems (ITS-88),* Montreal, p.97-102, 1988.
51. Woolf, B., and McDonald, D.D., Context Dependent Transitions in Tutoring Discourse. *Proceedings of the Annual Conference of the American Association for Artificial Intelligence (AAAI-84),* Austin, p.61-73, 1984.

2

Toward a Design Science of Education

Allan Collins
Bolt, Beranek & Newman Inc, Boston, Ma, U.S.A.

Abstract: We have had many technologies introduced in classrooms all over the world, but these innovations have provided remarkably little systematic knowledge or accumulated wisdom to guide the development of future innovations. Bolt, Beranek & Newman (BBN) Inc. is part of the new Center for Technology in Education located at Bank Street College in New York. A major goal of the Center is to synthesize research on technological innovation, to develop a methodology for carrying out *design experiments,* to study different ways of using technology in classrooms and schools, and to begin to construct a systematic science of how to design educational environments so that new technologies can be introduced successfully.

Historically, some of the best minds in the world have addressed themselves to education; for example, Plato, Rousseau, Dewey, Bruner and Illich. But they have addressed education essentially as theorists, even where they have tried to design schools or curricula to implement their ideas. What is different today is that some of the best minds in the world are addressing themselves to education as experimentalists: their goal is to compare different designs to see what affects what. Technology provides us with powerful tools to try out different designs, so that instead of theories of education, we may begin to develop a science of education. But it cannot be an analytic science like physics or psychology; rather it must be a design science more like aeronautics or artificial intelligence. For example, in aeronautics the goal is to elucidate how different designs contribute to lift, drag, manoeuvrability, etc.. Similarly, a design science of education must determine how different designs of learning environments contribute to learning, cooperation, motivation, etc.

There are, however, major problems with the kind of design experiments currently carried out that prevent our gaining much information from them. Typically the experiments are carried out by the people who designed some technological innovation, and so they have a vested interest in seeing that it works. They typically look only for significant effects (which can be very small effects) and test only one design, rather than trying to compare the size of effects for different designs or innovations. Furthermore, such experiments are so variable in their design and implementation that it is difficult to draw conclusions about the design process by comparing different experiments. Finally they are carried out without any underlying theory, and so the results are, for the most part, uninterpretable with respect to constructing a design theory of technology innovation in education. While we plan to look at past experiments in detail, we think only very limited conclusions can be drawn from them.

Our goal then will be to construct a more systematic methodology for conducting design experiments, and ultimately to develop a design theory to guide implementation of future innovations. The kind of methodology we anticipate will involve working with teachers as co-investigators to compare multiple innovations (different media and software) at one site with no vested interest in the outcome. The design theory we envision will identify all the different variables that affect the success or failure of any innovation, and will specify critical values and combinations of values with respect to the different variables. This paper will elaborate on these two goals of our work.

Keywords: design experiments, design theory, evaluation, methodology, multiple innovations

1. Methodology for Design Experiments

We will describe our initial ideas about a methodology for carrying out design experiments, but we expect to refine the methodology during the first years of the project. One difficulty is that there is a huge space of possible designs one might try out in schools. Therefore, a major goal of such a methodology must be to systematically explore the space of designs in relatively few experiments, so that one can extrapolate into the regions of the space that cannot be tested directly. At the same time there are a large number of constraints deriving from the school setting and the capabilities of administrators, teachers, and students to deal with new technologies, that limits our ability to try out different designs. So the goal must be to maximize the information gained within the limitations of any particular experiment.

There are several desiderata we think are critical in developing such a methodology:

1.1 Teachers as co-investigators

Any experiments must work within the constraints that the teachers involved think are necessary to be successful, and at the same time must address questions that the teachers would like answered. Hence it is absolutely critical that teachers take on the role of co-investigators helping to formulate the questions to be addressed and the designs to be tested, making refinements in the designs as the experiment progresses, evaluating the effects of the different aspects of the experiment, and reporting the results of the experiment to other teachers and researchers.

1.2 Comparison of multiple innovations

In order to assess the relative effects of different innovations it is important to try out multiple innovations at each site and across sites. Within a site it is possible to hold constant the teachers, students, school culture, etc. in order to make comparisons. Across sites it is possible to vary these same factors systematically.

1.3 Objective evaluation

In order to develop a design theory, we want to break the pattern of developers testing their innovations to see if they work. We need to address questions of how well different innovations work and under what circumstances. To do that we need to view different innovations objectively. While we will be testing some of our own technologies, they will be embedded in situations where other technologies are tried out for comparison and we will not include the developer in the design team for that site.

1.4 Testing technologies most likely to succeed first

In school settings, videotape, electronic-network, and tool-based technologies, such as word processors or graphing packages, are most likely to have wide application and be used most successfully, because they require least restructuring of the school milieu. Therefore addressing questions about their effective uses is most likely to have a high payoff.

1.5 Multiple expertise in design

In any design of a classroom (or larger unit) there are a vast number of different variables that may affect the outcome. The goal should be to all those variables as far as possible within the constraints of the setting. To accomplish this requires multiple expertise: teachers, designers, technologists, anthropologists, psychologists, etc. Sometimes several kinds of expertise may reside in the same person, but these multiple perspectives are necessary.

1.6 Systematic variation within sites

In order to test specific hypotheses about particular design questions, it is best to make specific comparisons within a site. In this way most variables can be held constant, while addressing a question about, for example, the structure of the classroom or the role of the teacher or the activities using a particular technology. The designs compared in this way should be as good as we can make them. The teacher(s) must be interested but neutral about questions addressed, and confident that they can execute the two variations successfully.

1.7 Flexible design revision

It may often be the case that the teacher or researchers feel a particular design is not working early in the school year. It is important to analyse why it is not working, and take steps to fix whatever appears to be the reasons for failure. In this way we collect information about failures, which are of equal value to successes, plus information gathered from the attempted repairs to the design, and whether they succeed or fail. It is critical to document the nature of those failures, and the attempted revisions, as well as the overall results of the experiment.

1.8 Multiple evaluation of success or failure

Success or failure of an innovation cannot simply be evaluated in terms of how much students learn on some criterion measure. There are a number of different kinds of evaluation that are necessary for addressing questions such as: how sustainable the design is after the researchers leave, how easy is it to realize the design in practice, how much the design emphasizes reasoning as opposed to rote learning, how the design affects the attitude and motivation of teachers and students, how much the design encourages students to help other students learn, etc. To evaluate these different variables, it is necessary to use a variety of evaluation techniques, including standardized pre and post-tests and ongoing evaluations of the classroom milieu. For these latter evaluations we anticipate using both observation and interview techniques, and perhaps primary trait scoring based on videotapes of the classrooms. Issues such as sustainability require follow-up studies to see what happens to the design in later years.

A major goal then is to develop a specific methodology incorporating these desiderata (and others we discover in the course of our research). Below, we describe a design experiment to give a specific idea as to the kinds of designs we anticipate might be viable in sites we have worked with in the past. It is not a final design, because teachers and other researchers must arrive at a final design given particular settings. But it at least concretizes the abstract principles described here.

2. What Are Design Experiments?

The best way to describe design experiments is to give an example of an experiment we may carry out. We have been thinking about developing a technology-based unit on the relative motion of the earth and sun and the seasons; i.e., why it is warmer in the summer and colder in the winter. Several of us have been working with fourth-grade classrooms in Cambridge (USA) with large numbers of minority children, observing teachers, developing materials, and interviewing students about the seasons. Even though the seasons are taught somewhere in most K-12 curricula, Philip Sadler has found from interviews with 24 graduating seniors at Harvard that only one understood the causes of the seasons correctly. In fact, one study found that 55% of adult Americans do not know that the earth revolves around the sun once a year. So clearly this is a topic students are failing to learn in school.

We propose to consider five technologies in developing a unit about the seasons:

1) The television series, The Voyage of the Mimi 2, developed at Bank St., has several programs devoted to astronomy, in particular, the relative motion of the earth and sun.
2) Associated with the Voyage of the Mimi series, Bank St. has developed a series of computer programs that allow students to explore different views of the earth-sun relationship (e.g., an orbital view with earth rotation and day/night cycles; a view out a window in different places, showing the sun's at different times of the year; a dome of the sky view showing how the sun moves across the sky in different places at different times of year; and finally a view of projected shadows at different times of the year).
3) The ELASTIC program developed at BBN for teaching students how to construct tables of data and to graph them in different ways.
4) A computer network such as Earth Lab or Kidnet to encourage students to communicate with other students about their findings.

5) Word processors and drawing programs that students can use to produce documents about their findings.

Our first step would be to observe a number of teachers, and to choose two who are interested in trying out technology to teach students about the seasons, and who are comparably effective, but use different styles of teaching: for example, one might work with activity centers in the classroom and the other with the entire class at one time. Ideally, the teachers should have comparable populations of students.

We plan to devise a unit that integrates the technology available as optimally as we can manage. For example, we might have students first watch the Voyage of the Mimi episodes, and then work with the various computer views. Students might then be encouraged to collect data on the sun's position at different times from their school and put these data in ELASTIC. Then they could compare their data with those in the window-view program from Bank Street, and perhaps with students in another location. Finally, they might produce books explaining their observations and understanding of the movements of the earth and sun and the causes of the seasons.

Assuming both teachers teach a number of classes, we would ask each to teach half her classes using the design we have developed. In the other classes, we would help the teacher design her own unit on the seasons using these various technologies, one that is carefully crafted to fit with her normal teaching style.

In evaluating the results of the experiment, we would look at a number of different aspects:

1) We would give students a pencil and paper test on the earth-sun motion and the causes of the seasons.
2) We would use structured interview as we have done with fourth graders, to analyze how well students understand the seasons and more generally scientific inquiry.
3) We would observe the classrooms to see how the designs were realized in practice.
4) We would ask the teachers to make daily notes as to which parts of the design she perceived to be working and which parts not, and what changes she implemented in the design to make it work better.
5) We would carry out follow-up studies in the following year's class to determine whether the teacher decided to teach about the seasons and if so, how and why.
6) We would follow up on the student's understanding after a year or two.

The purpose of the study is partly to determine the form a design theory should take: can it try to characterize the most effective designs in terms of activities and technologies, or must the theory differentiate designs in terms of teaching styles? Other similar issues are raised in the next section.

While the grain size of this experiment is at the individual classroom level, design experiments should also be done at the grade, school, and even district levels. Such larger experiments would permit variation in cooperation between teachers, length of class period, peer tutoring across grade levels, relations of community to school, etc., that cannot be viably altered at the classroom level.

3. A Design Theory for Educational Innovations

Our long-term goal in studying various technological innovations in schools and in carrying out a series of design experiments is to construct a design theory for technology innovation. This design theory will attempt to specify all the variables that affect the success or failure of different designs. Furthermore, it will attempt to specify what values on these variables maximize chances for success, and how different variables interact in creating successful designs. Crafting such a design theory for technology innovation in education has not been attempted heretofore, but we think it is the most critical kind of role that a center for educational technology can perform.

The first phase of our work in constructing such a theory will be to identify all the relevant variables: both dependent variables in which terms we measure the success or failure of any innovation, and independent variables, which are the variables we control in creating any design. Identifying the relevant variables will be a major goal of our analysis of different innovations that have been attempted to date. Because they have been so varied in their designs, they should have uncovered most of the critical variables needed for a design theory.

Some of the dependent variables we think are important are listed in the section on multiple evaluations above. The independent variables cover a wide range of things including the technologies, software, and associated activities, the number of machines and their configuration in the classroom, the roles that students and teachers play in working with the technologies, the maintenance and other kinds of support for teachers using technology, the amount of planning time and preparation for using the technologies, the organization of time and activities in the class period, etc. While neither list of independent or dependent variables is at all complete, the two lists do give a flavour of the space over which a design theory will be constructed.

The second phase of our work will specify how different independent variables interact to produce success or failure with respect to the different dependent variables. There are a vast array of issues surrounding the interaction of variables. For example:

— It may be the case that without sufficient time on the computer, any innovation is more costly in teacher time and disruption of ongoing activities than it is worth in terms of student learning, so that a low saturation of computers has negative effects.

— Perhaps the best deployment of technology in moderate saturation is based on activity centers in the classroom, whereas the best deployment in high saturation is to have students working for large amounts of time on projects with the teacher acting as a coach, and students sharing information.

— Programs designed to teach specific subjects, such as physics or geography, may be difficult to incorporate into classroom learning, no matter how well they are designed, because of the cost of turning the classroom over to the software's goals. Tool-based software may work better in classrooms to the extent that it supports more general goals of students and teachers.

Tables 1 and 2, which are based on interviews with Denis Newman and Andee Rubin, illustrate our first attempts to evolve a design theory. The interviews sought to determine what the respondents thought were critical factors affecting the success of technology in classrooms. What came out were a set of principles which at least tacitly specified three things: the scope of the principle (e.g., network-based software, computer technology), the dependent variable affected by the factor (e.g., adoption, continued use, learning), and the independent variable or factor itself (e.g., student-computer ratio, restart capability). Andee Rubin began to group factors together that affect a particular variable, such as adoption, because she has done some prior analysis. This kind of analysis leads to a systems-dynamic model, such as the models in econometrics or climatology.

These issues are only meant to be illustrative of the kind of issues a design theory must address: there are a very large number of such issues that have important consequences as to how we should deploy the technologies we develop and it is important that we start addressing such issues in a systematic way.

Table 1 Factors affecting success of technology: (from Denis Newman)*

For all technology, ***adoption*** depends on whether teacher has a lot of activities already, or is starved for innovative things to do. This variable might be thought of as *activity saturation*, and it depends on how much the teacher values the activities currently used.

Network-based software (e.g., Earth Lab, Kidnet) takes coercion to reach *critical mass* simultaneously to achieve ***continued use***. Have to have enough people communicating from beginning to hold people's interest. Critical mass requires both enough machines (~20 machines) and enough participants.

All technology used in projects requires the ability to stop work and restart easily on another machine (*portability or restart capability*) to achieve ***continued use***.

All computer technology requires multiple users for each machine (optimal between 2 to 1 and 4 to 1) in order to achieve ***cooperative learning***, (or kids teaching each other). This variable might be called *student-computer ratio*.

*Format: Scope, ***Dependent variable***, *Independent variable*

Table 2 Factors affecting success of technology (from Andee Rubin)

For any technology, ***initial implementation by teachers*** depends on:

Teacher interest in technology.
Some male teachers tend to be motivated by this variable, particularly if they have a computer at home.

Enhanced subject-matter learning.
If the teacher feels technology can help students learn a particular subject better, she is more likely to adopt the technology.

Teaching career enhancement.
If the teacher feels administrators expect or would value her using technology, she is more likely to do it.

Teacher interest in experimentation.
If the teacher wants to try something new, then technology has appeal.

For any technology, ***quality of implementation*** depends on:

Coordination between decision-makers.
Computer coordinators, curriculum specialists, and teachers are all involved in making decisions about how technology is used. Sometimes they are at different levels in the school district which make coordination difficult. Various decisions, such as who orders software, are assigned to different people in different systems.

For any technology, ***continued use by the teacher*** depends on:

Student enthusiasm.
To the degree that teachers see the students are enthusiastic and self-motivated to work on tasks, teachers are rewarded and are likely to continue use.

Student learning.
Not only do teachers want to see students enthusiastic, but in time (about a month) they want to see some tangible effects on learning. Again this affects continued use.

Teacher enthusiasm.
If the teacher likes the technology, and perhaps feels it improves her teaching, then she is likely to continue use.

Level of Use.
Susan Loucks identifies seven levels of expertize teachers move through as they gain greater ease and sophistication. Teacher training and professional development need to help teachers move through each of these levels.

Table 2 cont.

For any technology, ***institutionalization*** depends on:

Powerful advocate.
To the degree that there is a budget-controlling administrator who is a strong advocate, the more likely it is that institutionalization will occur.

There are some classroom management variables that affect both ***initial implementation by teachers*** and ***continued use by teachers*** of computer technology.

Activity-centered classrooms.
If teachers structure classrooms around activity centers, then it is easy to incorporate computers into classrooms by adding one or two computers to the activity centers. This style allows for effective use in low student-computer ratio settings.

Whole-class teaching.
If a teacher normally teaches to the whole class at one time, she has several options for trying to deal with the classroom management problem:

a) Some students miss the lesson.
If there are one or two computers in the classroom, the teacher may let a few students, who can afford to miss the lesson, work on computers at the same time as she conducts the lesson with the class. This can lead to problems about making up work. Teachers do not like to do this because they feel their lessons are important for everyone, and so this strategy works against continued use.

b) Works with whole class on computers together.
This is what happened in Columbus ACOT ("Apple Classroom of Tomorrow") classroom with 1-1 student-computer ratio (computers mostly sit idle). Normally this strategy is implemented by going to computer labs, which is somewhat disruptive of lesson continuity. This strategy works somewhat better than (a) for continued use.

c) Teacher uses computer for demonstrations.
If there is only one computer, then by using large screen projection, the teacher can run demonstrations on the computer. Effectiveness of this strategy depends on how much involvement the teacher can elicit from students.

d) Team turn-taking.
Tom Snyder's Search Series can be used where four teams take turns at a computer, and plan their next move while they wait for their next turn. This strategy is quite effective for continued use.

3

A Workbench for Discovering Task Specific Theories of Learning

Kurt VanLehn
Departments of Psychology and Computer Science
Carnegie-Mellon University, Pittsburgh, PA 15217 U.S.A.

Abstract: This chapter examines why learning theories expressed as artificial intelligence programs have not had much direct effect on education and training. It suggests a new research direction.

Keywords: ACM, ACT*, addition, arithmetic algorithms, Artificial Intelligence, CASCADE, CIRRUS, cognitive behaviour, cognitive science, generalization hierarchy, immediate feedback, impasse, knowledge representation, learning theories, machine learning, METADENDRAL, physics, psychology, SAPA, skill acquisition, SOAR, subtraction, task analysis, TETRAD, universal theories of cognition, workbench

1. Introduction

One long-standing aspiration of cognitive science is that education would benefit from the building of learning theories that are expressed, at least partially, as Artificial Intelligence (AI) programs. I have built several such programs [34,38], and others have built many more [1,19,11,5,21]. Although such work has profoundly changed our image of competence and intelligence, and that change has begun to seep into the educational system, it is fairly clear now that the resulting programs/theories have not had as much *direct* effect on education and training as could be desired. This paper examines the reasons why and suggests a new research direction based on that analysis.

The basic problem is that there seems to be an unavoidable tradeoff between the generality of learning theories and their utility to educators. Let us examine this tradeoff by starting with some recent general theories of learning and seeing what utility they have for education.

SOAR [19,16] and ACT* [1,2] aim to be universal theories of cognition. Their goal is to describe only the aspects of skill acquisition that are common to the acquisition of *all* skills. These theories are well suited for some purposes. Some examples are:

— explanations of speed and error patterns in transcription typing [12],
— explanations of the power-law increase in speed and accuracy that invariably accompany extensive practice. [24,1],
— explanations of transfer, as measured by savings in learning time caused by prior training on a similar skill [29,30,13].

However, the mechanisms of ACT* and SOAR do not in themselves tell us much about the students' *initial* acquisition of the skill. For instance, they do not tell us how students will read an instructional text, nor the effects of examples, nor the impact of specific pre-existing conceptual knowledge, nor the importance of having mental models in task domains that admit them, and so forth.

This is not an oversight on the part of the authors of ACT* and SOAR, but arises from the fact that initial acquisition of a skill seems to be a form of problem solving. Students, while engaged in various pedagogical activities such as studying a text or working some exercises, occasionally discover that their knowledge is incomplete or mistaken. This is a problem. They know many methods for solving the problem of ignorance, and different students may know different methods[1].

As always in problem solving, the behaviour of the subjects is determined mostly by the nature of the problem and the particulars of their knowledge. Neither of these is specified by ACT* or SOAR, as they aim to describe only the *universal* aspects of cognition. However, ACT* and SOAR should be consistent with the observed behaviour in that one should be able to specify (as ACT* or SOAR programs) a model of the individual subjects' knowledge and the task environment that will cause the architectures to accurately simulate his or her behaviour. Presumably, the particulars of ACT* and SOAR put some constraints on the specification of the knowledge, but the constraints imposed by the nature of the task are much stronger.

To put it differently, suppose an educator who is interested in teaching thermodynamics is not sure which of several ways of learning is typically used by thermodynamics students or could potentially be used by them. Trying these various options out on ACT* and SOAR will not reduce the educator's uncertainty one bit, because the architectures will probably be consistent with all learning methods the educator is likely to consider. In short, because these

[1]Some types of problems occur so often that their solution has become routine, and subjects hardly notice that they have found and rectified a point of ignorance. For instance, students might not initially understand the referent of a mathematical symbol while reading a text or example, but after a few second's reflection, they retrieve (or construct) its meaning, and continue their reading. Presumably, they learn something from such an experience. The experience can be analyzed as a brief episode of problem solving, even though the subjects may not have thought of it as such.

architectures aim at universality, they turn out to pretty useless as constraints on task-specific theories of initial skill acquisition.

To put the same point a third way, one view of pedagogy [4] is that a sufficient teaching method (but not, of course a necessary one) is to:

1. formalize as production rules (or some other type of rule) exactly what the students need to know in order to perform competently, and
2. design a curriculum whose lessons introduces these rules in small batches (cf. VanLehn, 1983) and
3. design lessons that explain the rules clearly and provide sufficient practice on applying them. (Immediate feedback is seen as particularly important for catching misunderstandings and rectifying them, but it is not essential to this method.)

The critical step in this teaching method is the task analysis that takes place in the first step. Task analysis is driven almost exclusively by the subject matter of the task domain. General cognitive theories, such as ACT*, provide a notation for the rules, but otherwise offer little guidance to the person conducting the analysis.

2. The essential problem, and three possible solutions

These deficiencies are not a fault of ACT* and SOAR per se. Rather, it seems that very little of our cognitive behaviour (as opposed to more peripheral behaviours) is determined by the fixed, unchangeable parts of our mind. Cognitive behaviours seem to be determined by our knowledge and the environment itself. Moreover, knowledge acquisition is a cognitive behaviour, which is itself determined mostly by knowledge and the environment. To put it in more traditional terms, because we humans are a highly adaptive species (i.e., we mould our behaviour to fit the environment), our higher level behaviour is determined mostly by our history of interaction with the environment (our knowledge) and by the environment at hand.

Unpacking the recursion here, it seems that the ultimate determinant of cognitive behaviours is the person's environment. (This is, of course, a gross simplification -- I am not proposing a tabula rasa here.) Presumably, one could explain cognitive behaviour by omitting descriptions of the various cycles of knowledge acquisition, etc. and just examine the relationship between the environment and cognitive behaviour[2]. Although this is one logically possible way to predict human behaviour, I suspect that such an explanation would be cumbersome and inaccurate, so I would not recommend pursuing it.

Logically, the only other option is to incorporate the environment into the theory. Thus, for example, a theory of physics learning would include task-specific terms like "forces" and "equations." Such theories blend psychology and the particulars of a task domain. In order to illustrate the notion of task-specific theories, let us examine some simple ones. The task of arithmetic calculation is fairly well understood. It divides cleanly into recall of arithmetic facts, such as 17-9=8, and execution of arithmetic algorithms, such as the algorithm for subtracting two multi digit numbers. We will consider a task-specific theory for recall and a task-specific theory for execution.

Siegler [26-28] has developed specific models of how students "recall" arithmetic facts. Each model has parameters that can be fit to a individual subject's behaviour, thus providing both a test of the models and a way to forecast the subject's behaviour. Each model is specific to one type of arithmetic operation, but they are all consistent with his general theory of strategy selection, which features a specific procedure for trading off retrieval and reconstruction of the item to be recalled. Reconstruction, in this context, might consist of using counting to generate

---

[2]This proposal is similar to Anderson's Rational Analysis [3], except that the time scales and phenomena are different. Anderson seeks to explain the fixed, unchanging part of a person's mind -- the cognitive architecture -- by assuming that it is the product of genetic adaptation to the demands of the environment. The proposal here is to explain an individual's knowledge as the product of adaptation to the environment that has been experienced since birth.

an addition fact. Moreover, the general theory specifies how memory traces are strengthened by practice, thus leading to the dominance of memory retrieval over reconstruction that characterizes the competent student's performance. Siegler's theory of recall seems quite general, for it has been successfully applied to analyze acquisition of spelling rules (Siegler, personal communication) as well as the major arithmetic operations. Of course, it is not as general as ACT* or SOAR, but it serves nicely as a simple illustration of the difference between a general theory, a task-specific theory/model (e.g., the model for addition, which has explicit reconstruction strategies for arithmetic facts), and a subject-specific model (the addition model, with its parameters fit to a given subject's data). Siegler's task-specific models are specific enough that one can envision designing a curriculum around them, and Siegler has recently begun to do just that (Siegler, personal communication).

My colleagues and I have developed models of the algorithms for multi digit arithmetic, concentrating especially on subtraction [7,33,36,40]. There is a general theory, which distinguishes between normal execution of a procedure and "error handling." According to the theory, when people reach an impasse, perhaps because their knowledge of the procedure is incomplete and they can not decide what to do next, they treat the impasse itself as a problem and attempt to resolve it. One impasse-resolving strategy is to ask for help or to consult a textbook. Another is to search through one's earlier work looking for an inadvertent error. These strategies depend strongly on the particulars of situation that the students are in and on their knowledge of the task domain. Another hypothesis of the general theory is that learning occurs whenever the resolution of an impasse is summarized and stored in memory as a new rule [38]. The general theory has been tested by developing a task-specific theory/model of [33,38]. The model has been fit to individual subjects' error data. The task-specific model makes predictions about pedagogies for subtraction, some of which have been tested [35]. This work again illustrates the difference between a general theory, which offers little specific guidance to educators, and task-specific theories/models, which provide crisp suggestions.

Neither of the "general" theories just mentioned are as general as ACT* or SOAR, so a better view of the world is to see theories as arranged in some kind of generalization hierarchy. SOAR, for instance, is a straightforward generalization of both Siegler's theory and mine, because it generalizes the notion of an "impasse" to cover both failures due to memory retrieval and failures due to flawed knowledge. On the other hand, SOAR offers even less guidance to educators than either Siegler's theory or mine, just because it has more generality. So the same generality-power tradeoff is evident, even though the binary distinction between general theories and task-specific ones has dissolved into a generalization hierarchy. Although I will continue to speak of "general" versus "task-specific" theories, one should keep in mind that this is a simplification.

It seems that task-specific theories offer a viable option for guiding pedagogy. But unfortunately, task-specific theories offer little help to people who are interested in other tasks (or at least, that is how the theories are treated: theories of arithmetic are pretty much ignored by everyone except those interested in arithmetic). Thus, while task-specific theories are much more helpful to some educators than general theories, they are not helpful to very many educators.

This leads to a third option (the first two were environmental theories and task-specific theories), which is to formulate a *method* for generating task-specific theories. Traditionally, a method is a prescription of the kinds of experiments to run, the kinds of analyses to make and the kinds of conclusions to draw. The later two items are actually a weak task-general theory. It is weak because it does not foreordain the conclusions, but merely provides some ideas or even some notations for stating the task-specific theory. To put it differently, a method provides (1) a general theory and (2) a means of instantiating the theory to fit a task domain, thus formulating a task-specific theory.

There are methods in education, but I believe it is fair to say that all of them are oriented towards prescribing instruction rather than constructing learning theories. The social sciences contain many descriptive methods, such as factor analysis and its associated theory of intelligence, or structural linguistics and its associated theory of syntax. However, as far as I know, there is no method for formulating task-specific theories of learning.

This does not bode well for a project aimed at formulating such a method. All the arguments presented above depend only on ancient concepts, such as the distinction between knowledge and its application. These arguments lead more or less inevitably to the project of formulating a method. Surely someone in the long history of education and psychology must have tried to formulate such a method. Maybe they tried and failed. Maybe such a method is just not feasible.

Some recent results in AI indicate that a method for formulating task-specific theories may indeed be feasible. Most of the work is aimed at replicating the reasoning processes behind human scientific discovery [17,25]. Although there is no denying that these programs produce the same hypotheses and experimental demonstrations that the human scientists did, there are still grave doubts about whether the simplifications assumed by these models are too strong. Pessimists would say that the machine discovery programs are not particularly intelligent, but the people who chose the simplifications for them were very intelligent. Since the pessimists could turn out to be right, it is prudent for those who wish to apply this new machine discovery technology to assume that a practical machine discovery system has a scientist/user who selects the simplifications and oversees the machine's reasoning. To put it crudely again, although the machine discovery work may or may not be able to build a mechanical scientist, it probably can build a mechanical research assistant. Such a tool could play a key role in a method for formulating task-specific theories of learning.

In short, it seems that the most promising option for finding theories of learning that are really useful to educators is to formulate a method that combines the talents of people and machine discovery programs in order generate task-specific theories of learning. This is a research option that I think should be pursued.

3. Workbenches: existing and proposed

Calling the research product a "method" makes it sound like a step-by-step prescription of how to construct a theory. I do not think *that* kind of method is feasible. What I have in mind is a set of integrated computer-based tools for analyzing data and building models. Such a "scientist's workbench" would be based on some task-general theory, such as ACT* or SOAR, or perhaps some moderately general theory, like Siegler's or mine. This section discusses some examples.

CIRRUS [39,14] is a workbench based on my theory about how people execute cognitive tasks. In addition to the hypotheses mentioned above, the theory includes the hypotheses that people are free to pick any goal that they can recall as the next goal to attend to, and their knowledge includes some policies concerning what types of goals to attend to in what situations [40][3]. CIRRUS is designed for analyzing protocol data within the framework of the theory by building a runnable simulation and comparing its behaviour to the given protocol[4]. Students' policies about goal selection are formalized as a set of goal selection preferences of the form "If condition C holds, then prefer goals of type A over goals of type B." The simulator uses such preferences to sort a list of pending goals and choose the goal that is preferred above all others. To use CIRRUS, the theorist must input a procedure, written in the knowledge representation language of the theory, that lacks goal selection preferences. CIRRUS must also be given primitives from which goal selection preferences can be built. Given a protocol, CIRRUS builds goal selection preferences that allow a maximally accurate simulation of the data. To put it in more traditional terms, CIRRUS takes a model with one parameter, and fits it to the given data. However, both the model and the parameter are non-numeric.

[3]This theory is slightly more general than ACT* and SOAR. Those theories claim that people invariably select one of the unsatisfied goals that was created most recently (i.e., both ACT* and SOAR have a last-in-first-out goal stacks)

[4]CIRRUS does not understand natural language; the protocol must be encoded by humans before giving it to CIRRUS.

When my collaborators and I use CIRRUS, we find it necessary to refine the model given to it many times before we are finally happy with the analysis it yields. Typically, we analyze one subject's data in some detail, then start our analysis of the next subject using the model developed for the first subject. After several subjects have been analyzed, commonalties in the subject-specific models emerge. At that point, we build a subject-general model and install parameters (typically, a system of switches that turn rules off and on) in order to capture the between-subjects variation. We stop the analysis when all the subjects have been analyzed and one subject-general model has been found. One of the model's parameters, the set of goal-selection procedures, is fit automatically by CIRRUS; the other parameters, which were created during the model refinement process, are fit by hand. This refinement process can be viewed as finding a theory that is specific to the task under analysis but general across subjects. In this fashion, CIRRUS helps the scientist/user discover a task-specific theory/model.

ACM [22,23] is similar to CIRRUS. It is based on the theory that problem solving is search through a problem space. It takes as its model a specific problem space, and builds a set of operator selection heuristics that will cause search through this problem space to simulate answer data given to the program.

SAPA [6] is somewhat like ACM, in that it is based on the theory of problem solving as search through a problem space. However, it does not to actually build a set of search heuristics that fit some data given to it. It already has some search heuristics in it, along with a particular problem space[5]. These search heuristics are intended, I suppose, to represent those of a prototypical subject's. At each cycle of the search, SAPA asks the user if the inference it has just made corresponds to the protocol. If it does, then the built-in, fully parameterized model is upheld. If not, then SAPA checks to see if the parameterization is wrong -- i.e., it has the right problem space but the wrong heuristics for that subject. It performs this check by suggesting alternatives until the user indicates that it has found one that corresponds to the protocol. If none of SAPA's suggestions work, then the problem space is deemed faulty, because no parameterization of the model will fit the data. Bhaskar and Simon used SAPA to test their task-specific theory of thermodynamics problem solving, and to test their model of a prototypical student's search heuristics.

All these workbenches, as well as several others (e.g., Debuggy [8], TETRAD [10] and METADENDRAL [18] have three components: (1) a general theory that is so deeply embedded in the workbench that it can not be changed, (2) a underdetermined model given to the workbench by the user, such as a problem space for thermodynamics problem solving, and (3) a process that fits the model to the data, making it more deterministic. The theorist tinkers with the underdetermined model in order to get a fitted model that analyzes the data satisfactorily. The result is a model that is both a generalization over several (hopefully, many) subjects' data and a specialization of the general theory. The model can be considered a task-specific theory.

Of course, such a model is interesting only to the extent that that task is interesting. Educators are interested in learning, but CIRRUS, ACM and SAPA all assume that learning does not occur during the protocols they are analyzing. Thus, they could be used in a longitudinal study to model snapshots of the learner's development, but they can not model the learning process itself. This leads to a proposal to build a workbench that can model the learning process.

I am currently involved in building a scaled-up version of CIRRUS, called CASCADE. CASCADE is being built in order to analyze a very large data set, donated by Micki Chi[9]. The data consist of 8 protocols, each about 200 pages long. They were collected from students studying the first four chapters of a college physics textbook. The protocols record the learning that a typical college student would undergo in the first few weeks of a college physics course.

[5]Although SAPA was build to handle only thermodynamics, it could be redesigned to have more task generality by allowing the user to input a problem space.

4. Expected benefits of the proposed research

The most important application of the proposed technology is providing a "front end" to projects that create training systems. According to Anderson, the first step in developing a training system is to analyze the task domain to see what good students should know when they have completed their training [4]. Workbenches such as CASCADE are intended to help a designer perform such a task analysis. Although this section suggests a few other benefits that might accrue, one should keep in mind that the main benefit is technological assistance in task analysis.

The task-specific, subject-general model that is created on the workbench could be the starting point of the development of a student modeller for an intelligent tutoring system. Also, the data analysis tools developed as parts of the workbench could be used as parts of the diagnostic module of an intelligent tutoring system.

The mere process of analyzing students' learning in the face of the given instructional material will usually reveal defects in the material that can be easily remedied. Anderson, for instance, has a written a textbook on LISP based on his task analysis. Since the analysis had only got as far as recursion when the book was written, the last five chapters in the text were not based on a task analysis. Anderson comments: "Since the writing of the book we have slowly began to create tutor material corresponding to those chapters. As we have done so we have started to realize the inadequacy of the information in the last five chapters." [3 ch. 4]. It is significant that task analysis of the initial segment of the curriculum, even by someone like Anderson, was not sufficient preparation for writing an adequate material for the second segment. It seems that there is no substitute for formal task analysis, even if the intended training vehicle is "just" a textbook.

Once a task-specific model of the student has been constructed, it often suggests new pedagogical strategies. Given the model, some will seem clearly beneficial. However, pedagogies whose benefits are less certain can be simulated; if the model is psychologically accurate, and the proposed benefit helps the model learn, then human students should learn better as well. For instance, on the basis of Siegler's model of addition, it seems that under certain circumstances, supervised drill can take advantage of the commutativity of addition and only teach half the addition facts. Unsupervised drill on the other half should suffice for learning them. This pedagogical regime should be tested on his model before being tried in the classroom.

So far, the importance of this work to education has been stressed. But there are other potential beneficiaries as well. Machine learning has recently turned towards scientific discovery as a source of new problems. Because a workbench is a program that participates in scientific discovery, it should be of some interest to research on discovery. One can even imagine taking protocols of scientists while they use it in order to understand the discovery-making process better.

In protocols of students involved in learning new material, such as the ones being analyzed by the CASCADE project, there are many instances of students making discoveries. These discoveries might suggest discovery methods that could be developed into full-fledged machine learning techniques.

Looking further ahead, machine learning has not yet produced interactive learners that can hold up their end of a training dialogue with their trainer. Formal work in the Valiant framework ("PAC learning") indicates that such interactivity is necessary for tractable learning [31], so eventually machine learning will have to build such interactive learners if it is to live up to its promises of delivering systems that acquire knowledge for expert systems. The current protocol studies show how interaction proceeds with human students. That should suggest styles of interaction to machine learning researchers.

Turning now to the benefits for psychology, we start with the traditional observation that applications usually push theories towards completion because application efforts do not have the luxury of ignoring parts of human behaviour that are difficult to explain. This application of cognitive theory will certainly push it towards completion. For instance, the physics task domain is richer in conceptual material than other task domains, such as LISP and geometry, that have been studied. Thus, the development of a task-specific theory in physics should illuminate the interaction between conceptual and procedural learning.

I have concentrated on workbenches for analyzing protocol data because such data will push cognitive theory along by explicating the mapping between theoretical events, such as impasses, and visible types of human behaviour. There are few published comparisons of protocols and models as detailed as the analyses in Human Problem Solving [20], and none that compare models and students who are learning. The CASCADE project, and others like it, should yield the first fine-grained analysis of human learning. From such analyses, we ought to uncover some unexpected theoretical problems, as well as strengthen known weak spots in the theory.

References

1. Anderson, J. R. *The Architecture of Cognition.* Cambridge, MA: Harvard. 1983.
2. Anderson, J. R. Skill acquisition: Compilation of weak-method problem solutions. *Psychological Review*, 94(2), 192-210. 1987.
3. Anderson, J. R. *The Adaptive Character of Thought.* Cambridge, MA: MIT Press. (in press).
4. Anderson, J. R., Boyle, C. F., Farrell, R., & Reiser, B. J. Cognitive principles in the design of computer tutors. *In Proceedings of the Cognitive Science Society Conference.* Hillsdale, NJ: Erlbaum. 1984.
5. Anzai, T. Doing, understanding and learning in problem solving. In D. Klahr, P. Langley, & R. Neches (Eds.), *Production System Models of Learning and Development.* Cambridge, MA: MIT Press. 1987.
6. Bhaskar, R. & Simon, H. A. Problem solving in a semantically rich domains: An example from engineering thermodynamics. *Cognitive Science*, 1, 193-215. 1977.
7. Brown, J. S. & VanLehn, K. (1980). Repair Theory: A generative theory of bugs in procedural skills. *Cognitive Science*, 4, 379-426.
8. Burton, R. B. Diagnosing bugs in a simple procedural skill. In D. H. Sleeman & J. S. Brown (Eds.), *Intelligent Tutoring Systems.* New York: Academic. 157-183. 1982.
9. Chi, M. T. H., Bassok, M., Lewis, M., Reimann, P., & Glaser, R. Self explanations: How students study and use examples in learning to solve problems. *Cognitive Science*, 13, 145-182. 1989.
10. Glymour, C., Scheines, R., Spirtes, P., & Kelly, K. *Discovering Causal Structure.* Orlando, FL: Academic Press. 1987.
11. Holland, J. H., Holyoak, K. J., Nisbett, R. E., & Thagard, P. R. *Induction: Process of Inference, Learning and Discovery.* Cambridge, MA: MIT Press. 1986.
12. John, B. *Contributions to engineering models of human-computer interaction.* Doctoral dissertation, Department of Psychology, Carnegie Mellon University. 1988.
13. Kessler, C. M. *Transfer of Programming Skills in Novice LISP Learners.* Doctoral dissertation, Department of Psychology, Carnegie Mellon University. 1988.
14. Kowalski, B. & VanLehn, K. Inducing subject models from protocol data. In V. Patel (Ed.), *Proceedings of the Tenth Annual Conference of the Cognitive Science Society.* Hillsdale, NJ: Erlbaum. 1988.
15. Kulkarni, D. & Simon, H. A. The process of scientific discovery: the strategy of experimentation. *Cognitive Science*, 12, 139-175. 1988.
16. Laird, J. E., Newell, A., & Rosenbloom, P. S. Soar: an architecture for general intelligence. *Artificial Intelligence*, 33, 1-64. 1987.
17. Langley, P., Simon, H. A., Bradshaw, G. L, & Zytkow, J. M. *Scientific Discovery: Computational Explorations of the Creative Process.* Cambridge, MA: MIT Press. 1987.
18. Lindsay, R., Buchanan, B. H., Feigenbaum, E. A., & Lederberg, J. *DENDRAL.* New York: McGraw-Hill. 1980.

19. Newell, A. *Unified Theories of Cognition*. Cambridge, MA: Harvard. (in press).
20. Newell, A. & Simon, H. A. *Human Problem Solving*. Englewood Cliffs, NJ: Prentice-Hall. 1972.
21. Ohlsson, S. Truth versus appropriateness: relating declarative to procedural knowledge. In D. Klahr, P. Langley, & R. Neches (Eds.), *Production System Models of Learning and Development*. Cambridge, MA: MIT Press. 1987.
22. Ohlsson, S. & Langley, P. *Identifying solution paths in cognitive diagnosis*. (Technical Report CMU-RI-TR-84-7). Pittsburgh, PA: Robotic Institute, CMU. 1985.
23. Ohlsson, S. & Langley, P. Psychological evaluation of path hypotheses in cognitive diagnosis. In H. Mandl & A. Lesgold (Eds.), *Learning Issues for Intelligent Tutoring Systems*. New York: Springer Verlag. 1988.
24. Rosenbloom, P. & Newell, A. Learning by chunking: A production system model of practice. In D. Klahr, P. Langley, & R. Neches (Eds.), *Production System Models of Learning and Development*. Cambridge, MA: MIT Press. 1987.
25. Shavlik, J. W. Learning classical physics. In T. M. Mitchell, J. G. Carbonell, & R. S. Michalski (Eds.), *Machine Learning: A Guide to Current Research*. Higham, MA: Kluwer. 1986.
26. Siegler, R. S. Strategy choices in subtraction. In J. Sloboda & D. Rogers (Eds.), *Cognitive Processes in Mathematics*. Oxford, UK: Oxford University Press. 1987.
27. Siegler, R. S. Strategy choice procedures and the development of multiplication skill. *Journal of Experimental Psychology: General*, 117, 258-275. 1988.
28. Siegler, R. S. & Shrager, J. Strategy choices in addition: How do children know what to do? In C. Sophian (Ed.), *Origins of Cognitive Skill*. Hillsdale, NJ: Erlbaum. 1984.
29. Singley, M. K. & Anderson, J. R. The transfer of text-editing skill. *International Journal of Man-Machine Studies*, 22, 403-423. 1985.
30. Singley, M. K. & Anderson, J. R. A keystroke analysis of learning and transfer in text editing. *Human-Computer Interaction*. 1988.
31. Valiant, L. G. A theory of the learnable. *Communications of the ACM*, 27(11), 1134-1142. 1984.
32. VanLehn, K. *Felicity conditions for human skill acquisition: Validating an AI-based theory* (Technical Report CIS-21). Xerox Palo Alto Research Center. Out of print, but available from University Microfilms, 300 North Zeeb Road, Ann Arbor, MI 49106. 1983a.
33. VanLehn, K. Human skill acquisition: Theory, model and psychological validation. In M. R. Genesereth (Ed.), *Proceedings of AAAI-83*. Los Altos, CA: Morgan Kaufmann. 1983b.
34. VanLehn, K. Learning one subprocedure per lesson. *Artificial Intelligence*, 31(1), 1-40. Reprinted in Shavlik, J. W. & Dietterich, T. G. (Eds.). *Readings in Machine Learning*. Palo Alto, CA: Morgan Kaufmann. 1987.
35. VanLehn, K. Toward a theory of impasse-driven learning. In H. Mandl & A. Lesgold (Eds.), *Learning Issues for Intelligent Tutoring Systems*. New York: Springer Verlag. 1988.
36. VanLehn, K. *Mind Bugs: The origins of procedural misconceptions*. Cambridge, MA: MIT Press. 1990.
37. VanLehn, K. Felicity conditions for cognitive skill acquisition: Tutorial instruction does not need them. *Cognition and Instruction*. Currently available as technical report PCG-17, Department of Psychology, Carnegie Mellon University.(submitted).
38. VanLehn, K. & Ball, W. Teton: An architecture for analysis of protocol data. In K. VanLehn (Ed.), *Architectures for Intelligence*. Hillsdale, NJ: Erlbaum. (in press).
39. VanLehn, K. & Garlick, S. Cirrus: An automated protocol analysis tool. In P. Langley (Ed.), *Proceedings of the Fourth Machine Leaning Workshop*. Los Altos, CA: Morgan Kaufmann. 1987.
40. VanLehn, K., Ball, W., & Kowalski, B. Non-LIFO execution of cognitive procedures. *Cognitive Science*, 13, 415-465. 1989.

4

Computers in Teaching and Learning: An Interpretation of Current Practices and Suggestions for Future Directions

David L. Ferguson
Department of Technology and Society
College of Engineering and Applied Sciences
State University of New York at Stony Brook
Stony Brook, New York 11794-2250

Abstract: Most efforts to describe the use of computers in education focus on isolated categories with little emphasis on how the categories relate. I discuss a conceptual framework for understanding current computer-based learning activities. The framework exploits the concept of "learner control" and orders computer-based learning activities on this dimension. Using this framework, I examine major issues for charting the direction of computer-based learning activities for improving higher-order thinking. Central issues in the assessment of learning are explored.

Keywords: applications tools, cognitive processes, cognitive science, cognitive skills, collaborative learning, computer-based learning, creativity, databases, design environments, design experiments, directed activities, drill and practice, educational assessment, educational objectives, educational technology, evaluation, exploratory environments, higher-order thinking, intelligent tutoring systems, kinematics, learner control, LOGO, micro (small) discovery activity, microcomputer-based laboratory, microworlds, motivation, programming environments, simulation, TURTLETALK, types of learning

1. Introduction

Typical ways of classifying the particular types of uses of computers in education do little to show the relationships between the types, or relate the particular uses to psychological models. In this paper, I explore a conceptual framework for understanding the different types of computer-based learning activities. In addition, I examine some of the major issues that must be clarified regarding the design, implementation and assessment of computer-based learning activities. It is important that we establish conceptual frameworks for linking the different uses of computers in education. Such frameworks can be important guides for designers, users and evaluators of computer activities. The structures will be an anchor for researchers, and indeed these frameworks may suggest new areas of research.

2. A Conceptual Framework for Understanding Current Computer Based Learning Activities

An important way of classifying computer-based learning activities is on the basis of the degree of learner control that the activities permit. Figure 4.1 shows my definition of categories in order of increased learner control as one moves from left to right.

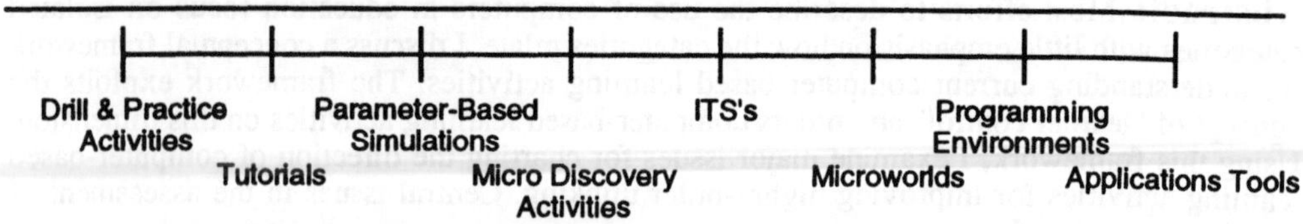

Fig.4.1. Computer based learning activities ordered according to degree of learner control (arranged from lesser to greater learner control)

I have used the term "directed activities" to refer to the two types of activities at the left-most part of the spectrum (namely drill and practice activities and tutorials). I have lumped the other activities under the term "exploratory environments." There are not always sharp boundaries between the types of activities. In addition, many software packages incorporate several types of computer-based learning activities.

3. Directed Activities

In the early days of the use of computers in teaching and learning most of the activities were directed activities. In fact, the activities were directed in two senses:

- Cognitive skills that students are supposed to develop are apparent. (Often, the skills are stated explicitly by the designers.)
- The way in which students are to acquire the cognitive skills is apparent. (There is very little learner control.)

The heart of drill and practice activities is repetition combined with a limited feedback system. The designer assumes one of the following instructional considerations:

- The user has been taught a set of explicit rules for performing a task (e.g., rules for multiplying signed numbers). (The aim of the drill and practice activity is to give the user experience at applying the rules).
- The user is expected to develop a skill (or understand a principle) by the repetitious performance of a "simple" task. (As an example, consider a variation of the game Decimal Darts [18]. A student who is learning about signed numbers may be asked to give the position of a balloon that is placed on the number line (see figure 4.2 below).

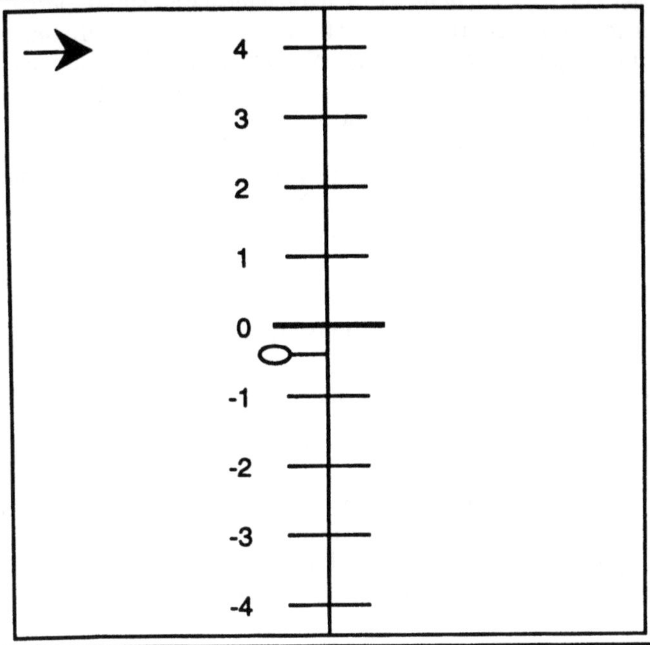

Fig.4.2. Use of drill and practice game to teach students about the number line

If the student gives the correct position the arrow goes over and punches a hole in the balloon. If a student gives an incorrect position, the arrow points to the incorrect position. Hence, there is a subtle feedback system that permits the student to adjust his/her behaviour.

Tutorials may offer a bit more learner control than drill and practice activities. This increased learner control results from a somewhat more extensive branching system. Hence, it is possible to handle a wider class of student responses. Different paths that students may follow are linked to a variety of "explanations." The explanations are generally brief and assume a fairly simple model of the rationale for the student's selection of a particular response.

4. Exploratory Environments

Exploratory environments, marked by considerable learner control, are generally characterized by several features:

- Clarification of the "objects" of the environments (These are the elements to be manipulated).
- Set of rules that define how the "objects" of the environment may be manipulated (In applications tools, the rules may have to be generated by the user).
- User-defined goals
- Effective feedback system

The feedback may be direct or indirect. In the indirect case, the user is expected to infer useful information by observing how the system responds. For example, in the LOGO environment, the user may make inferences about the appropriateness or inappropriateness of her/his actions by studying the graphics generated.

4.1 Parameter-Based Simulations

A simulation is a dynamic model that is useful in studying other underlying models. The simulation may represent an electric circuit, the automated supermarket system, cockpit of an aeroplane, or other physical systems. The simulation may represent economic or political systems and other complex phenomena. A parameter-based simulation is a simulation that permits the user to manipulate the values of a few parameters and study the effects on the system. The Yellow Light program is an example of this type of simulation [41]. This computer simulation of a traffic intersection is an environment for studying the effect of speed limit, yellow-light time, deceleration rate, width of intersection, etc. on stop zone, go zone and dilemma zone for a motorist who observes that the traffic light has just changed from green to yellow. The motorist must make a decision to stop or go. In the simulation, the student plays the roles of motorist and traffic engineer. As traffic engineer, the student attempts to manipulate the appropriate parameters (within reasonable values) so as to minimize the size of the dilemma zone.

4.2 Micro Discovery Activities

I use the term "micro (small) discovery activity" to refer to computer-based activities that are characterized by the following features:

- The designer has determined what the student is to discover via interaction with the activity
- The designer guides the student in the environment along paths that are believed to lead to the student's discovery.

We are often interested in the process by which students learn when they are placed in environments where they are expected to learn by discovery or through inquiry. How do students use the experiences gained from analyzing a few "simple" cases to make inferences or to arrive at generalizations? What is the characteristic of the sequence of cases that facilitates the students' ability to make "appropriate" inferences?

We are interested in the mechanics of rule induction and other forms of learning through discovery or inquiry. As an example of a model of how inference may be made in a particular context, one may consider the "guess my rule" activity. Here a student is expected to infer a particular relationship (usually mathematical) through observing input and output (black-box model). A model that might account for the student's ability to infer the rule is that a student has a repertoire of simple relationships in her/his head, and there is a constant attempt to match current experience to this repertoire of relationships. Some of these relationships might be constant added rule, constant multiplied rule, square relation, cube relation, logarithm, exponential, etc.

Some important learning may occur in environments where students are given considerable freedom to explore on their own. In some of these instances, we do not begin with a preconceived list of items that students are to discover, but somehow we expect them to explore and through such inquiry learn some significant things. It is this open-endedness that distinguishes inquiry methods from the somewhat more restrained notion of micro discovery.

4.3 Intelligent Tutoring Systems

A good human tutor has many capabilities:

- Subject-domain expertise.
- Ability to diagnose students' errors (and formulate appropriate models of the students' state of knowledge).
- Ability to use a variety of instructional approaches and adapt the approaches to the needs of the learner.
- Ability to present captivating tasks and sustain the interest of the learner over extended periods.

During the 1970's and 1980's there has been considerable effort to develop computer-based tutoring systems that exhibit "human-like" tutoring expertise. Efforts in this direction, regardless of the extent to which they actually meet their goals, have generally been described as intelligent tutoring systems.

Intelligent tutoring systems are usually characterized by a subset of the following features:

a) They attempt to teach the solving of problems that do not readily lend themselves to simple algorithmic solutions. (The task might be electronic trouble shooting, solving symbolic integration problems, solving certain classes of physics problems, solving algebra word problems, doing proofs in elementary Euclidean geometry, or tackling other problems in science, engineering, or a variety of other fields.)
b) The system accepts a wider range of "natural language" input than is normally expected of computing systems.
c) The system is able to use certain rules to make inferences or deductions, and hence arrives at new knowledge that may influence its subsequent behaviour.
d) The system exploits instructional strategies that partly mimic those of good human tutors. (Such abilities might include the capability to diagnose the student's misconceptions about a particular content area, and offer certain remedies.)
e) The system possesses some learning capabilities. (Notice that this is implied, in part, by item c) above.)
f) The system possesses a mechanism for accepting a wide range of symbolic representations (graphs and diagrams. informal language, formal symbolic language, etc.) and "reasoning" about such information.
g) The system possesses a feature of transparency that allows the user to "ask" the system for the "line of reasoning" that it used to arrive at a particular conclusion -- permitting the system to give a direct and detailed response to the query.
h) The system possesses a feature of extensibility that permits major changes to be made in the models that the system uses to solve problems, and in the instructional strategies that the system employs to aid students.

Individual chapters in this book by Reiser, Van Lehn and McCalla explore some of the problems and prospects of work in ITS. Numerous other sources explore major theoretical issues or immediate design issues in the development of ITS's. For example, [2-6.9,13,14,25,27,30,52,53].

Researchers in ITS must address some major issues:

a) What models of subject knowledge do students bring to bear on problem solving situations?
b) What models of subject knowledge might be preferred to enhance students' performance in a particular subject area?
c) What methods could be employed that would aid students in forming knowledge structures that would facilitate problem solving in specified domains.
d) What schemes will better allow for the accommodation of new knowledge in human and machine systems?
e) Given "appropriate" structures of knowledge, what models of the problem solving process would better facilitate performance in machines and people?
f) What is the relationship of central issues in artificial intelligence (e.g., natural language processing, general problem solving techniques, pattern recognition, and game playing) to the building of powerful ITS's?
g) Is ITS research fundamentally different in certain ways from other areas of AI research? (In particular, some researchers have suggested that the demand that ITS's be able to discern and represent different models of "state of knowledge" for different students and different models for the same student on different occasions represents a problem quite different from that encountered in other areas of AI research.)
h) How can models of problem solving and models of teaching be integrated to yield powerful ITS's?
i) What changes in the architectures of computers and in our conceptualization of software engineering might be needed as we attempt to address major issues in ITS design?
j) Can the cognitive impact of ITS's be demonstrated in "laboratory" settings? (Are the broader claims of ITS researchers attainable?)
k) Can ITS's be shown to be practical tools in the social context of school environments? (Let's assume that ITS's will make their way into the educational system in some form. Will the systems be compelling? Will students want to use the systems? What impact will such systems have on the humanistic dimensions of learning?)

l) How can the knowledge about teaching and learning, gained from research on ITS's, be used to influence teaching and learning in other areas of the use of computers and in non-technology instructional approaches? (ITS research must not be judged solely on the power of the systems that are developed or the paradigms that are generated, but on the total contribution of the field to our understanding of teaching and learning.)

4.4 Microworlds

The term "microworld" has been used by a number of researchers to describe computer-based learning environments that are highly visual and geared to open-ended problem solving. I think that most of the researchers' in this area were influenced in some way by Seymour Papert's Mindstorms [51]. Let us see if we can capture some of the meaning of "microworld" from Paperts' own writing.

> "We must ask why some learning takes place so early and spontaneously while some is delayed many years or does not happen at all without deliberately imposed formal instruction."
>
> "If we really look at the 'child as builder,' we are on our way to an answer. All builders need materials to build with. Where I am at variance with Piaget is in the role I attribute to the surrounding cultures as a source of these materials. In some cases the culture supplies them in abundance, thus facilitating constructive Piagetian learning. For example, the fact that so many things (knives and forks, mothers and fathers, shoes and socks) come in pairs is a "material" for the construction of an intuitive sense of number. But in many cases where Piaget would explain the slower development of a particular concept by its greater complexity or formality, I see the initial factor as the relative poverty of the culture in those materials that would make the concept simple and concrete. In yet other cases the culture may provide materials but block their use. In the case of formal mathematics, there is both a shortage of formal materials and a cultural block as well. The mathophobia endemic in contemporary culture blocks many people from learning anything they recognize as 'math,' although they may have no trouble with mathematical knowledge they do not perceive as such."

(from *Mindstorms* by Seymour Papert, Basic Books, New York, 1980 page 7)

Papert describes microworlds as self-contained worlds in which certain questions are relevant and others are not. According to Papert:

> "children get to know what it is like to explore the properties of a chosen microworld undisturbed by extraneous questions. In doing so they learn to transfer habits of exploration from their personal lives to the formal domain of scientific theory construction."

Seymour Papert's LOGO is the most classic example of a microworld. TURTLETALK, another microworld created by Papert, is a rich environment for studying laws of motion. Some general features of microworlds are as follows:

a) Microworlds are self-contained environments. (The environment is in some sense closed. In LOGO, the tools necessary to design are available in the environment.)
b) Microworlds are constrained environments. (The universe of discourse in LOGO is constrained by the language itself.)
c) Microworlds provide opportunities for multiple views and representations of real phenomena. (In LOGO, the computer program and graphical representations give different views.)
d) Microworlds make it easy to learn by constructing objects. (Students learn by "designing")
e) Microworlds are rich in the variety of questions that can be posed and potential solutions that can be explored.
f) Microworlds make it easy to learn via debugging activities.

One category of microworld is "design environments." In a special issue of the Journal of Machine-Mediated Learning devoted to design, researchers e.g., [7,22] describe a variety of microworlds that help students design in computer programming, music, genetics, architecture and geography. In all of these environments, students learn to "construct" using simple tools and by following some general rules or principles. The outcome of the design effort is a product (computer program, musical composition, experiment, etc.).

Some types of activities (for example, computer programming and the composing of music) are clearly design-oriented. However, we may use the word "design" in situation where the manipulation to be performed and the nature of the product to be generated are not so obvious. In her chapter "A Microworld-based Approach to Science Education" in this volume, White shows how a more subtle notion of design is used to teach students some intuitive notions about classic force and motion problems. This more subtle notion of design is used in ELASTIC, a software package for teaching informal statistical concepts and basic statistical reasoning [8].

Researchers would benefit greatly from a clarification of the use of the term "microworld." In particular, we need to answer the following question:

- How useful is the grouping of computer activities under the title of "microworld" (Are there useful constructs that run across projects? How can these constructs be more clearly articulated?)
- What useful subcategories could be formed under the general category of microworld (Several developers felt that the design metaphor was useful for communicating about cognitive skills, principles, instructional strategies and computer implementations across disciplines).
- What guidelines can be established for generating instructional activities? (For example, are there useful ideas for supporting learning via debugging activities? What should be the nature of feedback? What representational schemes would be helpful? How can we avoid the current practice of "starting from scratch" in the design of microworlds?)

4.5 Programming Environments

All of the computer-based learning activities that have been examined in earlier parts of this paper have been "general" activities. That is, they are applicable to a wide range of subject domains. In fact, it is likely that every subject may have parts for which each type of activity is relevant. Have we departed from general activities by now introducing the topic of programming environments? This is an open question. Several issues must be explored in regard to programming environments.:

- What are the cognitive skills and principles needed for effective programming? (Are these skills and principles different for different programming paradigms: procedural languages, list - processing orientation, logic programming, etc.)
- What is the role of visible programming environments and syntactic and semantic directed editors as aids for novice and expert programmers?
- How can computer-based activities, such as microworlds and ITS's, be used to enhance novices' learning of programming languages?
- What are the cognitive consequences of learning to program? (What general cognitive skills or principles are acquired?)

Some of the above issues are addressed in Soloway and Sleeman [58]. In the chapter in this book on "Towards More Versatile Tutors for Programming" Du Boulay discusses ITS for Programming.

4.6 Applications Tools

Examples of applications tools are word processors, databases, spreadsheets, graphics packages, statistical packages, modelling tools, (MBL) microcomputer-based laboratory materials, and authoring languages. Such tools, with the exception of MBL and educational authoring languages, are usually developed for business or industrial purposes. The "educational versions" of these tools are generally scaled-down versions of the business or industrial tools.

Microcomputer-Based Laboratory activities form an interesting class of applications tools. Microcomputer-Based Laboratory (MBL) activities may bridge the gap between the external physical world and computer-based tools for analysis. Through MBL and modelling software, students are able to study motion, sound, heat and temperature, biofeedback and other physical phenomena. Robert Tinker, who has led the design of MBL materials, argues that MBL offers opportunities for students to be scientists [62].

Careful studies of the impact of MBL on students' learning are just emerging. Some of the results are as follows:

- Linn, Layman and Nachmias report on middle school students' gain in graphing skills [42].
- Stein and Nachmias report gains in middle school students' understanding of science content [60].
- In the chapter (of this book) on "Tools for Scientific Thinking" Ronald Thornton reports on college students' gains in understanding kinematics.

There has been very little principled study of applications tools. Some major issues that should be addressed are as follows:

- What cognitive models underlie generic applications tools? (Every applications tool is based on principles or assumptions about the psychological and physiological characteristics of the user. We need to elucidate these principles and assumptions and question their validity.)

To what extent do we have educational application tools? (As indicated earlier, most applications tools were developed for business and industrial purposes).

- Is the category of "applications tools" a useful grouping from the point of view of designers and teachers?(Do the various parties that are involved in the development and use of applications tools have important things to say to each other? Are there general frameworks' for thinking about the development and use of applications tools?)
- Should we initiate a more systematic study of the design and use of educational applications tools?
- Will proficiency at a few general skills and understanding of a few principles lead to greater ability to learn new applications? (How does the learning of one database system influence the efficiency and effectiveness of one's learning of another database system? A similar question can be raised about the learning of word processors. Are there connections between learning to program and learning certain applications, such as query languages for database systems? What general skills must be developed, or general principles understood, to facilitate the learning of certain classes of applications?)
- What is the role of computer-based learning activities in teaching people how to use applications tools?
- What is the impact of specific uses of applications tools on students' ability to solve problems?

I have used the concept of "learner control" to order the types of computer-based learning activities. This same concept could be used to describe variations within a specific type of activity. For example, Duchastel [20] discusses learner control in the context of intelligent computer assisted instruction systems.

I have sketched only a few examples of the types of computer-based learning activities. More detailed examples are given in a number of sources (e.g. [1,10,50,64]. A variety of courseware catalogs feature pre-college packages for example, [61,48, Queue, 1988,40,17,28,47,55,49] Several sources provide useful directions for college/university courseware [23,56,57,59,32]. In addition, state-of-the-art use of computers are reflected in other chapters of this book. My intent has been to cast all of the efforts in the light of new conceptual frameworks.

5. Some General Design Considerations That Are Somewhat Independent of the Type of Computer-Based Learning Activity

In sections 3 and 4 of this chapter, I have discussed major issues related to current practices and future directions for the use of a variety of computer-based learning activities. In many ways the emphasis has been on activity-specific considerations. In this section, I turn to general consideration that are largely independent of the type of activity under consideration.

5.1 Affective Dimension

The novelty of computer use may have been sufficient to maintain students' interest in the early days of the use of computers in education. However, the more widespread use of computers demands that greater consideration be given to factors that will positively influence students' attitudes towards using the computer as a tool for learning.

One technique for gaining and sustaining motivation is through instructional games. Alessi and Trolip, [1] argue that the following features are present in varying degrees in games:

- goals (clearly stated or easily inferred)
- rules
- competition (The opponent may be another person or the computer)
- challenge
- fantasy
- safety (The game may be a safe way to engage in dangerous activities, such as contact sports, etc.)
- entertainment

Malone [44] presented an interesting study of intrinsically motivating features in games. There is a need to better understand the role of gaming environments in different types of computer-based learning activities.

Designers of computer-based learning activities must be in touch with the broader culture. The affective dimension should be sensitive to cultural diversity (gender, ethnicity, sub-cultures).

5.2 Representational Schemes and Mental Models

In any instructional process, decisions must be made about appropriate representations (words, graphs, diagrams, physical objects, etc.). We are barely beginning to understand the relative merits of different representations in specific contexts. In their chapter on "Mental Models and Understanding: A Problem for Science Education" in this book Frederiksen and White present an interesting perspective on representation, mental models and students' understanding of certain aspects of electricity.

5.3 Discourse

I shall use "discourse" in this context as the exchange between the instructional delivery system and the student. Some basic issues that must be addressed are as follows:

- Who should be in charge of the discourse?
- (How frequently and for what purpose should the student be interrupted?)
- What are appropriate representational schemes and mental models for the delivery system and the student?
- What aspects of the students' response are not addressed by the instructional system?

5.4 User Interface

The effective use of menus and icons, as well as the concept of direct manipulation environments prompted a movement in human-computer interaction. User interface, once thought to be an add-on to the basic computer activity, is now seen as central in the development of educational software.

6. Computer-Based Learning Activities and Higher-Order Thinking

The use of computers in education has helped to foster a reconsideration of the cognitive aims of education at every level, kindergarten through college. In particular, some investigators are beginning to propose new cognitive abilities for mathematics, science, writing and other areas. These new abilities relate largely to the students' capability to apply knowledge in a variety of contexts. The new tasks posed to students demand a flexible use of knowledge and require information processing and problem solving abilities described as higher-order thinking [54,45,67].

Some of the major issues regarding higher-order thinking which must be explored are as follows:

- What is higher-order thinking? (Is the category of "higher order thinking" sufficiently well defined to serve as a basis for communication? What subcategories of higher-order thinking are appropriate? How are the subcategories related?)
- What behaviours characterize higher-order thinking? (What observable behaviours might we say reflect higher-order thinking?)
- How similar or dissimilar is higher-order thinking across disciplines or across different subjects (or parts of subjects within a given discipline)?
- How can interactive computer-based learning environments help us to clarify students' understanding of subject matter?
- What types of computer-based learning activities can help to foster higher-order thinking?
- What new view of assessment of learning must be encouraged in light of efforts to get students to do higher order thinking?
- What are appropriate roles for the computer in creating test environments ("delivery" of tests) and in assessing students' performance? (How might the dynamics of interactive process oriented environments change the nature of the kinds of "items" that are given to students?)
- What are "tools" for thinking? (Are there basic tools that will give one a certain intellectual leverage? What about powerful individual metaphors for thinking versus general skills or principles across individuals?)
- What is the relationship between higher-order thinking and analytical approaches to the "world"?
- How should the educational system change to support the emphasis on higher-order thinking?
- What is the relationship between the affective dimensions and higher order thinking?

7. Context, Curricula, Creativity and Culture: Bridging the Gap Between Formal Education and Personal and Societal Interests

In the previous sections of this paper, I have tried to give a view of the development and use of computer-based learning activities. I have tried to give some indication of the problems, challenges and promises that lurk around the corner. However complex many of these issues may appear to be, they are dwarfed by the issues raised here.

Most computer-based learning activities are developed in ivory towers. In many instances the designers are isolated (maybe insulated) from the real educational environments in which the activities will ultimately be used. The developers identify themselves with various disciplines and few profess to keep an eye on general issues in education. A few issues I feel are critical to the ultimate success of computer-based learning activities in the "educational system":

- What is the "context" in which the activity is to be used? (What match or mismatch will exist between students' previous response to tasks and the aims of the current material (e.g. rote learning versus application of concepts)? What are students' and teachers' attitudes toward various types of learning activities? What is the level of knowledge of the teachers and students in relevant areas?)

- How does the proposed activity relate to the expressed or implied curriculum? (Will the proposed content fit? If not what are the opportunities for change? Are the proposed cognitive abilities similar or compatible with existing aims? If not, what is the rationale for the new emphasis and what is the likelihood of change? How can change be encouraged?)
- Does the proposed activity expand the opportunity for individual creativity? (If yes, then will the current assessment system permit it? If no, then does the activity foster the new emphasis on higher-order thinking?)
- What assumptions about culture are given explicitly or implied by the activity? (Have issues of gender, ethnicity, socio-economic levels, values, etc. been properly considered?) Several sources explore some of the issues raised in this section. [66,63,19,65]

8. Assessment of Learning Outcomes

One of the more significant benefits of the current effort to understand the significance of computers for education is the opportunity that it offers for us to examine attitudes and cognitive processes in particular as well as the educational environment in general. Evaluation, the act of assessing the impact of our actions in light of our goals and objectives, is fundamental to the proper deployment of computer-based technology to education and crucial to educational advancement in general.

Given the current level of use of computers in education and the rapid growth of that use, it is imperative that we develop better ways of assessing the impact of computer-based instruction on various audiences. Research on the effect of computer-based instruction on learning and teaching is encouraging. (33-39]. However, given the lack of specificity of the precise nature of the treatment used in various studies, many concerns have been raised about the meaning of the conclusions indicated by these studies [15].

There is a clear need to broaden our evaluation methods so that we are better able to assess the impact of simulations, microworlds, intelligent tutoring systems, and other types of "complex" computer-based learning environments. In addition, there is a striking need to assess the impact of computers on college/university level audiences and particularly to document the impact of computer-assisted instruction on higher order cognitive processes at every school level.

In this brief paper, we attempt to clarify some of the issues relating to the evaluation of computer-based instruction. In particular, we address some of the ways in which educators, designers, students, and others might cooperate to develop and implement evaluation plans that capture the relevant aspects of computer-based learning environments.

8.1 The Nature of Evaluation

It is not uncommon for one to hear designers and users of courseware say that they are not interested in evaluation. It is hard to believe that anyone who is engaged in any activity is not concerned about the ultimate impact of that activity. Hence, I really do not believe these people. I think that they are expressing their dissatisfaction with the rather narrow view of assessment that has been applied to the evaluation of computer-based instruction. Hence, any effort to broaden the audience of participants in the evaluation process must begin with a broadening and refining (no contradiction here) of the evaluation process so that it can be convincingly argued that the new scheme will better capture the relevant aspects of the learning environment.

Evaluation is a complex activity. It involves an identification of at least one audience who is interested in the process or product of the evaluation. More fully, evaluation is the act of:

- observing
- seeing the relevant
- documenting
- hypothesizing

- selecting or developing appropriate models
- selecting or developing appropriate paradigms
- selecting or developing appropriate instruments
- selecting (or possibly developing) appropriate experimental designs
- conducting "experiments"
- collecting and analyzing "data"
- interpreting results in light of existing or new conceptual frameworks
- discerning significant new directions
- communicating the results of the process and product of the evaluation so that the report is most valuable to a designated audience.

There is a concept that is very much akin to evaluation (we think that it is a part of evaluation) that notion is "documentation." What cognitive skills are addressed? What motivational factors are employed? What are the instructional strategies for helping the learner to develop the cognitive skills? etc. Answers to a wide range of such questions are crucial if a reader is to be able to interpret the meaning of experimental results. Treatment effects without clarification of what is the treatment are meaningless.

8.2 Need for Evaluation of Computer-Based Learning Activities

We need to know the following:

- What is the relevance of computer-based instruction to certain educational goals and objectives?
- What type of computer-based activity will be most appropriate for certain objectives?
- What types of treatments will be most appropriate for a given student audience?
- What will be the costs?

We can't reasonably answer these questions without a sensible evaluation plan.

8.3 In Search of More Meaningful Evaluations of Computer-Based Instruction

An evaluation may be meaningless for a number of reasons. The most obvious reason is the use of an unconvincing model or experimental design. However, there are many factors that may diminish the value of an evaluation study. We would like to outline some of the deficiencies that are all too prevalent in evaluations of computer-based instruction.

- Failure to define the treatment appropriately:

"Simulation to teach elementary algebra concepts" does not define a courseware package. Detailed cognitive skills addressed, specific motivational factors, and detailed instructional strategies are crucial elements of the treatment. The absence of such detail may render the courseware of little practical value to the teacher, and of little use to researchers who wish to replicate the study or generalize the results.

- Failure to give detailed demographics on the population:

The task of describing the population may indeed be much more difficult for college/university groups than pre-college populations.

- Failure to identify and assess unique attitudes and cognitive skills that may occur from the computer activities:

The computer-based instruction may offer opportunities for learning in addition to those conventional skills that it was designed to develop. Careful evaluation methods must attempt to capture this aspect of the learning experience.

In computer activities that use discovery/inquiry approaches, it may not be easy to identify and measure many of the outcomes. However, since students leave an "electronic trace" when they interact with certain computer activities, we have a better chance of documenting their actions. Of course, this type of monitoring must respect students' privacy.

- Intertwining instructional variables and effects of computer-based instruction:

Is the purpose of the study to show the effect of the instructional variables of interactivity, feedback, self- paced, etc.? Is it to show that the computer is an important tool for implementing certain instructional variables? Of course, one's answers to these kinds of questions will influence the choice of control.

- Failure to recognize the critical role of motivation in learning:

Can results be attributed primarily to increased motivation brought on through the use of the computer? How was motivation achieved in the computer environment?

- Failure to specify unambiguously questions that you hope to answer:

This failure is the root of other failures. If you don't begin with a set of clear questions, or at least find some along the way, your results are likely to be garbled and of little value to you or others.

The question of whether "computer-assisted instruction is better than conventional method X" may be unanswerable. Computer-assisted instruction refers to too many things and, in most contexts, so does X.

- Failure to recognize whether your study is or is not about computers:

Studies about instructional variables may go masked as studies about computer-based instruction. Clarifying the role of the computer is an important task.

8.4 Models and Paradigms for the Evaluation of Computer-Based Instruction

In an earlier part of this paper, evaluation was described as a complex activity. A significant part of this activity is the selection of appropriate models and paradigms. A model is the concrete realization of the ideological base from which the evaluation is derived. Evaluations may have their ideological bases in naturalistic inquiry, case study, anthropological approaches and a variety of other techniques, including classical experimental design [43]. We are using the term "paradigms" to refer to specific types of implementation of models.

The perturbations in social contexts and learning environments resulting from the introduction of computer-based instruction demand the full spectrum of evaluation models and paradigms. These perturbations may require documentation by teachers and participants, as well as the observations of designers and "external" evaluators. Until we can achieve this type of collective effort, our evaluations are not likely to capture much of the important changes in learning environments resulting from the "new" technology.

8.5 Reaping the Benefits of Better Evaluations

In order to achieve effective evaluation of computer-based instruction, we will be forced to confront important issues of motivation, cognitive skills, and instructional strategies. Instructional variables such as levels of interactivity, feedback, coaching, etc., may emerge as salient features in our investigation. The perturbations in social contexts and learning environments resulting from the use of computer-based instruction require the full spectrum of evaluation methodologies -- naturalistic inquiry, case study, anthropological approaches, classical experimental designs, etc.

Some of the fruitful outcomes of evaluative work may be the following:

- more effective ways for describing treatment
- mental measures for computer-based instruction
- validation of the role of certain instructional variables in meeting objectives
- models for assessing the learning that occurs in computer- based discovery/inquiry environments
- effective ways of communicating results to a variety of audiences
- ideas for abstracting general instructional ideas from computer studies

A number of process-oriented instructional activities and new methods of assessments that address higher-order thinking are emerging [16,46,24,45,67,68]. An interesting compilation of perspectives on more effective assessment is presented in the Proceedings of the 1987 Educational Testing Service Conference on Assessment in the Service of Learning (1987). In the chapter of this book entitled "Toward a Design Science of Education" Collins reports on a major effort to synthesize research on technological innovation with an aim toward developing a methodology for carrying out design experiments. Such experiments will be used to study different ways of using technology in classrooms and schools. In addition, the results will be used to construct a systematic science of how to design educational environments so that new technologies can be introduced successfully.

There is a strong tendency in educational assessment to report only studies that show a positive effect of treatment. In many instances, a result of "no effect" may be very significant if the conditions under which the "no effect" resulted are clearly articulated. Furthermore, educational evaluators often neglect the risks associated with particular instructional programs. Just as technologists in other areas must look at potential harmful effects of the technology, educational technologists must do effective risk assessments of specific uses of innovative technologies.

9. Nurturing the Design and Implementation of Computer-Based Learning Activities

By way of summary, I would like to indicate some of the major issues that must be addressed if we are to encourage the development and implementation of computer-based learning activities:

a) What are useful ideas for the design and interpretation of microworlds, ITS's and other forms of computer-based learning activities?

b) What is "Advanced Educational Technology"? (We want to be at the cutting edge. We need to understand what this means. One interpretation of advanced educational technology is super high-tech devices. Another interpretation of advanced educational technology is innovative uses of modest technology. We need to understand the role played by each of these views.)

c) What fundamental research in psychology and cognitive science is most relevant to advances in the development and implementation of computer-based learning activities? (Funding priorities dictate that funds allocated for educational technology cannot support all psychological studies. What "pure research" studies are so fundamental to success of educational technology that they must be considered competitive with the most impressive development activities.)

d) What are more useful assessment methods? (What changes must be made in our educational testing procedures? What new methods might better capture students' understanding? How can the impact of more open-ended computer-based learning activities be assessed?)

e) How can we understand the relevance of different computer-based activities to different instructional implementations (individual, small group, etc.) and cultural contexts?

f) Do "instructionism" and "constructionism" represent very different world views? (In a National Science Foundation's Director's Meeting in Pittsburgh, Pennsylvania (USA), in November 1988, Seymour Papert talked about "instructionism versus constructionism" Are the differences between ITS's and microworld-type environments reconcilable? How can these differences be reconciled? Some discussion of these issues are given by Henderson and Ferguson [29], Catrambone and Carroll [12].

g) How do we allocate resources (human, machine, textbook, etc.) so as to produce a cost-effective and desirable learning environment. (What should be the roles of human teachers, peer teachers, microworlds, ITS's, etc. in students' learning environments? What instructional bottlenecks might be opened through the allocation of resources for the development of ITS's for small domains? What areas of the curriculum should be relegated to textbooks?)

h) How can we establish learning environments that are captivating? (Have we lost sight of motivation, cultural differences, and other humanistic perspectives in our treatment of cognitive skills and learning of principles?)

i) What mix of "immediate impact" projects and "long-range" efforts is appropriate? (Teachers, students, parents, and often funding agencies look for activities that can be used immediately and whose impact on students' learning is immediate. Such demands may stifle the development of significant projects that may require several years to develop and may demand changes in the assessment system if the impact is to be realized.)

j) What are the implications of networks, telecommunications, and other technologies for offering instruction at a distance and fostering collaborative learning? (What are the cognitive and affective benefits of "team" approaches to problems?)

k) How might we better manage the use of educational technology? (Two types of management issues are of concern: micro-management and macro-management. I use the term "micro-management" to refer to the management decisions that must be made by the individual teacher in the context of selecting and utilizing appropriate resources (human teacher time, peer teaching, computer activities, etc.) for specific educational objectives. I use the term "macro-management" to refer to the management decisions that must be made by people who must direct the appropriate use of computers in individual schools, school districts, training departments within business or industry, or possibly regional or national projects.)

l) How can we keep the natural order of education first and technology second as suggested in the term "educational technology"? (The field of "educational technology" has an interesting mix of participants: educators, psychologists, computer scientists and the full spectrum of subject-matter specialists. Each has her/her own agenda in regard to the improvement of education. How can we direct the parts so that we move swiftly towards better educational practice? How can computer-based learning activities help to focus attention on higher-order thinking skills?)

Education is a complex human endeavour. The real potential of the computer in that endeavour is yet to be realized. However, we know that the computer has been a catalyst for rethinking educational goals. Furthermore, in our efforts to study the impact of computer-based learning activities, we have been forced to question our system for assessing learning. This search for effective uses of computers in education has brought together a force of cognitive psychologists, sociologists, educators, computer scientists, and subject-area specialists. Will the outcome of these efforts be a fragmented or a holistic view of education? The challenge for the next few years will be to create a symphony from the myriad of individual efforts.

References

1. Alessi, S. and Trolip, S., *Computer-Based Instruction: Methods and Development,* Prentice-Hall, Englewood Cliffs, New Jersey, 1985.
2. Anderson, J. R., Boyle, C. F., Farrell, R. G. and Reiser, B. J., Cognitive Principles in the Design of Computer Tutors, in P. Morris (editor) *Modelling Cognition,* Wiley, New York, 1987.
3. Anderson, J. R., Boyle, C. F. and Reiser, B. J., Intelligent Tutoring Systems, *Science,* Vol. 228, pp.456-462, 1985.
4. Anderson, J. R., Boyle, C. F. and Yost, G., The Geometry Tutor, *Proceedings of the Ninth International Joint Conference on Artificial Intelligence,* Los Angeles, California, 1985.
5. Anderson, J. R., Farrell, R. and Sauers, R., Learning to program in LISP, *Cognitive Science,* Vol. 8, pp. 87- 129, 1985.

6. Anderson, J. R. and Reiser, B. J., The LISP tutor, *Byte*, Vol. 10, pp.159-175, 1985.
7. Balzano, G., Restructuring the Curriculum for Design: Music, Mathematics, and Psychology, *Machine - Mediated Learning*, Vol. 2, No. 1 & 2, pp. 83-109, 1987.
8. Bolt Beranek and Newman Laboratories Incorporated, *Reasoning Under Uncertainty*, Technical Report No. 6774, Bolt Beranek and Newman, 1988.
9. Bonar, J. G. and Cunningham, R., Bridge: Tutoring the Programming Process, in J. Psotka, L. D. Massey and S. A. Mutter (editors), *Intelligent Tutoring Systems: Lessons Learned* Erlbaum, Hillsdale, New Jersey, 1988.
10. Brownell, G., *Computers and Teaching*, West Publishing, New York, 1987.
11. Bullough, R. V. and Beatty, L. F., *Classroom Applications of Microcomputers*, Merrill Publishing, Columbus, Ohio, 1987.
12. Catrambone, R. and Carroll, J. M., Learning a Word Processing System with Training Wheels and Guided Exploration, *Proceedings of CHI+GI '87 Human Factors in Computing Systems*, Association of Computing Machinery, New York, 1987
13. Clancey, W. J., Tutoring Rules for Guiding a Case Method Dialogue, in D. H. Sleeman and J. S. Brown (editors), *Intelligent Tutoring Systems*, Academic Press, London, 1982.
14. Clancey, W. J., *Knowledge-based Tutoring: The Guidon Program*, MIT press, Cambridge, Massachusetts, 1987.
15. Clark, R. E., Confounding in Educational Computing Research, *Journal of Educational Computing Research*, Vol. 1, No. 2, pp. 137-148, 1985.
16. Collins, A. Reformulating Testing to Measure Learning and Thinking, in N. Frederiksen, R. Glaser, A. Lesgold, and M. Shafto (editors) *Diagnostic Monitoring of Skills and Knowledge Acquisition*, Lawrence Erlbaum Associates, Hillsdale, New Jersey, 1988.
17. Conduit, *Catalog of Educational Software*, The University of Iowa, Iowa City, Iowa, 1988.
18. *Decimal Darts*, Control Data Corporation, Minneapolis, Minnesota, 1981.
19. Dreyfus, H. L. and Dreyfus, S. E. Mind Over Machine: *The Power of Human Intuition and Expertise in the Era of the Computer*, Free Press, New York, 1986.
20. Duchastel, P., Intelligent Computer Assisted Instruction Systems: The Nature of Learner Control, *Journal of Educational Computing Research*, Vol. 2, No. 3, pp. 379- 393. 1986.
21. Educational Testing Service, *Assessment in the Service of Learning*, Princeton, New Jersey, 1987.
22. Ferguson, D. L. and Henderson, P. B., The Design of Algorithms, *Machine-Mediated Learning*, Vol. 2., No. 1 & 2, pp. 67-82, 1987.
23. FIPSE Technology Study Group, Ivory Towers, Silicon Basements: *Learner - Centered Computing in Postsecondary Education*, Academic Computing Publications, 1988.
24. Frederiksen, J. R. and White, B.Y. Implicit Testing Within an Intelligent Tutoring System, *Machine-Mediated Learning*, Vol. 2, pp. 351-372, 1988.
25. Glaser, R., Raghavan, K. and Schauble, L., Voltaville: a discovery environment to explore the laws of DC circuits, *Proceedings of ITS - 88:* The International Conference on Intelligent Tutoring Systems, Montreal, 1988.
26. Hartley, *1988 Educational Software Catalog*, Dimondale, Michigan, 1988.
27. Hollan, J. D., Hutchins, E. L. and Weitzman, L., Steamer: An Interactive Inspectable Simulation-Based Training System, *AI Magazine*, Vol. 5, pp.15-28, 1984.
28. Houghton-Mifflin, *1988 Computer Software*, Boston, Massachusetts, 1988.
29. Henderson, P. B. and Ferguson, D. L., *Guided Algorithm Discovery*, Technical Report, Department of Computer Science, State University of New York-Stony Brook, Stony Brook, New York, 1987.
30. Johnson, W. L. and Soloway, E., PROUST: An Automatic Debugger for Pascal Programs, in G. Kearsley (editor), *Artificial Intelligence and Instruction: Applications and Methods*, Addison-Wesley, Reading, Massachusetts, 1987.
31. Kearsley, G. P. (editor), *Artificial Intelligence and Instruction: Applications and Methods*, Addison-Wesley, Reading, Massachusetts, 1987.

32. Kinko's Academic Courseware Exchange, *Low Cost Software for Higher Education,* Kinko's Service Corporation, Ventura, California, 1988.
33. Kulik, C.-L. C. and Kulik, J. A. Effectiveness of Computer-Based Education in Colleges, *AEDS Journal,* Vol. 19, pp. 81-108, 1986.
34. Kulik, C.-L. C., Kulik, J. A. and Shwalb, B. J., The Effectiveness of Computer-Based Adult Education: A Meta-Analysis, *Journal of Educational Computing Research,* Vol. 2, pp. 235-252, 1986.
35. Kulik, J. A. and Kulik, C.-L. C., Review of Recent Research Literature on Computer-Based Instruction, *Contemporary Educational Psychology,* Vol. 12, pp. 222-230, 1987.
36. Kulik, J. A., Kulik, C.-L. C. and Bangert-Drowns, R. L., Effectiveness of Computer-Based Education in Elementary Schools, *Computers in Human Behaviour,* Vol. 1, pp. 59-74, 1985a.
37. Kulik, J. A., Kulik, C.-L. C. and Bangert-Drowns, R. L., The Importance of Outcome Studies: A Reply to Clark, *Journal of Educational Computing Research,* Vol. 1, pp. 381-387, 1985b.
38. Kulik, J. A., Kulik, C.-L. C. and Bangert-Drowns, R. L. *Effectiveness of Mastery Learning Programs: A Meta-Analysis,* unpublished manuscript, Center for Research on Learning and Teaching, University of Michigan, Ann Arbor, 1988.
39. Kulik, C.-L. C. and Kulik, J. A., *Effectiveness of Computer-Based Instruction: An Updated Analysis,* Technical Report, Center for Research on Learning and Teaching, University of Michigan, Ann Arbor, 1988.
40. Learning Company, *1988 Fall School Catalog,* Fremont, California, 1988.
41. Liao, T. T and Piel, E. J., The Yellow-Light Problem: Computer-Based Applied Mathematics, in *Computers in Mathematics Education (1984 Yearbook-NCTM),* National Council of Teachers of Mathematics, Reston, Virginia, 1984.
42. Linn, M. C., Layman, J. and Nachmias, R., Cognitive Consequences of Microcomputer-based Laboratories: Graphing Skills Development, *Journal of Contemporary Educational Psychology,* 1985.
43. Madaus, G. F., Scriven, M. and Stufflebeam, D. L. (editors), *Evaluation Models,* Kluher-Nijoff, Boston, 1983.
44. Malone, T. W., What Makes Things Fun to Learn? A Study of Intrinsically Motivating Computer Games, *Cognitive and Instructional Sciences Series CIS-7 (SSL-80-11),* Xerox. Palo Alto, Ca: Palo Alto Research Center, 1980.
45. Marshall, S. P., *Assessing Schema Knowledge,* Technical Report, Psychology Department, Center for Research in Mathematics and Science Education, San Diego State University, San Diego, California, 1988.
46. Martinez, M. E. and Lipson, J. I. Assessment for Learning, *Educational Leadership,* April, 1989.
47. Merlan Scientific Ltd. *Merlan Micro Series,* Georgetown, Ontario (Canada), 1988.
48. MECC (Minnesota Educational Computing Consortium), *MECC Catalog,* St. Paul Minnesota, 1988-89.
49. Milliken, *Milliken Courseware,* St. Louis, Missouri, 1988.
50. O'Shea, T. and Self, J., *Learning and Teaching with Computers,* Prentice-Hall, Englewood Cliffs, New Jersey, 1983.
51. Papert, S., *Mindstorms,* Basic Books, New York, 1980. Queue, Inc., 1988 Educational Software Catalog, Bridgeport, Connecticut, 1988.
52. Reiser, B. J., Friedmann, P., Gevins, J. Kimberg, D., Ranney, M. and Romero, A., A Graphical Programming Language Interface for an Intelligent LISP tutor, *Proceedings of CHI '88, Conference on Human Factors in Computing Systems,* Association of Computing Machinery, 1988.
53. Richards, J. and Feurzeig, W., *Intelligent Tools for Algebra,* Technical Report, Bolt Beranek and Newman, Cambridge, Massachusetts 1988.

54. Schoenfeld, A. H., *Mathematics, Technology, and Higher-Order Thinking,* Technical Report, Graduate Group in Science and Mathematics Education, University of California, Berkeley, California, 1987.
55. Scholastic, Inc. *Microcomputer Instructional Materials* (1988/89), Jefferson City, Missouri, 1988.
56. Seiden, P., *The Elusive Mountain: Software Resources for Higher Education,* Academic Computing, pp.61-63, 1987a.
57. Seiden, P., *Directory of Software Sources for Higher Education: A Guide to Instructional Applications,* Princeton, New Jersey: Peterson's Guides, 1987.
58. Soloway, E. and Sleeman, D., (Editors). *Special issue of Journal of Educational Computing Research* (Vol. 2, No. 1). Baywood, Farmingdale, New York, 1986.
59. Spraggins, J., CAI and the College Curriculum: Five Cases, *Journal of Educational Technology Systems,* 1983.
60. Stein, J. S. and Nachmias, R., *Computers as Lab Partner: Students' Subject Matter Achievements,* Technical report, Graduate Group in Science and Mathematics Education, University of California, Berkeley, 1987.
61. Sunburst Communications, *Educational Computer Courseware*, Pleasantville, New York, 1989.
62. Tinker, R., Modelling and MBL: Software Tools for Science, in Conference Proceedings: *National Educational Computing Conference*, 1986.
63. Turkle, S., *The Second Self: Computers and the Human Spirit,* Simon and Schuster, New York, 1984.
64. Vockell, E. and Schwartz, E. *The Computer in the Classroom,* Mitchell Publishing, Santa Cruz, California, 1988.
65. Weir, S., *Cultivating Minds: A LOGO Casebook*, Harper and Row, New York, 1987.
66. Weizenbaum, J., *Computer Power and Human Reason: From Judgement to Calculation,* Freeman, San Francisco, 1976.
67. White, B. Y., *Thinker Tools: Causal Models, Conceptual Change, and Science Education,* Technical Report No. 6873, Bolt Beranek and Newman, Cambridge, Massachusetts, 1988.
68. White, B. Y. and Frederiksen, J. R., *Causal Model Progressions as a Foundation for Intelligent Learning Environments,* Technical Report No. 6686, Bolt Beranek and Newman, Cambridge, Massachusetts 1987.

5

New Directions for Educational Technology

Charles M Reigeluth
Indiana University
Bloomington, IN47405
U.S.A.

Abstract: I see three important areas of research for the future development of educational technology: instructional strategy prescriptions, tools to help designers, and applications (contexts). The purpose of this chapter is to identify specific new directions, within each of these three areas, that I think are most important for future research. However, before discussing these new directions for educational technology, I would like to briefly comment on some concerns I have regarding many of the chapters in this volume.

Keywords: affective learning, Artificial Intelligence, declarative knowledge, educational technology, expert system, formative evaluation, instructional management, Instructional theory, intelligent tutoring systems, mediational systems, motivational strategies, prescriptive instructional theory, procedural knowledge, sequencing, simulation, types of learning

1. Concerns

My primary concern is that many chapters represent a very narrow view of the field. Most of them are about intelligent tutoring systems (ITS). Although this is indeed an important new direction for educational technology, it is only one of many important new directions. As Merrill [9] has pointed out, tutoring (whether done by an experienced human or an artificially intelligent machine) is not always the best mode of instruction. Computer-based simulations provide a powerful environment with which the learner can interact to discover principles and develop methods for solving problems in a much more powerful way than a tutor could ever provide through dialogue alone. And for automatizing lower-order skills (procedural knowledge) and facts (declarative knowledge), drill-and-practice games are far more cost-effective and motivational than an ITS. We must not ignore such other aspects of educational technology when we discuss important new directions deserving of our time and funders' support.

The foundations of educational technology are based in media, and focused on the "hard technologies" to the exclusion of the "soft technology" of how to optimize the process of learning. We have gone through cycles of embracing a hard technology as affording a radically improved method of educating children, then having our expectations shattered, then embracing a new hard technology, and so on. We have seen radio come and go, followed by tape-slide and television, to name the most famous cases. Part of the problem comes from overhyping and overpromising, part is due to failure to recognize that the hard technology is not a universal tool that is equally effective for all types of learning, and part is due to failure to recognize the importance of the soft technology -- instructional theory -- for guidance as to what the instruction should be like regardless of the medium (the hard technology). As McCalla warns in his chapter in this volume, ITS is in danger of falling into this same trap.

Another concern is that many reports and presentations on ITS remind me of "show and tell." There seems to be little interest in developing and reporting generalizable prescriptions or rules which govern an intelligent tutor. What little generalizing is done is usually along the lines of descriptive theory (e.g., cognitive learning theory) rather than prescriptive theory (instructional theory). Although there are indeed few rules or prescriptions which would generalize to all learning situations, surely the vast majority generalize beyond a single topic. In this volume Collins discusses the need for a design science similar to aeronautics. ITS projects should contribute toward the building of such a prescriptive design science or theory.

The other side of this coin is the syndrome of "reinventing the wheel" to which McCalla also referred in his chapter. Most ITS projects seem to have ignored the existing knowledge base of instructional theory when designing their intelligent tutors. Instructional theory offers many validated prescriptions (rules) which should govern any effective instructional system, including an intelligent tutor. In his chapter, Ferguson discusses the distinction between instruction and construction, and suggests that the ITS people may ignore the existing instructional theory knowledge base because they perceive it as irrelevant to their focus on construction. I certainly agree that the construction mind-set is important for the more complex kinds of learning, and I have used it recently in my work to develop prescriptions for teaching "understanding" [11].

However, in adopting such a mind-set, we must be careful to maintain our interest in prescribing what a teacher or other instructional medium should do to facilitate construction. In other words, instruction is also required for construction -- they are not mutually exclusive terms. It is not sufficient to just describe what goes on (or should go on) inside a learner's head; it is important to prescribe what a teacher (or other medium) should do to make it happen. And much of what exists in the current instructional theory knowledge base is indeed relevant to facilitating construction of meaning by a learner. I have seen some features of ITS's touted as a great discovery, when they were in fact a clear implementation of an instructional theory prescription. Reiser, in his chapter, discusses a variety of general prescriptions for an intelligent programming tutor called GIL, including the timing of feedback and the use of examples. On the other hand, I have seen some ITS's which ignore some important principles of instruction. The quality of their tutoring would have been considerably improved if the developers had done some homework on instructional theory, or if an instructional theorist had been on the development team.

Another concern relates to the heavy reliance on observation of "experts" to derive rules to govern an ITS. More than half of my graduate students at Syracuse University were exteachers who were undergoing a career change. They typically had taught for as many as 10 to 15 years and were often among the best teachers. Universally, towards the end of my introductory course on instructional theory, several would comment, "If only I had known this when I was teaching, I would have been able to do so much better a job of teaching." To some extent, one could liken analysis of teachers' techniques now to the analysis of doctors' techniques a century ago. One could conclude, "Bloodletting is a common practice, so it must be good." There is a danger in analyzing current practice to prescribe what should be. It is but one of several approaches that should be used to build a sound prescriptive knowledge base (design science).

Another concern is the lack of emphasis on empirical comparisons to find out how good one's ITS really is. This is the flip side of the "show and tell" problem. Most projects have merely attempted to create a working ITS without concern for how well it compares with the most viable alternative approaches for teaching the same material. But, at the same time, much of the empirical research that is conducted by educational technologists is focused improperly on testing the validity of our methods. Whereas validity is the most important concern for descriptive theory, optimality is the most important concern for prescriptive theory. It is not a matter of whether a certain ITS can teach; rather, can it teach better than the best of the known alternatives. And even more importantly for a new technology, how can we improve it? The experimental study is terribly inadequate at providing empirical information to answer this question. But what are the alternatives? One possibility is a "formative evaluation" type of research which creates a piece of instruction solely on the basis of a prescriptive theory, then conducts one-on-one evaluations of the instruction to identify weaknesses and suggestions for improvement, which in turn reflect weaknesses and improvements for the theory itself [12]. Naturally, a representative sample of students is needed to assure reliability of findings. This form of research should yield a far greater wealth of information for improving a theory than an experimental study would, but much more work is needed to refine this research methodology.

A final concern is the lack of attention to system planning. Systems theory has been an important dimension of educational technology for several decades now. It is well understood that not only the effectiveness, but also the likelihood of adoption, of a new technology depends greatly on how it is to be used within the larger system of instruction. Again, an ITS project would be well advised to include an instructional theorist on its team.

In sum, I feel that ITS is indeed an important new direction for educational technology, but I have some serious concerns about some of the mind-sets which seem to be taking hold. First, there is the "narrow view" problem. ITS is but one important dimension of educational technology, and it is clearly not the best way to go for some educational needs. Furthermore, the hard technology and programming technology frequently receive too much attention relative to the soft technology of pedagogy or instructional theory. Second, there is the "show and tell" problem. There has been relatively little attempt to formulate generalizable prescriptions or rules (prescriptive theory). Third, there is the "reinventing the wheel" problem. All too often the existing knowledge base in educational technology (particularly instructional theory) has been ignored. Fourth, there is the "bloodletting" problem. Observation of experts should not be the only way we build our knowledge base. Fifth, there is the "lack of data" problem. To what extent is an ITS better than the best alternatives? Our research needs to focus more on optimality than validity to address this question. And finally, there is the "systems" problem. The design of an educational tool needs to be done with consideration for how it will be used within an educational system, rather than just developing it as a stand-alone entity.

Addressing these concerns is certainly one important "new direction" for educational technology. But what particular areas of research are most likely to advance our ability to improve education? As was mentioned at the beginning of this chapter, I see three important areas of research for the future development of educational technology: instructional strategy prescriptions, tools to help designers, and applications (contexts). Of these three, the area of strategy prescriptions is likely to be the most important, because it provides knowledge about how to effectively utilize the capabilities of the powerful new delivery systems to enhance learning.

2. Strategy Prescriptions

There are several important kinds of strategy prescriptions which are greatly in need of further development during the next decade: (1) prescriptions for types of learning which have been largely ignored by the field, such as understanding and generic skills; (2) prescriptions which take advantage of the unique capabilities of new technologies, such as simulations and intelligent tutoring systems; (3) prescriptions for structuring and sequencing a course or curriculum; (4) prescriptions for selecting mediational systems; (5) prescriptions for designing instructional-management systems; and (6) prescriptions for motivating learners.

2.1 Types of Learning

In our efforts to synthesize the current state of the art in instructional theory into a coherent, unified, prescriptive knowledge base, we have come to believe that there are in the cognitive domain four major types of learning which require very different methods of instruction [12]. In teaching these ideas to beginning graduate students, I have found that the most intuitive labels are: (1) memorizing information, (2) understanding relationships, (3) applying skills, and (4) applying generic skills. Memorizing information corresponds to Bloom's "knowledge," Merrill's "remember verbatim," and Ausubel's "rote learning," and is one aspect of Gagné's "verbal information." Understanding relationships is similar to Bloom's "comprehension," Merrill's "remember paraphrased," and Ausubel's "meaningful verbal learning," and is the other aspect of Gagné's "verbal information." Applying skills is the same as Bloom's "application," Merrill's "use-a-generality," and Gagné's "intellectual skills." And applying generic skills includes Bloom's "analysis," "synthesis," and "evaluation," Merrill's "find-a-generality," and Gagné's "cognitive strategies."

The various types of domain-specific content, such as concepts, procedures, and principles, can be acquired as any one of the first three types of learning: a concept can be memorized (either its definition or an example of it), or it can be understood (its relationships with other knowledge the learner has), or it can be applied (instances can be classified as examples or non examples of it). The fourth kind of learning is domain independent and generally requires more time to acquire. In our analyses of theories of instruction and learning, we have found that these four types of learning require greater differences in the instruction than any other categorization or factor.

The field of instruction (variously referred to as instructional psychology, instructional technology, instructional development, and instructional theory) has grown out of a behavioristic orientation which has focussed most efforts on prescriptions for memorizing information (association tasks) and applying skills (especially concept classification and procedure using). We have relatively very little in the way of validated prescriptions for facilitating the acquisition of understanding (meaningful learning). What work has been done has largely been on the development of descriptive learning theory, rather than prescriptive instructional theory. Considering recent advances in cognitive learning theory, it should be much easier now to develop useful instructional strategies for facilitating understanding. In fact, at Indiana University we have made progress recently on a project to develop prescriptions in this area [11].

Instructional theorists are already beginning to devote greater attention to generic skills: thinking skills, problem-solving skills, learning strategies, and metacognition. While much attention will continue to go to deciding what to teach in this area, it seems likely that instructional theorists will also place greater attention on figuring out how best to teach them. Of particular importance are prescriptions for designing a good simple-to-complex curriculum sequence for teaching a generic skill, and prescriptions for integrating such single-skill sequences with each other and with a range of domain-specific course sequences. We recently completed a project with Macmillan Publishing Company that worked on the development of both the sequencing and integrating prescriptions for a K-6 science program using the elaboration theory. This project resulted in some important new prescriptions for using the "simplifying assumptions" method to sequence generic skills and to integrate those sequences with the domain-specific sequences (biological, physical, and earth sciences) [13].

I hope and expect that we will see during the next decade much more work on these two areas of the cognitive domain (understanding and generic skills). But these areas are not the only types of learning which have been largely ignored by instructional theorists. Another type of learning is affective learning: attitudes and values, morals and ethics, social development, emotional development, personal development, and such. Martin and Briggs [8] have provided an excellent beginning for instructional prescriptions in this area. While much attention is also likely to be placed on deciding which ones to teach, there is a great need for advances on how to teach them. I hope the next decade will see considerable progress in this area, also.

However, the selection of instructional strategies should not just depend on the nature of the content. The nature of the learner is important, as well as the capabilities of the media that are available. In our work, we have found that the nature of the learner has a greater influence on decisions about what to teach than how to teach it. You don't want to teach things which the learner has already mastered, for that would be a waste of time and money, and it would demotivate the learner. On the opposite extreme, you don't want to teach things which are too far beyond the learner's current knowledge, for lack of important prior knowledge (including prerequisite skills -- [5] would make learning very difficult, if not impossible. The whole notion of "debugging" is basically a matter of deciding what to teach.

Perhaps the most important way that the nature of the learner influences the selection of instructional strategies is in making decisions about the amount of instructional support provided to the learner -- that is, how rich the instruction should be. It is important to assess the difficulty of the content based on the learner's ability and prior familiarity with it. The more difficult it is, the richer the instruction needs to be, including the use of more examples and practice, alternative representations (especially hands-on and visuals), attention-focussing devices, hints, and shaping (or successive approximations). A second way that the nature of the learner is important is in the selection of motivational strategies. A motivational profile of the learner is very important for selecting appropriate motivational strategies [6,7].

2.2 New Technologies

Clearly, instructional strategy prescriptions do not depend solely on the type of learning. Significant strides in information technologies are providing educational technologists with tools of a magnitude of power previously undreamed of. Most current instructional strategies were developed out of a "page" mentality. To take full advantage of the capabilities of new mediational systems, our thinking must advance beyond such a static, confining level. We need prescriptions which take advantage of the dynamic, interactive, and AI (Artificial Intelligence) capabilities of computers and interactive video.

Computer-based simulations possess great potential as one of the most powerful forms of instruction currently possible. But most simulations fall miserably short of their potential. Prescriptions for improving their quality are sorely needed. We recently completed a two-year project to develop such prescriptions [15]. But much more work remains to be done to test, refine, and further develop such prescriptions. I expect we will see considerable advances in this area over the next decade.

Advances in information technologies have also made possible the design of intelligent tutoring systems which can be used alone or in combination with simulations or other instructional approaches. Collins and Stevens [4] have identified a variety of strategies which are relatively unique to intelligent tutoring systems, including prescriptions for goal-setting, tracing consequences to a contradiction, and entrapping the student. The next decade should see continued advances in this important area.

2.3 Structure and Sequence

Another kind of prescription in great need of further development is how to structure and sequence a course or curriculum. Based on our efforts to synthesize the state of the art in this area, we have found considerable evidence that every pattern of sequencing is based on a single type of relationship within the content [14]. The chronological sequence is based on the time relationship among events, Gagné's hierarchical sequence is based on the learning prerequisite relationship among skills, the "forward-chaining" procedural sequence is based on the order relationship among activities, our elaboration theory's conceptual elaboration sequence is based on the "parts" or "kinds" taxonomic relationships among concepts, Scandura's shortest-path sequence (further developed and popularized by Paul Merrill) is based on the simple-to-complex relationship among paths of a procedure, and so forth.

We know relatively little about the kinds of relationships that are most important for a sequence to follow to maximize such goals as building stable cognitive structures, facilitating creative thought, and allowing for maximum appropriate learner control. New approaches to sequencing will probably be particularly important for generic skills, understanding, and effective learning. It seems likely that optimal sequencing "strands" will be developed for each of these types of learning, then interwoven with each other to form a complete course or curriculum sequence. As was mentioned earlier, we developed some prescriptions for doing this in our K-6 science project with Macmillan. We have continued this work on a project to redesign a course at Ithaca College [2], and we have found it easier than anticipated to integrate different strands to form a course sequence. Additional work is sorely needed in this area, and hopefully we will see much progress over the next decade.

Another dimension of structure is teaching the structure of a discipline to a learner. Synthesis is the process of explicitly teaching the relationships among ideas. Very little attention has been paid to developing useful prescriptions in this area. In our work on integrating prescriptions for macro methods, we have identified a variety of types of "pervasive" relationships -- relationships which exist on a continuing basis, such as "A is a kind of B, which is a kind of C, which is a kind of D...," and "M causes N, which causes O, which causes P..." see e.g., [16]. But these may be only the "tip of the iceberg" in relation to all the important kinds of relationships to teach. Again, this should be a fruitful area for future work.

2.4 Mediational Systems

Given that our field has strong roots in media, we have a tendency to constrain our instructional designs to certain mediational systems, particularly to such resources as print, computers, and video. However, it is helpful to keep in mind that many other types of mediational systems can be used. We should keep in mind that the source of instruction can be human or nonhuman, that a human source can be a professional or an amateur, that a nonhuman source can be instructionally designed or not created specifically for purposes of instruction, and that the intended receiver can be an individual or a group. These characteristics yield the kinds of mediational systems shown in figure 5.1.

		Source: Human		Source: Nonhuman	
		Professional	Amateur	Designed	Natural
Receiver	Individual	Tutoring	Peer Tutoring	Individualized Resources	Individual Projects
	Group	Lecture	Discussion	Group Activities	Group Projects

Fig.5.1. Eight kinds of mediational systems as defined by the nature of the source and receiver. The cell labels are merely the closest fit with the concept as defined by the nature of the source and receiver.

Please note that the labels in the boxes are familiar concepts that do not overlap completely with the concept as defined by the characteristics of the source and receiver. Furthermore, almost any medium (or combination of media) can be used within each of these categories. Instructional designers have had a tendency to use individualized resources without considering that another mediational system might be better. Cost-benefit analysis is likely to be very important in making informed decisions. This is another important new direction for educational technology.

2.5 Instructional-Management Systems

As instructional tools become more powerful and more varied, the task of managing the instruction becomes more formidable -- and more important. It is not just a matter of coordinating diagnosis-and-revision activities, although that is certainly very important. It is also a matter of deciding which kind of resource is important for whom and when, and which strategies are important for whom and when on each resource. A wide variety of considerations comes into play, including individual differences, mastery learning, record keeping, learner control, scheduling, incentives, and much more.

With the development of expert systems, it is possible to think of designing an "advisor" into computer-based instruction -- an advisor which will monitor the learner's Activities, intervene with advice when appropriate, answer questions about instructional management, and serve other instructional management functions. But what are the rules which should govern such an advisor? And what instructional management activities are best left to a human? These are important areas for work in the next decade.

2.6 Motivating Learners

There is increasing recognition of the importance of motivating learners. Motivational strategies were largely ignored by instructional theorists until very recently. John Keller has done excellent work to integrate the current knowledge about motivation into a set of prescriptions for instructional designers, but more work is needed in this area, particularly regarding motivational strategies which are uniquely possible with advanced technologies.

3. Designer Tools

The development of expert systems has made possible the creation of powerful tools to increase the productivity and quality of instructional designers' efforts. But, as with intelligent tutors, we need to operationalize our instructional prescriptions as a highly detailed set of rules before we can create such tools. We also need to find out the extent to which such expert systems can actually design the instruction for a designer versus serve as a job aid to help the designer do it. Furthermore, given the need for a designer to work with a subject-matter expert to design instruction, should another expert system replace the subject-matter expert? If so, how should the two expert systems be interfaced? Dave Merrill has made some progress in answering these questions [10], but much work remains to be done in this area.

4. Applications

Finally, with respect to applications (contexts), the field has shifted dramatically in the past ten years to an emphasis on corporate training, with lesser increases being registered for health education, government training, and various adult education contexts. Public schools are currently receiving relatively little attention. I expect this to change considerably over the next ten years, initially with work on textbook and courseware design and evaluation, but eventually with work on teacher training as well. But this will not be easy. We are finding that our powerful new learning tools are not being adopted by school systems the way they can and should be, because the structure of the school system works against it.

But even more important is the increasing recognition that the problems with our schools are ones which cannot be fixed by providing more of everything: more teacher training, more teacher pay, more school hours in a day, more school days in a year, and so forth. For a quantum improvement in education, we need to develop a better system [3].

With our field's emphasis on systems thinking, we are uniquely qualified within schools of education to help public schools to restructure, and along with this unique qualification comes a certain responsibility. Our field is beginning to awaken to this responsibility, as is demonstrated by the recent special issue of the Journal of Instructional Development on Instructional Development in the schools (Vol. 10, No. 4). At Indiana University we have recently become involved in helping the Indiana Department of Education to plan better ways to structure the Indiana public schools to meet the needs of an information society. And Bela Banathy [1] has been working on ways to bring about systems changes in the schools. But our knowledge base is woefully inadequate in this area. I hope we will see important advances here over the next decade.

In sum, I feel that the most important new directions for research in educational technology include advancing our instructional strategy prescriptions for:

1) Facilitating understanding, generic skills application, and affective learning,
2) Utilizing the unique capabilities of new technologies,
3) Structuring and sequencing a course or curriculum,
4) Selecting mediational systems,
5) Designing instructional-management systems, and
6) Motivating learners.

Other important new directions include:

7) Developing expert systems as job aids for, or even replacements for, instructional designers, and
8) Providing more help to the public schools, especially by applying systems thinking to the design of structural features that are more appropriate for the educational needs of an information society.

These kinds of advances in our knowledge base are not going to be easy to achieve. They are going to require vision and resources, communication and cooperation. But whatever the obstacles, those advances are strategically crucial for helping us to strengthen the most important economic resource in an information society: the knowledge of our people.

References

1. Banathy, B.H. Systems inquiry in education. *Systems Practice*, 1 (2), 193-211. 1988.
2. Beissner, K., & Reigeluth, C.M. Course sequencing with multiple strands using the elaboration theory. *Paper presented at the meeting of the Association for Educational Communications and Technology*, Dallas, TX. 1989.
3. Branson, R.K. Why the schools can't improve: The upper limit hypothesis. *Journal of Instructional Development*, 10 (4), 15-26. 1987.
4. Collins, A., & Stevens, A.L. A cognitive theory of inquiry teaching. In C.M. Reigeluth (Ed.), *Instructional-design theories and models: An overview of their current status*. Hillsdale, NJ: Lawrence Erlbaum. 1983.
5. Gagné, R.M. *The conditions of learning and theory of instruction* (4th ed.). New York: Holt, Rinehart & Winston. 1985.
6. Keller, J.M. Motivational design of instruction. In C.M. Reigeluth (Ed.), *Instructional-design theories and models: An overview of their current status*. Hillsdale, NJ: Lawrence Erlbaum. 1983.
7. Keller, J.M. Development and use of the ARCS model of motivational design. *Journal of Instructional Development*, 10 (3), 2-10. 1987.
8. Martin, B.L, & Briggs, L.J. *The affective and cognition for instruction and research*. Englewood Cliffs, NJ: Educational Technology Publications. 1986.
9. Merrill, M.D. The new component design theory: instructional design for courseware authoring. *Instructional Science*, 16 (1), 19-34. 1987.
10. Merrill, M.D. Knowledge engineering an instructional design expert system. Workshop presented at the meeting of the *Association for Educational Communications and Technology*, Dallas, TX. 1989.
11. Reigeluth, C.M. A model of instruction for understanding. *Paper presented at the meeting of the Association for Educational Communications and Technology*, Dallas, TX. 1989a.
12. Reigeluth, C.M. Educational technology at the crossroads: New mind-sets and new directions. *Educational Technology Research & Development*, 37 (1), 67-80. 1989b.
13. Reigeluth, C.M. Sequencing and integrating cognitive strategies with subject-matter content. *Paper presented at the meeting of the Association for Educational Communications and Technology*, Dallas, TX. 1989c.
14. Reigeluth, C.M. Prescriptions for designing a theoretical elaboration sequence. Paper presented at the meeting of the *Association for Educational Communications and Technology*, Dallas, TX. 1989d.
15. Reigeluth, C.M., & Schwartz, E. A prescriptive theory for the design of computer-based educational simulations. *Journal of Computer-based Instructional Systems*, 16 (1). (1989, winter).
16. Reigeluth, C.M., & Stein, F.S. The elaboration theory of instruction. In C.M. Reigeluth (Ed.), *Theories and models: an overview of their current status*. Hillsdale, NJ: Erlbaum Associates. 1983.

6

Formative Experiments on the Coevolution of Technology and the Educational Environment

Denis Newman
Bolt, Beranek and Newman Inc.
Boston, Ma, U.S.A.

Abstract: When new educational technology is put into actual use, new ways of using the technology and new ways of organizing instruction can emerge. This may create problems for standard evaluation techniques but at the same time it may present interesting opportunities for the designers. Levin & Kareev [9] report a delightful case in which two young boys appropriated the computer-running-a-space-game into their fantasy play, pretending it was the console of their space ship and they were space explorers who would investigate a planet (room of the house) then return to the console to transport them to another planet. Goals are not built into technology. They are things that people or groups of people have. How a new piece of educational technology gets used in a particular environment cannot always be anticipated ahead of time. It can be argued that what the environment does with the technology provides critical information to guide the design process.

Over a period of years there is a coevolution of technology and the environment that includes teachers and students, materials and topics, as well as the technologies. The environment changes as technology is introduced and technology can change to take fuller advantage of the new environment. Of course, this is not a natural process as the term "evolution" may imply. It all happens within an artificial system [18] designed for some purpose. But the fact that both the technology and the environment are human artefacts does not mean that the process of change is mechanical. Design of the technology and educational environment is goal-directed but is also very much a problem-solving task [15] which is ill structured and open-ended. An educational environment is inherently open-ended because *new goals* can enter the system. For example, goals associated with the workplace can enter the educational environment as the organization of instruction begins to resemble an apprenticeship. Consequently, it is not always possible to specify the objectives of a piece of educational technology and expect them to remain the same once the technology enters the educational environment. If the system falls into disuse or is used for an entirely different purpose, i.e., our system becomes extinct, we know radical redesign is needed. But, more likely, the system finds a niche serving possibly multiple purposes that need to be understood in future iterations of design.

This paper describes a set of examples illustrating the ways that the environment changes, sometimes unexpectedly, as a result of a piece of technology being used. I will start by outlining the method called a formative experiment and the theoretical approach on which it is based. The examples include a LAN environment designed for collaborative school work and intelligent instructional systems for use in training specific technical tasks.

Keywords: cognitive change, Cognitive processes, cognitive science, collaborative learning, databases, design experiments, educational objectives, educational technology, electronic mail system, Formative experiments, Intelligent instructional systems, Local Area Network, motivation, network interface system, personal workspace, scaffolding, student model, students' reflection, task analysis, zone of proximal development

1. Distributed Cognition as a Theoretical Basis for Formative Experiments

Recent work in the cognitive science of instruction has suggested that a unit of analysis larger than the individual person may be of value in understanding how cognitive change occurs [5,8,13,16]. Cognitive processes are usually distributed over several people and almost always involve tools for thinking such as writing or computers. The functional problem-solving system designed by the culture includes all these elements. A theory of change can take advantage of the interaction between the parts of the cognitive system to explain the emergence of new understandings. The same theoretical framework that provides important insights into cognitive change also provides a framework for changes on a larger scale, such as the introduction of educational technology.

Vygotsky's [21,22] developmental psychology provides important insights into instructional interactions. Vygotsky introduced the concept of a zone of proximal development in which children can work at problems that are beyond their competence as individuals. With "scaffolding" provided by others, children can solve problems interactively while they are in the process of learning how to solve them themselves. The knowledge and skills that become internalized, in this view, are the interactive processes by which the problem had been worked on. Observations of scaffolded problem-solving, in this view, provides a method for observing the origins of individual knowledge.

Observations of instructional interactions in which a teacher is helping a student or group of students indicates that teachers often do not have or apparently need an understanding of exactly how the students are approaching the task. Newman et al. (in press) describe teaching and tutorial sessions in which the teacher appropriates the students actions into her own way of understanding the task. The teacher has to find some way for the students to play at least a minimal role in the accomplishment of the task and give feedback in terms of the expert understanding of the task: what the goal is, what is relevant, why his move was not optimal and so on. In instructional interactions, both the student and teacher are necessarily somewhat ignorant of each other's mental state. All the student does is produce some move that in some way contributes (or can be understood as an attempt to contribute) to the task. The teacher does not have to know exactly what the student thinks he or she is doing as long as she can appropriate what the student does into the joint accomplishment of the task. Seeing how his or her action is appropriated provides the student with an analysis of task as the teacher understands it.

The basis for appropriation is the notion that human action is essentially a matter of interpretation [11]. Plans and goals are strategic fictions that help organize our work together [19]. The meaning of an action can be changed retrospectively by the actions of others that follow it [3]. The concept of appropriation provides a model for a range of interactions between two parties that have different interpretations of the initial situation. An apprenticeship, for example, involves an interaction in which the expert makes use of the novice's work even at the earliest stages of training when the novice has little understanding of the overall process.

An "intelligent" tool can also appropriate the actions of an inexperienced worker or student. For example, a system that provides a trace of the student's algebra problem-solving activities in effect takes the students actions and displays them in a framework that the student may not initially understand. By seeing how his or her actions are displayed, the student can come to understand, for example, that problem-solving is a process of successive attempts and backtracking. Teachers can appropriate an intelligent instructional system into their own lessons and classroom activities (although in this case we would not expect any cognitive change in the system as a result of its being appropriated.) Any tool can be appropriated by people's activities and thereby come to play a role somewhat different from that of the original designers of the tool. Just as students need not initially understand the teacher's task to which their actions are appropriated, a designer of educational technology need not entirely understand the educational environment to learn something about the environment and the technology by seeing how the environment appropriates the technology.

Formative experiments track the changes in goals and uses that occur when a piece of technology becomes a part of a new educational environment: how does the technology get used or understood differently from the original assumptions of the designers? How does the technology present new interpretations and ways of approaching the work not initially available in the environment? Formative research generally has the goal of improving the design of some product (TV show, software, curriculum materials) by having people use it. The experiments we have been conducting have a similar motivation but involve a much longer time frame and greater involvement in the context of use than is typically found in formative testing. Typically users are put in front of the prototype product for a few minutes to an hour in order to get feedback for the next stage of production. In contrast, instructional technology systems that involve teachers as well as students can be tested only by being put into use in actual instruction. This often involves elaborate arrangements including teacher training, curriculum development, and production of classroom materials in order to create the environment in which students and teachers can confront real instructional tasks. It is seldom the case that the technology can be inserted into a classroom without changing other aspects of the environment.

Our formative experiments also differ from the design experiments proposed by Collins in this volume. Our work has been less systematic than will be necessary for establishing a design science and the observations are done by the same group of people responsible for development. In other respects the point of view is very similar, e.g., the focus on the whole environment as a unit of analysis. Our observations thus provide hypotheses that a design science can pursue.

Often the impact of a formative experiment is found in new ways of teaching, different relationships between teachers and students, and new topics being taken up. The outcomes of these experiments go beyond what can be captured by the usual interview data or set coding scheme. The changes, especially when they impact the social organization, may require the experienced eye of the ethnographer as well as psychological observations and an understanding of the technology. What is of interest is the ways that people go beyond what was specifically designed for. Findings concerning where the people take the technology, how they appropriate it to their own goals, and how they change what or how they teach or learn provide the basis for designing the next version of the technology so as to provide specific support for these new ways of working.

2. A LAN Environment for Collaborative School Work

For the last three years, the Earth Lab project has been designing and observing the effects of a Local Area Network (LAN) system intended to facilitate collaborative work in elementary school earth science. The pedagogical rationale was that students should use technology the way real scientists do: to communicate and share data, i.e., to collaborate. In this project we were using educational technology specifically to change the educational environment from one that discouraged collaborative work among students to one in which collaborative work was used routinely. While we were moderately successful in this attempt, both the teachers and the students used the system in unanticipated ways.

Our plan was to create a prototype LAN system and demonstrate it in a public school using an earth science curriculum. A year-long formative experiment was completed in June, 1987. A LAN connected the 25 Apple IIe computers in the school to a hard drive which allowed for central storage of data, text, and programs. The Bank Street Writer word processing program was enhanced with an electronic mail system. The Bank Street Filer was another basic tool which made it possible for students to create databases which could be accessed from any computer in the school [12].

The electronic mail system opened up new channels for communication [4,10]. Students communicated with their teachers in ways other than through the discourse of the classroom lesson. Students communicated with other students both within their class and outside the school. Small groups of students collaborated to answer questions that the teacher sent after the lesson. Science activities were devised in which small groups invented questions for other groups to answer and these questions and answers were exchanged using the mail system.

Databases were shared among different groups in the class and were also created by groups and individuals for many different purposes. During the lunch hour, students invented databases of their favourite action figures. In social studies, students researched almanacs and other sources to fill in databases about countries of the world, and figures from Black history. In science, they examined databases of dinosaur fossils and earthquakes and created a database of the weather readings that small groups of students collected over a 3 month period. These activities were successful in large part because the computers were networked. Clearly, the electronic mail system was dependent on the connections among the computers. The database activities were also dependent on the connections since students shared different data with different students or groups in the school. A student may have data she shares with a science group, with a noon hour club, and with the whole class. It would not have been possible for each student to have her data on a floppy disk since the social organization of the data access required that multiple routes be possible into school's database. Management of the data organized by groups and individuals was the role of the network interface we designed.

The network interface program was designed to make it easy for individuals or small groups to store and retrieve data pertaining to their projects. Students and teachers identified by their homeroom class and a name could be assigned to any number of workspaces. Each workspace had a name which sometimes referred to the kind of work or activity for which it was used and sometimes was a distinctive name for a group of students who used the workspace. For example, workspaces with names like FRED.MARI were set up for pairs of students to work on writing assignments together. Other workspaces served clubs like YOUNG.ASTRONAUT. Each individual also had a personal workspace having the same name as his or her login name, such as FRED, MR.RHODES and so on. The science teacher, who had the students for two periods a week had the class form into groups of three or four for the purpose of conducting investigations in the science lab. The science groups gave themselves names such as STAR.WARS or PETITE.FOUR. These names later were made into group workspaces on the network.

Over the year, there was substantial movement toward more small group work. Teachers accepted fewer copies of the classroom materials since they realized that one copy was sufficient for a group. One classroom teacher for the first time conducted an activity with each small group in turn leaving the rest of the class to do set work on their own. Another teacher led several class discussions on how working in small groups was different than working alone or with the entire class. We found the science groups which originated in the science lab being used by the classroom teachers for a variety of social studies research activities, some of which were unrelated to the earth science curriculum. The network system produced these changes in an unexpected way: it made it possible for all teachers to assign classroom work to the science groups. The science group workspaces were a convenient means for organizing small group projects in other curriculum areas.

The classroom teachers were not entirely happy with the science groups since they would not have put those sets of students together, especially since the groups were all single-sex. Because our network interface system lacked an easy-to-use management utility, it was not straightforward to modify the groups or to easily create new groups. This was a source of frustration for the teachers who would have liked to reassign some of the students or even create new sets for other purposes. These inconveniences help to accentuate the fact that the science groups had become a resource across the school. Never had there been a mechanism by which a social organizational structure created by one teacher in this school could be used by other teachers as a resource for managing instruction.

The students also found unanticipated ways of using Earth Lab. Computers in the classrooms and in a central computer lab were all networked. We expected that projects would be started while the class was in the computer lab and would be continued in the classroom. We found the students were taking this flexibility another logical step. We observed two students working together at a classroom computer on individual book reports. They had not finished when it was their class's turn to go to the computer lab. Instead of dropping their work, they brought their notes with them and asked if they could continue their work at a lab computer while the rest of the class worked on other assignments. The students logged on and called up the file on which they had been working. The boundaries between one class period and another became permeable. This permeability was used by the students to pursue their own tasks.

Many students used the system extensively for their own work in addition to the work assigned as part of instruction. Students developed a sense of ownership to a greater extent than we anticipated. Some students accumulated hundreds of files in their personal workspaces over the course of the year. Earth Lab was also used for student-initiated collaborative work although it was not particularly well designed to facilitate it. In a year-end interview, we asked students to suggest improvements. One student, Mari, said she would like to create a new workspace to which she could give other students access. She explained that she often works with Alissa and they have to either work in her or Alissa's personal workspace. When one of them is absent, the other could not get at the work. This kind of user-creatable workspaces is a common feature of fileservers but had not been implemented on the Earth Lab system. For Mari, who had no familiarity with other fileservers, the idea was an invention based on a need that arose in her own attempts at collaboration. The extent to which both teachers and students appropriated the system into their own work gives us reason to believe that systems like Earth Lab will continue to modify the educational environment while pointing to the next generation of design.

3. Using Intelligent Instructional Systems in Real Contexts

Intelligent instructional systems we are currently developing and testing provide additional examples of how technology can change the organization of instruction in the educational environment. The two systems were designed to play a role in an army training school. In both cases a well-specified program of instruction was already in place in which instruction was divided between lecture presentation and practical exercises using conventional simulators and real equipment. Of interest is how this environment was modified with the introduction of the systems and the implications of these changes for the use of intelligent systems in real instructional environments. Unlike Earth Lab, the development of these systems did not have the explicit goal of changing the environment. Nevertheless, interesting changes occurred.

The intelligent instructional systems (IIS) we are working with are not conventional intelligent *tutoring* systems (ITS) since they do not contain an explicit model of the instructor or a model of the instructors model of the student.. They do contain a simulation of an operational system and a model of expert performance on the task that is the basis for intelligent feedback. They are meant to play a role in instruction as conducted by human instructors, hence the term IIS.

The first example is an IIS to train mechanics to repair a complex radar [7]. Mechanics use two sets of esoteric documents: a set of schematics and a book of fault isolation procedures (FIP). Having little background in the advanced electronics involved, the trainees are walked through the schematics in lectures and then attempt to follow the complex branching in the FIP during practical exercises. There is little opportunity to apply a theoretical understanding of how the radar works to the task of troubleshooting and graduates of the program have little understanding of the principles [7]. The IIS, called MACH-III, consists of a simulation of the radar represented in colour as an animated schematics and with the physical locations of all the parts represented spatially. If one component is broken, e.g., a wire is shorted, the simulation can indicate the change in information flow throughout the rest of the system. A second screen provides text information such as explanations, feedback, and guidance. Problems can be set for the student and a troubleshooting "expert" is available to provide critique and advice and/or display the troubleshooting steps, based on the FIP, in a tree diagram.

The initial formative research involved sitting pairs of students down at the system and having them troubleshoot simple problems. Besides the usual information about understandability, interface ease of use, etc. we were interested in how the students tackled the problem, for example, whether they would make use of the "expert" whether they would continue to consult their reference manuals, etc. We also sought advice from the instructors about how to organize the use of MACH-III. An issue that came up repeatedly from both instructors and students was a concern about the IIS turning into a crutch. It is not enough to learn to troubleshoot using the simulation, it is also necessary to learn to use the schematics and FIP. The IIS will be left at the school but the paper documents are the basic tool of the trade and are referred to even by very experienced mechanics in doing their work.

While the formative experiment on MACH-III is just now beginning, preliminary work both affected the design of the system to be tested and raised specific issues of interest in the experiment [6]. The IIS is being viewed both as a link between the lectures and the practical exercises (PE) and as a mediator between the students understanding of the radar and their understanding of the paper documents. Both lecturers and PE instructors are being given instruction on the use of the IIS. In addition, lecturers are using colour overheads in their classes which show various views of the radar as modelled by the simulation. Thus, the lectures are showing the link between the highly abstract schematics and MACH-III's more physically oriented representations of the same circuits. In the PE portion of instruction where the IIS is located, students continue to use their schematics and FIPs while working with the IIS. The "expert" refers to the FIP when suggesting a particular step. The research is concerned in part with whether the IIS can succeed in supporting the use of the documents.

The importance of the paper documents as a tool of the trade was not clear in the task analysis until the IIS with its "expert" alternative to consulting the documents was actually introduced and students and instructors were able to react to it. The goal of instruction defined narrowly as an understanding of the radar or the ability to troubleshoot was broadened to include a relationship to the documents which would be critical after the students left school. The role of MACH-III as a mediator rather than as an instructor emerged to deal with the need to provide tools for use in the field. The formative experiment considers how the program of instruction as a whole—including lectures, conventional PE and simulated troubleshooting—becomes more integrated and how the existence of the IIS changes the students' relation to the paper documents.

A second IIS trains students to operate an automated missile system [14]. A component of the existing program of instruction for this system was concerned with understanding its automatic operation using a conventional simulator. The usual task was to run the simulator in manual mode and get the student to mimic the automatic operation on the assumption that if they can do manually what the system does automatically, they will understand the automatic operation. The IIS, called INCOFT, provides a simulator of the system as well as feedback and "expert" demonstrations on the basis of an articulate simulation of the automatic operation which could be compared with the students performance. Feedback in the form of comments on each action (in comparison to what the system would have done) and a summary table listing all the actions listed not chronologically but clustered by each case the student was dealing with during a scenario.

As with MACH-III, INCOFT forms a bridge between the lectures and the practical exercises. Since INCOFT provides feedback on each action, it is possible to present subtle cases which illustrate specific problems covered in the lecture. Without the feedback there is no way of assuring that the student noticed the features of the case that are important for instruction. Also, since the IIS can articulate the "expert" process for any specific case in a scenario, it can serve as a vehicle for reviewing specific lecture material. The system feedback also cuts across the standard division of labour of the two system operators which is used as the basis for the sequence of lectures and practical exercises, i.e., first the students learn the officer's job and then they learn the assistant's job. From the system perspective, however, the division of labour is somewhat arbitrary and the IIS feedback concerning performance in one job is presented in terms of how it will impact the other job. This form of feedback becomes an opportunity for the instructors to point out the interdependence of the two jobs.

The instructor-student interaction with INCOFT is very different from that with the conventional simulator. In the conventional case, the instructors' role consists of walking students through some initial scenarios and then watching over the shoulder of students who are having trouble. With INCOFT, the instructor discusses the IIS feedback with the student, pointing out weaknesses and suggesting review and "expert" demos. Instead of providing feedback directly, the instructor is in the role of interpreting the feedback from the system. The cognition involved in providing feedback to the student is now distributed between the teacher and the technology. Research is continuing on the instructor-student interactions around the IIS and its feedback. Given the changing role of the instructor in relation to the technology we are considering tools which will support the new forms of interaction. Our interest focuses on how the IIS changes the goals for practical exercise, moving it more toward an integration of the information covered in lecture and toward considering the rationale for the system operation which is currently covered in on-the-job training if at all.

The two cases of IISs considered here are "schoolhouse" trainers used in formal instruction before on-the-job work begins. In both cases, however, students are expected to continue their training on-the-job so what happens in the school is obviously linked to the goals of the actual work. The goals of the school were quite modest and the graduates were far from fully competent. A change we might expect with IIS technology is the movement of more of the training into the school, producing more competent graduates. However, another possibility is that the IIS technology may find a more important role on-the-job as intelligent job aids that provide support and instruction for novice operators or mechanics. Such technology would support an apprenticeship allowing novices to gradually assume greater responsibility. But this would be a very different educational environment from the school. The advantages of learning in a meaningful context may support the migration of IISs into the workplace.

4. Conclusions

The cases described in this paper illustrate changes in the educational environment that go beyond the initial objectives. While we may consider ourselves engineers of the educational environment, we are never in full control, we seldom know what the environment is capable of given new tools, and we cannot always see how factors currently outside the environment can introduce new goals. As designers of the environment, our own goals change as we see the technology appropriated in new ways. For these reasons it is reasonable to describe the process as a coevolution of the technology and the environment.

Narrow definition of educational objectives in terms of test scores and the current classroom curriculum is attractive to administrators who must show quantifiable improvements. Applying advanced educational technology to goals so defined may not be the best approach ultimately since educational tasks with a meaningful relationship to the world outside the classroom may in the long run produce more useful knowledge and skills. It may also blind us to the ways that the environment takes the technology beyond the initial goals that we set based on the current educational environment. We cannot hold to a simple technological determinism that suggests that the environment will be controlled by the introduction of new technology. Very likely the technology will have an effect but it is an important empirical issue as to what the effect is and how it is achieved.

Our formative experiments suggest that an evolution toward a different educational environment is possible. Educational environments of the future may look very different from the schools of today. Advanced technology can increase the initiative of both students and teachers. Both parties in the environment can have a hand in appropriating the technology to goals that they define and in helping to evolve the goals of the environment so that they more adequately reflect the needs of a changing world.

Three possible directions for the co-evolution of advanced technologies and the environment appear, at this time, worthy of continuing investigation: integration of school and work, collaborative learning, and the use of technology for what Collins & Brown (1987) call a "tool for reflection."

Technology can present educational tasks that are more meaningful by virtue of their connections to real world data and tasks. It can open up channels of communication that allow new goals from the educational environment's context, such as the work environment, can be drawn in. For example, we find in an Earth Lab classroom that the teacher uses the networked database for keeping track of lunch money and students assist in this work context using the same database facility that they use in their science and social studies investigations. As with intelligent job aids that serve an apprenticeship function, the technology may increasingly merge education and work.

Collaborative learning using advanced technologies is likely to be a major feature of future educational environments not only because technology will continue to be a limited resource but, more importantly, because many educators consider collaborative learning to be educationally sound [2]. Even from a purely practical point of view, it is often useful to have two minds engaged collaboratively in interpreting the complex display of information provided by the technology. Having more than one student at the computer may appear to be a problem for the design of conventional intelligent tutoring systems since the student model is usually assumed to be a model of the individual. It may be that the social environment will lead to a redesign of the technology. Or it may be the case that a student model can apply as well to a group as an individual. This is an area for potentially interesting interactions between forces in the environment and technology design.

A third suggestion for how technology and the environment might coevolve is that instead of serving as a tutor, the ITS might become a tool that students use to learn with. Collins & Brown [1] have discussed the potential for technology to show students a trace of their own problem-solving processes and thus serve as a tool for reflection. The trace can also be used to deepen and enliven student-student and teacher-student interaction by providing a common object of conversation. From this perspective, a "student model" is also a trace of student performance as interpreted by the ITS. Ridgway [17] suggests that ITSs that can describe their own processes in coming to conclusions about students might turn out to be very useful as a tool for students' reflection on the learning process. As Ridgway suggests, ITSs can be designed to be more "transparent" in order to facilitate this method of using them. It will be interesting to see if ITSs begin to be used this way in instructional contexts.

An evaluation process for educational technology that watches for cases where the environment takes the technology beyond the designers' initial assumptions can help to guide a process of evolution toward more effective education. This chapter has provided some current examples and some speculations that illustrate directions a co-evolution may take.

References

1. Collins, A., & Brown, J. S., The computer as a tool for learning through reflection. in: H. Mandl and A.M. Lesgold (Eds.), *Learning Issues for Intelligent Tutoring Systems*, Springer-Verlag, New York, 1988.
2. Educational Researcher Editors, Cooperative learning: A research success story, *Educational Researcher 3*, March 1985.
3. Fox, B., Interactional Reconstruction in Real-Time Language Processing, *Cognitive Science*, Vol. 11, No. 3, pp. 365-387, 1987.
4. Goldman, S. V., & Newman, D., Electronic interactions: How students and teachers organize schooling over the wires. in: H. Mehan (Chair), Symposium on *Research*

perspectives on education via electronic networks. Annual meetings of the American Educational Research Association, New Orleans, 1988.
5. Hutchins, E., Learning to navigate in context. *Paper presented at the Workshop on Cognition in Context,* Stenungsund, Sweden, 1987.
6. Kurland, L. C., Design, development and integration of an ITS in the real world, *Paper prepared for the annual meetings of the American Educational Research Association,* San Francisco, 1989.
7. Kurland, L. C., and Tenney, Y. J., Issues in Developing an Intelligent Tutor for a Real-World Domain: Training in Radar Mechanics. in: J. Psotka, L. D. Massey, & S. A. Mutter (Eds.), *Intelligent tutoring systems: lessons learned,* Lawrence Erlbaum Associates, Hillsdale, NJ, 1988.
8. Lave, J., *Cognition in Practice; Mind, Mathematics and Culture in Everyday Life,* Cambridge University Press, Cambridge, 1988.
9. Levin, J. A., & Kareev, Y., Problem solving in everyday situations *The Quarterly Newsletter of the Laboratory of Comparative Human Cognition,* Vol. 2, No. 3, pp. 47-52, July 1980.
10. Newman, D., Local and long distance computer networking for science classrooms *Educational Technology,* Vol. 27, No. 6, pp. 20-23, 1987.
11. Newman, D., & Bruce, B. C., Interpretation and manipulation in human plans, *Discourse Processes,* Vol. 9, pp. 167-195, 1986.
12. Newman, D., & Goldman, S. V., Earth Lab: A local network for collaborative classroom science *Journal of Educational Technology Systems,* Vol. 15, No. 3, pp. 237-247, 1987.
13. Newman, D., Griffin, P., & Cole, M., *The construction zone: Working for cognitive change in school,* Cambridge University Press, Cambridge, in press.
14. Newman, D., Grignetti, M., Gross, M., & Massey, L. D., INCOFT: An ITS for operating an automated missile system *Machine Mediated Learning,* in press.
15. Pirolli, P. L., & Greeno, J. G., The Problem Space of Instructional Design. in: J. Psotka, L. D. Massey, & S. A. Mutter (Eds.), *Intelligent tutoring systems: lessons learned,* Lawrence Erlbaum Associates, Hillsdale, NJ, 1988.
16. Resnick, L. B., Learning in school and out. *Educational Researcher,* Vol. 16, No. 9, pp. 13-20, 1987.
17. Ridgway, J., Of course ICAI is impossible... worse though, it might be seditious in J. Self (Ed.), *Artificial intelligence and human learning: Intelligent computer-aided instruction,* Chapman and Hall, London, 1988.
18. Simon, H. A., *The sciences of the artificial* (2nd ed.), MIT Press, Cambridge, MA, 1981.
19. Suchman, L. A., *Plans and Situated Actions; The Problem of Human-Machine Communication,* Cambridge University Press, Cambridge, 1987.
20. Tenney, Y. J., and Kurland, L. C., The Development of Troubleshooting Expertise in Radar Mechanics. in: J. Psotka, L. D. Massey, & S. A. Mutter (Eds.), *Intelligent tutoring systems: lessons learned,* Lawrence Erlbaum Associates, Hillsdale, NJ, 1988.
21. Vygotsky, L. S., *Mind in society: The development of higher psychological processes* (M. Cole, V. John-Steiner, S. Scribner, & E. Souberman, Eds.), Harvard University Press, Cambridge, 1978.
22. Vygotsky, L. S., *Thought and language,* (A. Kozulin, Ed.), MIT Press, Cambridge, 1986.

7

Towards Intelligent Tutoring Systems that Teach Knowledge Rather than Skills: Five Research Questions

Stellan Ohlsson
Learning and Research Development Center
University of Pittsburgh
Pittsburgh, Pennsylvania 15260
U.S.A.

Abstract: This paper argues that five types of research are needed in order to develop a cognitive theory that can support the development of intelligent tutoring systems.

Keywords: abstract knowledge, abstract principle, ACT*, addition, alternative conceptions, Artificial Intelligence, assignment of blame problem, belief systems, bug library, cognitive conflict hypothesis, cognitive diagnosis, cognitive processes, cognitive science, cognitive skills, creativity, decision rule, declarative knowledge, DEDU, diagnosing, episodic knowledge, evaluation, expert system, explanation-based generalization, factual knowledge, generativity, gestalt, HS model, immediate feedback, impasse, induction hypothesis, instructional design, intelligent tutoring systems, interpretative productions, knowledge compilation, learning models, learning theories, LISP, machine learning, methodology, naturalistic study, one-one mapping, physics, principle of cardinality, procedural knowledge, psychology, rational learning, rule revision, schemata, simulation, skill acquisition, subtraction, symbolic computation, task analysis, theory-based design of instruction, theory-based instruction, think-aloud protocol, transfer test

1. Towards theory-based design of instruction

The design of instruction was until recently based on the instructor's expertise in the subject matter, supplemented with common sense ideas about learning. The effectiveness of an instructional design was investigated empirically, by using the material in a more or less realistic educational setting and measuring the learning outcome. This type of educational research is a form of trial and error. The researcher generates a design, and tries it out; if it does not work, he/she generates another design; etc. Since the space of possible instructional designs is rather large, progress can be expected to be slow.

The theory of human cognition that has emerged over the past three decades opens up the possibility *of theory-based* design of instruction. Theory-based instruction begins with a theory of the mental processes that are involved in learning a particular subject matter. Instruction is then designed to facilitate those processes. Theory-based instruction is based on the structure of the learner, rather than on the structure of the subject matter.

Consider, as an example, Kurt VanLehn's research on the acquisition of the algorithm for subtraction with regrouping. After extensive analyses of school childrens' answers to subtraction problems VanLehn proposed the hypothesis that school children induce the subtraction procedure from solved examples (rather than, say, construct it on the basis of the verbal explanation that accompanies those examples) [59]. If this hypothesis is correct, then the cognitive process involved in learning subtraction is functionally similar to the process that is known as *grammar induction* in Artificial Intelligence. Grammar induction is a well understood process, and it is known that the occurrence of *disjuncts,* alternative expansions of a node in the grammar, is a major obstacle for grammar induction. Multiple interacting disjuncts can make a grammar induction problem impossible to solve. The implication for the design of instruction is that a procedure should be presented in such a way that the learner has to deal with at most one disjunct at a time [58]. The principle follows from the nature of the hypothesized learning mechanism, not from the structure of arithmetic knowledge.

As a second example, consider the class of learning theories that view the acquisition of a cognitive skill as the construction of rules for searching a problem space. Several such theories have been proposed, see for example [26]. According to the central hypothesis of these theories the learner works practice problems by applying his/her current set of rules, and revises those rules on the basis of the feedback from the task environment. The process of rule revision has been the topic of intense research in both cognitive psychology and Artificial Intelligence, and it is known that a major obstacle for rule revision is the so called *assignment of blame problem:* If a cognitive skill consists of *N* rules, and the learner receives feedback from the environment to the effect that the performance generated by those *N* rules is incorrect, how does the learner know *which* rule to revise? The implication for the design of instruction is that the learner environment should provide *immediate* feedback. The feedback should arrive while the faulty rule is still active in order to help the learner identify which rule is to be revised. Since the application of a rule is a fast process—less than a second—the feedback has to arrive almost instantaneously to be effective. John Anderson and co-workers have designed and implemented intelligent tutoring systems for proof finding in elementary geometry and for LISP programming that incorporate this implication [7,53]. Field tests carried out with these tutors show that they provide more efficient instruction than regular classroom teaching.

Other learning theories have other implications for instructional design. For instance, the theory of discrimination learning proposed by Langley [29] implies that skill learning will be facilitated if the learner is supplied with both negative and positive examples of the rules he/she is supposed to learn. Both the theory of subgoaling proposed by Ohlsson [44] and the theory of chunking proposed by Laird, Rosenbloom, and Newell [38] claim that rule learning occurs when a subgoal is attained; hence, they imply that instruction in a cognitive skill should supply the learner with easy-to-reach subgoals. These instructional implications remain untested.

In short, the function of instruction is to help the cognitive mechanism in the learner's head to perform its task. Each type of learning mechanism has particular obstacles associated with it: If the learner is doing grammar induction, he/she might fail because of multiple disjuncts; If he/she is doing rule revision, he/she might have difficulties with blame assignment, and so on. Instruction should be designed to remove or circumvent those obstacles. Designing instruction in this way requires an explicit theory of the learning mechanism in the student's head. Only if the learning mechanism is described in detail can the obstacles associated with it be identified with enough precision to enable us to design instruction that circumvents them.

The most stringent test of an instructional design is that it can be implemented on a computer. If the instructional design is clearly stated, then it should be programmable. If it is based on a learning theory and that theory is accurate, then the design should be sufficient to produce learning. Furthermore, strict empirical test of an instructional design requires that the instruction delivered during the test consistently and faithfully adheres to the prescriptions of that design, a requirement that human teachers will find hard to fulfil, but which is guarantied to be fulfilled if the instruction is delivered by a computer. For these reasons, there is a close connection between theory-based design of instruction and the implementation of intelligent tutoring systems.

It is no accident that the examples to date of theory-based instructional design involve *cognitive skills* such as arithmetic calculation, proof finding, and computer programming. Current cognitive theory is mainly a theory about cognitive skills. Consequently, its instructional implications pertain mainly to skill training. The emphasis on skills is clearly visible in the topics that are being addressed in research on intelligent tutoring systems: algebraic manipulations, arithmetic calculation, electronic trouble shooting, game playing, geometry proof finding, medical diagnosis, operation of complicated machinery, use of electronic mail systems, word processing, etc. (see for example Wenger [62]). The main pedagogical activity of the current generation of intelligent tutoring systems is to monitor practice.

In this paper I take the position that cognitive skills are *not* what we want students to learn in academic (as opposed to vocational) schooling. Consider elementary mathematics. The skills of elementary mathematics are not pedagogical objectives in their own right. For example, it is of no practical interest to know how to carry out numerical calculations when calculators and personal computers are everywhere. As a second example, consider arithmetic word problems. It has been pointed out repeatedly that the situations described in such problems are artificial and unrealistic. The skill of solving arithmetic word problems is not a worthwhile learning target *per se*. Other mathematical skills, such as proof finding, are even less relevant as pedagogical objectives. Only students who become professional mathematicians will ever construct mathematical proofs after they leave school. This point is not limited to mathematics. For instance, the problems posed in physics textbooks contain so many unrealistic and artificial assumptions and simplifications that the skill of solving such problems has no value in itself. In short, the skills that we teach in schools are typically not worth knowing.[1]

We do not give students practice problems because we believe that the skill of solving them is worth knowing, but because we believe that *the activity of solving practice problems forces students to deepen and consolidate their understanding of the concepts and principles that underlie the solutions to those problems.* Mathematics teachers want students to solve arithmetic word problems in order to acquire a better understanding of numbers. Physics teachers ask students to solve problems because they believe that seeing the laws of physics in operation, working out their application to concrete cases, facilitates understanding of those laws. Geography teachers ask students to mark crops and climates on maps to illustrate the principle that the economic activity of a region is a function of the physical nature of that region, not because map colouring is a useful skill. And so on. Mastery of the concepts and principles– *the*

---

1 There are, of course, exceptions to this sweeping generalization. Reading and writing are the obvious examples. The fact that there are exceptions does not invalidate the generalization.

abstract knowledge of– a domain constitutes the primary pedagogical objective in academic schooling. In summary, *skills are needed in order to solve practice problems, but the solving of practice problems is not an end, but a means for teaching concepts and principles.*[2]

The topic of this paper grows out of the tension between the fact that our current theory deals mainly with cognitive skills and the fact that the purpose of schooling is to teach conceptual understanding. We cannot use theories of skill acquisition to design instruction in concepts and principles. In particular, we cannot use a theory of skills to design intelligent tutoring systems that teach abstract knowledge. However, this conclusion is not an argument against theory-based design of instruction, but only an argument against using our *current* theory as the basis for it. We want to progress towards theory-based instruction while keeping in mind that knowledge, rather than skills, is our primary pedagogical objective. Therefore, our main task at this time is to develop a theory of the acquisition of abstract knowledge that is precise enough to support instructional design. The ultimate test of such a theory is that its instructional implications can be embedded in an intelligent tutoring system that can teach conceptual understanding of some topic.

The paper has two main sections. The first section develops the distinction between abstract knowledge and cognitive skill in more detail, and provides evidence that the power of abstract knowledge cannot be captured in procedures. Developing a theory of abstract knowledge requires answers to the following five research questions:

1. What is the *nature of* abstract knowledge? What is a unit of abstract knowledge? What different kinds of abstract knowledge are there?
2. What is the *function of* abstract knowledge? If abstract knowledge does not consist of procedures, why is it useful? How does abstract knowledge interact with the performance system so as to facilitate and improve problem solving and learning?
3. How is abstract knowledge *acquired?* When, under what mental circumstances, do people construct new concepts and principles?
4. What methods of *task analysis* are required to identify the abstract knowledge that underlies a particular cognitive skill? What are the concepts and principles of any given subject matter topic?
5. What methods of *cognitive diagnosis* are required to track the acquisition of abstract knowledge? How do we assess whether a student knows a particular concept or principle?

The second section develops these questions in detail, and reviews some relevant arguments, theories, and experiments.

2. Abstract knowledge vs. cognitive skill

The first purpose of this section is to develop the three-way distinction between procedural, episodic, and abstract knowledge in some detail. The second purpose is to argue through examples that the power of abstract knowledge cannot be captured in procedures.

2.1 Characteristics of procedural, episodic, and abstract knowledge

The knowledge embedded in a cognitive skill is often called *procedural knowledge,* or knowledge *how.* Procedural knowledge consists of *decision rules,* often called *heuristics* in the context of problem solving. A rule encodes a self-exhortation or a piece of internal advice. The general form of a rule is *if my current goal is so-and-so, and the current situation has such and such properties, then I should consider this or that action.* For instance, *if I want to cross the street safely, and there is heavy traffic, then I should consider waiting until the light turns green.* Decision rules have the following general characteristics:

---

[2] This conclusion only holds for academic schooling. In vocational training the skills are the primary pedagogical objectives. Medical diagnosis, electronic trouble shooting, monitoring of nuclear power plants, and piloting of jet airliners are good examples of skills that are worth knowing per se.

— A rule is indexed in memory under the relevant goal (e.g ., *cross the street safely)*, and it is accessed by activating that goal.
— A rule specifies some action that the agent knows how to perform (e.g., *wait until the light turns green)*[3] . It asserts that performing the specified action in such and such a situation will lead to the attainment of the relevant goal. Procedural knowledge is knowledge about the activity of attaining goals. It does not assert anything about the world.
— Rules vary in how appropriate or useful they are. Following a rule leads to attainment of the relevant goal with a higher or lower degree of efficiency (e.g., since cars sometimes run red lights, your safety is not guaranteed by waiting until the light turns green, it is only increased to some degree).

One objection to the claim that procedural rules do not assert anything about the world is that effective procedures must operate in the world and are constrained by the world. A rule that recommends action A for attaining goal G in situation 5 implicitly asserts the proposition that *the world is such that performing* A *in S will get you closer to* G, or, shorter, *doing A works*. However, this proposition is distinct from a description of those properties of the world that causes action *A* to be appropriate. For instance, the heuristic if *it is dark, and you need to see, then flip the switch beside the door is* very different from the proposition *the switch beside the door is connected to the lamp through an electric wire.*

The analysis of procedural knowledge is one of the major contributions of cognitive science to the understanding of human cognition. Detailed analyses of cognitive skills in terms of collections of rules have been carried out for many task domains, and sophisticated techniques - computer simulation, complexity analysis, etc. - are available for investigating the properties of such collections. I believe that this contribution is permanent in the sense that future theories of human cognition will incorporate and extend on, rather than replace, these analyses.

However, before the emergence of the information processing perspective the term *knowledge* was understood to refer to declarative rather than procedural knowledge, knowledge *that* rather than knowledge *how*. Theory and practice, science and craft, thought and action, understanding and skill have been kept separate in discussions of knowledge ever since Aristotle introduced the distinction between theoretical and practical logic. Declarative knowledge contrasts with procedural knowledge in at least the following ways:

1. Declarative knowledge is not goal-indexed. Its power lies in the fact that a particular proposition can be useful or relevant for many different goals, *including goals which the agent had never thought of at the time of storing the knowledge in memory*. Hence, declarative knowledge cannot be stored in memory under particular goals.
2. Declarative knowledge refers to objects, properties, and events. Declarative knowledge is about the world (rather than about the activity of attaining goals).
3. Declarative principles vary in how accurately they describe the world (rather than in how useful they are).

In short, procedural knowledge is goal-indexed, imperative, and more or less efficient, while declarative knowledge is goal-independent, descriptive, and more or less accurate.

Declarative knowledge can be further divided into knowledge about particulars and knowledge about universals. Some propositions describe *particular* events or objects. For instance, when I remember a particular walk in the park, I am remembering a spatiotemporal context in which certain events took place, and in which particular objects with such and such properties were present. This kind of knowledge is traditionally called *factual* knowledge, but is now also called *episodic* knowledge, or, if the agent was a participant in the situation, *autobiographical* knowledge. Other propositions describe *universal* properties of the world. This kind of knowledge is what I refer to as *abstract* knowledge. I shall use the traditional term "principle" to refer to a unit of abstract knowledge.

---

[3] Rules that prescribe actions that the agent cannot perform, e.g., if you are in a hurry, then travel faster than light, are obviously not useful.

Figures 7.1 and 7.2 contain principles from a variety of knowledge domains. Inspection of the examples verifies the properties listed above: Principles do not contain any reference to particular goals, nor is their validity or usefulness limited to the context of particular goals or situations. They refer to the world rather than to the actions of some agent, and they vary with respect to the accuracy with which they represent the world. Each principle is a unit in the sense that it expresses a single idea or conceptualization.

Principles of physics:
— The *principle of inertia* which says that an object will continue in uniform rectilinear motion unless a force acts on it.
— The *Pauli principle* which says, roughly, that two elementary particles cannot have the same quantum numbers.
— The *second law of thermodynamics* which says that the entropy of the universe can only increase, not decrease.

Principles of social science:
— The law of *supply and demand* which says, roughly, that if the supply is greater than the demand, prices will go down, and vice versa.
— The principle of *historical materialism* which says, roughly, that when new tools for the manufacturing of economic goods appear, there will be a political revolution which transfers political power from the owners of the old tools to the owners of the new tools, followed by a restructuring of political and social institutions to fit the new manufacturing tools.
— *The Peter Principle* which says that, in the limit, all positions in a bureaucracy will be incompetently handled, because each employee will rise through the hierarchy until he/she gets assigned a position that he/she performs badly; he/she will then fail to get promoted, and, hence, remain at that position.

Principles of cognitive psychology:
— The principle of *limited capacity* which says that only a small portion of a person's knowledge is active at any one point in time.
— *Ohlsson's bet* which says that knowledge consists of abstract principles.

Principles of mathematics:
— The principle of *place value notation* which says that the value of a digit in a numeral is a function of its place in the numeral.
— The principle of *the density of real numbers* which says that for any two real numbers there is a real number that lies between them.
— The principle of *commutativity of multiplication* which says that the product of any two numbers is the same regardless of the order in which they are multiplied.
— The *side-angle-side* theorem which says that if two sides and the angle between them are congruent to the corresponding components of another triangle, then the two triangles are congruent.

Principles of logic:
— *Modus tollendo tollens* which says that if Q is an unavoidable consequence of P, and Q is not the case, then P cannot be the case either.
— *Modus tollendo ponens* which says that if two alternatives P and Q are exhaustive and mutually exclusive, and P is not the case, then Q must be the case.

Fig.7.1. Examples of principles from academic knowledge domains.

The principles in figure 7.1 illustrate the content of academic subject domains like science, mathematics, and logic. Principles like these constitute the core of the subject matter of these domains. For instance, a student is supposed to walk away from physics instruction knowing that objects continue in uniform rectilinear motion unless interfered with, that elementary particles must distribute themselves over the space of quantum numbers, and that the total entropy of the universe is always increasing. Similarly, a student is supposed to learn from mathematics instruction that numbers and geometric figures have non-obvious structural properties that are necessary consequences of the way they are defined. Whether the student can apply these ideas in problem solving or not is less important. It is the ideas themselves that constitute the core of the curriculum, not their applications.

The notion of an abstract principle is not limited to the highly developed knowledge domains that are taught in schools. The principles in figure 7.2 exemplify abstract knowledge in non-academic knowledge domains. It is significant that we can identify abstract principles in domains that are very action-oriented such as architecture, body building, ethics, and management. It is particularly intriguing that we can think with principles that we know are irrelevant, false, or purely imaginary. For instance, if we read a fantasy story involving unicorns, we expect the story to be consistent with our principled knowledge about unicorns. Finally, principles are not necessarily known explicitly. Intuitive and common sense knowledge also consists of abstract principles. In short, ideas, not skills, are the building blocks of both academic and non-academic knowledge.

A principle of architecture:
— The Frank Lloyd Wright *principle of organic architecture* which says that the exterior of a building should be an expression of the function(s) of the interior spaces of the building.

A principle of body building:
— The Joe Weider *overload principle* which says that a muscle grows stronger only in response to a resistance or a pressure that it cannot overcome.

A principle of moral conduct:
— The *Golden Rule* which says that you should behave towards others as you want them to behave towards you.

Principles of management:
— The motivation level of a project staff is directly proportional to the effort on the part of the project leader vis-a-vis the project.
— Eighty percent of the work gets done in twenty percent of the time.
— Every task takes more time than you expect; this remains true, even if you revise your expectations to take into account the fact that every task takes more time than you expect.
— *Murphy's* Law which says that if something can go wrong, it will.

A principle of fantasy land:
— Unicorns can only be tamed by virgins.

Principles of common sense:
— Two objects cannot occupy the same space at the same time.
— If a closed container is moved, any object inside the container is moved as well.
— If a given whole is cut into equal-sized parts, then the more parts there are, the smaller each part will be.
— If B is immediately to the right of A, and C is also to the right of A, then C is further to the right than B.
— There is no such thing as a free lunch.

Fig.7.2. Examples of principles from non-academic knowledge domains.

2.2 The power of abstract knowledge

Neither the contrast between abstract and procedural knowledge described in the previous subsection nor the examples of abstract knowledge in figures 7.1 and 7.2 prove that the distinction between knowledge and skill is fundamental. First, one might object that principles and procedures are just two different *formats* for expressing knowledge, rather than two different *types of* knowledge. Every principle, according to this view, can be rewritten as a rule, and *vice versa*. Second, one might object that although the distinction is valid in principle, people do not, in fact, have abstract knowledge. According to this view the distinction is not relevant for cognitive psychology, and procedural representations suffice to describe human cognition.

The issues involved in refuting these objections are deep and difficult, and a conclusive rebuttal cannot be attempted in this paper. The purpose of this subsection is to make the objections implausible by discussing examples that illustrate the power of abstract knowledge.

Example 1. Abstraction

Consider the following common sense principle taken from figure 7.2

Two objects cannot occupy the same place at the same time.

This principle constitutes the rationale underlying the following procedure[4] for putting an object in a particular place:

If the goal is to put object 0_1 in place X, and some other object 0_2 is currently in place X, then consider moving 0_2 to some other place before attempting to put 0_1 in X. (The remove obstacle rule.)

The relation between the principle and the rule is very close: Since the two objects cannot both occupy the relevant place, one has to be removed in order to make place for the other. The relation is so close that the principle and the procedure appear to be two formulations of the same piece of knowledge. Admittedly, the rule mentions the goal of putting 0_1 in X and the action of removing 0_2 and the principle does not. However, one could argue that the goal and the action are implicit in the principle, since the entire impact of the principle is captured in the notion that you cannot put an object in an already occupied place.

However, this cannot be the case, because the principle also constitutes the rationale for the following rule for *preventing* an object from occupying a particular place:

If the goal is to prevent object 0_1 from occupying place X, and place X is currently empty, then consider moving some other object 0_2 into X. (The blocking rule.)

Given a different goal, the principle implies the *opposite* action: moving an object *into* instead of *out* of the relevant position. Since the principle implies two rules with contradictory goals and actions, it cannot be identical to either one of them. Hence, the principle abstracts from goals and actions.

Example 2. Generativity

Consider the fact that

The city of Uppsala is 100 kilometers straight north of Stockholm.

This fact is the rationale for the rule that

If you are in Stockholm, and you want to be in Uppsala, then travel 100 kilometers straight north.

The same principle also dictates the opposite rule:

If you are in Uppsala, and you want to be in Stockholm, then travel 100 kilometers straight south.

But the set of rules implied by the proposition is not exhausted by these above rules. For instance, here is yet another rule that builds on the fact that Uppsala is 100 kilometers straight north of Stockholm:

If you are mid-way between Uppsala and Stockholm, and you want to be as far away from both as possible, then travel straight west or straight east.

I want to suggest that *the set* of *procedures that can be derived from this simple fact is infinite.* The only limitation on the set of procedures that follow from this fact are the limits on our imagination in thinking of contexts in which the fact is relevant. Here are two additional

[4] Procedures usually consist of collections of a number, sometimes a very large number, of rules. The simple procedures discussed in this subsection consist of only a single rule each.

examples of heuristic rules that work because the distance between Uppsala and Stockholm is 100 kilometers:

If you want to build a railroad between Stockholm and Uppsala, and you haven't bought your supplies yet, then consider buying 100 kilometers worth of rail.

If you want to start a domestic airline in Sweden, do not consider providing a service between Stockholm and Uppsala.[5]

It is entirely implausible that even thousands of rules could exhaust this one simple fact. Regardless of how many rules we have generated, all we need to generate yet one more rule is to think of yet another context in which the distance and direction between Uppsala and Stockholm is relevant.

Example 3. Creativity

Consider the following problem situation:

The Glass Jar Problem: I want to open my marmalade jar to make breakfast, but the jar is brand new and the lid is screwed on too tight. I am in a hurry, nobody stronger than me is around, and I don't want to break the jar. What do I do ? The jar is made of glass and the lid is made of metal.

The most elegant solution to this problem is to heat up the jar by putting it in hot water. The lid will come loose, because metal expands more than glass when heated.

The Glass Jar Problem is an example of a so-called insight problem. The typical characteristics of an insight problem are (a) the problem is unfamiliar to most people in the sense that it cannot be subsumed under some well known type of problem, (b) a competent adult has the knowledge necessary to solve the problem, (c) the problem is nevertheless difficult, and (d) the solution is typically obtained after an extended impasse. Insight problems were originally researched by Gestalt psychologists, but have recently caught the attention of information processing psychologists [30,43].

Procedural knowledge:
- If I want to loosen the lid on a glass jar and the lid is made of metal, then I should consider heating up the jar.
- If I want to heat up an object, and the object is small enough to fit into the kitchen sink, then I should consider putting it in hot water.

Declarative knowledge:
- Episodic knowledge:
- Last Monday morning, John Smith opened a marmalade jar by putting it in hot water in his kitchen sink.
- The marmalade jar in front of me is made of glass and has a metal lid.

Abstract knowledge:
- Material objects expand when heated; furthermore, metals expand more than glass.
- Heat flows from hotter to colder objects.

Fig.7.3. Procedural, episodic, and abstract knowledge for the Glass Jar Problem.

Figure 7.3 shows three groups of knowledge items that are relevant for the Glass Jar Problem. The three groups illustrate procedural, episodic, and abstract knowledge, respectively. Each group is sufficient to produce the solution to the problem. First, the solution can be constructed by executing the simple procedure consisting of the two rules at the top of figure 7.3: The first rule recognizes the situation as one in which we should consider heating up the jar, and the second rule generates the action of putting the jar in hot water. Second, the same solution can also be constructed by establishing an analogy with the episode described in the

[5] Because the distance is too short to make air travel a convenient alternative.

middle part of figure 7.3: Since John Smith opened his marmalade jar by putting it in hot water, perhaps I can open mine by doing what he did. Finally, the solution can be constructed by deriving it from the two principles at the bottom of figure 7.3: The lid can be loosened by heating the jar, because metal expands more than glass when heated. The jar can be heated by putting it in hot water, because heat flows from hotter to colder objects.

The claim that there is no fundamental distinction between principles and other types of knowledge implies that the third way of constructing the solution can be reduced to either the application of a procedure or to the construction of an analogy. But this is entirely implausible. First, the procedure can only be known if the problem is familiar. The first rule in figure 7.3 already contains the essence of the solution, namely to use heat.[6] Hence, if the problem is truly unfamiliar, there is no reason to expect the agent to have a procedure like the first rule in figure 7.3. The same is true of the episodic knowledge The memory of what John Smith did already contains the essence of the solution. Thus, both the procedural and the analogical solutions presuppose that the problem is *not* unfamiliar; the solution is, in a sense, already known. The abstract principles at the bottom of figure 7.3, on the other hand, contain no reference to the problem of getting lids off jars. Knowledge of those principles does not in any way depend on having encountered a previous instance of the Glass Jar Problem. In short, the principles support the process of creating a novel problem solution, but neither the rules nor the episode do.

```
(defun count (set)
(prog (object number)
(setq number 0)
STEP
(cond ((empty set)(return number)))
(setq object (select set))
(setq number (update number))
(setq set (remove object set))
(go STEP)))
```

`(empty set)` **tests whether** `set` **is the empty set or not**
`(Select set)` **selects a randomly chosen element of the set**
`(update number)` **retrieves the next number in the number line**
`(remove object set)` **removes the** `object` **from the** `set`

Fig.7.4. A LISP procedure for unordered counting.

Example 4. Flexibility

Consider the simple but fundamental task of counting. In *unordered counting* the elements in a set are counted without regard to the order of the elements. The procedure for this task is entirely straight forward. Each step consists of testing whether the set of objects to be counted has been exhausted, and, if not, to select an object, generate the next number in the number sequence, pair the object with that number, and remove the object from the set. This continues until the set is exhausted, in which case the procedure returns the last number generated. figure 7.4 shows the procedure for unordered counting as represented in the programming language LISP.[7]

[6] Instead of rotational force, which, of course, is everybody s first reaction to the problem of getting a lid off a jar.

[7] It is not written in the way in which a LISP programmer would actually program it, but in a way that illustrates the point of the example as clearly as possible.

```
(defun count (sequence)
(prog (object number)
(cond ((empty sequence)(return 0)))
(setq object (getfirst sequence)
(Setq number 1)
STEP
(cond ((equal (getlist sequence) object))(return number)))
(setq object (getnext object sequence)) (object number (update
number))
(go STEP)))
(empty sequence) tests whether the sequence is the empty sequence
(getfirst sequence) finds the first element in the sequence
(getlast sequence) finds the last element in the sequence
(getnext object sequence) finds the object in the sequence that follows the object
```

Fig.7.5. A LISP procedure for ordered counting.

The abstract principles that underlie this procedure have been identified by Gelman and Gallistel [15]. The two most important ones are the *principle of cardinality* which says that the last number assigned to an object during counting denotes the cardinality of the counted set, and the *one-one mapping principle* which says that correct counting requires that each object is assigned exactly one number. These two principles define correct counting, and hence must underlie all correct counting procedures.

As an example of a second procedure for counting, consider the LISP procedure for *ordered* counting shown in figure 7.5. Ordered counting is similar to unordered counting, except that the objects are counted in a particular order that is given by pairwise *next* relations between the objects. This procedure takes as input the first object in the sequence to be counted; it proceeds by generating the next object in the sequence, generating the next number, and pairing them up; this continues until the last object has been counted. The procedure returns the last number generated.

There is nothing in the codes for the two procedures in figures 7.4 and 7.5 that reveals that they are two procedures for performing the same task under two different circumstances. The codes contain many differences, and they generate different sequences of actions. The only aspect of the two procedures that is the same is that both achieve a one-to-one mapping between objects and numbers. However, we can nevertheless recognise that the two procedures are two different counting procedures, or procedures for two different counting tasks. *The fact that we can see this relation between them shows that we have access to a representation of counting that is more abstract than the procedures themselves.* Since the only aspect of the procedures that is the same is that they both honour the principles of cardinality and of one-one mapping, our ability to recognize them as similar shows that we know those principles.

I want to suggest that this observation is paradigmatic. For instance, consider the question of what all addition algorithms have in common. What are the properties that make them addition algorithms? Comparison of the abacus algorithm for addition with the algorithm for counting on one's fingers with the place value algorithm quickly reveals that there are *no* concrete aspects - no goals or actions - that are general, i.e., that recur in each algorithm. Hence, the fact that we regard them all as addition algorithms proves that we have a representation of addition that is more abstract than the algorithms themselves.

Consider next a learner who knows the procedure for unordered counting, and who is confronted with the task of counting a set of objects in a particular sequence. By comparing the representation in figure 7.4 with the representation in figure 7.5 we can identify the revisions that are required to construct this transformation. First, the argument to the LISP procedure for unordered counting is a *set,* while the argument to the LISP procedure for ordered counting is a *sequence.* Second, the procedure for ordered counting needs to test whether there are any elements in the sequence, a step that is not needed in the procedure for unordered counting. Third, the procedure for ordered counting has to initialize the object variable by retrieving the first element in the given sequence, a step that is not needed in the case of unordered counting. Fourth, the procedure for ordered counting needs to initialize the number variable to unity rather than to zero. Fifth, in unordered counting objects are selected randomly; in ordered counting they are selected by following the *next* links. Sixth, in unordered counting the set of objects to be counted has to be revised in each step by removing the counted object; no corresponding operation is needed in the case of ordered counting. Seventh, the halt condition for unordered counting is that *the set of objects to be counted is empty;* this has to be replaced by the halt condition for ordered counting which is that *the current object is the last object in the given sequence.* figure 7.6 summarizes these changes for the LISP representation of the two procedures.

1.	***Change the input variable:***	
	replace	`set` ***by*** `sequence`
2.	***Test the input:***	
	insert	`(cond ((empty sequence) (return 0)))`
3.	***Initialize the variable "object":***	
	insert	`(setq object (getfirst sequence))`
4.	***Initialize the variable "number":***	
	replace	`(setq number 0) with (setq number 1)`
5.	***Update the variable "object":***	
	replace	`(setq object (select set))`
	by	`(setq object (getnext object sequence))`
6.	***Update the variable "set":***	
	delete	`(setq get (remove object set))`
7.	***Change the halt condition:***	
	replace	`(empty set)`
	by	`(equal (getlast sequence) object)`

Fig.7.6. Revisions for transforming unordered into ordered counting.

The changes described in figure 7.6 are unconnected both with respect to form, function, and location. *There is nothing in the revisions themselves that reveal that they constitute a coordinated set of changes that enables the revised procedure to perform a different version of the same task.* The purpose of the revisions is to guarantee that the one-one mapping between numbers and objects is honoured in the new problem situation. It is entirely implausible that a learning system could compute those revisions when confronted with the ordered counting task *without knowledge of the one-one mapping principle.* Empirical research has shown that children can easily adapt their counting procedures to a variety of changes in the task demands [16,17].

I want to suggest that this observation, too, is paradigmatic. Flexible adaptation of a procedure to changing task demands cannot be done by syntactic editing of the code for the procedure. It requires knowledge of the principles that underlie that procedure.

2.3 Discussion

In summary, the knowledge embedded in cognitive skills--procedural knowledge--is goal-indexed, imperative, and more or less efficient. The unit of procedural knowledge is the decision rule. In contrast, abstract knowledge is goal-independent, descriptive, and more or less accurate. The unit of abstract knowledge is the principle. Although principles constitute the rationale for rules, the former cannot be exhaustively represented by the latter. Principles abstract from goals and actions. Principles are generative in the sense that a principle can be the rationale for an infinitude of procedures. Principled knowledge is required for the creation of solutions to unfamiliar problems, and for the flexible adaptation of an already learned cognitive skill to changing task demands.

The questions of whether principles are true or not, what it would mean for them to be true, and how one could know that they are true - these questions are not relevant for the current discussion. For instance, whether, say, the law of supply and demand is in fact true is a question for economics, rather than for cognitive psychology. Similarly, the questions of what it means for a principle to be true, and how one can know that it is true are questions for epistemology. The psychological questions are what principles a person believes in, how those principles function in his/her cognition, and how they are acquired.

The distinction between declarative and procedural knowledge has been abandoned by researchers in Artificial Intelligence as not fruitful for their enterprise. The problem with the distinction from their point of view is that any expression becomes executable, hence procedural, if one programs an interpreter for it; conversely, the code for any procedure can be treated as data by other procedures, and hence function declaratively. But these observations are not directly relevant to cognitive psychology. The question whether the human mind has the procedural-declarative distinction embedded in it or not is an empirical question that cannot be settled by reference to the properties of programming languages.

3. Five Research Questions

The subject matter of academic knowledge domains consists of abstract knowledge rather than of cognitive skills. Theory-based design of instruction in such domains requires a theory of the acquisition of abstract knowledge that is at the same level of precision as today's theories of skill acquisition. To develop such a theory is to answer the five research questions discussed in this section.

Question 1: What is the nature of abstract knowledge?

Two basic questions that a scientist can ask about a phenomenon X are *What is a unit of* X? and *What types of X are there?* Cognitive science has attacked these questions with respect to procedural knowledge. The production rule is becoming the standard unit for the analysis of cognitive skills [26] and there are several systematic attempts to classify procedures into functionally different types (see, e.g., [32],[38 p. 834-847],[39]).

However, cognitive science has little to say about abstract knowledge. The two most common units of abstract knowledge, *concepts* and *principles,* are inherited from logic and philosophy. Traditional analyses distinguished between class concepts, which were discussed in terms of class membership and class inclusion, and relational concepts, which were discussed in terms of the properties treated in relational logic (symmetry, transitivity, etc.). A concept was supposed to be created by a definition which states the necessary and sufficient conditions for something to be an instance of that concept. It is generally agreed today that this theory of concepts is radically inadequate, partly because most concepts are neither class concepts nor relational concepts in the classical sense, and partly because nobody has succeeded in stating the necessary and sufficient conditions for any interesting concepts. Similarly, traditional analyses cast principles as propositions, i.e., true or false assertions. Many cognitive theories, particularly memory theories, are based on the notion of propositions.[8] It is generally agreed that the classical notion of a proposition is unsatisfactory, partly because the concepts of truth and falsity are problematic.

Traditional analyses of knowledge recognized at least five categories of abstract knowledge: knowledge of nature, mathematical knowledge, logical knowledge, moral knowledge, and knowledge of social conventions. Simon [56] has added knowledge of the artificial to this list, to make up a total of six categories:

---

[8] Hayes [21] has pointed out that schemas are only syntactic variants of the logical notation for propositions.

— *Knowledge about nature*. The core examples in this category are the theories of the natural sciences. Distinguishing features of this type of knowledge are that it purports to refer to things that are independent of human beings, and that observational evidence plays an essential role in its construction.
— *Knowledge about the artificial.* Knowledge about the products of human actions, primarily society, but also complicated machines, natural language, etc. The status of observational evidence is problematical in this type of knowledge, because we can choose to alter our own creations.
— *Mathematical knowledge.* Knowledge about mathematical objects, primarily numbers. Mathematical objects are peculiar in that they are not perceptually available, and yet seem to have objective existence. The ideal character of mathematical objects enables the mathematician to draw necessary conclusions about them, a type of result that is not available in the empirical sciences. Consequently, mathematicians tend to progress by accumulating results, rather than by replacing old theories with new and hopefully better ones. Furthermore, observational evidence plays a heuristic rather than justificatory role. Observations can suggest a new theorem, but neither prove nor disprove it.
— *Logical knowledge.* Some principles, traditionally called tautologies, seem to be true by virtue of their internal structure, and hence are knowable without recourse to either observations or arguments. The classical examples are the laws of propositional logic.
— *Moral knowledge.* While the previous four categories of knowledge are descriptive, moral knowledge is prescriptive. Exactly how one gathers evidence for or against a moral principle and on what basis one should prefer one moral principle over another is unclear.
— *Knowledge of conventions.* Some principles are the result of decisions on the part of human beings. Traffic laws are prototypical examples. Conventions are arbitrary in the sense that they would be different if human beings had made different decisions.

Each of these categories of principles are illustrated in figures 7.1 and 7.2. Cognitive science has as yet neither verified, improved, nor produced a grounded rejection of this classification of knowledge.

A central feature of the different kinds of knowledge is that they are constructed with different methods, and that choices between principles are based on different types of grounds. Physicists, sociologists, mathematicians, logicians, and moral thinkers use different kinds of evidence and argue in different ways. It is a plausible conjecture that these differences have implications for how we should teach the different kinds of knowledge, although we do not yet understand the differences well enough to say what those implications are.

The type of research needed to improve our understanding of the nature of abstract knowledge is what we might call *naturalistic* studies of knowledge. By a naturalistic study I mean the collection and detailed description of principles from real knowledge domains. Figures 7.1 and 7.2 show a number of examples of principles. If we understood those examples, we would have made considerable progress towards an understanding of abstract knowledge. However, since the purpose of those figures is to show that principles occur in all domains of knowledge, they are unrealistic in that they show only a single principle from each domain. But principles do not come one by one, but typically occur in *belief systems,* clusters of principles that belong together (dietary regulations, ethical systems, logical systems, mathematical theories, political ideologies, religions, scientific theories, etc.). Even very small belief systems turn out to be quite complex. Analysis of the system of spatial principles that are embedded in concepts such as *left, adjacent, between,* etc. revealed more than a hundred distinct principles [41]. Current work on the belief systems that underlie fractions arithmetic [47] and naive conceptions of physical motion[9] indicate that these systems of principles are even more complicated.

Question 2: What is the function of abstract knowledge?

[9] Stellan Ohlsson and Nina Robin, the impetus theory of physical motion, in preparation

The main question with respect to abstract knowledge is why such knowledge is useful. Since abstract principles, by definition, do not refer to particular goals, situations, or actions, how can principles be helpful in the solving of particular problems? How do abstract principles interact with the cognitive performance system so as to facilitate problem solving and procedural learning? In short, what does understanding buy you? There exists a small body of empirical studies that try to pinpoint the interaction between abstract knowledge and performance, as well as a handful of attempts to propose formal theories of that interaction.

3.1 Empirical research on the function of abstract knowledge.

The empirical studies reviewed below show that (a) correct performance is possible even in the absence of knowledge about the underlying concepts and principles, (b) knowledge about concepts and principles does not *guarantee* correct performance, and that (c) knowledge of principles *does* facilitate performance and procedural learning under some conditions. Each group of studies will be summarized in turn.

Performance in the absence of abstract knowledge. Mathematics instructors frequently observe a lack of connection between principles and procedures in children's mathematical performance [22,37]. It is commonplace that students who consistently produce correct answers to mathematical problems upon questioning reveal that they do not understand the meaning, purpose, or justification for the operations they carry out. They have memorized the relevant cognitive procedure independently of, or in the absence of, any abstract knowledge about numbers. There is also evidence that young children who not only *lack* the principle of commutativity of addition, but who actively *deny* this principle, nevertheless do not hesitate to switch the order of the addends in order to simplify an addition problem [8]. The lack of connection between conceptual understanding and algorithmic performance is perceived by many mathematics educators as *the* central problem in mathematics instruction.

A similar phenomenon has been discovered in physics instruction [40]. Students who consistently attain the correct solution to physics problems often lack conceptual understanding of the principles of physics that provide the rationale for the problem solving procedures they are applying. Physics students operate with ideas - variously called misconceptions, alternative conceptions, or naive conceptions - that contradict the principles of the physical theory that is supposed to be applied in the problem solving exercises. For instance, students may believe in the impetus principle, rather than in the principle of inertia. They nevertheless manage to solve mechanics problems, using problem solving procedures that are disconnected from their beliefs about the physical world.

The procedural knowledge of students who solve problems correctly but without understanding is similar to the procedural knowledge in so-called expert systems, Artificial Intelligence systems that solve complex tasks at the level of a human expert. The typical expert systemcontains a large amount of procedural knowledge, but has no representation of the principles of the relevant domain. In fact, the methodology of expert systems was invented precisely to enable the construction of Artificial Intelligence programs that operate in task environments for which a so-called deep theory - a theory consisting of abstract principles is not available. Expert systems are brittle, i.e., they work well on problems that instantiate some problem type that the knowledge engineer designed the system to do, but they cannot handle problems with novel features. Similarly, students who learn arithmetic or physics by memorizing problem solving procedures typically do not know what to do when faced with an unfamiliar problem.

Abstract knowledge without effect on performance. The problem of understanding the interaction between knowledge and performance in human cognition is further complicated by two bodies of evidence that show that the possession of abstract knowledge does not guarantee correct or successful performance. Resnick and Omanson [54] have observed schoolchildren who were capable of explaining the steps in an arithmetic procedure - who had the requisite knowledge for correct action - but who nevertheless did not perform the relevant procedure correctly. Some of their subjects made errors even in the presence of abstract knowledge that is sufficient to rule out those errors.

A second body of evidence about the lack of performance in the presence of abstract knowledge was produced by the Gestalt school of psychology[10]. The Gestalt psychologists constructed a family of problems, commonly known as insight problems. Competent adults in our culture have all the requisite knowledge required for their solution, but they are nevertheless difficult to solve. For instance, in Maier's Two-String Problem the objective is to tie together two strings hanging from the ceiling at a large distance from each other. Competent adults know that swinging a rope makes its end point travel a distance to the side--the core idea in the most elegant solution to this problem--but this principle is generally not accessed without considerable cognitive strain on the part of the subject. The characteristic solution process for an insight problem consists of a long period of floundering, followed by swift attainment of the solution (followed by a feeling of stupidity for not having seen the solution sooner). The solution to a so-called insight problem typically follows directly from some principle that the subject knows very well; the entire difficulty of an insight problem is in accessing that principle. The ease with which people can be tricked into spending large amounts of time rummaging around in the wrong corner of their knowledge store highlights the fact that the application of abstract knowledge in performance is far from simple or direct. There is no guarantee that the perception of a problem situation will access the abstract knowledge that is needed to solve that problem.

Interaction between abstract knowledge and performance. The two groups of results reviewed above might be taken to imply that abstract knowledge is an epiphenomenon, that there are no connections between abstract and procedural knowledge, and that abstract knowledge therefore has no function in performance and learning. According to this hypothesis, so-called abstract knowledge is just the skill of reciting or paraphrasing certain natural language sentences.

However, there are examples of situations in which performance and learning does unfold under the influence of abstract knowledge. The first psychological study that was explicitly designed to determine the effect of knowledge of a principle on performance was a series of experiments by Katona [24]. Subjects learned to sort a deck of cards in a manner that supports a particular card trick. The sorting task was learned under two conditions: Either the learner was told the principle that underlies the card trick, or else he/she was simply asked to memorize the procedure for sorting the cards. The same paradigm was used in a series of studies of match stick problems. The results were that procedural learning, transfer, and retention were much improved by knowledge of the underlying principle. The same effect was obtained in a small set of studies of mathematics learning, in which students who acquired a principle performed much better on a computational task than subjects who tried to learn the skill by rote [13,33].

The strongest case for knowledge-based procedure learning has been made by Gelman and co-workers [15,16,17] with respect to learning how to count a set of objects. Gelman and co-workers have identified the principles underlying the correct procedure for counting. They include the one-to-one mapping principle (each object should be assigned exactly one number), and the cardinality principle (the last number to be paired with an object is the cardinality of the set). They argue that the construction of counting procedures in children proceeds under the influence of these principles. The main grounds for this claim is that children can readily adapt their counting procedures to changes in the task demands, e.g., a demand to associate a particular object with a particular number.

In short, there is evidence that abstract knowledge interacts with performance, although the evidence is not extensive. Indeed, Brooks and Dansereau [9] comment in their review of what they call content-to-skills transfer that the influence of abstract knowledge on performance "has been the subject of a surprisingly small amount of research" (p. 134). The research programme conceived by Katona [24] is still valid: We need experimental studies in which one group of

[10] See Ohlsson [42] for a summary of the Gestalt theory of problem solving.

subjects are taught one or more principles and their subsequent performance compared to the performance of subjects who have not been taught those principles.

3.2 *Theoretical research on the function of abstract knowledge*

Many simulation models of human cognition deal with educationally relevant task domains, but only a handful of them are *learning* models [46]. A learning model differs from a performance model in that it includes one or more learning mechanisms that enable it to learn as it runs. Furthermore, most learning models simulate either the process of learning from examples or practice effects. To the best of my knowledge, there are only four runnable learning models published to date that deal with the function of abstract knowledge.

Anderson [6] has proposed a learning mechanism called *knowledge compilation*. Knowledge compilation operates in the context of ACT*, a production system architecture that is intended as a model of the human cognitive architecture [5]. The main phenomenon addressed by knowledge compilation is how a verbally stated principle, such as a geometry theorem, can be transformed into a procedure for doing a particular task, such as finding geometry proofs [3,4]. The model assumes that the verbal statement of the principle gives rise to a declarative structure in memory. The transformation of that structure into a set of production rules involves two distinct processes, proceduralization and composition. During *proceduralization* the declarative knowledge structure is used by general inference procedures that Anderson call *interpretative productions*. When an interpretative production is executed, it creates a new production rule that is a copy of itself, except that all variables that were bound to expressions in the declarative knowledge structure are instantiated. Through this mechanism proceduralization creates a collection of task specific production rules. In the second learning step, called *composition*, the newly created production rules are combined into more compact rules that carry out the functions of several rules in a single production system cycle. Composition does not make use of the declarative knowledge structures.

The learning mechanism of the DEDU model proposed by Ohlsson [45] is similar to the proceduralization mechanism in that it assumes that principles appear as declarative knowledge structures in memory, and that they function as input into general inference procedures that create new task specific production rules based on the local context in which they apply. The performance mechanism of the DEDU model is also a production system architecture. The learning method of the DEDU model is called *rational learning* to emphasize that learning is based on abstract knowledge about the relevant domain (as opposed to a collection of instances or examples). The main phenomenon explained by the DEDU model is the succession of strategy shifts on the three-term series problem. Subjects have been shown to shift from an initial imagery strategy to a propositional strategy, and from the propositional strategy to a perceptual pattern strategy. Unlike the interpretative productions in ACT*, the interpretative productions in the DEDU model are looking for *patterns of relations* between principles and already existing production rules in order to identify *learning opportunities*, e.g., situations in which the principles indicate that some improvement in the current procedure is possible.

Greeno and co-workers have proposed a model of the function of abstract principles in the context of planning [18,57]. Principled knowledge is encoded in *action schemata*, abstract actions that have pre-requisites (conditions that have to be true for the schema to apply), co-requisites (conditions that have to remain true while a schema is being applied), post-requisites (conditions that have to be true in order to for the schema to have been applied successfully), and results and effects (conditions that are guaranteed to be true, if the schema has been applied successfully). The phenomenon explained by the action schema model is childrens' flexibility in adapting their counting procedures to a variety of changes in the task demands, e.g., to count in such a way that a specified object becomes associated with a specified number. The counting principles are encoded in action schemata which are used as inputs to a planning mechanism that poses the goal of counting a set of objects in a particular situation or *setting*, and tries to build a plan that can achieve that goal by searching for a schema that has the desired outcome as result, and then posing its pre-requisites as subgoals, etc. When the plan is finished, it is executed to generate a performance.

There are three differences between the action schema model, on the one hand, and the ACT* and DEDU models, on the other. First, while the ACT* and DEDU models assume that principles are encoded as general propositions, the action schema model introduces a non-propositional knowledge unit. The notion of an abstract action has been proposed repeatedly throughout the history of psychology - it is, for instance, central to Piaget's work - but the theory by Greeno and co-workers is the first attempt to define this concept within an information processing framework. Second, while the ACT* and DEDU models assume that principles appear as structures in memory, and hence are known explicitly, the action schema model is intended as a model of implicitly known principles. Third, unlike the ACT* and DEDU models, the action schema theory is a competence theory rather than process model. The authors do not claim psychological reality for the planning mechanism included in the model, only for the action schemata.

Ohlsson and Rees [50] have recently described a learning model called HS that differs in significant respects from the three models discussed above. The performance component of the HS model consists of a production system architecture that operates by searching a problem space. Abstract knowledge is encoded in terms of *state constraints,* knowledge units that constrain the set of valid search states. A state constraint consists of two patterns that are pattern-matched against search states. If the *relevance* pattern matches against a state, then the *satisfaction* pattern must also match, otherwise that state violates the constraint. Hence, the first function of abstract knowledge in the HS model is to monitor the performance component and to detect errors. The second function of abstract knowledge in the HS model is to specify how the existing rules should be revised. The learning mechanism uses a variant of goal-regression to compute the appropriate revisions of rules that cause constraint violations. The main phenomena explained by the HS model is the flexibility of children's counting behaviour (i.e., the same phenomenon addressed by the action schema model), and the self-correction of subtraction bugs on the part of a knowledgeable learner.

The HS model differs from the three models discussed above in that the abstract knowledge is applied in the *evaluation* of the current procedure, rather than in its *generation.* HS learns from it mistakes, while the learning mechanisms of both ACT* and DEDU operate in the context of correct performance. HS learns while doing, i.e., it begins by performing its current task through trial and error and constructs a procedure as it goes, while the action schema model constructs an entire procedure before it starts performing its current task. Like the action schema model, but unlike the ACT* and DEDU models, the HS model is intended as a model of implicitly, rather than explicitly, known principles. Finally, the unit of abstract knowledge in HS, the state constraint, differs from the units used in the other three models in subtle ways. Implicational propositions and action schemata both contain the input-output relation of a procedure, albeit in disguise. The antecedents of an implicational statement are the truth conditions for its conclusion, and the pre-requisites of an action schema are the conditions under which the schema can produce its effects. However, a state constraint does not imply that the content of the satisfaction pattern can be inferred or constructed when the relevance pattern is true. It implies that if the relevance pattern is true, then the satisfaction pattern *ought* to be true, otherwise a mistake has been made. Hence, state constraints are further removed from actions than other units of abstract knowledge.

Artificial Intelligence research has now focussed on a type of learning that is called *explanation-based generalization* [12,36]. The basic idea of explanation-based generalization is that in order to learn from an example of a concept, the learning system needs to know why the example is an instance of that concept. A variety of learning systems have been proposed that use abstract knowledge--a domain theory--in the form of a collection of implicational propositions to construct an explanation of why a given object or event is an example of some concept. It then uses a regression algorithm to generalize the significant features of the example into an efficient procedure for recognizing other instances of that concept.

In short, current theories of the function of abstract knowledge postulate three different units of abstract knowledge: implicational propositions (used in the ACT* and DEDU models, as well as in explanation-based generalization), action schemata, and state constraints. The knowledge encoded in these constructs are used in a variety of processes, such as proceduralization, planning, rule revision, and the construction of explanations. However, only a handful of phenomena have been modelled by these theories, and the fit between the behaviour of the models and human behaviour has not been investigated in depth[11]. There is need for simulation models that (a) build on an explicitly stated performance model, (b) have separate representations for procedural and abstract knowledge, (c) postulate some mechanisms by which abstract knowledge can influence performance, and (d) generate testable predictions about the kind of behaviour we should expect to see in human learning.

3.3 Discussion

The empirical and theoretical research reviewed above deals with the question of how abstract knowledge *functions* in performance and procedural learning. The learning issue investigated in this research is how abstract knowledge facilitates the acquisition of cognitive skills. The empirical studies manipulate knowledge of the principles through instruction, and observe the effects on the learning of some problem solving skill. Similarly, the simulation models reviewed assume that the relevant principles are available. The process they model is the construction of a procedure on the basis of those principles, not the process of acquiring the principles themselves. In short, the research reviewed above does *not* address the question of how abstract principles are learned.

One might believe that the problem of how principles are acquired is, or should be, the primary question, and that the question of how principles function once they are acquired is, or should be, the secondary question. This is a mistake, however. The reason is methodological. Researching the question of how abstract knowledge is acquired presupposes some way of tracking the acquisition process. In order to test hypotheses about the acquisition of principles, we must be able to assess when a principle has been acquired. But we cannot test such an hypothesis against observations, unless we know what to look for, i.e., unless we know what effects a principle would have on performance, if indeed it were learned. Hence, a theory of the function of abstract knowledge is logically and methodologically prior to a theory of the acquisition of abstract knowledge.

Question 3: How is abstract knowledge acquired?

The question of how abstract knowledge is acquired is, of course, the key question for the enterprise outlined in this paper. To repeat the argument from the introduction: Unless the learning mechanisms involved in the construction of knowledge are known in detail, the obstacles to learning cannot be identified with enough precision to inform the design of instruction. If our aim is to teach abstract knowledge rather than skill, we need a theory of how such knowledge is acquired. When, under what mental circumstances, does a person construct a new principle (or grasp a new idea, as common sense would say)?

Cognitive psychology has inherited two hypotheses about the origin of principles from philosophy[12]. The *induction* hypothesis claims that a general principle is constructed by extracting recurring features from a set of instances. Induction certainly has some psychological validity--obviously people generalize over examples *sometimes--but* it cannot be the main

---

11 The ACT- model has been subject to extensive empirical testing. However, those aspects of the model that have been tested are not the aspects that are of interest here, namely the properties of the proceduralization mechanism. The empirical tests of the proceduralization mechanism that have been published to date consists of impressionistic matchings between the model and (unpublished) think-aloud protocols from a handful of subjects learning geometry proof finding.

12 Philosophy also considered a third hypothesis, namely that at least some principles are innate. This hypothesis has not been influential within psychology.

source of new principles. Most interesting principles cannot be construed as summaries of features that recur in a set of examples. For example, the principle of inertia cannot be construed in this way, because nobody has ever observed even a single example of a body moving without any forces acting on it. Also, the induction hypothesis does not explain how people select which set of examples to generalize over.

The second hypothesis about the origin of principles that cognitive psychology has inherited from philosophy is *deduction*, i.e., the idea that new principles are constructed from previously learned principles by logical reasoning. People might occasionally construct principles in this way, but deduction cannot be the main source of new principles. Experimental investigations have revealed that our ability to carry out logical arguments is rather limited. Indeed, one investigator has concluded that people *never* reason deductively [23]. Also, since deduction creates new principles out of old, some principles must be given at the outset. Deduction cannot explain where those very first principles come from.

In short, neither induction nor deduction is a psychologically valid hypothesis about the acquisition of abstract knowledge. This is not surprising, since these hypotheses were originally proposed by philosophers in response to epistemological problems. There never was any reason to expect these hypotheses to solve psychological problems.

The main hypothesis about the origin of principles that has been proposed from within psychology is that *new ideas arise from the resolution of cognitive conflicts*. This hypothesis has been put forward repeatedly in a variety of contexts. For instance, Piaget's theory of cognitive development postulates that development occurs because the child is trying to restore equilibrium in his/her cognitive structures [51,52]. The cognitive conflict hypothesis was vigorously developed by social psychologists in the 1950's and 1960's under the name of cognitive consistency theory [2]. Unfortunately, this branch of cognitive psychology has now died out [1]. Cognitive conflict is also a central concept in the study of insight problems [42], and the history of science [27]. The notion of cognitive conflict has recently been taken up in Artificial Intelligence research on non-monotonic reasoning [34] and discovery [55], as well as in philosophical research on belief revision [14,20]. The main difficulty in formulating a formal theory based on the cognitive conflict hypothesis is to specify precisely what is meant by a conflict between *systems of* principles, rather than between pairs of principles.

In short, there is a scarcity of ideas about how abstract principles are constructed. The classical notions of induction and deduction have some psychological reality, but neither is tenable as the main source of new principles. The hypothesis that principles arise in the resolution of cognitive conflicts has not yet been formulated precisely within the information processing framework.

Question 4: What methods for task analysis?

One of the most striking and dramatic results of modern research into cognition is the discovery that *we do not know the content of even the most well-analyzed knowledge domains*. For instance, number theory has been studied for thousands of years; the theory has been reformulated and restated repeatedly; it has been axiomatized for over a century. Nevertheless, if we ask what concepts and principles a student must know in order to learn arithmetic, expositions of number theory do not provide the answer. figure 7.7 show some of the concepts and principles that we now believe that students must acquire in order to learn arithmetic. But these principles do not appear in systematic treatments of the number system. Cognitive scientists everywhere find that the first item on their agenda is to identify the content of the knowledge domain they are interested in, be it mechanics [63], electricity [19], medical diagnosis [11], or computer programming [Reiser, this volume]. Once the content of the knowledge domain has been identified it is possible to proceed with research on the cognitive processes involved in the acquisition and utilization of that knowledge, but the expositions of domain experts are of little help in the identification of the knowledge.

Principles of whole numbers:
— The coordination between cardinality and ordinality: The cardinality of a set corresponds to an ordinal position in a linear ordering.
— The principle of cardinality: The last number to be assigned to an object during counting denotes the cardinality of the counted set.
— The one-one mapping principle: In counting each object must be assigned exactly one number.

Principles of integer arithmetic:
— The interpretation of integer addition: The sum of two numbers can denote either the result of combining two quantities, or the result of changing one quantity by a specified amount.
— The principle of additive decomposition: Any number can be expressed as a sum of other numbers.

Principles of fraction arithmetic:
— Relation between number of parts and size of parts: If a quantity is partitioned into equal sized parts, then the more parts, the smaller the parts and vice versa.
— Equivalent fractions-1: If two fractions denote the same rational number, they are equivalent.
— Equivalent fractions-2: The combination of N quantities of size x can result in the same quantity as the combination of M quantities of size y.

Fig.7.7. Concepts and principles of arithmetic.

Part of the difficulty of task analysis, or, more accurately, knowledge identification, is that the relation between skills and knowledge, between principles and procedures, is obscure. The skills of a particular domain are relatively easy to identify. A domain of knowledge is typically associated with one or more canonical problem types, and we recognize experts in the domain by the fact that they have the skills required to solve those problem types. The canonical task in arithmetic is to perform calculations, the canonical tasks of medicine are to diagnose and to apply treatment, and so on. An Artificial Intelligence system that can solve a canonical problem is often a decent first approximation to how experts solve that problem.

However, identification of the principles that underlie a skill is difficult. How does one know what the rationale is for a particular skill, and, conversely, how does one know what skills a given principle imply? For example, suppose that somebody denied the claim by Resnick and Omanson [54] that the principle of additive decomposition is part of the rationale for the standard subtraction algorithm. *How would we defend the claim?* What would count as evidence in such a debate? If we can construct a competence theory in the form of a running computer program that can derive the procedure from the principle is that supporting evidence? Such a program only proves that the principle is sufficient but not that it is necessary. If experts agree that the principle forms the rationale for a procedure, does that prove the claim? If so, what are we supposed to conclude if the experts turn out to disagree? If it can be shown that children can learn the procedure without having been taught the principle, is that counter evidence? Or does that only show that children can discover the rationale for the procedure on their own? If we teach children the principle, and then observe them fail to learn the procedure, is that counter evidence? Or does that just show that children can know the principle without also knowing how to apply it? The current author confesses bafflement in the face of these questions.

In summary, it is a minimal requirement for theory-based design of instruction in a particular subject matter that we can identify the content of that subject matter. However, no systematic methods have yet been developed for identification of the concepts and principles of a given knowledge domain. Subject matter identification is still an art form: Someone who understands the domain[13] writes down whatever concepts and principles he/she intuits as belonging to the

[13] or believes he/she understands the domain.

domain. We would not expect paintings by different artists to look alike, and they don't: The reader is invited to compare Kieren [25], Ohlsson [47] and Vergnaud [61], three knowledge identification artists who have painted rather different pictures of the concepts and principles of fractions arithmetic. Our inability to identify the knowledge we are supposed to be studying and teaching is a major obstacle for cognitive research as well as for instruction.

Question 5: What methods for cognitive diagnosis?

Theories of the acquisition of abstract knowledge cannot be tested against observations, unless we have methods for diagnosing whether a particular concept or principle has been learned or not. Similarly, instruction in abstract knowledge requires methods for assessing instructional outcomes. The problem of cognitive diagnosis can be stated in the following general form: *Given a person's performance on a set of problems, infer the knowledge state of that person.* This formulation covers both the problem of how to interpret data from laboratory subjects, and the problem of how to diagnose students in order to provide individualized instruction. (See VanLehn [60] for a review of cognitive diagnosis in the context of intelligent tutoring systems.)

Educators have developed two methods for the diagnosis of abstract knowledge, namely explanation questions and transfer tasks. *Explanation questions* require the learner to verbalize the rationale for a procedure or a step in a procedure, or to explain an event. The obvious difficulty with this approach is that concepts and principles might be known implicitly rather than explicitly. Furthermore, empirical research has shown that it is possible to know a principle without knowing how to apply it. In these two types of cases, diagnosis through explanation questions will give a conservative estimate of the person's level of understanding, a frequent criticism of Piaget's early attempts to diagnose children's abstract knowledge with so-called clinical interviews. Conversely, a concept or principle might be memorized, and hence verbalizable, without being fully understood. To complicate matters further, one cognitive scientist has recently argued that the verbalization of a principle, e.g., the impetus principle of physical motion, does not necessarily imply that the principle is known[14] by the person verbalizing it. Instead, it might be constructed in the course of answering the question. In these types of cases, diagnosis based on verbalization will overestimate the person's knowledge of principles.

The second traditional test of understanding is the *transfer test,* in which the student is asked to apply what he has learned to a novel problem. The obvious objection to the transfer test is that *some* procedural learning is involved in mastering the transfer task (otherwise it is not an unfamiliar task). Hence, failure to solve the transfer task might simply indicate failure to construct the procedure for the transfer task, rather than an absence of the principles that are supposed to underlie performance on both the training and the transfer tasks. Without formal models of the relevant procedures it is difficult to know how much cognitive work is involved in adapting to the transfer task. Also, without formal models of the adaptation process, there is no proof that the adaptation to the transfer task involves the knowledge that is supposed to be diagnosed. The selection of transfer tasks is, like knowledge identification, an impressionistic art form at this time. As a result, the transfer test is likely to underestimate the student's knowledge.

Cognitive science has generated several approaches to cognitive diagnosis. The diagnostic method invented by Newell and Simon [38] takes a think-aloud protocol as input, maps the protocol onto a path through a problem space, and induces production rules on the basis of regularities in the path. The result is a collection of production rules that can reproduce the observed performance. This method has only been applied to a handful of domains [38,48]. It is very laborious, and its inter-judge reliability is unknown, i.e., we do not know the extent to which different researchers analyzing the same protocol would construct the same collection of production rules. The diagnostic method used in the BUGGY/DEBUGGY [10] system for

[14] diSessa, personal communication.

automatic diagnosis of subtraction errors is based on a pre-defined library of bugs, i.e., faulty subtraction procedures. The input to the BUGGY/DEBUGGY system is a set of answers to subtraction problems, and the output is a listing of the most plausible explanations, i.e., the best-fitting bugs or bug combinations. The construction of a bug library is a tedious task. However, Ohlsson and Langley [49] demonstrated that a bug library is not always necessary. They implemented a system for bottom-up diagnosis of subtraction errors which first searches for a psychologically plausible solution path to explain the observed answers, and then applies machine learning methods to infer production rules that can produce that path. The main problem with these approaches to cognitive diagnosis from the point of view of the present paper is that they diagnose cognitive skills, rather than abstract knowledge.

A different approach to cognitive diagnosis has been suggested by Langley, Wogulis, and Ohlsson [31]. Representing principles as constraints, they propose to match the constraints against a solution path in order to decide whether that path violates or conforms to those principles. If a certain constraint is consistently violated by the student's solutions, then it is reasonable to infer that the corresponding principle is not known by that student. This method of diagnosis is currently being implemented in the HS model [50] but no results as to its effectiveness are as yet available.

In short, both research and individualized instruction requires methods for diagnosing knowledge states. The traditional methods for assessing abstract knowledge, explanation questions and transfer tasks, suffer from several weaknesses. Cognitive science has recently proposed several new methods for cognitive diagnosis, but those methods are only relevant for the diagnosis of procedural, as opposed to abstract, knowledge.

4. Conclusion

The advances of modern cognitive psychology in general, and the advances towards theory-based instructional design in particular, are consequences of the collective decision to view human cognition--thinking, remembering, learning--as symbolic computation. The symbolic computation metaphor provides us with a rich conceptual apparatus for talking about and dissecting procedures: agenda, AND/OR tree, architecture, compilation, complexity function, control structure, data-flow, evaluation function, execution cycle, frame, goal-subgoal hierarchies, heuristic, means-ends analysis, rule, search schemes, stack, strategy, variable binding, etc. This explosion of conceptual power had the unfortunate side-effect that researchers focused their attention almost exclusively on procedural knowledge. As a result, current cognitive theory is a theory of cognitive skills rather than a theory of knowledge, and its instructional implications pertain mainly to skill acquisition.

However, the metaphor of symbolic computation does not provide us with equally powerful notions of abstract knowledge. Information processing ideas about knowledge are poor and weakly articulated. Consequently, current cognitive theory is not very useful for the design of instruction in abstract knowledge. In particular, it is not very useful for the design of intelligent tutoring systems that teach concepts and principles. Hence, if we want to provide theory-based instruction in abstract knowledge, we need to develop a theory of the acquisition of abstract knowledge.

In order to develop a cognitive theory that can support the development of intelligent tutoring systems that teach knowledge rather than skills, we need to carry out five types of research. First, we must study the nature of the abstract knowledge. In what units should knowledge be discussed, what different types of knowledge are there, and what are the psychologically essential properties of belief systems? Second, we need to invent hypotheses about how abstract knowledge facilitates problem solving performance and procedural learning, and carry out experiments in which performance under the influence of knowledge can be compared to performance in the absence of knowledge. Why is knowledge useful? Why do people act under the influence of knowledge in some situations, but not in others? Third, we need to generate new ideas about how concepts and principles are acquired. What are the mental circumstances under which a person grasps a new idea? Fourth and fifth, we need to extend our repertoire of methods to enable us to identify the concepts and principles of any given knowledge domain, and to diagnose to what extent those concepts and principles are known by a subject or student. The ultimate test of a theory of abstract knowledge is that it can be the basis for the design of an intelligent tutoring system that can teach concepts and principles.

References

1. Abelson, R. P. Whatever became of consistency theory? *Personality and Social Psychology Bulletin, 9,* 37-54. 1983.
2. Abelson, R. P., Aronson, E., McGuire, W. J., Newcomb, T. M., Rosenberg, M. J., & Tannenbaum, P. H. (Eds.), *Theories of cognitive consistency: A sourcebook* Chicago, Ill.: Rand McNally. 1968.
3. Anderson, J. R. Acquisition of cognitive skill. *Psychological Review, 89,* 369-406. 1982.
4. Anderson, J. R. Acquisition of proof skills in geometry. In R. S. Michalski, J. G. Carbonell, & T. M. Mitchell (Eds.), *Machine learning: An artificial intelligence approach.* Palo Alto, CA: Tioga Publishing Co. 1983a.
5. Anderson, J. R. *The architecture of cognition.* Cambridge, MA: Harvard University Press. 1983b.
6. Anderson, J. R. Knowledge compilation: The general learning mechanism. In R. S. Michalski, J. G. Carbonell, & T. M. Mitchell (Eds.), *Machine learning: An artificial intelligence approach (Vol. 11,* pp. 289-310). Los Altos, CA: Morgan Kaufmann Pub., Inc. 1986.
7. Anderson, J. R., Boyle, C. F., & Yost, G. The geometry tutor. *Proceedings of the International Joint Conference on Artificial Intelligence,* Los Angeles, 1-7. 1985.
8. Baroody, A. J. & Gannon, K. E. The development of the commutativity principle and economical addition strategies. *Cognition and Instruction, 1,* 245-296. 1984.
9. Brooks, L. W., & Dansereau, D. F. Transfer of information: An instructional perspective. In S. M. Cormier, & J. D. Hagman (Eds.), *Transfer of learning: Contemporary research and applications.* New York: Academic Press. 1987.
10. Burton, R.B. Diagnosing bugs in a simple procedural skill In D.H. Sleeman and J.S. Brown (eds) *Intelligent Tutoring Systems.* New York; Academic, 157-183. 1982.
11. Clancey, W. J. *Knowledge-based tutoring. The GUIDON program.* Cambridge, Mass.: MIT Press. 1987.
12. DeJong, G., & Mooney, R. Explanation-based learning: An alternative view. *Machine Learning, 1,* 145-176. 1986.
13. Egan, D. E., & Greeno, J. G. Acquiring cognitive structure by discovery and rule learning. *Journal of Educational Psychology, 64,* 85-97. 1973.
14. Gardenfors, P. *Knowledge in flux. Modelling the dynamics of epistemic states.* Cambridge, MA.: MIT Press. 1988.
15. Gelman, R., & Gallistel, C. R. *The child's understanding of number.* Cambridge, MA: Harvard University Press. 1978.
16. Gelman, R., & Meck, E. Preschoolers' counting: Principle before skill. *Cognition, 13,* 343-359. 1983.
17. Gelman, R., & Meck, E. The notion of principle: The case of counting. In J. H. Hiebert (Ed.), *Conceptual and procedural knowledge: The case of mathematics* (pp. 29-57). Hillsdale, NJ: Erlbaum. 1986.
18. Greeno, J. G., Riley, M. S., & Gelman, R. Conceptual competence and children's counting. *Cognitive Psychology, 16,* 94-143. 1984.
19. Haertel, H. A qualitative approach to electricity (Technical Report, August 1987). Palo Alto, Calif.: Institute for Research on Learning. 1987.
20. Harman, G. *Change in view. Principles of reasoning.* Cambridge, Mass.: MIT Press. 1986.

21. Hayes, P. J. The logic of frames. In R. J. Brachman & H. J. Levesque, (Eds.), *Readings in knowledge representation*. Los Altos, Calif.: Kaufmann. 1985/1979.
22. Hiebert, J. (Ed.). *Conceptual and procedural knowledge: The case of mathematics*. Hillsdale, NJ: Erlbaum. 1986.
23. Johnson-Laird, P. N. *Mental models. Towards a cognitive science of language, inference, and consciousness*. Cambridge, Mass.: Harvard University Press. 1983.
24. Katona, G. *Organizing and memorizing: Studies in the psychology of learning and teaching*. New York: Hafner Pub. Co. 1967.
25. Kieren, T. E. Personal knowledge of rational numbers: Its intuitive and formal development. In J. Hiebert & M. Behr, (Eds.), *Number concepts and operations in the middle grades*. Hillsdale, NJ: Erlbaum. 1988.
26. Klahr, D., Langley, P., & Neches, R. (Eds.). *Production system models of learning and development* Cambridge, MA: The MIT Press. 1987.
27. Kuhn, T. *The structure of scientific revolutions*, second ed. Chicago, Ill.: University of Chicago Press. 1970.
28. Laird, J. E., Rosenbloom, P. S., & Newell, A. *Universal subgoaling and chunking: The automatic generation and learning of goal hierarchies*. Boston, MA: Kluwer. 1986.
29. Langley, P. A general theory of discrimination learning. In D. Klahr, P. Langley, & R. Neches (Eds.), *Production system models of learning and development* (pp. 99-161). Cambridge, MA: The MIT Press. 1987.
30. Langley, P. & Jones, R. A computational model of scientific insight. In R. J. Sternberg, (Ed.), *The nature of creativity. Contemporary psychological perspectives*. Cambridge: Cambridge University Press. 1988.
31. Langley, P., Wogulis, J., & Ohlsson, S. Rules and principles in cognitive diagnosis. In N. Frederiksen (Ed.), *Diagnostic monitoring of skill and knowledge acquisition*. Hillsdale, NJ: Erlbaum. (in press).
32. Lenat, D. B. Toward a theory of heuristics. In R. Groner, M. Groner, & W. F. Bishop, (Eds.), *Methods of heuristics*. Hillsdale, NJ: Erlbaum. 1983.
33. Mayer, R. E., Stiehl, C. C., & Greeno, J. G. Acquisition of understanding and skill in relation to subjects' preparation and meaningfulness of instruction. *Journal of Educational Psychology, 67*, 331-350. 1975.
34. McDermott, D. & Doyle, J. Non-monotonic logic 1. *Artificial Intelligence, 13*, 41-72. 1980.
35. Michener, E. R. Understanding understanding mathematics. *Cognitive Science*, 2, 361-383. 1978.
36. Mitchell, T. M., Keller, R. M., & Kedar-Cabelli, S. T. Explanation-based generalization: A unifying view. *Machine Learning, 1*, 47-80. 1986.
37. Nesher, P. Are mathematical understanding and algorithmic performance related? *For the Learning of Mathematics, 6*, 3-9. 1986.
38. Newell, A., & Simon, H. A. *Human problem solving*. Englewood Cliffs, NJ: Prentice-Hall, Inc. 1972.
39. Nilsson, N. J. *Problem-solving methods in artificial intelligence*. New York: McGraw-Hill. 1971.
40. Novak, J. D. (Ed.), *Proceedings of the Second International Seminar on Misconceptions and Educational Strategies in Science and Education, Vols. 1-111*, July 26-29. Ithaca, NY: Cornell University. 1987.
41. Ohlsson, S. Competence and strategy in reasoning with common spatial concepts (Technical Report No. 4). Stockholm, Sweden: The Cognitive Seminar, Department of Psychology, University of Stockholm. 1980.
42. Ohlsson, S. Restructuring revisited. 1. Summary and critique of the Gestalt theory of problem solving. *Scandinavian Journal of Psychology, 25*, 65-78. 1984a.
43. Ohlsson, S. Restructuring revisited. 11. An information processing theory of restructuring and insight. *Scandinavian. Journal of Psychology, 25*, 117-129. 1984b.

44. Ohlsson, S. Transfer of training in procedural learning: A matter of conjectures and refutations? In L. Bolc (Ed.), *Computational models of learning* (pp. 55-88). Berlin, Federal Republic of Germany: Springer-Verlag. 1987a.
45. Ohlsson, S. Truth versus appropriateness: Relating declarative to procedural knowledge. In D. Klahr, P. Langley, & R. Neches (Eds.), *Production system models of learning and development* (pp. 287-327). Cambridge, MA: The MIT Press. 1987b.
46. Ohlsson, S. Computer simulation and its impact on educational research and practice. *International Journal of Educational Research, 12, 5-12*. Oxford: Pergamon Press. 1988a.
47. Ohlsson, S. Mathematical meaning and applicational meaning in the semantics of fractions and related concepts. In J. Hiebert & M. Behr, (Eds.), *Number concepts and operations in the middle grades.* Hillsdale, NJ: Erlbaum. 1988b.
48. Ohlsson, S. Trace analysis and spatial reasoning: An example of intensive cognitive diagnosis and its implications for testing. In N. Frederiksen, R. Glaser, A. M. Lesgold, & M. Shafto, (Eds.), *Diagnostic monitoring of skill and knowledge acquisition.* Hillsdale, NJ: Erlbaum. (in press).
49. Ohlsson, S., & Langley, P. Psychological evaluation of path hypotheses in cognitive diagnosis. In H. Mandl, & A. Lesgold (Eds.), *Learning issues for intelligent tutoring systems.* New York: Springer-Verlag. 1988.
50. Ohlsson, S., & Rees, E. *An information processing analysis of the function of conceptual understanding in the learning of arithmetic procedures* (Tech. Report No. KUL-88-03). Pittsburgh, PA: University of Pittsburgh, Learning Research and Development Center. 1988.
51. Piaget, J. In P. H. Mussen, (Ed.), *Handbook of child psychology. Vol 1: History, theory, and methods.* New York, NY: Wiley. 1983.
52. Piaget, J. *Experiments in contradiction.* Chicago, Ill.: Chicago University Press. 1986.
53. Reiser, B. J., Anderson, J. R., & Farrell, R. G. Dynamic student modelling in an intelligent tutor for LISP programming. *Proceedings of the Ninth International Joint Conference on Artificial Intelligence,* Los Angeles, 8-14. 1985.
54. Resnick, L. B., & Omanson, S. F. Learning to understand arithmetic. In R. Glaser (Ed.), *Advances in instructional psychology(Vol. 3,* pp. 41-95). Hillsdale, NJ: Erlbaum. 1987.
55. Rose, D. & Langley, P. Chemical discovery as belief revision. *Machine Learning, 1,* 423-452. 1986.
56. Simon, H. A. *The sciences of the artificial.* Cambridge, Mass.: MIT Press. 1969.
57. Smith, D. A., Greeno, J. G., & Vitolo, T. M., A model of competence for counting. *Cognitive Science.*(in press).
58. VanLehn, K. *Learning one subprocedure per lesson* (Tech. Report No. ISL-10). Palo Alto, CA: Xerox PARC. 1985.
59. VanLehn, K. Arithmetic procedures are induced from examples. In J. H. Hiebert (Ed.), *Conceptual and procedural knowledge: The case of mathematics* (pp. 133-179). Hillsdale, NJ: Erlbaum. 1986.
60. VanLehn, K. Student modelling. In M. C. Polson & J. J. Richardson, (Eds.), *Foundations of intelligent tutoring systems.* Hillsdale, NJ: Erlbaum. 1988.
61. Vergnaud, G. Multiplicative structures. In J. Hiebert & M. Behr, (Eds.), *Number concepts and operations in the middle grades.* Hillsdale, NJ: Erlbaum. 1988.
62. Wenger, E. *Artificial intelligence and tutoring systems.* Los Altos, Calif.: Morgan Kaufmann, Inc. 1987.
63. White, B. Designing computer games to help physics students understand Newton's laws of motion. *Cognition and Instruction, 1, 1-4.* 1984.
64. Winograd, T. Frame representations and the declarative/procedural controversy. In D. G. Bobrow & A. Collins (Eds.), *Representation and understanding. Studies in cognitive science* (pp. 185-210). New York: Academic Press. 1975.

8

The Present and Future of Intelligent Tutoring Systems

Ernesto Costa
Dept. Engenhavia Electrotechnica,
Universidade Coimbra Portugal

Abstract: The goals of this chapter are twofold. First, we will show how the use of machine learning techniques can greatly improve the dynamic construction and updating of student models. Then, we will discuss the underlying principles of the traditional design paradigm for Intelligent Tutoring Systems (ITSs) and will argue that they are, partially, responsible for the difficulties felt by present day ITSs. We maintain the thesis that the teaching (and learning) situation is a particular instance of the general case of interaction among intelligent agents. As a consequence of this point of view, we sustain that new principles for building ITSs are needed, based on the idea of belief systems.

Keywords: ACM, Artificial Intelligence, belief systems, diagnosing, discrimination trees, expert system, explanation-based learning, intelligent tutoring systems, knowledge communicating system, knowledge representation, machine learning, methodology, student model, student module, subtraction, tutorial strategies

1. Introduction

Today the important role played by Artificial Intelligence in Education is well accepted and recognized [14], in particular with the so called Intelligent Tutoring Systems (ITS for short) [11]. The maturity of this new area of research and application can be inferred from the enormous number of books, magazines and conferences dedicated to the subject. One of the most significant outcomes after some years of work was the emergence of a consensus around a common architecture for an ITS. It consists mainly of three modules (domain, student and pedagogue), reflecting what is called the "what, whom and how" paradigm for tutoring, plus an interface for student/system communication [15,17].

The domain module represents what is being teached and contains usually a set of facts and/or rules representing the knowledge we have about the domain. Sometimes this part of the system is also responsible for the automatic generation of examples. A lot of attention has been paid to the problem of domain knowledge representation, the solutions ranging from declarative (frame-like) to procedural ones (production rules).

The student module, the whom part, stands for the accurate definition of the student is current knowledge state (what he knows - either correct or incorrect - and does not know). It can be a (static) data structure, representing a subset of the domain knowledge mastered by the learner (an overlay model), or it can be a set of (possibly wrong) procedures describing the student past behaviour (a buggy model).

The pedagogue module determines, at each stage of a teaching session, how to proceed, that is, which type of interaction should be used so that learning might become more effective. It is usually expressed as a set of meta-knowledge rules stating the knowledge the system has about teaching and learning.

ITSs are a big step beyond traditional computer-aided instruction in the sense that:

- there is no need for a priority specification of a complete set of tasks to be executed by the student;
- pairs of question/answer need not be pre-coded. They are constructed whenever necessary;
- teaching is sensitive to the characteristics of each particular student. This is achieved by means of a (dynamic) student model maintained by the tutoring system.

Usually the design of a tutoring system follows a sequence of three steps. First, the domain module is built, normally around an expert system. A lot of time is spent structuring and representing the domain knowledge. Second, the student module is constructed. Traditionally, the student model is heavily dependent on the previous step, being either a subset of the domain knowledge (the ideal model) or a perturbation of this knowledge expressed within the same framework. Third, if we arrive to this last step, some general tutoring principles are incorporated into the tutor. Only in a few cases is the system build around a learning theory.

Each of this aspects is a difficult task of its own. So the nonexistence of a ITS integrating in a satisfactory way these different components is not surprising.

In this chapter we will present and discuss two main points. In the next section, we will show how the use of machine learning techniques can greatly improve the dynamic construction and updating of the student model. Then, we will discuss the underlying principles of the design paradigm for ITSs presented above, and will argue that they are, partially, responsible for the difficulties felt by present day ITSs.

2. Machine Learning and Intelligent Tutoring Systems

One definition of Machine Learning (ML) is that area of Artificial Intelligence concerned with the development of computational models of learning. There are at least three main areas for application of ML [2]. The first one consists in the automation of the process of knowledge acquisition for expert systems; the second one is used to test general (human) theories of learning; the third one applies to the design of ITSs. According to Michalsky [12], learning strategies can be classified with respect to the power of the inferences made by the learner. The main ones are learning by deduction, learning by analogy and learning by induction.

Machine Learning has been used in education for the construction and maintenance of the student model [8], using either inductive techniques [10] or deductive ones [6]. The reason for that is the fact that student modelling has long been recognized as the most difficult and crucial part of an ITS. Moreover, the two classical approaches (overlay and buggy) are not satisfactory. The overlay approach assumes that students knowledge is a subset of the (ideal) teacher model. This methodology, focussing on what the student knows and does not know, is unable to deal with what the student incorrectly knows. Solving this last problem, that is, analyzing deviations from a correct behaviour, is the ultimate goal of buggy approaches. The student model will be a set of correct and incorrect procedures. The later ones come from a set of "mal-rules" which were compiled off-line, and are chosen for their predictive power regarding students answers. In order to work well, this method needs to have a set of complete buggy rules. This is, in general, an impossible task. Consequently, we need new ways for constructing, dynamically, a student model which expresses what the learner knows, does not know and knows incorrectly in a particular moment.

2.1 Machine Learning and Inductive Techniques

Langley et al. [10] developed a program, called ACM (for Automatic Cognitive Modelling), which is able to generate buggy rules automatically. It works on the domain of subtraction. The system is based on a particular type of inductive learning called learning by examples. This technique can be described as follows: given a set of positive and negative examples of a concept or rule, find an intentional definition of this concept or rule so that it covers all positive instances and none of the negative. The definition must be able to correctly classify future instances. ACM uses this methodology to learn incorrect procedures (the mal-rules). The authors follow the search space paradigm for problem solving, viewing the task of student modelling as a heuristic search problem, where the heuristic knowledge is represented by a production system. The search space is composed of psychologically plausible procedures, that is, procedures that can be used by students during a problem solving task. The goal of ACM is to determine what conditions should be added to initial subtraction operators (like find-difference below) so they account for students behaviour.

Example 1: initial rule for find-difference (Langley et al. 1984)

find-difference
if you are processing column1
and number1 is in column1 and row1,
and number2 is in column1 and row2,
then find the difference between number1 and number2,
and write this difference as the result for column1

The idea is: given a subtraction problem, apply in all possible ways a set of initial operators to that problem. This is done by using an exhaustive breadth-first search control mechanism. Assuming that the initial operators included those used by the student, it insures that the system will be able to generate the same answer as the learner. The conditions satisfied by the problem along the solution path, when an operator was used, are considered to be a positive instance for proposing that operator. Those leading one step off the solution path are, on the contrary, considered to be negative instances. The conditions tested are previously given to the system and are of the type, for example, (greater number number), (above row row) or (added-ten number). For instance, for the problem of subtracting 54-23 we have the search tree of figure 8.1. It corresponds to the correct answer 31.

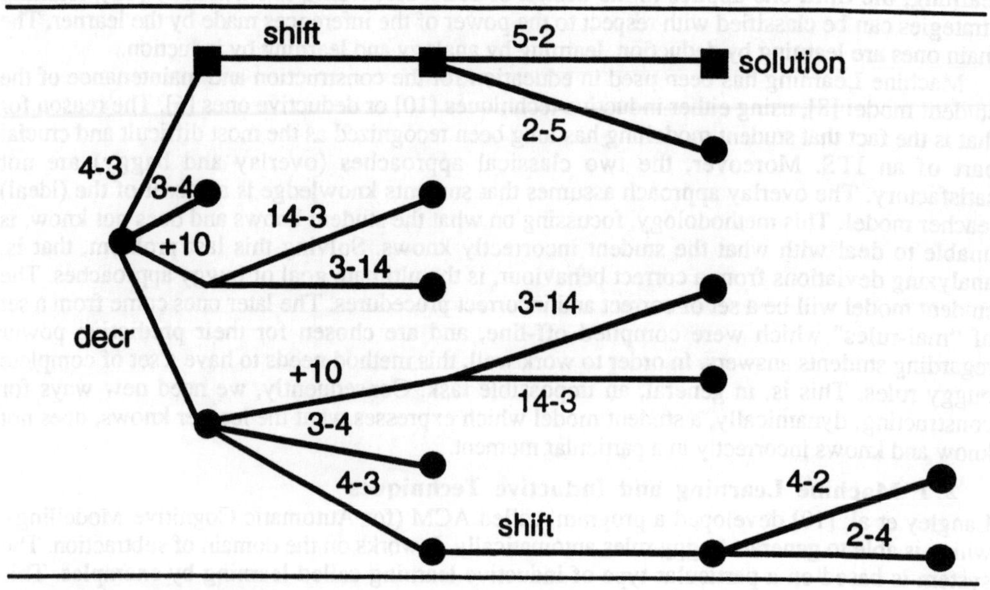

Fig.8.1. Search Tree

If we try to see which version of the find-difference operator was used by the learner, we must look to the positive (4-3 and 5-2) and negative (3-4 and 2-5) examples of application, and seek for conditions discriminating the two situations. In this simple case they are (greater number1 number2) and (above row1 row2) (see table 1)

Table 1

	4-3 (+)	5-2 (+)	3-4 (-)	2-5 (-)
above (N1,N2)	X	X		
greater (N1,N2)	X	X		

From this table we can conclude that the find-difference rule used was the one below.

Example 2 - learned find-difference rule (Langley et al. 1984)

find-difference
if you are processing column1
and number1 is in column1 and row1,
and number2 is in column1 and row2,
and row1 is above row2,
and number1 is greater than number2,
then find the difference between number1 and number2,
and write this difference as the result for column1

In more complex cases, when several examples are analyzed at the same time, a more sophisticated technique based on discrimination trees is required. This technique uses an evaluation function to calculate the most discriminating condition. Once discovered, the

condition splits the examples into two disjoint subsets (one satisfying it and the other not). The principle is applied recursively to the rest of conditions. The process stops when each of the subsets generated contains only instances of the same kind (either positive or negative). The conjunction of the conditions leading from the root to a leaf containing only positive examples will form the additional premises of the operators. If there is more than one such a set we form the disjunction of the conjunctions.

Like others methods, this one is also biased: the level of initial procedures and the conditions tested determined the type of procedures that are learned. Nevertheless, rules can be organized into an hierarchy reflecting different levels of detail and, consequently, different types of students. Also, the number of conditions used is substantially less than the number of mal-rules that must be used for subtraction.

2.2 Machine Learning and Deductive Techniques

Deductive learning is based on the existence of a language in which we can express axioms (a theory) and inference rules. These rules are used to produce all valid consequences of the axioms. Recently a particular kind of deductive learning, called Explanation-Based Learning (EBL), has been proposed [13,17]. This method works by generalizing a proof which explains why a particular example is a positive instance of the concept. The explanation-based learning methodology is defined in table 2.

Table 2 *EBL methodology*

Given
1) a goal concept, e.g. a concept definition which describes the concept to be learned,
2) a training example of the goal concept,
3) a domain theory, e.g. a set of rules and facts about the domain,
4) an operational criterion, e.g. a predicate over concept definitions, specifying the form in which the learned definition should be expressed,

Determine
A generalization of the training example that is a sufficient concept definition of the goal concept and that satisfies the operational criterion.

There is today a research effort in order to overcome the difficulties of EBL to deal with imperfect theories, that is, theories which are incomplete, intractable or inconsistent. If we look to human mental states as expressing a theory, these are typical cases of incomplete and inconsistent sets of facts and rules.

MORE is an experimental system, implemented in Prolog [4], which uses explanation-based learning techniques to build the student model. MORE is able to cope with the problem of incomplete theories by means of an oracle, and it is now being extended to deal with the problem of inconsistencies. We have chosen a non-procedural domain to test the principles and ideas underlying our system, the domain of French XVII century history. It is clear, however, that our approach can be used in procedural domains as well.

Knowledge Representation

The knowledge embedded in the system is organized as a hierarchy of contexts (or worlds or situations). Each context is in fact a theory divided into two parts: episodic and semantic memory. In semantic memory, each piece of knowledge has bound to it the following additional information: the context number, the contexts it depends on, the dependent contexts and a flag indicating the state of the student regarding the part of knowledge mentioned (see example 3).

Example 3 - A context in MORE

```
prof_sm(2, [0], [], (wig(X,Y) :- people(X), disguise(X)),0)
prof_sm(2, [0], [], (have_fun(X) :- people(X), disguise(X)), 0)
prof_sm(2, [0], [21], (go_party(X) :- disguise(X), 0)
```

The knowledge of a context is inherited by low level contexts.

All contexts have their own semantics attached, given by a predicate with six arguments, each argument referring to a particular dimension: context number, time, space, actors, events and theme (see example 4). Theme refers to the intended meaning of the context in which events occur (in a definite place and time) involving several agents.

Example 4 - context semantics

```
w_type(1, [middle_age], [france], [louis_XIV], [using_wig],
[social_position])
w_type(21, [night], [clubs], [people], [music, drinking], [party])
```

As it is shown in the example 4, each dimension may be looked from several different points of view. For instance, the dimension time may refer to historical time (middle age) or daytime (night). Moreover, they aren't defined quantitatively. This aspect is very important for tutoring systems if we want to understand students' misconceptions [5].

Diagnosing

MORE works by putting a question regarding some particular knowledge belonging to a certain context. Then, it tries to understand the answer given by the student within this context. If it is unable to do it, the system tries another related context. During this task it may happen, as the theory is incomplete, that the explanation for the answer can only be produced if some piece of knowledge at the present time unknown to the system is true. Now, the system asks the learner for that knowledge. After the explanation is produced, the knowledge contained in it is considered to be part of student's knowledge and it is generalized before being added to his/her model.

So, diagnosing is a two step procedure. First, the context where the student is reasoning is fixed, second, the theory formed by the facts and rules used in the explanation is generalized by a goal-regression technique so that the model can cope, in the future, with more situations.

Using explanation-based concepts we have the definition of table 3.

Table 3 EBL and student modelling

Given
goal concept: an unknown context;
domain theory: the hierarchy of contexts plus context semantic predicates;
training instance: the pair question/answer
operational criterion: the context definition may include knowledge from system contexts plus knowledge given by the learner;
Determine
A context definition consistent with the domain theory and respecting the operational criterion.

Notice that, contrasting with usual EBL, we don't have, at the beginning, a goal definition to rephrase. As a consequence, we can not say that the result produced by the tutor is "correct"

Let us see with a small example how the system works.

Suppose that the system asks "why does Louis XIV use a wig?" and the answer is, "because he wants to have fun" Using its domain knowledge (see table 4), the system starts a resolution like proof for the answer (that is why the system is called MORE - Modelling by Resolution).

Table 4 *Example of System's domain knowledge*

```
prof_sm(0, [], [1,2,3], (people(X) :- man(X)),0)
prof_sm(1,[0],[],(wig(Y,X) :- man(X), noble(X),
live(X,cent_17)),0)
prof_sm(1,[0], [], (wig(Y,X) :- man(X), judge(X)),0)
prof_sm(1,[0],[], (noble(X) :- judge(X)),0)
prof_sm(2,[0], [], (wig(Y,X) :- people(X),
disguise(X)),0).
prof_sm(2,[0], [], (have_fun(X) :- people(X),
disguise(X)),0)
prof_sm(2,[0], [21], (go_party(X) :- disguise(X)),0)
prof_sm(3, [0], [], (wig(Y,X) :- woman(X), bald(X)),0)
prof_em(man(louis_XIV))
prof_em(noble(louis_XIV))
prof_em(live(louis_XIV,cent_17))
prof_em(wear(louis_XIV,a))
prof_em(wig(a,louis_XIV))
```

The concrete proof is obtained by going to context 2 (where there is a reference for having fun) and asking a reason for the unknown fact disguise (Louis XIV). After the explanation of the student we obtain the concrete student model of figure 8.2.

```
[(have_fun(louis_XIV) :- people(louis_XIV),
disguise(louis_XIV)), 2, prof_sm)]
[(people(louis_XIV) :- man(louis_XIV)) 0, prof_sm]
[man(louis_XIV), _, pro_em]
[(disguise(louis_XIV) :- wear(louis_XIV,a),
wig(a,louis_XIV)), _, stu_rule]
[wear(louis_XIV,a), _, prof_em]
[wig(a,louis_XIV), _, prof_em]
```

Fig.8.2. Concrete model

Using a goal regression technique [9] the more general student model is obtained. This model must be integrated with the old one.

```
[(have_fun(X) :- people(X), disguise(X)), 2, prof_sm)]
[(people(X) :- man(X)) 0, prof_sm]
[man(X), _, pro_em]
[(disguise(X) :- wear(X,Y), wig(Y,X)), _, stu_rule]
[wear(X, Y), _, prof_em]
[wig(Y, X), _, prof_em]
```

Fig.8.3. Abstract model

Tutorial Strategies and Agendas

In MORE, tutorial strategies are defined using an agenda of ordered contexts. It is initialized by the tutor designer and is modified dynamically by the system during a teaching lesson. At any moment, the agenda reflects the initial goals of the system and also the content of the student model. For instance, before the question about the wig, the agenda was:

Example 5 - Initial agenda

```
agenda([[0, generic], [1, social_position], [2, fun], [3,
aesthetic]]
```

After the student's answer, the agenda is modified reflecting the idea that the system is now interested in confirming if the learner is in fact in the context 2, which has the semantics "fun":

Example 6 - Agenda after the first interaction

```
agenda([[2, fun], [0, generic], [1, social_position], [3,
aesthetic]]
```

Automatic examples generation

MORE is also able to generate automatically the examples it presents to students. To that end it uses the agenda to choose a context and a theme. Notice that, the agenda, as said above, reflects implicitly the student's model. After a context is chosen, the system picks up a rule, not yet used by the student in that context, and instantiates it with the events, actors, time and space of its knowledge. In doing so the system takes great advantage of the way knowledge is organized. In fact, a context being a set of Horn clauses it can be executed directly. Instantiation is then a side effect of running one rule. In order not to repeat questions the system has memory of the past interactions.

Conclusion

MORE is an experimental system in which there are still some problems to be solved. For instance, it is not guaranteed that the student's hierarchy is a subset of the systems's hierarchy. In fact, in general, this is not the case. This introduces the problem of building new contexts and integrating them with previous ones. One idea could be to use inductive learning techniques. This may introduce inconsistencies that must be solved in some way. Another aspect refers to the "wild" generalization produced by the goal regression step. This way of generalizing lacks psychologic validity. We must constrain the goal regression procedure using semantic information. For example, generalizing Louis XIV to a noble instead of generalizing him to a man. Finally, MORE, like other systems, is biased. This is due to the way context and semantics are initially given. Nevertheless, as the system is interactive, we can start with a small set of contexts, refining and augmenting them during the course of a teaching lesson.

To conclude, we would like to point out two good things about MORE. In first place, MORE is able to understand deep misconceptions by a simple mechanism of context's semantics comparison. Second, because it is a theory, the student model is runnable. It is thus possible to know the consequences of the student knowledge by just executing the theory representing it.

3. Do We Need a New Design Paradigm?

The existence of a common paradigm for ITSs was, in part, responsible for the emergence of a large number of systems of good quality. In fact, as a result of a common framework, designers can link the problems they have to a particular module, on which they would concentrate their efforts. It is possible, for instance, to have a system concerned only with the problems modelling and diagnosing the student (like the system MORE above). However, as it always happens with paradigms, after some time they become conservative: we always try to solve the problems encountered within our model, refusing to question if these problems are not a consequence of the approach itself. It is interesting to observe that the majority of ITSs developed today deal with procedural skills (algebra, programming, and so on) contrasting with the "old days" systems, like SCHOLAR [2] and WHY, [16] more concerned with concepts. There must be some reason for this shift of attention and for the fact that we don't have systems specialized in domains like history or philosophy, to name just these two. It is our aim in this section to put forward some questions about our present ideas on ITSs. We are aware that there aren't any easy answers to these questions nor do we have these answers. So what are those problems?

3.1 What are the Goals/Foundations of Learning?

If we try to formulate the main goal of teaching using an ITS, as expressed by several authors, this goal is clearly the one of transforming every student into an expert on a particular domain with, it is hoped, the same level of expertise of the teacher. This point of view is arguable.

Students are different in their ability to understand teachers solutions. A good teacher can improve the student's comprehension by adapting a particular type of tutoring (text, concrete or abstract examples, analogies) which had proved in the past to be tailored for that apprentice. This is already done in some ITSs [18]. But, what the expert system approach seems unable to accept is the fact that concrete students do have limitations. This means that sometimes they will be unable to understand the system's solution whatever method we use to explain it. So, a good ITS would be the one that is able to adopt as good a student's solution even if it is not the best one. As a corollary, modelling a student is not only detecting what s/he knows or does not know. It is also establishing the limits of comprehension of the student. This is a very hard task.

Another aspect of the same underlying assumption is the idea that an ITS is just a knowledge communicating system [19]. This means that we have, on one side, an expert teacher and, on the other side, an ignorant learner. Learning is the result of the one way flowing of knowledge: from teacher to learner. An important consequence of this point of view is the fact that every time the student doesn't give the answer expected by the teacher, this must be explained in terms of student's lack of knowledge. That is why, in part, student models are so important.

If we change our view, assuming that the goal of teaching is just to aid students to (re)construct their own view of the world and science, then we will transform ITSs into knowledge interaction systems. We must assume then, that misconceptions are not only due to learner's lack of domain knowledge but also a consequence of how teachers plan and present the material. That is, misconceptions implicitly may reflect the way the student perceives the learner. This point raises the question of the need for something we can call a teacher model.

3.2 What is the Characteristic Shared by both Teacher and Learner?

Another neglected aspect in the literature, a consequence of the expert system approach, is the fact that students come to a teaching session with a lot of world knowledge. This common sense knowledge, which is not necessary knowledge about the domain being taught, strongly influences students in their comprehension of notions like time, space or causality. Students, as teachers, must be viewed as belief systems. They both are intelligent autonomous agents with intentions, plans and beliefs. We must drop the idea of a teacher as an expert (system) and a student as a ignorant knowledge recipient. We must look at teaching/learning as the process by which two agents, given their intentions, and using interaction come to an agreement concerning their mutual beliefs.

4. Conclusions: What Should Be Our Research Directions?

The application of machine learning techniques to the question of student modelling is an improvement on past solutions presented to that problem. We have shown two methods, one based on inductive techniques and the other on deductive techniques. Each one has its strengths and weaknesses. We think that a combination of the two methodologies should be worth trying: inductive techniques could enable the enrichment of the theory, while deductive techniques would direct the system to the sources of student problems more quickly. Another point, not discussed above, is the fact that human beings, when they learn, use analogies extensively. This is an aspect where, again, machine learning techniques can be very useful.

So, ITSs researchers, should, in the future, look upon the efforts made by ML researchers in their tentative integration of inductive, deductive and analogic learning.

We think, also, that we must abandon our vision of ITSs built around the ideas of expert system and communication of knowledge. We should shift to a view of learning and teaching stressing the interaction between beliefs systems.

As a consequence, ITSs researchers, should try to incorporate into their work the results from natural language understanding [1], man-machine communication [17] and psychological theories of belief [20]. Within this framework, user modelling will be equivalent to belief revision.

References

1. Allen, J., *Natural Language Understanding*, Benjamin/Cummings Publishing Co., Menlo Park, USA. 1987.
2. Carbonnell, J. and Langley, P. Machine Learning, in *Encyclopaedia of Artificial Intelligence,* S. Shapiro (Ed.), John Wiley and Sons, New York, USA. 1987.
3. Carbonnell, J.R. and Collins, A "Natural semantics in artificial intelligence." *Proceedings of the Third International Joint Conference on Artificial Intelligence,* Stanford, California 1973.
4. Coelho, H. and Cotta, J. *PROLOG by example*, Springer-Verlag, New York, USA. 1988.
5. Costa, E. Artificial intelligence and education: the role of knowledge in teaching *Proceedings of the European Working Session on Learning* - EWSL-86, Orsay, France. 1986.
6. Costa, E., Duchénoy, S. and Kodratoff, Y. A resolution based method for discovering students' misconceptions in *Artificial intelligence and human learning: intelligent computer-aided instruction*, chapter 9, John Self (Ed), Chapman and Hall, London. 1988.
7. DeJong, G. and Mooney, R. Explanation-based learning: an alternative view *Machine Learning,* 1, nº2, 145-176. 1986.
8. Gilmore, D. and Self, J. The application of machine learning to intelligent tutoring systems in *Artificial intelligence and human learning: intelligent computer-aided instruction,* chapter 11, John Self (Editor), Chapman and Hall, London. 1988.
9. Kedar–Cabelli, S. and McCarthy, L. Explanation-based generalization as resolution theorem proving *Proceedings of the Fourth International Workshop on Machine Learning,* University of California, Irvine, pp. 383-389. 1987.
10. Langley, P., Ohlsson S. and Sage S. *A machine learning approach to student modelling* Technical Report CMU-RI-TR-84-7, Carnegie-Mellon University, Robotics Institute. 1984.
11. Mandl, H. and Lesgold, *A. Learning issues for intelligent tutoring systems*, Springer-Verlag, New York, USA. 1988.
12. Michalsky, R. Understanding the nature of learning: issues and research directions in *Machine Learning: an artificial intelligence approach,* Michalsky, R. Carbonnell, J. and Mitchell, T. (Eds.), chapter 1, Morgan Kaufman, Los Altos, USA. 1986.
13. Mitchell, T., Keller, R. and Kedar–Cabelli, S. "Explanation-based learning: a unifying view" Machine Learning, 1, nº1, 47-80. 1986.
14. O'Shea, T. and Self, J. *Learning and teaching with computers: artificial intelligence in education,* Harvester Press, UK. 1983.
15. Polson, M. and Richardson, J. (Eds), *Foundations of Intelligent Tutoring Systems,* Lawrence Erlbaum Associates Pub., Hillsdale, USA. 1988.
16. Stevens, A and Collins, A The goal structure of a socratic tutor. *Proceedings of the national ACM Conference*, Seattle, Washington. Association for Computing Machinery, New York. 1977.
17. Suchman, L., *Plans and situated actions: the problems of human machine communication,* Cambridge University Press, Cambridge, USA. 1987.
18. Viccari, R., *An intelligent tutoring system for the PROLOG language,* Ph. D. Thesis,. 1988.
19. Wenger, E., *Artificial Intelligence and tutoring systems: computational and cognitive approaches to the communication of knowledge*, Morgan Kaufman Pub. Inc., Los Altos, USA. 1987.
20. Wilks, Y. and Bien, J., Beliefs, points of view and multiple environments *Cognitive Science*, 7, 95-116. 1983.

9

Intelligent Tutoring Systems: Navigating the Rocky Road to Success

Gordon I. McCalla
ARIES Laboratory
Department of Computational Science
University of Saskatchewan
Saskatoon, Saskatchewan S7N 0W0
CANADA

Abstract: This paper is concerned with basic methodological and sociological factors which increasingly may affect the success of research into intelligent tutoring systems. In particular, seven factors which could impede progress in the field are presented: the limited number of success models, the lack of shared perspectives among researchers, the inability to transfer methods and results between research projects, the field's weak theoretical foundations, the inadequate methodologies used to validate research, the poor research and reporting practices of researchers, and the lack of understanding of intelligent tutoring systems by people external to the field. The nature of each of these obstacles is analyzed in detail, not only showing how each obstacle may now or in the future impede progress in the field, but also examining how it can be overcome. The paper concludes with optimism about the future of intelligent tutoring systems as a research area, an optimism which is tempered by the realization of just how daunting some of these obstacles are.

Keywords: Alternate Reality Kit, architecture, Boxer, computer science formalisms, educational technology, evaluation, expert system, external validation, GUIDON, immediate feedback, instructional design, intelligent tutoring systems, internal validation, learning outcome, LISP, LISP Tutor, logic-based knowledge representation, LOGO, methodology, MYCIN, physics, PLANNER, PROSPECTOR, protocol analysis, PROUST, psychology, Recovery Boiler Tutor, SCENT, self improving instructional planner, SIIP, SOPHIE, success models, validation, XCON

1. Prologue

In this paper I would like to discuss a set of issues that it seems to me are important to the long term future of research into the application of artificial intelligence to education. These issues are not at the technical level. They do not pertain directly to such deep problems as representing a student model, figuring out computationally precise pedagogic principles, incorporating learning into a tutoring system, understanding the cognitive mechanisms directing a student's learning, exploring appropriate interaction styles for tutoring, etc. Instead they are meta-issues of a sort, issues that are about the state of the science itself. They are concerned with the basic assumptions which underlie this particular field of scientific inquiry, the perceptions of the field held by the scientists themselves and others outside the field, the ways in which scientists in this field communicate their results to each other, the motivations which drive researchers onward, the means of measuring progress in the field.

The scientific field with which I am concerned I will call "intelligent tutoring systems" This term will be used comprehensively to include such activities as building working systems that teach intelligently in some sense, performing experiments to determine how human cognition works in a teaching/learning situation, constructing computational learning environments that encourage discovery learning, postulating formal computationally-oriented theories of aspects of the teaching/learning process, working out any of the components of a teaching system (like the student model, the interface, the controller, the expert module, etc.), and so on. The term "intelligent tutoring systems" (or ITS), while it is often used quite narrowly, seems to me to be a more accurate description for the entire field than any of the alternatives I have seen. Certainly, "artificial intelligence and education" the main competitor, while being inclusive, does not designate one field, but two, and gives no sense of the synergy which has occurred between these two fields. Perhaps the biggest roadblock on the road to ITS success is finding a suitable name for the field!

ITS is a diverse field, but probably no more so than any other large area of science. It is a field that promises, through the use of computation and the computational metaphor, to shed new light on many long-standing problems in teaching and learning. Moreover, ITS is a field that is very exciting right now. This is due to the confluence of a number of factors, especially the radical changes that have occurred over the last decade in computer power, computer cost, and software effectiveness; and the burgeoning set of techniques that are emerging from artificial intelligence (AI) research which can be applied to ITS. People in the field are extremely enthusiastic, and are willing to tackle just about any problem that comes their way. The field is zealously experimental, and systems with impressive performance have been constructed (albeit typically on limited domains). Progress over the past decade has been steady: the capabilities of the systems constructed have improved, and there has been a growing understanding of what is required of an intelligent tutoring system and what it takes to fulfil these requirements. Many different sub-fields of ITS have evolved, including investigations into the cognitive modelling of students' learning, the construction of discovery learning environments, explorations into coaching and tutoring, building flexible large courses, etc. As in many scientific fields, results discovered in one sub-discipline often find applicability in others, and there is much work which is fundamentally interdisciplinary in that it tries to bridge gaps between sub-fields. In fact many of the papers in this volume are a testament to the growing sophistication of the field, and its growing confidence in the appropriateness of computation as a means of understanding what happens during teaching and learning.

Thus, the field of ITS has burgeoned into a large, highly experimental, highly interdisciplinary enterprise. Unfortunately, its very success has led to a number of problems. It is becoming more and more difficult to keep track of what is going on in the field, to judge what is deep and interesting and what is merely flashy, to be able to understand how results garnered in one research project may apply to another, to ferret out basic truths which apply widely across ITS. There is an increasing need for theoretical frameworks which allow a wide variety of research to be put into perspective and which suggest new research directions which might be promising; for shared research methodologies which can allow results to be transferred among projects; for rigorous techniques with which to validate ITS research claims; for mechanisms which enhance communication and information flow among ITS researchers. Some of these issues are pressing, others will become really serious only in the longer term. These issues are the subject of this paper.

Let me conclude this prologue with a few words about my motivations for writing this chapter. It has been written in the hopes of stimulating discussion within the field. It is by no means a complete or definitive analysis of all of the problems confronting ITS, but it is my reaction to what I see as a growing crisis in the field. My own predilection is for experimental research, for making forays into unknown scientific territory through constructing programs whose behaviour sheds light on parts of this territory. In this I share a common perspective with many other ITS researchers. However, when I try to integrate what my research has taught me about ITS with lessons learned by other ITS researchers, I have difficulties of the kind mentioned above. This has led me to step back from my immediate technical concerns, and to look at the science of ITS itself, to try to understand limitations in the underlying assumptions of ITS research, and to try to spot roadblocks impeding progress in the field. The remainder of this chapter will consider these various obstacles to ITS success and suggest possible approaches to overcoming them.

2. Obstacles Impeding the Success of ITS

2.1 Limited Number of Success Models

Important to the success of any scientific field is the presence of success models which can serve as role models for further developments and which can serve as examples of the field's potential. These success models are particularly important if the field is to be taken seriously and to be funded adequately. They are also important for attracting researchers into the field, and for maintaining the morale of those who are already there. It is thus important that ITS have success models. What characteristics would such success models have? An interesting analogy can be made with AI, which provides instructive lessons about the nature of success models, and how they are useful.

An outsider to AI might say that until 1980 AI was only an academic pursuit, without much practical to offer and with little potential. Then, success models like MYCIN, DENDRAL, PROSPECTOR, and R1, came along and showed the possibilities for the field, especially for commercial success. But, DENDRAL [6] has been around since the late 1960's, MYCIN [32] since the early 1970's, and PROSPECTOR [10] since the mid to late 1970's. Only R1 (now XCON --- McDermott [23] can really be said to coincide with the 1980 boom period. Moreover, even before these systems were developed, AI had already had plenty of successes throughout its early history. There had been game playing programs which could beat human experts at intellectually challenging games (e.g. Samuel's [31] checker playing program dating from the late 1950's; symbolic algebra systems developed by Project MAC at MIT in the late 1960's [22]; theorem proving systems of some generality already up and running in the late 1960's, based on Robinson's [30] resolution principle; and natural language systems such as ELIZA [34] or Winograd's [37] system (later dubbed SHRDLU) which were realistic in their language behaviour. Further, there had been major successes spun off from early AI investigations. These included the invention of new and influential programming languages (e.g. LISP, developed in the early 1960's by McCarthy and his colleagues at MIT for use in AI, and PLANNER, an early logic programming formalism dating from the late 1960's, developed by Hewitt); the creation of innovative operating systems (e.g. the timesharing systems developed at the MIT AI Laboratory in the early 1960's); and the development of tools for human-computer interaction (e.g. the complex on-line editing and debugging packages associated with MACLISP at the end of the 1960's). Despite all of these successes, AI was still perceived as being largely irrelevant and impractical by the great mass of computer scientists and computer users until success models such as DENDRAL, MYCIN, PROSPECTOR, and R1 came along. Why?

The answer to this question sheds considerable light on the issue of what constitutes a success model. First, these four success models were successful because they were generally perceived to be of importance. Theorem provers, symbolic algebra systems, and computerized game players weren't at the time deemed to be anything more than academic toys (despite the later explosion of popular interest in computerized games, and the now widely popular use of symbolic algebra systems). A second important attribute of the four success models listed above concerned their prospects for commercial success. PROSPECTOR helped to discover a multi-million dollar mine; DENDRAL was used to help referee academic papers in molecular chemistry; R1 had the potential to save millions of dollars through enhancing computer companies' abilities to configure computers. A third attribute of the success models was that they were still considered to be part of the field of AI. The various spin-offs mentioned above were rapidly hived off as technologies in their own right, and the early influence of AI was soon forgotten. DENDRAL, MYCIN, PROSPECTOR, and R1, on the other hand, were systems that continued to be considered to be AI, both by AI people and others.

A fourth reason that these systems became success models, where other systems did not, was that they seemed to constitute general solutions to the problems they solved. It seemed clear that they could be adapted as the world in which they operated changed. For example the "production system" architecture on which R1, PROSPECTOR, and MYCIN were based could be easily updated and modified. In contrast, the SHRDLU program was tailored to a particular microworld, and could not be easily adapted to new situations even within the same domain. A fifth characteristic of the success models was that their methodologies could be generalized beyond their own domain. The very fact that three of the models share the same architecture proves out the generality and abilities of this architecture. So pervasive is this impression that often today the term "expert system" is used interchangeably with the term "rule-based expert system". ELIZA, the simulated psychiatrist, however, was completely restricted to its domain. Its illusion of competence depended totally on the fact that psychiatrists can in various situations say very bizarre things or nothing at all, so that what would be anomalous behaviour for any other natural language system would be acceptable behaviour for ELIZA. A final characteristic of these success models had to do with vast amount of publicity which descended upon them. Once a success model has met most of the other requirements, it needs a final "push" in order to be generally recognized. Publicity breeds more publicity, and a hype feedback loop eventually embeds a success model deeply into a field's psyche.

Are there success models for ITS? Like AI, ITS has had a long history, and has produced a number of very successful systems. These include the BIP programming tutor [36], PROUST [14], the SOPHIE electronic trouble-shooter [5], the BUGGY arithmetic diagnosis system [4], the WEST [7] and WUSOR [12] game coaches, and in fact many of the systems discussed in Sleeman and Brown's [33] classic collection. None of these systems, however, is likely to be a success model in the terms discussed above since none is commercial enough, and all of them are typically designed using techniques that are not generalizable either within or beyond their domains. Like AI, the field has also produced a number of "spin-off" technologies, including LOGO and its paradigm of student initiative learning; system development aids such as Programming by Rehearsal [11] which allow flexible instructional programs to be created; learning environments such as Boxer (diSessa) and the Alternate Reality Kit (ARK); and, arguably, much of the Smalltalk and hypermedia line of development. In fact, current directions and issues in the ARK and in hypermedia are discussed elsewhere in this volume by Smith and Jonassen, respectively. While important as well as commercially successful, these systems are often considered to be outside the scope of ITS, even though under the inclusive definition of ITS given in the introduction, they should still be part of the field.

There do appear to be several candidates for success models which satisfy most, if not all, of the criteria above. Although by no means an exclusive list, certainly the LISP Tutor [2] GUIDON [8] and the Recovery Boiler Tutor [38] come immediately to mind. The LISP Tutor deals with an important area and is commercial (in fact it is now being sold as a product). Its model tracing methodologies, being based on production systems, are adaptable and generalizable (a geometry tutor was built using the same approach). GUIDON has become very influential. It deals with teaching medical diagnosis, an area of great relevance and commercial potential, although it hasn't been made into a commercial product. One of its main goals is to prove that generalizable methodologies can be realized in ITS, that an ITS can be "strapped onto" a production system-style knowledge base to teach the expertise in that knowledge base. In fact, a number of other systems have been modelled along the lines of GUIDON e.g. [28]. Thus, it satisfies the fourth and fifth criteria above. The Recovery Boiler Tutor deals with teaching a complex industrial process and has been applied in a number of real world establishments. Its methodologies are not as general as those of the LISP Tutor or GUIDON, but its emphases on incorporating simulation-based reasoning and providing an interactive, menu-based interface that emphasizes student-controlled learning are emulated throughout ITS. And the good news is that all three systems are still considered to be part of ITS.

The bad news, unfortunately, is that there is still much controversy surrounding these systems. For example, the Recovery Boiler Tutor has not been around all that long, GUIDON is considered to have been a "failure" relative to its goals by many ITS researchers, and the LISP Tutor has been roundly condemned for its "fascist" interaction style (its immediate feedback features often seem intrusive and counterproductive). Of course, research is progressing on improving some of the approaches used by these systems. For example, Reiser's chapter discusses enhancements to the LISP Tutor's methodologies which will allow explanations of the tutor's reasoning to be dynamically generated by the tutor as needed. Moreover, criticisms are not uncommon for any success model, especially in fields involving the automation of human intellect, where to explain is to explain away, and where a working system often provides a conveniently precise target to attack for its failures to achieve everything. Systems need not be perfect to be success models.

All three of these systems are now widely cited and emulated, and are thus becoming role models for their particular approaches. Thus, it seems possible that they will become success models for the entire field of ITS. What is still missing is the hype that allowed AI to soar about 1980, and that only came about after the Japanese announced their 5th Generation Project. ITS seems to be where AI was around 1978 or 1979 a number of systems which could serve as success models for the promotion of the field have been developed, but this promotion hasn't yet happened. Perhaps, the NATO Advanced Educational Technology programme will help to serve this purpose! If it does, it isn't altogether clear that this is a "Good Thing" The AI boom of the early 1980's has now been replaced by a certain amount of AI doom and gloom, as the early expectations have been perceived to have been unfulfilled. A similar fate could befall ITS if its possibilities are promoted without proper caution. Like AI, ITS still has many other problems to overcome (in fact many of the same problems). These problems have the potential to bring great disillusionment with the field should too much hype about ITS be promulgated now. The remainder of this paper will deal with some of these problems.

2.2 Lack of Shared Perspectives

The varying perspectives of the researchers in the field constitute a second major roadblock on the road to ITS success. These perspectives differ along a number of dimensions. The most fundamental dimension concerns the research background and training of ITS researchers. Researchers in ITS can be initially trained in vastly different schools of thought: a person educated in computer science and artificial intelligence looks at the world differently from a person with a cognitive psychology background and both of these view things differently from a person with training in education. This early training establishes paradigms for choosing a research problem to work on, for selecting a methodology with which to carry out an experiment, and for determining the success or failure of the experiment. Too strong an adherence to a paradigm can obstruct understanding of the other paradigms, and can lead to research that is ignorant of relevant work in other paradigms. Worse, it is sometimes the case that methodologies of another paradigm are more appropriate for a given research problem than are the methodologies of the researcher's own paradigm, but the researcher can be unaware of this. For example, empirical validation is often poorly done (or not done at all) by computer scientists, in part at least due to their ignorance of the methods of psychology.

If differences in training can lead to different global research paradigms, differences in objectives have led to a variety of local research paradigms internal to ITS. Thus, there are ITS researchers who are exploring the automation of the tutoring or teaching process; others are involved in using the computer as a tool for enhancing their understanding of the processes of teaching and learning, but don't really care about building a tutoring system; still others are interested in the effect on teaching and learning of teaching computation; and there are those (exemplified by the LOGO school) who are involved in the creation of rich, computational learning environments (see White's chapter in this volume for a discussion of the use of such environments for students learning Newton's laws of motion). Naturally, these different local research paradigms within ITS can lead to much misunderstanding both inside and outside of the field about what the field stands for. In fact, these differences are largely responsible for the lack of a generally agreed upon name for the field.

A third major difference in perspective that can lead to misunderstandings is that different researchers in the field can have markedly different mindsets. Some researchers are fundamentally engineers, and are interested in the nuts and bolts of actually building something that works, never mind any theoretical import. Others are more theoretically inclined, and carry out research with a view to long term understanding of the issues of ITS, never mind whether their ideas can be applied. This trend is exemplified in AI more generally in the distinction between the "scruffies" and the "neats" who often assail each other's approaches without really understanding how practice can inform theory and vice versa. Although ITS is still largely an experimental, engineering-orientated field, there seems to be a growing scruffy/neat dichotomy, one that may be increasingly emphasized as engineering results become more and more difficult to publish in the increasingly neat AI literature. Those ITS researchers who also want to be considered to be AI researchers may be more and more often pushed in a neat direction, which may in the future exacerbate the neat/scruffy dichotomy within ITS.

While the varying perspectives above can cause great difficulty, it is important to note that with care the very diversity of ITS can be turned into a strength. As Kuhn [16] has pointed out, many of the most important discoveries in science have come about when two paradigms of research have been integrated. If researchers in ITS can deeply understand the various global and local paradigms in the field, and can make use of the dynamic tension between theory and practice, then the field may be able to evolve a new paradigm for research which is in some ways more powerful than any of the paradigms out of which it has been fashioned. The development of such a paradigm is crucial to sustained progress in the field, since without it researchers will continue to have the Herculean task of maintaining a vigilant knowledge of far too many disciplines and will continue to have difficulty communicating with each other.

Is there any hope that a new "super paradigm" for ITS is coming about? There are a number of positive signs. One of these is the fact that many of the chapters in this volume deal explicitly with issues involving the integration of ideas from two or more paradigms. For example, Reigeluth and Jones argue persuasively for the incorporation of instructional design principles (developed in education) into intelligent tutoring systems. Collins outlines the possibility of a design science of education which draws on ideas from many arenas. Another good sign is that there seems to be an increasing number of researchers being attracted to the field who have degrees in more than one discipline (e.g. education and computer science, or psychology and artificial intelligence). Such people have a deep and comprehensive knowledge of issues in all of their fields of training, a necessary prerequisite to synthesis among these fields. A third positive sign is the establishment of large, interdisciplinary research groups (for example the Institute for Research on Learning in Palo Alto or the Center for Technology in Education at Bank Street College in New York described in Collins' chapter). These groups bring excellent scientists from a wide variety of perspectives together, thus establishing another of the necessary preconditions for the development of an ITS paradigm. In addition to their research activities, such centres are often able to provide integrated education to graduate students who may be associated with the centres. The recent publication of many books in the field (e.g. Kearsley [15], Lawler and Yazdani [17], Mandl and Lesgold [21], Polson and Richardson [27],[29] is also useful in helping to achieve the necessary shared knowledge that is prerequisite to mutual understanding. Wenger's [35] book is especially impressive, since it is much more than just an edited collection, and in fact attempts to integrate the many diverse threads of ITS. Finally, the relatively recent establishment of a regular international conference series in AI and Education is encouraging, as is the creation of a new journal in the field (no matter that there is still debate as to what it is going to be called!) Whatever shape the new paradigm takes, it promises to revolutionize the kinds of research done in ITS and to enhance the influence of ITS.

2.3 Non-Transferable Methods and Results

One of the greatest problems in doing ITS research is the fact that it is so difficult to build research results on top of one another. Methods used by one researcher are not easily transferred to problems being considered by another researcher; lessons learned in one research project are ignored in another research project; results gleaned from one experiment are not built upon in future experiments by other researchers. This transferability problem is partially due to the differences in research perspectives discussed above. It is also partially due to innate human laziness: it can be easier to recreate the wheel than to understand how somebody else has built it. The fact that so many wheels are recreated so often has led to a plethora of different notations for similar things, further obfuscating knowledge transfer within ITS.

Perhaps the major obstacle to the transfer of methods and results between research projects, however, is the fact that so much work in ITS is validated through the construction of programs. While they are precise and unambiguous, programs do not specify a semantics for the theory that they are encoding. In fact, many of the programming languages in which these programs are written do not themselves have a formal semantics, which means theories built on top of them are built on something akin to quicksand. Programs do not allow the theory they are encoding to be viewed at varying grain sizes—-they are uniform, fairly low-level, large, and often very cumbersome implementations of the theory. They do not illuminate any of the meta-issues about where a theory applies and doesn't apply, and what the theory's strengths and weaknesses are. In short, programs are not theories. This makes it very difficult to understand what a program does; in order to understand a piece of research implemented by a program, other researchers must rely on the often inadequate higher-level description of the program provided by the researcher who created the program.

How can this problem be overcome? Once again, AI provides an interesting analogy since it has faced (and still faces) this problem. AI has essentially taken two different approaches, one exemplified in expert systems and the other in logic-based knowledge representation. One of the main reasons for the great success of expert systems derives from the methodologies used in their construction, particularly the production system architecture. The production system architecture allows programs to be described at a higher level of detail than the code level, in terms of "if - then" rules that fairly directly encode the theory being represented in the expert system. The ability to directly encode a theory in such a high-level representation scheme allows the knowledge contained in these rules to be readily transferred to anybody who wants to understand what has been represented. The fact that production systems are widely applicable is a further bonus, since it means that the methodology itself is now well-honed, and that the number of practitioners familiar with the methodology is sizeable.

The other approach taken by AI is to attempt to borrow methodologies from other disciplines with which to formalize various AI theories. This is an especially prevalent strategy in the area of knowledge representation, where different kinds of logic have been adapted for use in representing knowledge. A knowledge representation scheme expressed in logic has a number of nice features, including provable properties, a secure foundation from which to reason, and most importantly for this discussion the ability to allow mutual understanding of the knowledge representation scheme since the semantics of a logic-based scheme are precise and commonly understood. To be sure, there are doubts as to whether logic has the power required for general knowledge representation (see [18]), and logic is at one fairly low-level grain size which makes for difficulty in understanding a large knowledge base implemented in logic. Nevertheless, it is undeniable that the various logics provide universal languages which are widely (and deeply) understood, thus enhancing the transferability of results among those using the logics.

Returning to ITS, are there any signs that commonly agreed upon architectures are being elaborated which might make information transfer easier? There are several interesting architectures which are beginning to find favour in ITS. One of these is, in fact, the production system architecture, which underlies a number of ITS systems (including the LISP Tutor, the geometry tutor, and GUIDON). Another is a somewhat related architecture, the blackboard architecture which allows large, distributed systems to be easily built, and described component by component without much worry about how the components interact. This has been used, for example, by Macmillan and Sleeman [20] in the self improving instructional planner (SIIP) and by Ng and McCalla [24] in the SCENT program advisor. A third popular shared methodology involves the use of standard planning techniques, especially for tutoring purposes (see [26] and [20], for example). Greer and McCalla [13] suggest that granularity hierarchies may be useful mechanisms for representation and recognition in many areas of ITS. These methodologies have two main attributes in common. First, they are widely applicable. Second, a system can be described in terms of the abstractions used by these methodologies, rather than at the code level, thus enhancing transferability of information.

There seems to be no apparent use of formal methodologies in ITS corresponding to the use of logic in knowledge representation. This is likely due to the experimental nature of ITS right now, the small grain size of logic-based knowledge representation schemes, and the fact that it seems premature to spend a lot of effort formalizing what is as yet not well understood (it is interesting to note that formal logic came along in knowledge representation only after many years of experience using more informal approaches had set the stage). A further discussion of logic will ensue in the next section in the context of the search for an underlying foundation for ITS research.

2.4 Weak Foundations

The discussion of logic in the last section points out that the field of ITS does not have a strong theoretical foundation. Part of the problem is that the field does not share a paradigm (as was pointed out in section 2.2). ITS is still relatively unexplored; thus, as was mentioned in the last section, it may be premature to formalize the field. Another explanation is that the researchers in the field tend to be experimentalists, not theorists. Whatever the explanation, the absence of a strong foundation is problematical in ITS since it makes it very hard to understand what a result in the field really means, and since it makes it difficult for researchers to rationalize where they should be spending their efforts. Moreover, a strong theoretical foundation will become a necessity for putting flesh on the bones of any shared paradigm that might evolve in ITS; that is, it will describe in a deep fashion the shared principles and rules underlying the paradigm.

What does it mean for a field to have a strong foundation? There are two aspects: first, the field needs a formalism in which to express concepts; and, second, the field needs a set of rules described in this formalism which specify the formal ground rules for the field. A good example is Newtonian mechanics. Newtonian mechanics is built on the formalism of mathematics in which are formulated rules like "F=ma".

The parallel common underlying thread in ITS is the use of programs to describe theories, that is programs are the formalism underlying most ITS systems. Unfortunately, as discussed in the last section, this is inappropriate to communicate what the theory is about, due both to the fine grain size of a program description and the inherent imprecision in specifying the semantics of a program. For these same reasons, a programming language, *per se*, is not particularly appropriate as the formalism in which to specify the foundations for ITS, although with the choice of a relatively formal programming language this problem can be played down. Far more serious, however, is the lack of commonly agreed upon rules for an ITS; that is, although most ITS research projects are described in a programming formalism, more general computational principles that precisely specify the theory being proposed in the research project are not postulated.

Can the gap in ITS between high-level general theories and low-level computation be overcome? Consider the "parent" fields of ITS. Computer science can provide insight at the level of describing the underlying computational formalism, but gives very little help when trying to specify the higher order rules. It may be possible to work bottom-up from computer science formalisms towards the development of theories described computationally. This seems to be what is happening in the area of qualitative reasoning e.g. [3] where the need to understand the reasoning processes of naive human beings has led to the rapid evolution of computationally precise theories of such reasoning. Such qualitative reasoning theories may be particularly useful in providing foundations for student modelling in ITS, although it is hard to see how they might apply elsewhere in the field. An alternative approach is to work top-down from existing higher-level education and psychology theories, attempting to reformulate them in computational terms. Education theories tend to be general, and quite far removed from the computational level in which they must be described (e.g. pedagogic rules like "be relevant" are irrelevant in computational terms). Thus, despite the pleas of Reigeluth and Jones elsewhere in this volume, it will be very hard to translate instructional design principles into computational terms. Psychology, perhaps, provides the best bet for theories that make commitments to higher level distinctions, but that are formulated rigorously enough that it is possible to describe them computationally. For example, Anderson's [1] ACT* theory presents a high level psychological theory parts of which have been made computationally precise through implementation in the LISP and geometry tutors developed at Carnegie-Mellon University. VanLehn's chapter on task-specific theories of learning further elaborates the issues dividing general theories of cognition such as ACT* and SOAR from task-specific theories of learning which are more immediately useful.

However, there is still a long way to go before ACT*, SOAR or any other theory can be fully elaborated computationally, and applied widely to ITS. It is likely that feedback from attempts to elaborate such theories experimentally will affect the nature of the theories being implemented, and will thus lead to revisions at the theoretical level. In the long term, it is to be hoped that full blown formal foundations for ITS (or at least aspects of ITS) will evolve. In the short term, however, it is probably premature to envision such foundations. There is simply not enough yet known about ITS to formulate comprehensive foundations for the field. In fact, an ITS-wide commitment to any single such proposed foundation would, at present, be dangerous. It would seriously impede the diversity of research that is needed to gather data that will form the basis for solid, widely useful theoretical foundations for the field.

2.5 Inadequate Validation Methodologies

Another roadblock on the road to ultimate ITS success is the lack of good methods for validating ITS research. Following Littman and Soloway [19], there seem to be two kinds of validation necessary for an ITS: internal and external. Internal validation is necessary to prove that an ITS is internally consistent ; that it is correct; and that it implements its requirements specifications. External validation is necessary to prove that the ITS behaves appropriately; that it teaches what it set out to teach; that its performance is good; and that its requirements specifications are in fact appropriate.

Internal validation of ITS systems is normally carried out through implementation. Since implementation has well-known weaknesses (see above), internal validation is often augmented with written and verbal argumentation. Very occasionally it is possible to prove things about an ITS using mathematical methods such as algorithm analysis or graph theory techniques (for example the granularity hierarchies of Greer and McCalla [13] are specified with enough formality that it should be possible to prove properties associated with recognition at many grain sizes). Presumably, if work continues on computational formalisms, and especially if the field can eventually elaborate firm foundations as discussed in section 2.4, it should become increasingly possible to carry out reliable internal validation of an ITS.

A far more difficult problem arises in externally validating an ITS. Even with a firm theoretical foundation for the field, ITS systems must still be validated with respect to the real world in the same way that a completely elaborated physics theory (such as a unified field theory) must be proven out experimentally before it is fully accepted. ITS has borrowed its external validation methodologies from psychology and education. Unfortunately, many of these methodologies are not easily adapted to the requirements of ITS validation.

Consider attempting to directly validate an ITS by showing the conditions under which it behaves just as a human teacher would behave. Classic experimental design would suggest carrying out this process as a series of experiments, changing various variables one at a time, until a detailed map has been worked out which shows the strengths and weaknesses of the ITS for each variable. Unfortunately, it is nearly impossible to set up a controlled experiment in anything approaching classic terms since there are so many variables and so little chance of controlling them. Students and teachers come to a tutoring session with numerous preconceptions which can never be precisely known. The interaction between student and teacher is subject to many unpredictable influences including attention span problems, personality differences, interference from external factors such as noises, interruptions, etc. Between sessions, students and teachers can access new sources of knowledge, can learn, or can otherwise change in ways that are unpredictable. All of this means that a controlled experiment is extremely difficult to achieve; the best that can be done is to reduce the number of variables as much as possible and, regardless, to be careful in whatever conclusions are drawn.

It should be noted that all of these problems also occur if data is being gathered in order to initially design an ITS, rather than being gathered simply to test an existing ITS. This implies that the knowledge engineering of an ITS is even more difficult than the knowledge engineering of a traditional expert system. At least an expert system has a focused set of expertise to be extracted, and most of the factors affecting the expertise can be made explicit as the expert system evolves.

Returning to the problem of external validation, a second means of validating an ITS may involve performing an "outcomes analysis" where the effectiveness of an ITS in teaching students is compared to the effectiveness of alternative schemes. Standard psychology methodology suggests that this be done using a double blind experiment, where neither experimenter nor student is aware of which scheme is being employed in any given experiment. Even a single blind experiment is clearly impossible in an ITS situation, where it is obvious to all involved whether or not an ITS is being used. Moreover, there are many other questions which are difficult to answer in such an experimental design. How can learning outcomes be measured? Which outcomes are important, which not so important? Is speed of learning a factor? Is efficiency of the teaching process important? What are real effects and what are merely artefacts? Thus, outcomes analysis is also faced with formidable difficulties as an approach to ITS validation.

Perhaps the problems of ITS external validation can be overcome through a third technique, protocol analysis, where a panel of randomly chosen judges is asked to evaluate whether the input/output behaviour of an ITS is realistic. Since this approach does not even attempt to figure out which variables affect ITS performance, the variable control problems of the first kind of validation above are circumvented. Since this approach makes no reference to any desired outcomes of the teaching process, the problems of defining the nature of an outcome in the second kind of validation are avoided. Thus, there is some hope that this approach will work. There are two ways of carrying out this kind of protocol analysis: through direct questioning of the judges, or through a modified Turing test, where students are asked to distinguish ITS input/output from input/output of a human teacher. Both of these approaches lead to problems. Direct questioning is notoriously subjective, with judges telling experimenters what they want to hear. In contrast, use of a modified Turing test could be carried out using a double blind methodology. Unfortunately, (at least at this stage of ITS research) for the double blind to be effective, modifications will be required to the input/output of the program to remove "obvious" computerese which might give away the program for non-pedagogical reasons. Similarly, modifications will also be needed to the human protocol to eliminate "noise" and other verbal behaviours which might unduly mark the protocol as human generated. Such "editing after the fact" leaves the final interpretation of the experimental results open to question: were similarities or differences that were noted by the judges due to real similarities or differences, or merely artefacts of the post hoc editing?

Regardless of external validation methodology, sources of bias like the Hawthorne effect (that any change in a standard environment is perceived by individuals in that environment to be positive) are likely to get in the way of objective analysis. When faced with using an ITS, students will by definition work and learn more effectively due to the very novelty of the ITS, rather than particular attributes of the ITS. This problem has bedevilled scientific attempts to prove that LOGO, for example, is a better way of teaching mathematical reasoning than more traditional approaches.

It seems clear that major work will have to be done in formulating experimental methodologies expressly tailored for the difficult requirements of ITS creation and validation. It is interesting to note that Alan Collins in his chapter argues for the development of a systematic science of how to design educational environments so that new technologies can be introduced successfully into classrooms. Part of the evolution of this design science will certainly involve the construction of good evaluation techniques in the sense discussed in this section. Thus, there is some hope that progress can be made on this front.

2.6 Poor Research and Reporting Practices

Regardless of any foundational difficulties with the field, ITS researchers still must behave responsibly in conducting and reporting their research. Unfortunately ITS researchers are not always responsible. Sometimes, incomplete research is published; poorly formulated research projects are promulgated; research is carried out with little awareness of relevant related research; papers are badly written; inadequate or inappropriate experimentation is performed; conclusions are drawn which are not supported by the evidence presented; research duplicating other research is carried out and reported upon; essentially the same paper is published numerous times in various outlets; exaggerated claims are made. Often papers take on a "show and tell" ambience (as Reigeluth called it during the workshop out of which this volume has evolved) which makes it difficult to understand how the research being reported upon relates to more general issues of ITS. These problems, of course, are not unique to ITS or even to AI. Nevertheless, there is still cause for concern, especially given that the rejection rate of ITS papers submitted to the AAAI-88 conference in Minneapolis was over 90%, and the new AI and Education journal had to delay publication for a year, in part due to the high rejection rate of its initial submissions. These high rejection rates are, in some sense, a positive indication in that high standards are being enforced, but they are a negative indication in that the quality of the research and reporting being carried out in ITS could stand improvement.

The multiple paradigms of ITS research, and the diverse backgrounds of researchers in the field certainly contribute to these problems. The lack of ITS-specific journals, and the shortage of conferences focused on ITS issues, exacerbate these problems still further. That is, it is extremely difficult to maintain uniform research and reporting standards when there are no flagship journals and conferences leading the way. It is to be hoped that the recent creation of a new journal in the field and the recent expansion in the number of high quality ITS conferences will help the field to better establish its standards.

The need for strong ITS research and reporting standards will be especially critical should an ITS boom be about to explode upon the scene. If the recent AI boom is any indication, this would mean that the field would attract many "born again" ITS researchers, short on ITS training and experience but long on incautious promises about the field's potential. The consequent avalanche of poorly done research could seriously impair the field's credibility if adequate standards are not maintained. Boom or no boom, however, it is important if ITS is to be considered to be a legitimate field of inquiry, that ITS scientists try to achieve the highest research and reporting standards.

2.7 Lack of Understanding of ITS by People External to the Field

No research discipline lives in a vacuum. This is especially true for a diverse effort such as ITS. Research in the field impacts (and is impacted by) many other disciplines; applications spun off from ITS research have the potential to seriously affect the "real world" perhaps even (eventually) to revolutionize the way society educates, trains, and re-trains its citizens. Thus, the way in which others, both scientists and "jus' plain folks" perceive ITS is important. Funding decisions will be affected by these perceptions. Political ramifications may ensue. A lack of understanding by other scientists, educators, politicians, and the general public of the nature of ITS, its goals, its current capabilities, and its potential could thus be problematical for the field.

Current external perceptions of the field, insofar as there are any at all, do not seem to correspond with the viewpoints of scientists doing ITS research. The general public, although largely unaware specifically of ITS, seems to view educational technology from two quite opposite and polarized perspectives: either as an instant "quick fix" for fundamental problems in education, or as over-hyped window dressing, irrelevant to education. The latter perception has led many to turn away from technological solutions and to advocate a return to some halcyon earlier golden era when teachers could teach and students could learn. The former perception has often led to grandiose expectations about the introduction of technology, almost as often followed by disillusionment and the adoption of the latter perception! In general, ITS scientists are cautious about the current capabilities of ITS, while they are optimistic that AI approaches to educational problems can eventually have fundamental and far reaching impact. Unless public awareness of the role that research can play in improving education can be increased, there will be little pressure to increase funds for educational research, let alone for ITS research.

Politicians know they must voice concern about education if they are to get the support of voters. Business people claim to be acutely aware of the costs of training. For various reasons, however, this doesn't seem to translate into an increased investment by these politicians in public education or by these business people in training. Even more rarely does it result in an investment in research into educational issues. One reason, as discussed above, is the lack of public support for such investment. Another reason is the fact that education and training slip between the cracks. Government funding agencies are often divided along rigid disciplinary lines, leaving interdisciplinary endeavours like ITS to be overlooked by each funding agency as "somebody else's responsibility". Companies view training as an activity that is secondary to their main goals (to find oil, to produce widgets, or whatever). A company which might invest millions of dollars in carrying out their primary mandate, may not deem it important to invest in research into how to train their employees, even if this would lead to great productivity increases. This slipping between the cracks is further exacerbated in a multi-tiered political system, where federal, provincial (or state), and municipal responsibilities for education are often ill-defined or inappropriately defined, allowing crucial decisions to be fumbled among the various jurisdictions. This also allows the costs of education to be divided among many budgets, thus hiding the extraordinary size of the overall education investment (which in many countries is greater than military investment). These difficulties make it hard to set national priorities on education, and hard to get industrial backing for a major investment in training and education research.

Professional educators have much more awareness of educational issues than do the general public, politicians, and business people, but they also often represent vested interests, and always have strong opinions as to what's right and what's wrong with education. Unfortunately, many of these vested interests and strong opinions do not correspond well with ITS views of education. The growing (at least in North America) "back to the basics" movement, with its emphasis on rigid structure and competency-based training, seems the very opposite of the individual empowerment metaphor which underlies most ITS perspectives. The search for a "golden era" which has garnered so much public popularity seems to have gained a toehold among professional educators as well. If the professional education community increasingly deviates from goals of individual fulfilment in instruction, arguments for increased funding of ITS will fall increasingly on deaf ears.

Even research colleagues in disciplines related to ITS have much misunderstanding of the field. Education researchers often fail to see how the precision of a computational model can firm up their theories, and be used as a tool for thought. Psychologists and computer scientists often fail to realize the incredibly rich domain that ITS is investigating, the possibilities for discovering deep problems in learning and representation, and the potential for creating innovative new techniques with widespread application outside of ITS. Even the characterization of ITS as a "subset" of AI is misleading. David Littman remarked at the Third International Conference on AI and Education in Pittsburgh in May of 1987 that, contrary to popular opinion, "ITS is a superset of AI" since the ideal ITS system presupposes the solution of most problems in AI as well as an understanding of pedagogic and student modelling issues. John Seely Brown, at the International Conference on Intelligent Tutoring Systems held in Montreal in June of 1988, considered that in many ways the "forcing functions" for ITS are more relevant than those for AI, i.e. that the kinds of questions that must be asked in order to build an intelligent tutoring system may result in more interesting research directions being explored than the standard kinds of questions asked in AI. If even researchers in fields closely allied to (part of?) ITS do not understand its importance and significance, then what hope is there for more general understanding of and support for the field?

So, what can be done to improve the profile of ITS to those outside of the field? Here are a few modest suggestions! There needs to be much more public debate about the field. The Pea and Soloway report abstracted in [25] advocating the establishment of "Centers for Interactive Technologies in Education" is an important watershed in this regard, since it puts the ITS case forward in the kind of public document which might actually garner attention in the corridors of power. Proponents of ITS need to continue to lobby various government agencies for their share of the public purse. Companies have to be constantly harassed and shown how some of the practical spin-offs from ITS research can be of immediate benefit to them in reducing training costs and increasing training effectiveness. ITS researchers must continue to write papers for a wide variety of journals, and must attend a wide variety of conferences (even if there are now international conferences specifically in the field), in order to explain the importance of ITS to colleagues in related disciplines (and, not insignificantly, to learn something from these related disciplines!) Some of these conferences should be conferences which attract practising education professionals --it is important that such people be made aware of ITS and that ITS researchers be informed of the real problems confronting those who are on the teaching frontlines. Of course, there is nothing like time and increasing success (both practical and theoretical) for helping increase the profile of a field!

A final question must be asked before leaving the issue of external awareness of IT --should there be a formal society to promote the aims of ITS? This society could coordinate the biennial international conference, could produce a newsletter to keep members informed, and could in general raise the profile of the area. It might, however, have the drawback of taking up a lot of valuable research time for those involved in society organization, and could ultimately lead to an unhealthy "group think" about ITS issues. One of the delights of the field right now is its very anarchy, the tumult of its ideas, the freewheeling explorations of this exciting subject. It would be ironic if a society initially set up merely to rationalize certain organizational problems ended up impeding the excitement of the field.

3. Epilogue

The problems discussed in this paper are not unique to ITS. Most other scientific fields have at some time in their history confronted problems similar to these; many still are struggling with one or more such problems. The fact that others may have these problems, however, doesn't mean that ITS researchers don't need to try to grapple with them, even if many of the problems won't be totally resolved for years to come.

It isn't necessary, of course, to overcome all of these problems in order to make progress in the field. Despite its many problems, ITS seems to be making steady advances as the requirements for intelligent tutoring are better understood, and the basic components of an intelligent tutoring system are fleshed out. Hopefully, the explicit recognition of some of the obstacles discussed in this paper will make it easier to get over them, slide under them, or slip around them. If so, the energy and excitement that has permeated the field virtually since its inception nearly twenty years ago will continue, and all of us in the field can look forward to a stimulating future.

Acknowledgements

Most of the ideas in this paper have been vaguely stirring in my subconscious for some years. I have been immeasurably helped in trying to make them more precise by my interactions with many other people, although they, of course, bear no responsibility for any misconceptions or mistakes which still remain. I would like to thank my AI and ITS colleagues over the years who have engaged in fierce discussions with me (and each other) over the nature of AI and ITS. In particular I would like to thank my ARIES colleagues, Jim Greer and Marlene Jones, and all of my graduate students past and present for being good sounding boards for my ramblings, and for trying (although not always succeeding) to bring me around to common sense whenever I went too far. Some of the ideas in this paper were thoroughly hashed over in a panel discussion entitled "What's Wrong with ITS Research?" that I chaired at the International Conference on Intelligent Tutoring Systems in Montreal in June 1988---I would like to thank Bill Clancey, Gerhard Fischer, Marlene Jones (again), and David Littman for serving on this panel, and for inspiring the idea of writing this paper. Last, and certainly least, I would like to thank Rogatien "G." Cumberbatch for all the terrible papers he has written over the years which have provided me with "failure models" that I can ponder. I have been able to draw on these whenever I have desperately needed an example of bad research methodology or slip-shod reporting. The financial support of the Natural Sciences and Engineering Research Council of Canada for all of my research endeavours is gratefully acknowledged.

References

1. Anderson, J. R., *The Architecture of Cognition*, Harvard University Press, Cambridge, Massachusetts, 1983.
2. Anderson, J. R. and Reiser, B. J., The LISP Tutor *BYTE*, Vol. 10, No. 4, pp. 159-175, 1985.
3. Bobrow, D. G., editor, *Qualitative Reasoning About Physical Systems*, MIT Press, Cambridge, Massachusetts, 1985.
4. Brown, J. S. and Burton, R. R., Diagnostic Models for Procedural Bugs in Basic Mathematical Skills *Cognitive Science*, Vol. 2, pp. 155-191, 1978.
5. Brown, J. S., Burton, R. R. and deKleer, J., Pedagogical, Natural Language, and Knowledge Engineering Techniques in SOPHIE I, II, and III in Sleeman and Brown [1982], pp. 227-282, 1982.
6. Buchanan, B., Sutherland, G. and Feigenbaum, E. A., Heuristic DENDRAL: A Program for Generating Explanatory Hypotheses in Organic Chemistry in Meltzer, B. and Michie, D., editors, *Machine Intelligence 4*, Edinburgh University Press, Edinburgh, 1969.
7. Burton, R. R. and Brown, J. S., An Investigation of Computer Coaching for Informal Learning Activities in *Sleeman and Brown [1982]*, pp. 79-98, 1982.
8. Clancey, W. J., *Knowledge-Based Tutoring: The GUIDON Program*, MIT Press, Cambridge, Massachusetts, 1987.
9. DiSessa, A. Boxer., A reconstructible computational medium, *Communications of the ACM*, 29(9), 859-868. 1986.
10. Duda, R., Gashnig, J., Hart, P., Konolige, K., Reboh, R., Barrett, P. and Slocum, J., Development of the PROSPECTOR Consultation System for Mineral Exploration Final

Report, *SRI Projects 5821 and 6415,* SRI International Inc., Menlo Park, California, 1978.
11. Finzer, W. and Gould, L., Programming by Rehearsal *BYTE* , Vol. 9, No. 6, pp. 187-210, 1984.
12. Goldstein, I., The Genetic Graph: A Representation for the Evolution of Procedural Knowledge in Sleeman and Brown, pp. 51-77, 1982.
13. Greer, J. E. and McCalla, G. I., Formalizing Granularity for Use in Recognition *Applied Mathematics Letters,* to appear.
14. Johnson, W. and Soloway, E., Intention-Based Diagnosis of Programming Errors *Proc. AAAI-84,* Austin, Texas, pp. 162-168, 1984.
15. Kearsley, G. P., *Artificial Intelligence and Instruction: Applications and Methods,* Addison Wesley, Don Mills, Ontario, 1987.
16. Kuhn, T., *The Structure of Scientific Revolutions,* U. of Chicago Press, Chicago, Illinois, 1962.
17. Lawler, R. W. and Yazdani, M., *Artificial Intelligence and Education: Volume 1, Learning Environments and Tutoring Systems,* Ablex, Norwood, New Jersey, 1987.
18. Levesque, H., guest editor, Open Peer Commentaries on Drew McDermott's A Critique of Pure Reason Taking Issue Section, *Computational Intelligence,* Vol. 3, No. 3, pp. 149-237, August 1987.
19. Littman, D. and Soloway, E., Evaluating ITSs: The Cognitive Science Perspective in Polson and Richardson [1988], pp.209-242, 1988.
20. Macmillan, S. A. and Sleeman, D. H., An Architecture for a Self-Improving Instructional Planner for Intelligent Tutoring Systems *Computational Intelligence,* Vol. 3, No. 1, pp. 17-27, February 1987.
21. Mandl, H. and Lesgold, A., *Learning Issues for Intelligent Tutoring Systems,* Springer-Verlag, New York, New York, 1988.
22. Mathlab Group, MACSYMA Reference Manual Technical Report, Laboratory for Computer Science, M. I. T., Cambridge, Massachusetts.
23. McDermott, J., R1: A Rule-Based Configurer of Computer Systems *Artificial Intelligence,* Vol. 19, pp. 39-88, 1982.
24. Ng, T. H. and McCalla, G. I., A Plan-Based Approach to Blackboard Control in an Intelligent Tutoring System *Proc. International Computer Science Conference '88 on Artificial Intelligence Theory and Applications,* Hong Kong, 1988.
25. Pea, R. and Soloway, E. The State of the Art in Educational Technology R&D: Policy Issues and Opportunities (Extended Abstract), *Proc. International Conference on Intelligent Tutoring Systems,* Montreal, Quebec, pp. 16-17, 1988.
26. Peachey, D. R. and McCalla, G. I., Using Planning Techniques in Intelligent Tutoring Systems *Int. J. of Man-Machine Studies,* Vol. 24, No. 1, pp. 77-98, 1986.
27. Polson, M. C. and Richardson, J. J., *Foundations of Intelligent Tutoring Systems,* Lawrence Erlbaum Associates, Hillsdale, New Jersey, 1988.
28. Prasad, B., Wood, H., Greer, J. E. and McCalla, G. I., A Knowledge-Based System for Tutoring Bronchial Asthma Diagnosis Unpublished Manuscript, 1988.
29. Psotka, J., Massey, L. D. and Mutter, S. A., *Intelligent Tutoring Systems: Lessons Learned,* Lawrence Erlbaum Associates, Hillsdale, New Jersey, 1988.
30. Robinson, J. A., A Machine-Oriented Logic Based on the Resolution Principle *J. ACM,* Vol. 12, pp. 23-41, 1965.
31. Samuel, A., Some Studies in Machine Learning Using the Game of Checkers in Feigenbaum, E. A. and Feldman, J., eds., *Computers and Thought,* McGraw-Hill, New York, pp. 71-108, 1963.
32. Shortliffe, E., *Computer-Based Medical Consultations: MYCIN,* North-Holland, 1976.
33. Sleeman, D. and Brown, J. S., eds, *Intelligent Tutoring Systems,* Academic Press, Toronto, Ontario, 1982.

34. Weizenbaum, J., ELIZA - A Computer Program for the Study of Natural Language Communications Between Man and Machine *C. ACM*, Vol. 9, pp. 36-45, 1966.
35. Wenger, E., *Artificial Intelligence and Tutoring Systems*, Morgan Kaufmann, Los Altos, California, 1987.
36. Westcourt, K., Beard, M. and Gould, L., Knowledge-Based Adaptive Curriculum Sequencing for CAI *Proc. ACM National Conference*, Seattle, Washington, pp. 234-240, 1977.
37. Winograd, T., *Understanding Natural Language*, Academic Press, New York, 1972.
38. Woolf, B., Blegan, D., Jansen, J. and Verloop, A., Teaching a Complex Industrial Process *Proc. AAAI-86*, Philadelphia, Pennsylvania, pp. 722-728, 1986.

10

Designing Hypertext for Learning

David H. Jonassen
Professor and Chair of Instructional Technology
University of Colorado at Denver
U.S.A.

Abstract: This paper describes hypertext, and its potential as a technology that can effectively facilitate learning.

Keywords: addition, cognitive overhead, dynamic text, expert system, fine tuning, free recall protocols, graphical browsers, hypertext, integration of information, navigation, restructuring, schemata, semantic networks, sequencing, simulation

1. Hypertext

Hypertext is non-linear or dynamic text. Although its antecedents date to 1945, the term hypertext was coined by Theodor Nelson [9,11] to describe non-sequential writing. In traditional text the readers/learners are expected to follow the author's style and organization of text, which reflects the author's knowledge structure. Hypertext, on the other hand, allows the user immediate access to any piece of text or information in the knowledge base. In hypertext, readers are not constrained by the subject matter structure or by the author's organization of the text. Since an individual's knowledge structure is unique, the ways that individuals prefer to access, interact with, and interrelate information is also distinct. So, access to and organization of information should be under the control of the learner. In hypertext, users may explore information and even alter it in ways that make the information more comprehensible.

Characteristics of Hypertext

Hypertexts possess some or all of these characteristics:

- Nodes or fragments of information
- Associative links between the nodes
- Network of ideas formed by the link structure
- Organizational structure that describes the network
- Ability to represent explicitly the structure of information in the structure of the hypertext
- Dynamic control of information by the user
- High level of interactively with the user
- Database-like structure for storing information
- Multi-media information environment (hypermedia)
- Multi-user access to the information.

Hypertext research and development work is expanding rapidly. Most of the hypertext projects of the 1980's, such as Intermedia, IBIS, Neptune, and Notecards, are powerful multi-user problem solving environments that run on main-frame computers. Within the past two years, hypertext editors for personal computers have expanded the interest in and applications of hypertext greatly. For more information about hypertext and its application, see [1] or [5].

2. Designing Hypertext

Although most researchers and developers of hypertext contend that it possesses great potential as a learning environment, few verified principles of design are available. Hypertext development has largely been by the seat-of-the-pants. In this paper, I will discuss the design of hypertext using two separate approaches. In the first, I describe some verified problems in using hypertext and then recommend some possible solutions. In the second approach, I will start by describing a model of learning and then describe how hypertext can facilitate the processes in that model and how hypertext might be designed based upon that model.

Problems in Using Hypertext

Some very significant problems plague hypertext users. These problems need to be accommodated in the design of instructional hypertext.

Navigation

Perhaps the best established problem is navigation through the hypertext. Hypertext documents often contain thousands of nodes, each with multiple links to other nodes. It is easy for users to get lost in that morass of information. Users become disoriented, unaware of the route they took or of how to find their way out of the hypertext. What navigational tools or guidance should be provided to the user?

Accessing Information

A related problem is how and where do users access information in the hypertext? Most hypertexts provide an array of options to the user, usually providing no suggestions or recommendations about where the user should begin. How will their access points to the hypertext affect their understanding of the information contained therein? What sorts of access structures are necessary to provide alternate meaningful access points? What types of decision aids are needed to guide the user?

Integrating Information into Knowledge Structures

An issue related to navigation and access is the problem of integrating the information acquired in the hypertext by the learner into their own knowledge structure. That is a psychological requirement of meaningful learning. As users navigate through the hypertext, how will they relate that information to what they already know? In the absence of the author's top level structure imposed upon the text, will learners develop their own knowledge structures and use them to accommodate the new information? How can hypertext be structured to replicate content structures or knowledge structures of experts that will map more directly on the knowledge structures of the learners? How likely are users to assimilate these structures or accommodate to them? What forms of hypertext structure are necessary to facilitate or supplant those processes? I contend that the less structured the hypertext is, the less likely users are to integrate what they have learned into their own knowledge structures.

Synthesizing Information

Once information has been acquired from a hypertext, it needs to reorganized by the user to create new knowledge structures. It also must be applied and refined. Learners must synthesize new knowledge structures for all of the information contained in the hypertext. How can learners be aided in the reconstruction of knowledge and its generalization to contexts outside the hypertext?

Cognitive Overhead

Dede [2] also cites the problem of cognitive overhead. The exponentially greater number of learning options available to learners places increased cognitive demands upon the learners that they are often unable to fulfil. "The richness of non-linear representation carries a risk of potential intellectual indigestion, loss of goal-directness, and cognitive entropy" [2, p.8].

Hypertext Processing Strategies

Since hypertext is a relatively new technology that places increased demands upon the user, most users find it difficult to develop the skills required to use hypertext. In addition to navigating and integrating information, users must monitor their own comprehension of information. They also need to set goals for themselves, estimate task difficulty, and other metacognitive skills. Sophisticated users do develop strategies for searching, comparing information and solving problems. Yet these individuals are well educated. How generalizable are these skills to normal and below-normal populations? Can hypertexts be structured well enough to supplant many of these strategies?

3. Design Solutions

Hypertext design is theory-rich and research-poor. Cognitive psychology provides rich conceptualizations to guide the production of hypertext. In fact, hypertext offers a powerful environment for conducting studies in cognitive psychology. Yet there is very little empirical research available to guide the practice of hypertext design. My bias is that hypertext needs to be structured in such a way as to facilitate the acquisition, integration, and synthesis of knowledge. The following approaches to designing hypertext for learning will provide some approaches to guide future designs.

Empirical Designs

One approach to designing hypertext is to observe how users navigate through relatively unstructured hypertext. Execute audit trails of the learner's navigation to find out how do they assimilate information from hypertext. Are there patterns of access and do those patterns relate to individual differences that may be used as predictor variables? Start by providing learners with access to unstructured, node/link hypertext and audit the users' paths through the hypertext. Develop a path analysis to classify the prominent paths or routes that learners take through the hypertext. Finally, relate those paths to individual differences, such as field articulation, serialist/holist learning style, etc. The paths that are generated by the most productive learners may provide the best design or sequences for guided tours.

Structured Hypertext

Using various conceptual models, prescriptions for hypertext designs are obvious. These include chunking the nodes into conceptually related units that model the structure of those units or the information processing demands required to learn that information. For instance, using the Node Acquisition and Integration Technique [3], organize the hypertext into blocks consisting of concept, descriptor, antecedent, consequent, subset, superset, and examples nodes. A Cross Classification Strategy is a matrix strategy where information is classified in a two-dimensional matrix to enable the learners to compare and contrast concepts based upon their attributes. Hypertext can easily be structured in this manner.

Having designed a structured hypertext, you need to assess the effects of the alternative structures on the learners' comprehension of the material. This may require prepositional analysis of free recall protocols in order to assess learning. It is also important to assess the users' knowledge structures. If the advantages of hypertext are structural, then learning of structural knowledge should profit most. What advantages of structuring hypertext do accrue to the learner? Differences in the knowledge structures of learners exploring structured vs. unstructured hypertext should provide some useful design heuristics. But how do we best assess changes in knowledge structure?

New tools for assessing knowledge structures are gaining prominence. One option is to use semantic networking software. A previous study [7] showed that it is possible to map cognitive structure using a paper-and-pencil mapping technique. A similar technique has now been implemented in a computer environment. Programs such as Learning Tool [8] and SemNet [4] are capable of mapping the semantic network (i.e. cognitive structures) of learners. These programs require some skill, but that skill can be trained easily.

Map the Structure of Knowledge/Information on the Hypertext

If we assume that learning is the mapping of the expert's knowledge structure on the learner, then an obvious method for structuring hypertext is to structure it in a way that overtly reflects the knowledge structure of the expert. This is the basis for graphical browsers in hypertext- to map the structure of the knowledge. Most graphical browsers show a structure, but often they are not based upon any coherent conception of the knowledge base. A few methods for reflecting the appropriate structure are presented below.

Quantitative method.

The first method is to develop a cognitive or semantic map of the expert's knowledge using quantitative methods. This method requires the expert to complete word associations of all of the related concepts in the content domain. The intercorrelations are multi-dimensionally scaled to generate a structural map (see Jonassen, [7] for a description of this technique). This structural map would then be used as a graphical browser or concept map for accessing information in the hypertext.

Semantic networking software.

The content map may also be generated using semantic networking software described above.

Intelligent front end using expert systems.
Expert system tools are now available that can define and depict the knowledge of an expert. These are known as frame-based systems, which define frames or schemas and instantiate those with information that enable them to inherit information from other frames. These systems are practical replications of schema theory. They enable you define the knowledge of the expert as well as converting that knowledge into a production system of if-then rules. Rather than instantiating the frames with information, instantiate the frames with the addresses of the nodes in the hypertext. That would, in effect, map the expert's knowledge directly onto the hypertext. It would also be important to assess learner's cognitive structures to assess the extent to which they reflected the expert's.

4. A Model for Designing Hypertext for Learning

A central hypothesis of this paper is that hypertext is a technology that can effectively facilitate learning, because its access and information structures closely resemble the learning process. Hypertexts that are designed to facilitate learning should reflect models of learning. Learning involves the construction of schemas or networks of schemas, schemata. These schemata are constructed, according to the LNR group, by a process which includes accretion, restructuring, and tuning and results not only in the accumulation of facts but also the reorganization of the learner's knowledge structure [12].

Schema Theory and Semantic Networks

Learning is a normally conceived to be a reorganization of knowledge structures. Knowledge structures refer to the organization of ideas in semantic memory. Ideas are referred to as "schema" A schema for an object, event, or idea is comprised of a set of attributes. Attributes are the associations that an individual forms around an idea. Most of us have a schema for "aeroplane" that includes wings, fuselage, seats, jet engines, flight attendants, cardboard snacks, and so on. Each individual possesses a unique schema for objects or events depending upon their experiences. Each schema that we construct represents a mini-framework in which to interrelate elements or attributes of information about a topic into a single conceptual unit [13]. These concepts are all arranged in a network of interrelated concepts known as our semantic network.

Our semantic networks our represent our knowledge structures. The schemata in our semantic network are linked together by way of various associations. These interconnections enable learners to combine ideas, infer, extrapolate or otherwise reason from them. Probably the most universally accepted method of modelling semantic networks is the "active structural networks" [14]. Structural networks are composed of nodes (schema) and ordered, labelled relationships (links) connecting them [13]. These networks describe what a learner knows, which provides the foundations for learning new ideas, that is, expanding the learner's semantic network.

Accretion

Accretion describes the accumulation of information in order to fill existing memory schemas. The learner adds information (arguments or attributes) to the knowledge structure that exists. For instance, if a medical student acquired additional facts about a particular disease, that information would be added to his or her schema for that disease. Accretion can also result in the addition of new schemas that use existing schemas as their model. No re-organization of knowledge occurs in the learner's cognitive structure during accretion. Accretion is pre-requisite to restructuring.

Restructuring

As knowledge is acquired, the learner's schemas expand to a point where they are unable to adequately accommodate all of the information. The learner begins to restructure his or her knowledge by adding schemas or developing new conceptualizations for existing ones. While restructuring of knowledge is the least common learning activity, it is the most important. Restructuring is facilitated instructionally by the use of metaphors, analogies, and inferences, all of which are mentally difficult activities. In hypertext, they can be easily included as part of the structure (for example, analogy or metaphor buttons that immediately access an appropriate metaphor for the learners). The result of restructuring are new knowledge structures, which enable the learner to interpret or access their knowledge in new ways. The ideas are rearranged sufficiently to provide new meanings to ideas. A personal observation of the disease, for instance, may provide enough new information through accretion that it causes the medical student to revise his or her understanding of the disease. This new experience, parenthetically, can easily be added to a hypertext. Restructuring is the activity that is necessary for the learner to truly understand the information. It is a process that can be facilitated by hypertext.

Tuning

After all of the schemas have been developed and re-organized by the learner into a coherent knowledge base, minor adaptations are made in order to make performance more efficient. Through practice or consistent use of new knowledge structures, they are tuned or finely adjusted. Behaviour based upon the existing knowledge structures may become automated. This automaticity requires a fine tuning of the schemas that enable it. Schemas are modified to meet specific task demands or adapted to particular knowledge domains or contexts. Tuning might entail the refining of a procedure, filling-in of inferences, or adapting the schemas to new situations. After having witnessed and treated a number of victims of a disease, the medical student's diagnostic and prescriptive skills become sharpened. The student may easily recognize different manifestations of the disease. Tuning is an on-going process, where schemas may continue to be fine tuned over a lifetime. Practice in using the schemas or procedures is the best instructional intervention to facilitate the tuning process.

Sequence

The sequencing of these processes is not invariant. Typically, the learner begins with accretion or the building up of information until it forces restructuring, which occurs for some time. Over time and with practice, the learner tunes his or her knowledge structures, so that it is the dominant mode during the latter stages of learning. However, these processes are carried out simultaneously. While restructuring some schemas, the learner may also be adding new information to other information while fine tuning other topics. Although schemas are developed in the accretion-restructuring-tuning sequence, all three modes are usually present. Also, the learner may recycle through some stages. Even after developing finely tuned schemas, the learner may enter the accretion mode later when new information becomes available. If that new information is substantial enough, it may elicit some additional restructuring.

5. Hypertext Environments that Foster Learning

A learning environment that facilitates accretion, restructuring, and tuning must be able to simulate and facilitate each of these processes but also must be dynamic enough to permit the learner to switch modes and schemas. Most computer learning environments, including tutors and simulations, seek to effect closure on one idea or objective before moving onto another. So, they do not permit browsing or changing the direction of their learning. Hypertext is the ideal environment for this. Hypertext is an information environment that can most directly reflect the accretion-restructuring-tuning model of learning. I will briefly describe the characteristics of a hypertext project that reflects these modes of processing [6].

Accretion

Accretion of information is the basis for hypertext. Information is chunked in nodes which makes it more accretable. Accretion implies more than acquisition. It also implies adherence or attachment to a knowledge structure. Providing a basic hypertext structure, as discussed above, and making the relationship of the nodes to the structure obvious through the link structure will facilitate accretion. In the Instructional Systems Design Hypertext, I have developed a map of the primary concepts in our field and organized those into a graphical browser. The arrangement of ideas in the browser was generated by multi-dimensionally scaling relatedness coefficients produced by pairwise rating of all the concepts by researchers in the field. At the concept level, the user may explore examples, applications, implications, and terms related to each foundational concept. In addition to facilitating navigation, the hypertext should facilitate the accretion of information. Hypertext is a natural accretion medium. The problems, as discussed above, come with restructuring.

Restructuring

The problem of integration of information into the learners knowledge structure (discussed above) relates to the learning process of restructuring. Learners must be able to explicitly reorganize their own ideas in order to better accommodate new information. The most effective way to do this will be to include semantic networking components in the hypertext or to launch that type of software from the hypertext. Semantic networking programs enable the learner to create maps of concepts and describe the links in between, much like hypertext. The software that we are launching from HyperCard is SemNet [4]. Requiring the learners to generate their own semantic maps forces them to analyze their own knowledge structures. It will also allow us to follow the development of the learners' knowledge structures.

Tuning

Tuning is the most difficult of the learning processes to simulate in any system. We will use an iterative loop consisting of practice items requiring first near and then far transfer of the information accreted from the hypertext followed by semantic analysis using SemNet. The learners will receive near transfer and recall questions first followed by semantic analysis. Then they will receive a series of far transfer questions requiring the learners to generalize from the knowledge that they have acquired followed by semantic analysis once again.

6. Conclusion

Hypertext is a powerful instructional environment. With the exception of Intermedia project at Brown University and Project Perseus at Harvard, the most common applications of hypertext to date have not been in the instructional area. However, a number of potentially powerful instructional applications are being investigated. What is needed is a set of design prescriptions for designing hypertext for learning.

References

1. Conkin, J. Hypertext: An introduction and survey. *Computer*, 20(a), 17-14. 1987.
2. Dede, C. *The role of hypertext in transforming information into knowledge*. Paper presented at the annual meeting of NECC Dallas, TX, June 1988. 1988.
3. Diekhoff, G.M., Brown, P., & Dansereau, D.F. A prose learning strategy based on network and depth of processing models. *Journal of Experimental Education*, *50*(4), 180-184. 1983.
4. Fisher, K.M., Faletti, J., Thornton, R. Patterson, H., Lipson, J., & Spring, C. *Computer-based knowledge representation as a tool for students and teachers*. Paper presented at the annual meeting of the American Educational Research Association, New Orleans, April, 1988.
5. Jonassen, D.H. *Hypertext/hypermedia*. Englewood Cliffs, NJ: Educational Technology Publications. 1989a.
6. Jonassen, D.H. *Designing an instructional systems design hypertext*. Paper presented at the annual meeting of the Association of Educational Communications and Technology, Dallas, TX, February 1-4, 1989b.

7. Jonassen, D.H. Assessing cognitive structure: Verifying a method using pattern notes. *Journal of Research and Development in Education, 20* (3), 1-14. 1987.
8. Kozma, R.B. The implications of cognitive psychology for computer-based learning tools. *Educational Technology, 28* (11), 20-25. 1987.
9. Nelson, T.H. *Dream machines*. South Bend, IN: The Distributors. 1978.
10. Nelson, T.H. Electronic publishing and electronic literature. In E.C. DeLand (Ed.), *Information technology in health science education*. New York: PLenum. 1974.
11. Nelson, T.H. *Literary machines*. Swarthmore, PA: The author. 1981
12. Norman, D. A. *Studies in learning and self-contained education systems*, 1973-1976. Tech Report No. 7601. Washington, D.C.: Office of Naval Research, Advanced Research Projects Agency. (ED 121 786). 1976.
13. Norman, D.A., Gentner, S. & Stevens, A.L. Comments on learning schemata and memory representation. In D. Klahr (Ed.), *Cognition and instruction*. Hillsdale, NJ: Lawrence Erlbaum Associates. 1976.
14. Quillian, M.R. Semantic memory. In M. Minsky (Ed.), *Semantic information processing*. Cambridge, MA: MIT Press. 1968.

11

A Prototype Futuristic Technology for Distance Education

Randall B. Smith
Xerox Palo Alto Research Center
3333 Coyote Hill Rd.
Palo Alto, California, 94304
U.S.A.
and
Rank-Xerox EuroPARC
61 Regent St.
Cambridge, CB2 1AB
England

Abstract: I describe a system called SharedARK (for Shared Alternate Reality Kit,) which may serve as a prototype for a future distance education technology. In SharedARK, each single-user site consists of a computer workstation, an audio headset, a video monitor, and video camera. Each site is physically isolated from the others and are connected via a computer-switchable audio-video and high performance computer networks.

The system is quite literally based on a shared virtual world model. Users may roam through this world, encountering each other to act together in a collaborative task while communicating over an audio-video link, or users may move off by themselves to work in isolation. The system is intended to support a wide range of activities currently part of conventional distance education (such as editing and sharing text and graphics, and viewing prepared video material) plus activities that are currently unavailable (such as realtime interactive collaborative use of simulated laboratories or video links among students and teachers.) I present the motivations for the virtual world model, describe the system and its implementation, and discuss the issues raised by the current prototype.

Keywords: visual programming, Alternate Reality Kit, ARK, computer-based collaborative learning, distributed software systems, local area network, Media Space, motivation, object-oriented, real-time video links, SharedARK, Smalltalk-80, textual programming, virtual reality

1. Introduction

Recent research emphasizing the role of collaboration in learning and current interest in computer supported cooperative work reinforce the importance of investigating the area common to these two fields: computer-based collaborative learning. Many existing collaborative systems are intended to supplement situations in which participants are in the same room for part or all of their working sessions. However, when users are unable to meet in the same room, face-to-face interaction is impossible. This is the domain of distance education, in which most or all of the interpersonal interactions among students and teacher are mediated by some form of technology. Institutions such as the various "open universities" already exist primarily to provide distance education, and ways to supplement distance education with interactive technologies such as electronic mail, computer-based conferencing [6], [7], and real-time video links [10] are being explored.

I will describe a rather futuristic educational environment called 'SharedARK' (for 'Shared Alternate Reality Kit') a system under development at the Xerox Palo Alto Research Center and at Rank-Xerox EuroPARC in Cambridge. SharedARK is based on a collection of physically isolated, single-user sites. Each site consists of a video camera, a video monitor, an audio headset-microphone, and a computer workstation. The sites communicate over a computer-switchable audio-video network and a high performance computer network. The primary purpose of this project is to explore what might lie in the future, beyond conventional images of students sitting at terminals and typing messages at each other. It is based on the assumption that both the computing power available in today's high-end workstations and the bandwidth available in today's local area networks will continue to improve while becoming inexpensive and ubiquitous. In this paper I report on the motivations for SharedARK's design (section 2), describe the system (section 3), and discuss the issues raised in taking the system further towards the motivating goals (section 4).

Users of spread sheets or word processors are often free to adopt some alternative if they find the interface obscure or intimidating. In distance education, users have no choice but to use the shared, given technology. Consequently, I believe it is crucial to provide interfaces to distance education technology that are easily learned and intimidate the user as little as possible. So the primary motivation is to support a wide range of collaborative learning activities in distance education with a natural and easily learned interface. SharedARK attempts to achieve this by providing a virtual reality in which students and teachers move about, coming together to form collaborative groupings, separating to work on their own.

In SharedARK, students and teachers wander within a pseudo-physical space, and communicate over audio-video links. SharedARK creates a virtually infinite two-dimensional "flatland" within the computers: each workstation only sees a few square feet of territory at a time. Each user has a mouse-operated "hand" for manipulating objects, and a type-out object for creating text from the keyboard. As users wander within the space they may come into contact with each other and cause audio and video links to be established. The intent is to create a very real sense of space within which users move about, manipulating virtual objects and directly encountering each other.

Distance education students typically engage in a broad range of activities: they may read some material, view a video presentation, write a report, and communicate with a tutor, all as part of a single course. SharedARK is intended to support this wide range of educational activities, all of which can be happening concurrently: some students may be working together on a simulated chemistry lab, while a few dozen (virtual) yards away, another student works alone, possibly writing a report for a literature class or viewing a videotape.

I will comment in this chapter on experiences with users, although much of this experience so far is based on a single-user version.

2. Motivations

Why video? It may seem that bandwidth requirements would make video connections a luxury that one could do without. However, currently available video compression hardware enables a signal to be transmitted with less than 100 kbs, much less than is required by most local area networks. But even if video connections do become inexpensive, why use them at all? There are three motivations.

First, prepared video has been found to be a successful technology in many distance education courses. In SharedARK this technology can play its traditional role. But because access to authored videotape and videodisk is embedded in the SharedARK environment, it is possible to imagine new settings, in which playback of the video material is synchronized with material within the computer.

Second, in educational settings, situations routinely arise in which students or teachers wish to refer to objects in their environment. For example, a teacher may wish to perform a physics demonstration. Or a student may wish to use a hand gesture to clarify a question. Subtle cues such as facial expression and tone of voice can be transmitted by audio video technology -- such cues are not really available in a textual medium. All of these kinds of communication are an important part of the educational process.

Third, education is at least partly a social process. Interactions between people often play a dominate role in learning. Use of audio-video connections is partly an attempt to give participants a sense of personal connectedness akin to what they have come to know from the real world. A technology which provides audio and visual contact enables people to exchange ideas while feeling "in touch" in a more familiar way, addressing a frequent criticism of distance education.

Within the Computer.

The computer-based component of this system provides the synthetic world in which students and teachers co-exist. SharedARK is based on a physical world metaphor. But what is the motivation for using the real world as a model? I believe that the physical world has three properties that make it worthy of imitation: familiarity, uniformity, and extensibilty.

The physical world is *familiar*. Even an infant knows a considerable number of the world's operating rules. If one mimics the real world within the computer, one might hope to capture the real world's property of being familiar. Such a computer system should be easily learned, and might be less intimidating.

The real world is *uniform*. By this I mean that there is a single underlying set of rules governing all that happens. A student in the physical world can use the same pen and notebook for a creative writing exercise and for working a mathematics problem. Many computer systems are unfortunately non-uniform: a student reading a mathematics problem is normally unable to copy the text into a report or to integrate it into electronic mail. A uniform computer system has one set of functions and data structures serving the users in all areas of their work. A uniform system, requiring only a single set of tools and methods, will be more easily learned, and will avoid barriers that artificially divide activities into preconceived categories.

Finally, the real world is *extensible*. New things can be made from within reality itself. Many educational computer systems do allow users to create new documents and "files," but to add something really new, if possible at all, normally requires one to leave the current application and invoke a "programmer's interface." This is a completely different domain with different rules and a different representation of the application.

If an instructor is able to use the system for creation of new objects, he or she will not have to learn a special interface for "programming" tasks. Direct creation of new objects is typically more concrete, and has been found in ARK to be faster than using a purely text-oriented mechanism [11]. In addition, extensibility allows the instructor to include a wider range of creative activities as part of the curriculum.

I readily admit that these motivations will cause problems if taken too far. For example, the environment probably should not be so extensible that even the network operating code is changeable by any user. And if uniformity were adhered to with total rigor, even minor, task-specific specializations of software would be forbidden.

If the system were completely familiar, the users would encounter nothing new at all, wasting the computer's ability to provide useful capabilities whose analog is impossible in the real world. This is of course an interesting design tradeoff in trying to make powerful systems for novices: how does one make it useful yet easily learned?

Nevertheless, I believe familiarity, uniformity, and extensibility are important principles that help to make learnable and functional systems that support a wide variety of activities. The current SharedARK prototype embodies two of these attributes fairly well I think, but extensibility is problematic. Some of the difficulties that arise in building the prototype will be discussed in greater detail in section 4.

3. Description of SharedARK

SharedARK can be thought of as a multi-user, multi-workstation version of the Alternate Reality Kit [12,13] which has been enhanced with a computer-controlled audio-video network. Like ARK, the computer-based component of SharedARK is an interactive, animated environment, in which everything is presented as a visible physical object with velocity and mass. Users employ a mouse-operated hand to press buttons, to carry and even to throw objects across the enormous two-dimensional surface. SharedARK has been combined with a distributed, computer-controlled audio-video network called the "Media Space" [14] at PARC in Palo Alto, or the "Interactive Intermedia Facility" at EuroPARC in Cambridge. Using compressed video and high bandwidth phone lines, SharedARK has been used in real-time collaborative activities between workstations 600 miles apart.

Imagine an infinite two dimensional plane, populated by clusters of objects. Your computer screen serves as a window onto a rectangular portion of this plane, and your mouse operates a hand with which you can press buttons, operate sliders, or carry and throw any object across the surface. A thrown object left alone will drift off the edge of your screen. However, you are able to "scroll" your window so that you can chase after the object to retrieve it. While exploring this plane, you are likely to encounter other hands wandering into view. Each hand represents a user at a workstation like your own. You can directly speak with any user through a "phone operator's headset," and users can connect video monitors and cameras to put themselves in visual contact. Users can work together to carry out a simulated physics experiment, or jointly edit graphics using simulated pens and tablets. The keyboard at each workstation operates a type-out object which drops pieces of text into the SharedARK world so that collaborative (or single-user) text-editing is also supported.

Both ARK and SharedARK have hosted novice users in a variety of experimental settings. It has been found [9], [11] that novices can learn how to use the interface with a few minutes of instruction. Many seem to find the system engaging, and sometimes explore on their own. I believe this is attributable to the physical world metaphor, providing uniformity and familiarity.

SharedARK currently provides extensibility through textual programming. Objects or buttons can be created or modified by writing appropriate Smalltalk code. More in keeping with the metaphor would be to abandon text completely, and do extensions by directly manipulating the SharedARK objects. This also has been tried. Problems with these approaches will be discussed in section 4.

Special objects enhance the usefulness of the environment. Pairs of objects whimsically called "Teleporters" can instantly transport objects between locations, possibly over many miles of intervening virtual space. Teleporters can operate on your hand, so you can "step through" these doorways as well. Objects called "regions" denote rectangular areas of the plane which can be locked by users for privacy: other users can be excluded from moving their hands or other objects into these regions, and can be prevented from seeing the region's contents by an obscuring cover which is transparent only to the owner. A "Radar View" at the top of each screen gives the user a miniature picture of the off-screen surrounding space.

Virtual video tape recorders, video disk players and switching devices are part of the Media Space, and can be controlled from within the environment: by activating virtual buttons and connecting virtual devices together, users have considerable flexibility in their ability to view and record combinations of live and recorded video material. Although currently user-to-user video and audio connections are typically not changed throughout a session, it would be easy to establish these connections automatically based on proximity in the virtual world. As an individual comes within range of your radar view, a video connection might be established between the two monitors and cameras. If users come so close that their main views overlap, audio connections could be established.

One of the interesting capabilities in ARK and SharedARK is the ability to represent normally intangible and abstract entities as concrete, physical objects. Thus, the speed of light can be made to appear as an object whose value can be changed by a slider control. Even fundamental laws of nature, such as the conservation of energy, can be experimentally violated. The concreteness and malleability of abstractions as presented in this system creates educational possibilities that are unavailable in the real world.

3.1 Extrapolating from the Current System:

Before I discuss the limitations of the current implementation of SharedARK which hamper the full realization the motivating vision, I will indulge in describing an extrapolation from the current SharedARK prototype.

It is possible to imagine twenty or more students working for an extended period, each at a workstation which is physically many miles away from his or her nearest classmate. Some students could be working in isolation while others work (virtually) together. A teacher could roam around the world offering help where needed.

If bandwidth is sufficiently cheap, students need not "log out" at the end of "school:" by retreating to a "home," perhaps many miles away across the infinite plane, students would be free to do homework in privacy. Teleporters and private regions would be useful here. Extra-curricular collaborations between students which are currently not feasible due to physical separation could become commonplace. Because instantaneous leaps across miles of space are simply a button press away, forming collaborative groups is very "light weight."

Notice the role of uniformity: there is no separate computer interface for physics simulations and text editing. The metaphor of direct manipulation of physical objects serves for making graphs in mathematics and for making graphics in a written report. There is no need for electronic mail -- a typed "letter" can be carried and dropped off at the "home" of any user. Specializations of teleporters could be used for creation of "distribution lists:" letters dropped into a central port could be copied and delivered to many destination ports. "Bulletin boards," normally the subject of separate software, can be created with no extra support whatsoever. Again, uniformity is a great benefit here: ANY object, not just "letters" can be copied and "posted." Because it is a virtual world, the system supports all the phases of educational activity, including preliminary task definitions and the final interpretative activities.

3.2 Implementation

SharedARK is implemented in Smalltalk-80 [4], a high-level, object-oriented language. In Smalltalk, computations are performed by message passing between objects. SharedARK is currently running on a version of Smalltalk-80 on Sun 3 workstations.

All the objects in the SharedARK software are replicated on each participating machine. The SharedARK objects are represented identically within each computer. In addition, an input state broadcast process on each host lets all the machines on the network know its host's current mouse and keyboard state. Thus, each computer always has a self-contained and up-to-date representation of the entire virtual world.

In addition to exchange of input state packets, there is a small amount of network traffic for synchronizing the worlds on each machine. SharedARK executes in an animation loop, during which each object in the world is given a chance to do some characteristic activity, and to draw itself on the screen. Before each step in the loop, network packets are exchanged so that each host is certain that all the other hosts are ready to execute the next animation step.

Thus the number of packets on the network scales as the square of the number of hosts. The amount information sent from each machine is very small -- typically just a few bytes. But the real-time character of the interaction demands low-network latency. This is discussed below.

4. Issues For Future Research

4.1 Extensibility

The current mechanism for creating new objects and new methods is sufficient as a matter of principle, but it requires one to learn Smalltalk-80 syntax and semantics. More "physical" mechanisms for programming have been tried out in ARK, but have met with only limited success -- these could be studied further and brought into SharedARK.

One win in ARK's "visual" programming comes in making new kinds of objects: a copy-and-modify scheme is used, which is more concrete and faster than the corresponding Smalltalk approach in which one must define a subclass, describe initialization, and finally instantiate. One is also able to make small programs by combining buttons together in ARK, but programs requiring large amounts of mathematics code, for example, are extremely tedious to make and are visually hard to understand.

In neither SharedARK nor ARK is there a "line" beyond which it is unsafe to travel: as in LISP, Smalltalk, and many modern languages, much of the system can be modified from within itself. Because, for example, it is possible to redefine the compiler and to reimplement the fundamental animation algorithms, it is also possible in principle to crash the entire system. Where and how to provide appropriate protection is a difficult question.

4.2 Current Technological Limitations

The current implementation of SharedARK has a virtual extent far in excess of billions of miles and can support an arbitrary number of users. However, present-day network and computational performance limitations prevent the system from working well with more than three or four users and more than a few dozen objects.

The animation rate slows down under the full-scale scenario in which dozens of students and teachers interact with hundreds or thousands of objects. It is possible that distributing the software load in a different way amongst the various computers on the network could enhance performance. Rather than the current replicated-object implementation described in section 3, one might use a "distributed object" strategy, in which each object resides on one machine only. In this case, message sends between objects may involve the network. Of course, some combination of replication and distribution might be used. Naturally, these techniques are an area of research in distributed software systems [2,3,5,8]: moving towards distribution lowers the per-node computational demands, but raises network bandwidth requirements and increases the system's vulnerability to node crashes. Distributed implementations also require attention to load balancing amongst the various hosts if one is to optimize overall performance.

The real-time interactive character of the system pushes the limit of network latency more than bandwidth. For example, a half second may be required for a send and reply in such cases involving geo-synchronous satellites, a factor of 5 too great for reasonable animation. The future may bring low-orbit satellite systems or undersea optical fibre, which with faster gateways, would suffice.

4.3 Integrating Audio and Video with the Computer Interface

Despite the talk of uniformity in section 2, the computer-based component and the audio-video component of the current SharedARK prototype are glaringly disjoint. First, the audio/video is output to a device completely separated from the computer screen. Second, the computer and audio/visual domains have no way to communicate their subject matter to each other.

Based only on informal observation, the first problem (separate displays for video and computer) seems to cause the video to be somewhat neglected. Users are often intently focused on the computer screen -- the video monitor can seem so far from the point of action as to be irrelevant. There are available technologies in which video images are incorporated within the computer's display. Instead of just a "hand" icon representing the user, the user's video image might somehow be incorporated. How to make this natural in a "flatland" setting like that of SharedARK is an interesting challenge.

The exchange of video and computational substance would seem to be very difficult to provide, but it would bring intriguing capabilities. Integration of the substance of video and computation would mean that any video image would correspond to a data structure in the computer. A video image of a document could ideally be made to correspond to an appropriate data structure within the computer. Once captured in this form, the document could be edited, stored and copied as needed -- such capabilities are becoming commercially available today. But carrying this further, a video image of a ball might correspond to a software object representing the ball's position and velocity. If this correspondence were tracked in real time, then real-world physics experiments could be mapped directly into the computer where they could be monitored and measured by "soft" instrumentation under student control. Integration would ideally run the other way as well: the computer would be able to display the ball's velocity vector on top of its video image. These capabilities are of course the subject of a great deal of current research in document recognition and real-time scene recognition.

4.4 Video and Large Numbers

One final challenge in the use of video is how to deal with large numbers of users, engaging in a group discussion for example. Conference calls are frequently used in current distance education practice, but providing the video analog presents a problem. The current audio-video networks do provide a "picture in a picture" facility so that multiple video sources can be displayed on a single monitor, but it is unclear what might be done to support a large number of simultaneous interconnections. A sense of eye-to-eye contact can be created for the case of two users by employing a half-silvered mirror so that the optical axis of the camera and video monitor are made to coincide [1]. But how can one use a single monitor to accurately represent a discussion among, say, five students in which heads turn to face the current speaker? It seems likely that vigilant fidelity to the real world may have to be sacrificed in these cases.

5. Conclusions

The purpose of this prototype is to demonstrate and test certain intuitions, and to raise issues for further research. The underlying intuition is that a virtual reality which allows users to directly see and hear each other, and allows them to directly act together in a shared world, is easily learned and minimally threatening. The virtual reality metaphor provides a uniform and flexible substrate which can support a wide range of activities.

The system has somewhat broad implications, raising issues from the sociological aspects of remote collaboration to the computer science aspects of distributed implementations. How to support the extensibility of the system in a safe and natural way is a difficult question. A more immediate challenge is, I believe, how to most effectively integrate the video world of appearance with the computer's world of activity.

Currently, SharedARK is a prototype -- a system intentionally slightly before its time. The technology needed to support a truly useful version is rapidly falling in price, and I believe there are no fundamental barriers to the full realization of a distributed distance education system based on the SharedARK model.

6. Acknowledgements

Thanks to Carl Waldspurger who wrote most of the code promoting ARK to shared status, to Amy Lim who implemented the text objects and paper objects in ARK, and to Tim O'Shea for his helpful comments.

References

1. Acker, S. R. and Levit S. R., Designing videoconference facilities for improved eye contact. *Journal of Broadcasting and Electronic Media,* (Spr), Vol. 31(2), pp. 181-191. 1987.
2. Bennett, J. K., The design and implementation of Distributed Smalltalk. *Proceedings. OOPSLA '86,* Orlando, Florida, Oct. 4-8 , pp. 318-330. ,1987.
3. Black, A., Hutchinson, N., Jul, E. Levy, H., Object Structure in the Emerald System. *Proceedings. OOPSLA '86,* Portland, Oregon, Sept. 29-Oct. 2 , pp. 78-86. 1986.
4. Goldberg A. and Robson D., *Smalltalk-80, the Language and its Implementation.* Addison Wesley, Reading, Massachusetts, 1983.
5. Jones, M. B., and Rashid, R. F., Mach and Matchmaker: Kernel and Language Support for Object-Oriented Distributed Systems. *Proceedings. OOPSLA '86,* Portland, Oregon, Sept. 29-Oct. 2 , pp. 67-77. 1986.
6. Kaye, T., Computer conferencing and electronic mail, in Thorpe, M. and Grugeon, D. (eds) *Open Learning For Adults,* Harlow, Longman, pp. 186-193. 1987.
7. Mason, R., Computer conferencing: a contribution to self-directed learning. British *Journal of Educational Technology* Vol. 19 (1), pp. 28 -41. 1988.
8. McCullough, P. L., Transparent forwarding: first steps. *Proceedings. OOPSLA '86,* Orlando, Florida, Oct. 4-8 , pp. 331-341. 1987.
9. O'Shea, T. and Smith R. B., *Violating the laws of nature: experiments in understanding physics by exploring alternate realities.* (in progress)
10. Ringstead, M., *On-The-Job-Training: a multimedia experiment in distance education.* Technical report of Arhus Technical College, Arhus, Denmark.
11. Scanlon, E. and Smith, R. B., A rational reconstruction of a bubble chamber simulation using the Alternate Reality Kit, *Computers and Education,* Pergamon Press, 1988.
12. Smith, R. B., Experiences with the Alternate Reality Kit: an example of the tension between literalism and magic. *Computer Graphics and Applications,* Sept. 1987, pp. 42-50, also in *CHI+GI '87 Conference proceedings,* Toronto, April 5-9, 1987, pp. 61-67. 1987.
13. Smith, R. B., The Alternate Reality Kit: an animated environment for creating interactive simulations. *Proceedings. IEEE Computer Soc.* Workshop on Visual Languages, June 1986, Dallas, Texas [CS-IEEE, Los Altos, Calif.,] pp. 99-106. 1986.
14. Stults, R., *Media space.* Technical report of System Concepts Lab, Xerox PARC, 1986.

12

Tools for Scientific Thinking: Learning Physical Concepts with Real-Time Laboratory Measurement Tools[1]

Ronald K. Thornton
Center for Science and Math Teaching
Tufts University
Medford, MA 02155
U.S.A.

Abstract: Learner-controlled explorations in the physics laboratory with easy-to-use real-time measurement tools give students immediate feed-back by presenting data graphically in a manner that can be understood. Using Microcomputer-Based Laboratory (MBL) sensors and software students can simultaneously measure and graph such physical quantities as position, velocity, acceleration, force, temperature, light intensity, sound pressure, current and potential difference. Using these MBL tools provides a mechanism for more easily altering physics pedagogy to include methods found to be effective by educational research. The ease of data collection and presentation encourage even badly prepared students to become active participants in a scientific process which often leads them to ask and answer their own questions. The general nature of the tools enable exploration to begin with the students' direct experience of the familiar physical world rather than with specialized laboratory equipment. The real-time graphical display of actual physical measurements of dynamic systems directly couples the symbolic representation with the actual physical phenomena. Such MBL tools and carefully designed curricula based on educational research have been used to teach physics concepts to a wide range of students in universities and high schools. Data show substantial and persistent learning of basic physical concepts, not often learned in lectures, by students who use MBL tools with carefully designed curricular materials.

Keywords: cognitive science, computer-based learning, evaluation, kinematics, laboratory curriculum, mechanics, Microcomputer-Based Laboratory, physical intuition, physics, probes

---

[1] Paper Based on an Invited Talk by Ronald K. Thornton at the Conference on Computers in Physics Instruction, North Carolina State University, July, 1988.

1. Some Problems With Physics Education

There has been strong evidence that introductory physics students in the usual college and university lecture courses are not learning concepts necessary to their understanding of the physical world. This paper will present some additional evidence. Traditional science instruction in the United States, refined by decades of work, has been shown to be ineffective in altering student misconceptions and simplistic understandings. Even at the university level, students, science majors and others, who take post-secondary physics courses, enter and leave the courses with fundamental misunderstandings of the world about them essentially intact: their learning of facts about science remains within the classroom and has no effect on their thinking about the larger physical world. The ineffectiveness of these courses is independent of the apparent skill of the teacher, and student performance does not seem to depend on whether students have taken physics courses in secondary school e.g. [2,3].

One of the reasons that traditional science courses have failed in this respect is that they do not make strong connections to the everyday experiences of the students nor to the incomplete "understandings" which serve students well within limited domains but do not lead to the general principles underlying deeper scientific understanding. These principles can sometimes seem to counter naive ideas built from everyday experiences. It would appear that unless a course is planned carefully to examine simple understandings and to build to general principles while addressing misconceptions, students' ideas will not change.

1.1 Developing Physical Intuition in the Physics Laboratory

Even successful physics students who can solve all of the problems at the end of the chapter generally lack physical intuition—a reliable accurate response to the physical world based on an understanding of its underlying principles and physics honours students have been shown to have fundamental conceptual difficulties [7]. In contrast, students who develop physical intuition will have a conceptual, qualitative understanding which can be applied outside of the classroom in their everyday interactions with the physical world. Thus it is likely to be fruitful to alter the way most science students are taught --to begin with what students can learn by arranging their interaction with the physical world around them, and then to connect that learning to the underlying principles which constitute scientific knowledge.

A well-designed science laboratory can provide the sorts of experiences necessary to correct misconceptions and to develop useful physical intuition. It is one of the few places where students can truly participate in the processes of science; gaining first-hand knowledge of physical phenomena, constructing for themselves the theories necessary to understand the physical world, and formulating their own questions which further engages them in the learning process. To alter misconceptions that were first generated by interaction with the physical world requires additional interaction. Recent developments in cognitive science and education substantiate the importance of empirical, heavily phenomenological experiences in learning science skills and concepts e.g.,[6]. One of the ways Arnold Arons [1] suggests for increasing student learning is by providing the means for students to form concepts from concrete experience.

In fact, laboratories are often omitted from or de-emphasized in physics courses because the teaching laboratory is not thought to be a place where students can learn physics but a place for developing laboratory skills of limited academic usefulness. Many laboratory instruments are hard for the student to use as well as unreliable. The reality of many science laboratories is that exploration is not encouraged. Instructions are "cookbook" and seemingly unrelated to physics concepts, calculations are time-consuming, and the results that emerge after an enormous amount of effort are what one would expect anyway. The traditional physics teaching laboratory is often pedagogically ineffective, ignored by faculty and disliked by students. Laboratories of this sort are better omitted from courses because they discourage students, provide no new information about nature, and give an incorrect view of the process of science. Yet science laboratories are not a frill that can be discarded without consequence. The absence of the direct experience afforded by the laboratory can make science less interesting and less accessible to students.

Scientists rarely "preach what they practice." Science is exciting to scientists because they are engaged in discovery and in creatively building and testing models to explain the world around them (the practice). In most courses, students "do" no science and only hear lectures about already validated theories (the preaching). Not only do they not have an opportunity to form their own ideas, they rarely get a chance to work in any substantial way at applying the ideas of others to the world around them.

Direct experience with physical phenomena is especially important to the students in introductory courses and although the teaching laboratory can allow the novice to actively participate in a scientific investigation, the problems with teaching labs described above are compounded when they are used for inexperienced students. Because such students have not developed sophisticated laboratory techniques, honed investigative skills, or become familiar with analytical skills, it is difficult to construct laboratory experiences where they can successfully ask and answer questions that interest them. The effort to insure that students with minimal laboratory skills get the "right" answer has led to the overly explicit instructions for exercises which direct students through routine steps in confirming known answers to uninteresting questions.

1.2 Tools for Scientific Thinking

The "Tools for Scientific Thinking Project[2] of the Center for Science and Mathematics Teaching at Tufts University is addressing some of the problems outlined above by introducing Microcomputer-Based Laboratory (MBL) tools and curricula at the college level. Powerful, easy to-use, scientific tools with which students can collect physical data and display it in a manner that can be remembered, manipulated, and thought about can go a long way toward making teaching laboratories engaging and effective for developing useful scientific intuition. It is just this sort of MBL tool that was first developed at the Technical Education Research Centers (TERC)[3] , and is now readily available[4] . MBL tools can eliminate the drudgery associated with data collection and display and allow students to concentrate on the scientific ideas that are the goal of their investigations. MBL tools can be structured to encourage an inquiry approach to science and thereby help avoid the "cookbook" laboratory. Because of their ease of use and pedagogical effectiveness, well-designed MBL instruments are especially well-suited to the revitalization of science laboratories for students of all levels because such tools make an understanding of physical phenomena more accessible to the naive science learner and because they expand the investigations that more advanced students can undertake.

MBL instruments with the aforementioned characteristics give the science learner unprecedented power to explore, measure, and learn from the physical world. They do not simulate physical phenomena, but are the means of changing inexpensive computers into instruments for student-directed exploration of the physical world which allow data acquisition, display, and analysis. MBL instruments of the type developed by TERC make use of inexpensive microcomputer-connected probes to measure such physical quantities as temperature, position, velocity, acceleration, sound pressure, light, force, and physiological indicators such as heart rate. Measurements taken by the probes are displayed in digital and graphical form on the computer monitor as the measurement is taken. Data can also be transformed and analyzed, printed, or saved onto disks for later analysis. Carefully developed software makes these laboratory tools easy to use even for the first time. MBL tools dictate neither what is to be investigated nor the steps of an investigation. Consequently, students feel in control of their own learning. Moreover, these general tools can be used with many different curricula by both physics majors and non-majors.

---

2 This work was partially funded by The Fund for the Improvement of Post Secondary Education (FIPSE, US Department of Education) under the Tools for Scientific Thinking Project at Tufts University.

3 Technical Education Research Centers (TERC), 1696 Massachusetts Ave.,Cambridge, MA 0213

4 HRM Software, Queue, 562 Boston Avenue, Room S, Bridgeport, CN 06610

As part of the Tools for Scientific Thinking Project, laboratory curricula and MBL tools have been tested at varied institutions including California Polytechnic State University, Dickinson College, Massachusetts Institute of Technology, Muskingum College, University of Oregon, Tufts University, and Xavier University. The project is making available microcomputer-based laboratory modules and curricula which emphasize the role of the physics teaching laboratory . The materials are designed to give students the means to build physical intuition (a conceptual, qualitative, usable understanding of the physical world). Such laboratories will be accessible to the naive science learner, and will provide a foundation for the restructuring of science courses for non-majors as well as majors. The project is funded by the Fund for the Improvement of Post secondary Education (FIPSE) of the US Department of Education. This project is linked to another FIPSE funded project, Workshop Physics, which is developing an entire introductory physics course sequence that will replace the traditional physics course, with its separation of lecture and laboratory, with a workshop format designed to enhance student interaction with the physical world[5] .

1.3 Learning Kinematics Concepts with MBL Tools and Curricula

University and high school students have successfully learned kinematics concepts that they did not learn in lectures using a motion detector designed by TERC and curricula developed by the Tools for Scientific Thinking Project at Tufts. The motion detector (hardware and software) is able to measure, display, and record the distance, velocity, and acceleration of any object. The hardware was developed from a sonic transducer used in Polaroid cameras. The motion probe is essentially a SONAR unit that sends out short pulses of high frequency sound (50 kHz), then detects and amplifies the echo. A microcomputer is then programmed to measure the time between the transmitted and received pulse and to calculate the position, velocity and acceleration of the object causing the reflection (much as a bat is able to do). Any one of these quantities may be displayed on the computer screen as the data are taken and all are available after the measurements are completed. The motion detector can accurately detect objects between 0.5 and 6 meters. It detects the closest object in a roughly 15 degree cone. The motion detectors used in the following were connected to Apple II computers.

The kinematics laboratory curriculum was designed using guidelines and beliefs common to curriculum in all of the various subject areas on which the project has been working. A fundamental belief is that physical concepts can be and often are best learned in a laboratory setting. The curriculum is heavily based on research and uses a guided discovery approach that makes use of student predictions, pays attention to student alternative understandings, supports peer learning, and provides opportunities for students to construct knowledge for themselves. Substantial use was made of the students own motion to teach kinematic concepts. (See Thornton, [9] for additional description of the curriculum and the motion detector.)

1.4 Student Understanding of Simple Kinematics

Early on we tested students' knowledge of simple concepts in kinematics and classical mechanics so that we could address difficulties in the laboratory e.g. [5]. Work by other researchers and our own teaching had made us aware of the standard alternative understandings and student difficulties. In spite of this knowledge we were not prepared for the large percentage of university students who seemed to have trouble with even the most basic qualitative concepts. To confirm our findings we decided to collect results from a larger sample of physics students. Because it is difficult to convince physics professors to give up any course time and to make evaluation less subjective, we decided to use short answer questions. From earlier work with students involving questions requiring written answers and the drawing of graphs we evolved a set of short answer questions that give a reasonable indication of students' basic knowledge about kinematics and its graphical representation. The questions were such that most university physics professors were sure that no more than 10% of their students would miss them. Most professors also agreed that students who could not answer questions

[5] Priscilla Laws, Director, Dickinson College, Carlisle PA 17013

such as these did not have a basic understanding of kinematics. In fact there was considerable concern that giving such questions was a waste of time and an insult to the intelligence of the students.

For this study the source of the data was actual college and university physics teaching laboratories of members of the Tools for Scientific Thinking Project. The student population was primarily students enrolled in introductory algebra or calculus-based physics courses. In general students were given two kinematics labs lasting between 2 and 3 hours. These labs replaced standard university laboratories. In one case, students were given one laboratory lasting only 1 hour and 15 minutes. The motion detector connected to an Apple II series computer was used with curricula designed to guide students to explore fundamental motion concepts. Additional characteristics of the curriculum are described above. Students worked in small groups (2 to 4 students). Homework related to the lab was assigned. The labs do not depend explicitly on knowledge gained in lectures or textbooks. The labs covered the position and velocity of moving objects well and introduced acceleration. The relationship between force and acceleration was not covered.

The following figures give some of the results of this study. All data presented here, pre and post-MBL were taken after students had had the usual kinematics lectures and (in most cases) had done the usual problems. (Other data from smaller student samples seem to show that there is no effect from lectures on how well students do in the labs. If the labs are done first, class discussions in smaller classes seem to indicate more interest and understanding.) Almost always the average error rates on a question are given. We wish to focus on areas of student difficulty. Error rates greater than 15% on simple conceptual questions such as these are probably cause for altering the curriculum.

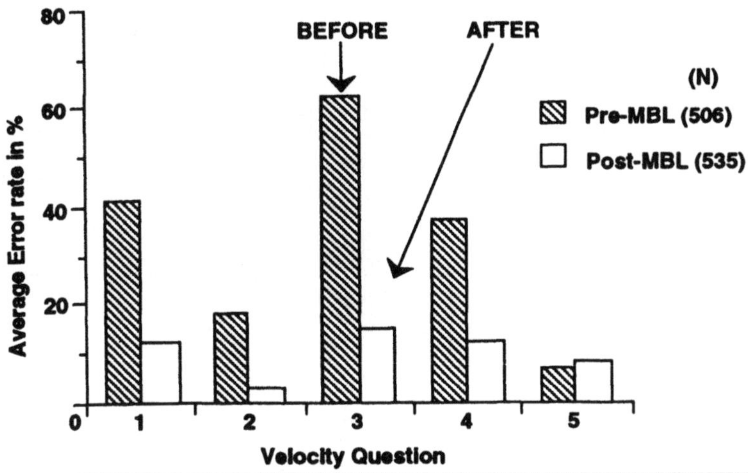

Fig.12.1. Weighted Average Error BEFORE and AFTER MBL (all after Lectures)

The dark bars in figure 12.1 show the weighted average error rate for 506 physics students from four different universities who answered the simple questions shown in figure 12.4. The large error rates are even more surprising since these students had recently heard the standard kinematics lectures and worked the problems associated with them. figure 12.2 shows the error rates for the questions above for each of the 6 student populations making up the weighted average. The pattern is remarkably stable across different student populations.

The large error rates associated with questions 1 and 3 are not the result of the wrong choice of "sign" which only accounts for a few percent of the answers. The most common error is the choice of the "distance analog" graphs A and B. Such a choice is not always made consistently by the students as the different error rates for questions 1 and 3 show.

The error rates for the same five questions after one or two MBL motion laboratories are shown in figure 12.1 as the white bars. Note that the pre and post-MBL populations are not identical. The six different populations making up the post-MBL results are shown in figure 12.3. The pre-MBL sample is 45% physics-with-calculus students while the post-MBL sample is only 28% physics-with-calculus students. Calculus students do better than non-calculus students on the pretest but the effect is only about + or - 10% from the average error rate. Post-test results are much closer. In addition, the 52 Tufts students included in the post-MBL sample were in a "Physics for Humanists" science course which did not generally emphasize kinematics. Their MBL lab exposure was only one short lab (about 70 minutes). No pre-test was given because most students had not had physics and many could not read graphs (see [8,9] for more information). The post-MBL data also include two different post-tests on the Oregon students-one of which is delayed (the mid-term). Either one can be removed without greatly changing the weighted averages shown in figure 12.1 These Oregon data will be examined more closely in what follows.

Smaller sample studies have shown that post-tests given as part of the homework produce essentially the same results as post-tests given in class for the kind of question above. In general the students do slightly better when the post-test is given in class which is the reverse of what we would have predicted. Smaller sample studies also show that students who are given the same questions for a pre-test and post-test do not do better than students given only the post-test.

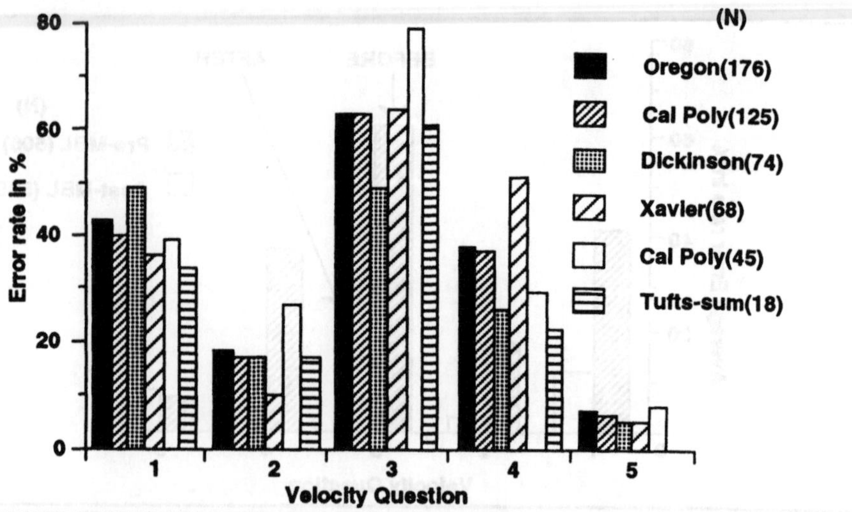

Fig.12.2. Error rate BEFORE MBL but after Kinematics Lectures

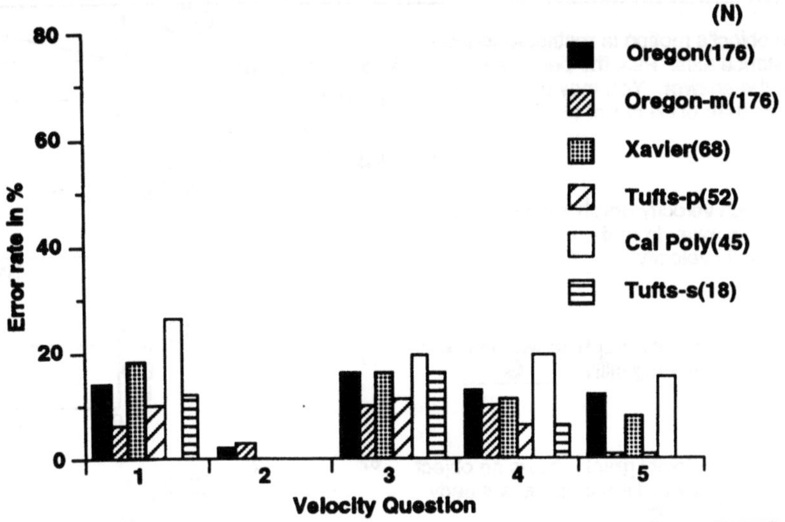

Fig.12.3. Error rate AFTER MBL and after Kinematics Lectures

Questions 1 through 5 (shown in fig 12.4) are the questions referred to in figures 12.1-12.3. The order of the questions and the graphs were sometimes changed.

2. The Oregon Kinematics Results

Thanks to Professor David Sokoloff we were able to do more intensive studies with students at the University of Oregon. Figure 12.5 (overleaf) shows the results on these questions for 172 Oregon students (36% were enrolled in a physics with calculus course (the text was the first edition of Tipler) and 64% in an algebra-based course (Sears, Zemansky and Young-- College Physics, 6th Edition). All students had finished kinematics when they took the pre-MBL test. The students were given two labs using the motion detector, with correlated homework questions. The labs primarily concentrated on the distance and velocity of moving objects including the students' own bodies. Acceleration was introduced but not as systematically. The post-MBL questions were given as part of the homework which was graded and returned. (Answers, however, were not posted.)

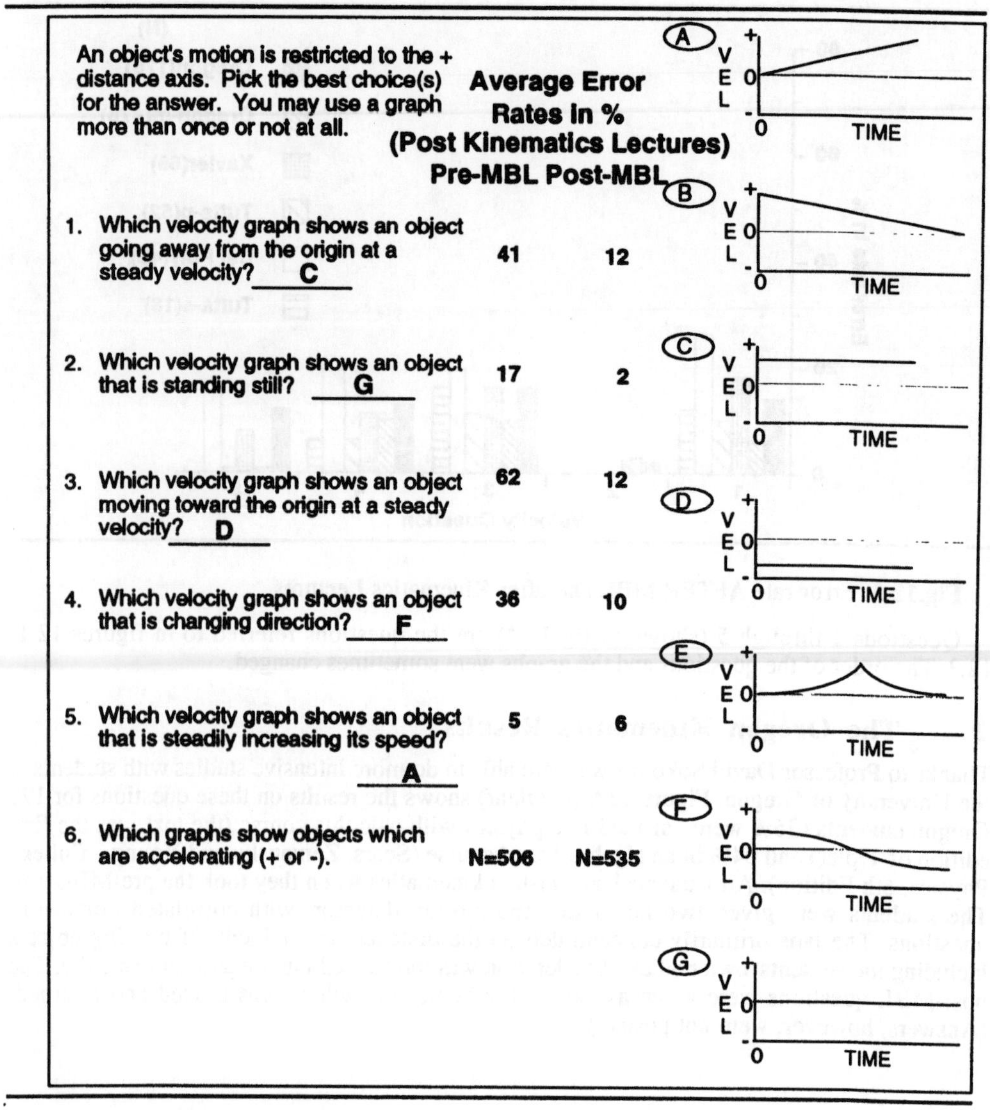

Fig.12.4. Velocity time graphs

About three weeks later, the same questions, rearranged, were given as part of the mid-term. The results of this delayed-post test are also shown in figure 12.5. The results would seem to indicate that the homework helped them to understand kinematics. Is it possible that students have "memorized" the questions after seeing them twice before? Evidence was mentioned earlier that giving a pre-test does not help students get better scores on a post-test. The rearrangement of the questions would prevent strict memorization. The students also did as well on other, different, questions, making memorization even less likely to account for the improvement. Therefore, it seems more likely that they now understand these simple concepts.

We were able to give the first four questions (again rearranged) to a small sample of noncalculus students (37) as part of their final exam at the end of the term. The results, shown also in figure 12.5, seem to indicate that their understanding is retained over a substantial period of time.

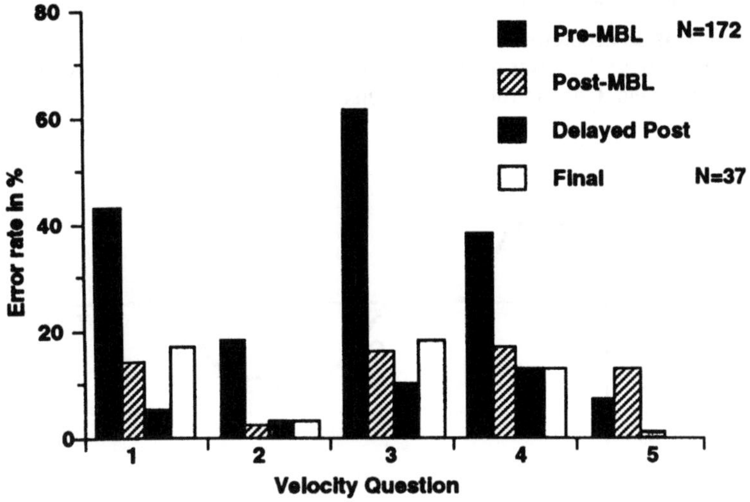

Fig.12.5. Oregon - Velocity Error Rates

Questions on acceleration were asked even though acceleration was only introduced and not as systematically covered in the labs. Some results are shown in figure 12.6.

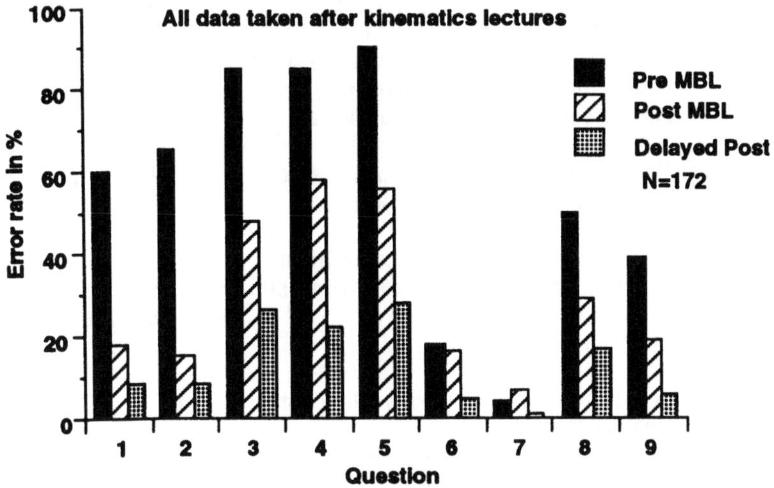

Fig.12.6. Oregon - Error Rate on Acceleration Questions

The questions follow
University of Oregon-176 students (36% calculus, 64% non-calculus All data taken after students completed lectures in kinematics.

Acceleration-Time Graphs

The graph below is an acceleration-time graph for a car, the motion of which is restricted to the + distance axis. Choose the letter of the section of the graph which could correspond to each of the following motions. Choose the one best answer. If you think that none correspond, write N.

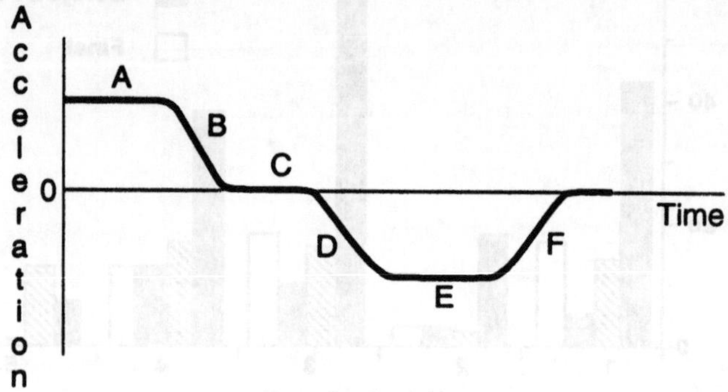

Correct Answer			Error Rates in % Pre-MBL	Post-MBL	Delayed Post
A	1.	The car could be speeding up at a steady rate, moving away from the origin.	59	16	7
C	2.	The car could be moving at a constant speed away from the origin.	63	14	7
E	3.	The car could be slowing down at a steady rate, moving away from the origin.	84	47	25
C	4.	The car could be moving at a constant speed toward the origin.	84	56	21
E	5.	The car could be speeding up at a steady rate, moving toward the origin.	90	54	25

Acceleration

Consider the acceleration in each of the following situations. For each of the following descriptions of the motion of an object, write a "+", "-" or "O" in the space to indicate that the acceleration is positive, negative or zero.

-	6.	A car is moving in the positive direction and comes to rest.	19	17	4
+	7.	A car starts from rest and begins to move in the positive direction.	3	5	2
+	8.	A car is moving in the negative direction and comes to rest.	51	27	15
-	9.	A car starts from rest and begins to move in the negative direction.	38	18	10

2.1 Comparison of Students Who Had MBL Laboratories to Those Who Did Not.

Figure 12.7 shows the student error rates for 11 questions on the final exam for 90 students who attended the same lecture session of the algebra-based physics course. The 53 students who did not do the two MBL kinematics laboratories had substantially higher error rates. The lectures were the same for all students. The table below summarizes the average error rates for each category of question.

Average Error Rates for Students in the Algebra-based Physics Course

Topic	Questions	with MBL	without MBL
Velocity	1,3,4	13%	39%
Acceleration	5-9	36%	56%
Force	10,11	55%	55%

The "with MBL" results are quite consistent with the coverage of the MBL laboratories. The MBL labs covered distance and velocity well; introduced, but did not emphasize, acceleration, and did not cover the relationship between force and acceleration. The four velocity questions were selected from the ones described earlier. The error rates of the "MBL" students increased a few percent compared to the delayed post-test, but retention over the two month period is very high. The error rates for the "no MBL" students are unfortunately consistent with the pre-MBL error rates taken earlier in the course, except that the students apparently did learn through the standard treatment to recognize the velocity graph of an object standing still (question 2). Questions 5 through 11 are shown below in figure 12.8. No students had seen these exact questions previously.

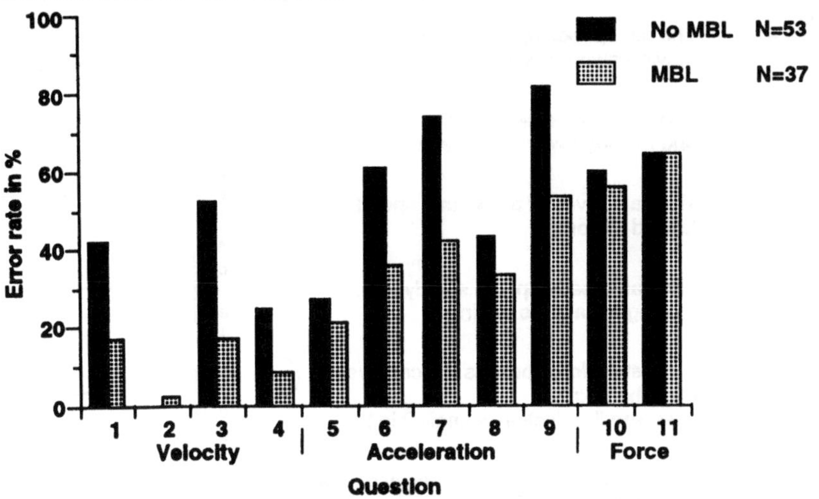

Fig.12.7. Oregon -- Final Exam -- Non-Calculus

2.2 Is MBL Software Pedagogically Successful?

There has been considerable discussion about whether computer-based learning offers substantial advantages over any other method. There has been very little evidence in the literature of pedagogically successful software. Is there a sense in which the MBL software discussed in this paper could be considered pedagogically successful? This paper has shown evidence for substantial persistent learning of very basic physical concepts by students using a particular set of curricular materials. These same simple physical concepts were not learned by large numbers of students when they listened to "good" traditional physics lectures, read respected textbooks, and did the traditional algorithmic problems at the end of the chapters. The laboratory curriculum used by these students was made possible (or at least practical) by the use of a microcomputer-based motion tool which used the power of the computer to allow students to see actual measurements of physical phenomena displayed in real-time as graphs. The immediate coupling of the graphs to the physical phenomena seems to lead the students not only to understand graphing as a useful scientific symbol system but also to aid their understanding of the physical concepts when they are guided to examine appropriate phenomena. What happens when beginning students use MBL tools to do more or less traditional physics experiments? The students are pleased, they may do additional exploration, and they do a better job in general. Preliminary evidence show that they do not, however, learn fundamental physical concepts unless the means of teaching them are structured into the experiments. We can certainly say that the MBL software and hardware tools are pedagogically successful for teaching such physical concepts when used in combination with appropriate curricular materials.

Questions 5-11 refer to the motion of a toy car which is restricted to the + distance axis. Choose the letter of the one correct acceleration vs. time graph which could correspond to the motion of the car described in each of the following. If you think that the name is correct, answer N. You may use a graph more than once.

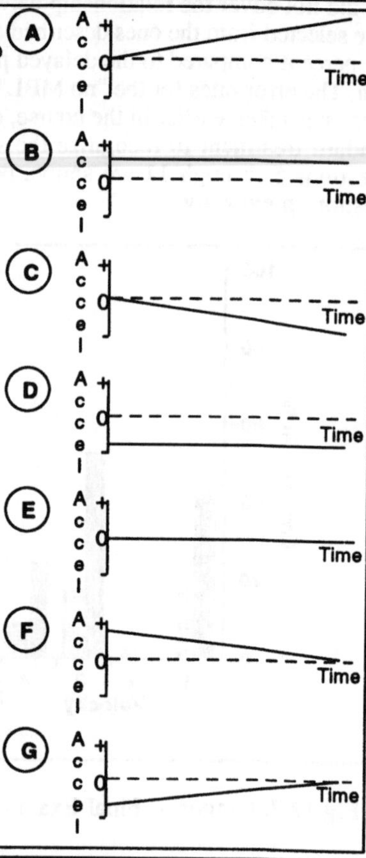

__E__ 5. The car moves at a constant speed away from the origin.

__B__ 6. The car speeds up at a steady rate, moving away from the origin.

__D__ 7. The car slows down at a steady rate, and moving away from the origin.

__E__ 8. The car moves at a constant speed toward the origin.

__D__ 9. The car speeds up at a steady rate, moving toward the origin.

__B__ 10. A constant force pushes the car away from the origin. (Assume that friction is negligible.)

__E__ 11. The car was given a push, released and now moves away from the origin. Which graph corresponds to the car's acceleration after it was released? (Assume that friction is negligible.)

Fig.12.8. Questions 5-11 Given to All Students on the Final Exam

References

1. Arons, Arnold. *Achieving wider scientific literacy*. Daedalus. 112, No. 2, pp. 91-122. 1983.
2. Halloun, I. A. & Hestenes, D. Common sense concepts about motion. *American Journal of Physics,* 53: 1056. 1985a.
3. Halloun, I. A. & Hestenes, D. The initial knowledge state of college physics students. *American Journal of Physics,* 53:1043. 1985b.
4. Laws, Priscilla. *Workshop physics--replacing lectures with real experience.* Dickenson College, PA 1988.
5. McDermott, L.C. Research on conceptual understanding in mechanics. *Physics Today,* 37, N 7, p. 24. 1984.
6. McDermott, L.C., Rosenquist, M.L., & van Zee, E.H. Instructional strategies to improve the performance of minority students in the sciences. *New Directions for Teaching and Learning* 16. 1983.
7. Peters, P.C. Even honours students have conceptual difficulties with physics. *American Journal of Physics,* 50:501. 1985.
8. Thornton, R.K. Access to college science: microcomputer- based laboratories for the naive science learner. *Collegiate Microcomputer,* V. No. 1, February, 1987 1986.
9. Thornton, R. K. Tools for scientific thinking: microcomputer-based laboratories for physics teaching. *Physics Education.* 22:230. 1987.

13

Constructing Student Knowledge in Science[1]

Robert F. Tinker
Technology Center
The Technical Education Research Centers, Inc.
1696 Massachusetts Ave., Cambridge, MA 02138
U.S.A.

Ronald K. Thornton
Center for Science and Mathematics Teaching
Lincoln-Filene Building
Tufts University
Medford, MA 02155
U.S.A.

Abstract: A drift towards increased content expressed in texts and tests, driven by the growth of science and a demand for results and measurable progress, has trivialized science education. Three technologies are suggested to address this problem.

Keywords: Boxer, collaboration, collaborative science, constructionism, constructivism, constructivist curriculum, constructivist educational strategies, creativity, databases, factual knowledge, graphs, kinematics, MBL tools, microcomputer-based laboratory, microcomputer-based labs, microworlds, modelling, physics, probe, science education, science misconceptions, science teaching, seismology, sensor, simulation, spreadsheets, STELLA, telecommunications, TERC, transducers

---

[1] This work was supported in part by grants from the National Science Foundation grants DPE-8317155, MDR-8550373, and MDR-8652120 to TERC, the Fund for the Improvement of Post-Secondary Education(FIPSE) through the Tools for Scientific Thinking Project at Tufts University, the Board of Regents of Massachusetts, and donations from Apple Computer, Inc. The findings and opinions reported here are those of the authors and do not necessarily reflect the views the funding agencies.

1. Introduction

The Educational Crisis

Numerous indicators have signalled that math and science education in the United States are in serious trouble. The dual problems of poor student performance and lack of well-qualified faculty have been documented in many studies over the last five years [9]. The evidence strongly indicates that something is basically wrong with mathematics and science instruction in today's schools. Most students have fundamental science misconceptions which remain unchanged by instruction [4,8,12,26]. Many teachers are unaware of these problems and attempt to teach concepts that are far above their students' level [7,11,22,24,26]. The performance level of many high school and college students is very low–they often cannot interpret graphs and cannot solve simple ninth grade algebra problems, even after passing courses "covering" this material. If students have failed to acquire the rudiments of math and science from earlier courses on these topics, then additional or advanced instruction, if continued in the same mode, will also fail to improve the performance of the vast majority of students. "For young people who have not fared well in school, a regimen of 'more of the same' may result in less learning" [6]. As long as teachers subscribe to the educational philosophy that science is a collection of facts to be memorized, there is too much to teach and too little time to teach it. If teachers plan a curriculum by merely making a list of the key vocabulary and the few critical classes of problems that they want students to learn, they will find there is already far too much content for the usual time allocated. The usual course is a rushed survey of facts and formulas that lead very few students to any understanding of science. Texts which cover so many topics and the standardized tests which measure a breadth of factual knowledge at the expense of process skills and deeper understanding, all create an almost irresistible pressure on teachers to cram more topics into courses. This results in a facts-and-formula approach to teaching, one which not only fails to convey the more human side of science, but which often gives students limited and negative views of science. For example, students learn that trajectory problems use a particular group of equations, and some students learn to manipulate these equations but most of these students have little understanding of the connection of these equations to the physical world or the importance of Newtonian mechanics as a world view. Fewer still have had any time to think about the implications of Newtonian determinism and its usefulness, or lack thereof, in describing the world around them. Even students who do well with algorithmic manipulation report that they really do not understand why or what they are doing, and hence come away with a sense that they are not interested in science, or perhaps are unsuited for it.

Most teachers agree that there should be more to a science course than vocabulary and a series of problem types; that it would be better for students to get a sense of what it is like to be a scientist; that they need some laboratory experience in addition to reading a textbook. Some smaller number of teachers would also agree that students ought to have a sense of the social and ethical issues raised by science and an idea of the history and culture of science. We would add that, most importantly, as the amount of scientific knowledge explodes and the fraction of science content that can be taught in any course shrinks, students should learn how to learn. But these "soft" topics are hard to quantify and measure, and really will not help the students on the usual exams so they are usually consigned to benign neglect. Thus, the vast bulk of science instruction proceeds with facts and formula courses only superficially altered from generation to generation because that is what everybody else is teaching, that is what the texts offer, that is what the tests measure, that is what defines the prerequisites to the next course. There is almost no pressure to alter the textbooks because no textbook publisher can afford to leave out a topic that might be important to someone and the books must cover all the facts on the standardized tests.

While there is debate on the source of the larger social forces that are at the root of the present practice in science education, there is widespread agreement that the proximal problem is that **students are not being actively engaged in learning**. They passively listen to lectures, skim huge, poorly written texts and have decreasing access to laboratory experiences. Because learning is an active process that requires attention, active participation, communication, inquiry and thought, it is not surprising that these trends have resulted in poorer student performance. Learning science, like the conduct of science itself, must be active.

2. Constructivism

> I'm convinced that one could develop a marvellous method of participatory education giving a child the apparatus to do experiments and thus discover a lot of things by himself...For me education means making creators.... Piaget quoted in [3]

While dominant educational practices have followed from a view of knowledge which defines knowledge as a set of unchanging facts about the world, modern science has contributed to a shift in the way knowledge itself is viewed. We have come to understand that knowledge is not absolute, that the knower is part of the known, and that knowledge is what knowers make of their world through the questions they ask and the means of inquiry that they use to answer them. From this perspective, it is impossible to consider knowledge in any area without considering the activities and processes of the knower. And it is impossible to obtain knowledge without being actively involved in its construction.

A constructivist perspective posits that students learn best through active engagement in their own studies in an environment that encourages them to construct and communicate their own knowledge and understandings. Such a perspective precludes the use of the facts-and-formula approach to learning science. Students who are thoroughly engaged in original projects, having selected the topic, decided on the approach, performed the research, drawn the conclusions, and communicated the results, are *doing* science. They are seeing science not as a noun, an object consisting of facts and formulas, but as a verb, a process, a set of activities, a way of proceeding and thinking. Thus, a constructivist educational framework is not only good pedagogy, but good science. It can convey not only the content of science but its process. In this model, students' communication with peers, teachers, and collaborators about their work and about the process of learning itself is an indispensable part of the learning experience.

Technology in the Service of Constructivist Educational Practice

There has been considerable recent work that indicates how new educational technologies, including innovative uses of the microcomputer and telecommunication networks, can serve a constructivist approach in science education. Papert [17] describes a constructivist educational theory and an instructional strategy, which he labels *constructionism*, that emphasizes technology used to support student project work, creativity, autonomy and communication. He suggests a vision of how school could be better, and of how technology could be used to facilitate the improvement of science education.

Initial applications of computers focused on technology as in the more rote and mechanical aspects of learning. The new vision focuses on using technology to support excellence in learning. In this vision, students would tackle much harder problems, they would work on larger-scale, more meaningful projects, they would have a greater and more reflective responsibility for their own learning and they would be able to work in a variety of styles whose differences reflect gender, ethnicity or simply individual personality. Much of the earlier thinking saw the computer as replacing at least some of the functions of the teacher. The new vision sees the technology as supporting excellence in teaching; it seeks enhancement–not replacement–of the support teachers offer learners [16,21].

3. Software and Hardware Tools That Enable

Technology by itself cannot correct the serious trouble in which science education finds itself, but it can be an indispensable part of a constructivist solution.

The vast majority of software designed for science education supports facts-and-figures instruction. Such software is relatively easy to create, easy to find, and easy to integrate into instruction. There is a role for software that supports fact-and-formula science, just as there is a role for fact-and-formula science. Simulations, tutorials, drill-and-practice, when well-constructed, do work. They lead to improvements in student performance, and some efficiencies in classroom management.

If we seem to lack enthusiasm for this class of software, it is because the path to substantially better science education, as we suggested above, will not be found by trying to improve facts-and-formula instruction. The appropriate use of technology from our point of view are those uses that enables active student construction of knowledge, not drill. The technology that best supports such learning is tool-like, because tools are general, powerful, flexible, and easily used. The most effective use of constructivist software tools is to engage students in projects with the maximum feasible student independence and ownership of these projects.

Technology has something to offer for every aspect of constructivist student activities; it can expand the range of possible projects, offer new opportunities for collaboration and communication, simplify acquiring and displaying data, provide mechanisms to control experiments, increase the sophistication of the theory-building, modelling and data analysis, provide new outlets for creative expression, and grant access to vast databases of information. Without the technology, practical issues of classroom management and limitations in the scope of potential student projects make student-centered activities difficult to offer and sustain. Technology gives students a wide range of tools they can apply to their investigations, and new collaborators via electronic networks with whom to communicate and learn. Furthermore, teachers' imagination and background can be stimulated and expanded with mentors and collaborators on networks.

The constructivist approach to education is not fundamentally new, but the advent of inexpensive microcomputers and telecommunications adds new power to the approach, allowing the use of better learning strategies while simplifying their implementation. The technologies that offer such promise involve a few tools that are easily mastered by students and teachers:

— Communication tools. Word processors and telecommunications packages, preferably integrated to combine writing, reading, data-base searching, and electronic communication. This combination is easily the most important set of tools for academic and business research and communications, and represents the most accessible tools for students.

— Interface tools. The computer is a powerful aide for investigations when interfaced so that it can control and measure the environment. Microcomputer-based labs (MBL) and interfaces to mechanical systems like LEGO/Logo and the Capsela IR link allow students to record easily a wide range of phenomena and control the conditions under which these measurements are made.

— Theory-building tools. Spreadsheets, graphing and data-display utilities, microworlds and modelling environments are computer-based computational tools that increase students' ability to create and understand theories. This ability greatly enhances the potential learning that can be derived from student projects.

— Creativity tools. Word processors, video interfaces, music and graphics tools, and hypermedia all give students new ways to express themselves. Enhancing student communication, an essential part of the constructivist model.

— Database tools. Telecommunications packages, CD ROMs, and videodisks all give students access to unprecedented volumes of information. Hypermedia tools make that access easier and more responsive to student investigations.
— Programming tools. Programming languages continue to be important because they give students the greatest control of computers, putting that resource at their disposal in service of student-originated activities. It is important to note that programming options are just below the surface in powerful applications like HyperCard, many word processors, and more advanced databases. As a result, programming concepts are increasingly important.

While many of these tools are available on the microcomputers found in schools, their systematic use to empower students has not been widely explored nor followed to the conclusions that will inevitably alter and expand the curriculum.

Technology-enhanced, constructivist educational strategies based on these tools have many practical advantages. They are:

— Adaptable. Learners with different styles and abilities work comfortably together on projects and long-term activities.
— Interdisciplinary. Projects often require input from a variety of technical fields, use many forms of communication, and profit from the creative arts.
— Integrative. Students see how disciplinary studies fit together to solve problems and address issues.
— Pre-professional. Constructivist activities and their use of technology tend to mirror those of the adult world and thus give students an unusually accurate view of the professions.
— Motivational. Activities selected by students and pursued in depth can be extremely interesting for students and can call on skills and motivation that standard classroom instruction leaves untapped.
— Effective. Constructed knowledge that comes from self-selected topics or self-directed inquiry has unusual staying power.
— Efficient. The proposed use of technology offers the greatest chance for major improvements in learning "efficiency" using a definition that honours the amount of deep learning and problem solving skills students acquire.
— Implementation ease. The small number of tools makes them easier to purchase, distribute, support and learn to use. Because these tools are available for all computers, one is freed from the need to support one family of hardware.

In the sections that follow, three examples of constructivist tool use will be presented in detail.

4. Some Examples of Technology in the Service of Science Learning

Microcomputer Based Labs

An approach TERC has termed microcomputer-based labs, or MBL, converts a microcomputer equipped with a small collection of transducers and general-purpose software into a universal laboratory instrument.

Educational Use of Computer Interfaces

While the computer is seen as an indispensable lab tool in science research, it has taken years of persuasion, first by TERC and then many other innovators, to get educators to see the advantages of using the computer in the teaching laboratory. Variously known as "microcomputer-based labs," "MBL," "probeware," or "laboratory aids," these computer applications are beginning to be seen as a valuable part of science education.

Microcomputer-based labs–the use of microcomputers for student-directed data acquisition, display, and analysis-represent one of the most promising new developments in science instruction enabled by emerging technologies. With appropriate hardware and software, the microcomputer-based laboratory gives students unprecedented power to explore, measure, and learn from the material environment. This power enables the earlier and more thorough treatment of science topics while also fostering science process goals. Constructivist use of MBL has shown the way to substantially reorganized and revitalized science curricula in which much more science was covered much earlier in ways that increased both content learning and an appreciation of the process of science.

Educational Importance of MBL

MBL eases many of the problems that inhibit the more widespread use of laboratory for science learning. The computer can be used to present the measured data in meaningful way while it is being collected and to speed the computations while leaving students the choice of data to collect and which computations to employ. With its general measurement techniques, MBL tools eliminate the need for special-purpose, inflexible and expensive apparatus and enhance the range of student choice. Because MBL tools reduce the time spent on calculations, making more time is available for "messing around" and experimenting. One can now give students a flexible instrument that was only a dream a few years ago; an instrument that can measure force, light, pressure, temperature, heart rate, speed, acceleration, response time, brain waves, muscle signals, and many, many other phenomena in the world about us. These measurements can be performed by powerful, general-purpose software that speeds analysis and provides real-time feedback. MBL can make meaningful science instruction possible earlier and at a much more profound level than many educators would have believed possible.

MBL Can Be a Natural Extension of the Senses

One of the important advantages of MBL to the student, particularly the very young student, is its ability to connect abstract measurements directly to concrete actions that are available to the students direct sensory perception. For example, by simply giving students a sensor that measures temperature and immediately graphs it as a function of time on the screen, even very young students can, within minutes, learn how to control the temperature recorded, how to generate interesting graphs of temperature against time, and how to interpret those graphs. What is going on is that these students are "calibrating" what they see on the screen against their own sensory perceptions of temperature. They immediately learn that there is a close similarity between what they sense is hot and what causes the graph to rise.

Almost as quickly as they learn to understand the data from the temperature probe, students encounter situations where something seems to go wrong. In attempting to heat the probe, they put it in a glove which they assume is hot. The probe does not seem to record properly and yet they quickly can test whether something is wrong by touching the tip of the probe and seeing the temperature rise again. Why aren't gloves hot? Immediately important scientific question are raised which can lead to further investigation and learning. In fact, one of the more interesting aspects of the use of MBL in classrooms is the number of "what if..." questions stimulated. Students begin–without prompting, without long lectures about the scientific method–to apply their common sense to elucidate the phenomena they observe. That is the essence of science and we see science happening at a phenomenal rate when students have access microcomputer-based laboratory instrumentation.

Making a Computer into a Laboratory Instrument

With the addition of interface electronics, even the simplest computer can be used to gather and analyze data. The interface consists of transducers, analog circuits, and analog-to-digital converters. The transducer detects some physical input and converts it to an electric analog signal. This signal is then processed by analog circuitry to produce a signal that is convenient for the next component. This signal is finally converted by an analog-to-digital converter into a digital signal, which the computer can then use. The computer stores these data in memory and can process them just as any other numbers can be processed. The computer can control all aspects of the data-gathering process including its initiation and timing. With suitable transducers, the data gathered can represent force, pressure, time, temperature, light level, humidity, air flow, water flow, position, velocity, acceleration, and much more.

The computer with a laboratory interface is a powerful and flexible instrument. Using a graphical output to display results that it has accumulated, it becomes a storage oscilloscope. Using the timing capabilities that are inherent in all computers, it can be a timer that measures the time between external events, or a frequency counter that counts the number of external events in a fixed period of time. By simply displaying the voltages and currents that it senses, it becomes an ammeter or a voltmeter.

Because these functions are realized as part of a single instrument, they can be combined to create versatile measurement and control systems. Data gathered can also be transformed by the computer to generate displays that are more meaningful and easier to interpret than outputs from conventional instruments. Students do not need to know anything about computers to use MBL tools because menu-driven software can make the use of the tool self-explanatory.

MBL hardware and software for use in teaching can be constructed from common parts, from kits, or purchased. MBL is increasingly available commercially, although there is a wide range of performance and cost, and no single system yet combines the power and flexibility that is possible. The Northwest Regional Laboratory produced a good review of MBL and developed useful criteria for its evaluation. TERC provides current information about MBL material and workshops.

Misconceptions Concerning MBL

A computer used with laboratory instruments is sometimes described as "emulating" or "simulating" instrumentation. This terminology is misleading since it seems to imply that the computer is not *really* the instrument. It is easy to confuse this description with the idea of a simulated laboratory, where experiments are not actually performed but rather are simulated with software. It is more accurate to say that the computer with MBL hardware and software is just as real an instrument as an oscilloscope or light meter.

More thoughtful critics have criticized MBL as automating the lab and consequently stifling student thought and initiative. This is a danger posed not by MBL itself, but by its implementation. Like any technology, MBL creates options, and one option is complete automation. One can imagine a parody of MBL in which students would turn on the computer and watch it pick up a ball, drop it, measure the distance and time, compute the acceleration of gravity and print out the result. One can imagine a similar technology configured as a general-purpose photogate counter and timer that would be used in many student explorations of motion, among them falling balls. These two approaches to the same technology and educational goals would have completely different educational outcomes that can be traced to differences in educational theory, not to MBL. This is why it is important to stress a constructivist approach to choose among the options technology offers.

Features of Constructivist MBL Applications

A good implementation of MBL supports constructivist applications by being a flexible and responsive tool. A crescent wrench is a good model for MBL tools. This is the adjustable wrench that has a knurled worm gear near its movable jaw. Its operation is obvious and simple; the knurling invites finger adjustment of the jaw opening. Designed for tightening and loosening nuts, it can also be used as a hammer, bottle top opener and window prop. It can be used by young and old, learning-disabled and Nobel prize winners, for both simple and sophisticated jobs. There is no instruction manual packed with it and there is no right or wrong use of it. It is relatively unobtrusive and rarely the focus of much attention. And, while it helps remove nuts, it certainly does not remove them automatically. The choice to use it, its setting and manipulation require thought and planning by the user.

There are several performance characteristics of microcomputer-based laboratory instruments that make them useful tools analogous to the Crescent wrench:

— **Ease of Control**. MBL instruments can be designed for easy control by students. Prompts, menus, explanations, and dialogs should be used to help students easily control the instrument so that their attention can be focused on the scientific investigation.
— **Intelligent Operation**. Some basic operation should be possible as soon as the application is started. The software should respond intelligently to the probes and actuators selected.
— **Fast Response**. Data must be collected, stored and displayed in real time in a convenient and obvious format so students can easily comprehend the result of any action or change.
— **Display Flexibility**. Outputs should be available in many forms: tables, graphs, histograms, or three-dimensional projections.
— **Modularity**. Both the hardware and software should adhere to a set of standards and conventions so that the same ideas and the same equipment can be used in many different applications.

Research on MBL

The capabilities of MBL have broad applications to science teaching. To begin to explore the implications of these capabilities, Tinker and Barclay [25] initiated a series of clinical classroom trials of MBL in the fall of 1980. The primary goal of this work was to determine whether elementary and junior high school students could use MBL, and whether its use could facilitate cognitive development in science. Additional goals were to develop instructional strategies adapted to the capacity of MBL and to observe whether there were any sex-based preferences for this approach.

The results of the exploratory research were quite encouraging. Students in grades four through eight were able to understand MBL and use it to understand scientific phenomena. The students demonstrated a keen interest in the experiments; the participating teachers were impressed with the ease of students mastery of the technology and the richness of the learning that ensured. Students were attracted to the equipment, quickly and naturally learning to control it through play and exploration. With guidance, these explorations stimulated an enormous number of questions which, in turn, led to both discussions and further exploration. No sex bias in student preference, use, or learning was detected.

Since that initial research, numerous studies have increased our understanding of MBL and its educational value. MBL applications have been carefully studied in classrooms. Qualitative observations confirm that by reducing the time and effort required by repetitive operations and calculations, MBL helps student understand the relation between phenomena and their representations [27]. Quantitative studies have also confirmed the value of MBL. In a series of extended studies at many high schools and colleges, physics students showed significant increases in understanding classical mechanics and thermodynamics as a result of short exposures to MBL [22-24]. More detail on these studies and their results are given below.

One strand of educational MBL research has focused on graphs, since many MBL applications use graphs as the primary output display. Because it is well known that most entering college freshmen have difficulty interpreting graphs even if they can produce them, questions were raised about starting at the 4th grade with MBL applications which used graphs. It turned out that, because of the dynamic nature of real-time applications, students learned the conventions of graphing very quickly in MBL applications, and, as a consequence, easily learned how to interpret graphs. Research [2] has shown that high school physics students' graph comprehension went up measurably in one forty-minute exposure to the HRM Motion Unit. The result depended on the real-time nature of the display—neither software with a twenty second delay nor non-computer activities resulted in measurable learning. This research indicates that graph production and graph interpretation are separate skills and illustrates how conventional instruction focussing on graph production fails to teach comprehension.

We are nearing a time when students could have a shoe box filled with a few dozen transducers that could measure a very wide range of physical phenomena. One or more of these could be plugged into a universal interface and be recognized by a single, powerful software package that would combine all the features of an expensive storage oscilloscope, function generator, pulse analyzer and a rack full of other electronics. This would provide the ideal environment for student-initiated projects.

Using MBL to Enhance Student Conceptual Learning in Physics

It is difficult to affect any change in the way students are taught because it is always easier and much less risky to continue using accepted methods. Demonstrating that any particular way of teaching a subject or a topic is ineffective may be the first necessary step to change but it is only a small step. A much more difficult next step is to demonstrate an acceptable, effective way of teaching the material. Beyond these initial steps to educational change are many more. It is now possible to take the first two steps within a limited number of topics in physics. The following discussion is designed to show that a constructivist use of currently available MBL tools and curricula provide an effective means of teaching physical concepts, not ordinarily learned by a majority of students in lecture courses, to high school and college students. The curricula and tools described below have been used for a number of years by over thirty high schools and ten colleges and universities as part of the Tools for Scientific Thinking Project of the Center for Science and Mathematics Teaching described in the previous chapter by Thornton.

Students and professors are in general very enthusiastic about using MBL. Additional studies have shown that student learning persists at least to the end of the semester, that homework correlated with the laboratory work increases the learning, and that students do almost as well drawing the graphs as choosing among the given graphs. Smaller sample studies also show that students who are given the same questions for a pre-test and post-test do no better than students given only the post-test [23,24].

An object's motion is restricted to the + distance axis. Pick the best choice(s) for the answer. You may use a graph more than once or not at all.

	Average Error Rates in % (Post Kinematics Lectures) Pre-MBL	Post-MBL
1. Which velocity graph shows an object going away from the origin at a steady velocity? C	41	12
2. Which velocity graph shows an object that is standing still? G	17	2
3. Which velocity graph shows an object moving toward the origin at a steady velocity? D	62	12
4. Which velocity graph shows an object changing direction? F	36	10
5. Which velocity graph shows an object that is steadily increasing its speed? A	5	6
	N=506	N=535

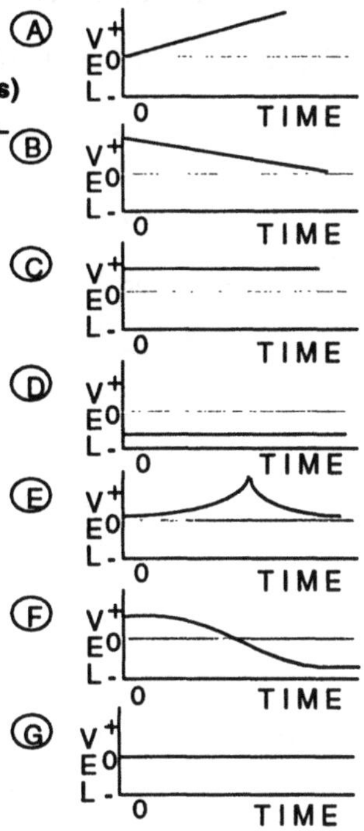

Fig.13.1. Velocity-time graphs

High School Kinematics Results

The data that follow are the result of using a very similar curriculum to that described in the previous chapter by Thornton with students in standard and honours physics courses at eight different Massachusetts high schools as part of project (primarily funded by the Massachusetts Board of Regents) at the Center for Science and Math Teaching. The five velocity questions are the ones shown in figure 13.1. Even though the pre-MBL error rates are higher, the post results are as good as those for university students. This particular sample of students did not have kinematics lectures.

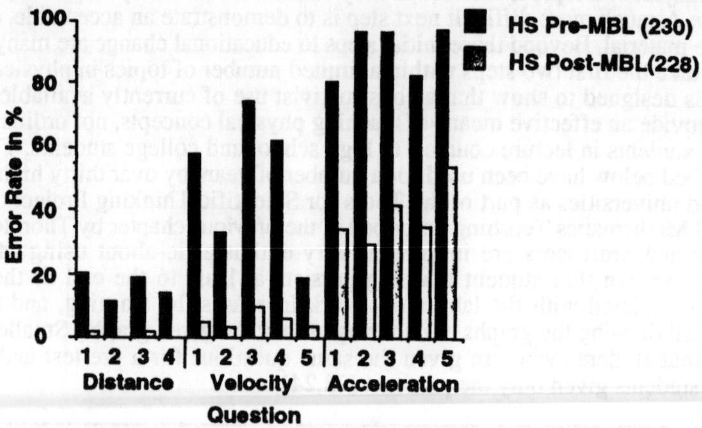

Fig.13.2. Massachusetts High Schools 1988 Motion Results

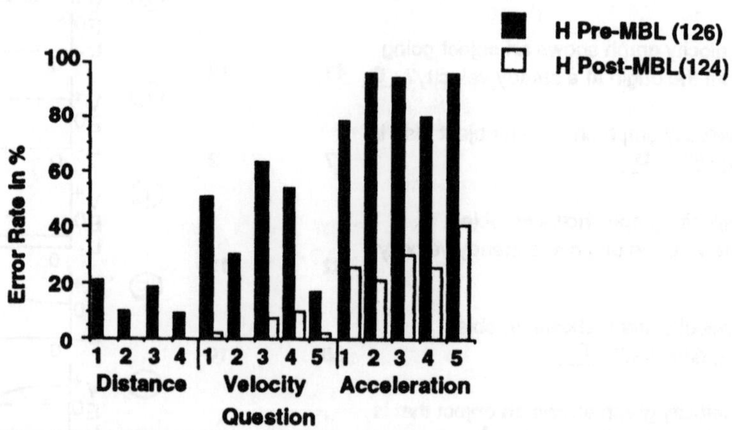

Fig.13.3. Massachusetts High Schools 1988 Kinematics -- Honors Classes

A toy car can move in either direction along the + distance axis. Choose the letter of the acceleration-time graph which could correspond to the motion of the car described in each of the following. You may use a graph more than once or not at all. If you think that none is correct, answer J.

__1. The car moves away from the origin at a constant velocity.

__2. The car moves away from the origin, speeding up at a steady rate.

__3. The car moves away from the origin, slowing down at a steady rate.

__4. The car moves toward the origin at a constant velocity.

__5. The car moves toward the origin, speeding up at a steady rate.

__6. A constant force pushes the car away from the origin. (Assume that friction is negligible.)

__7. The car was given a push, released and now moves away from the origin. Which graph corresponds to the car's acceleration after it was released? (Assume that friction is negligible.)

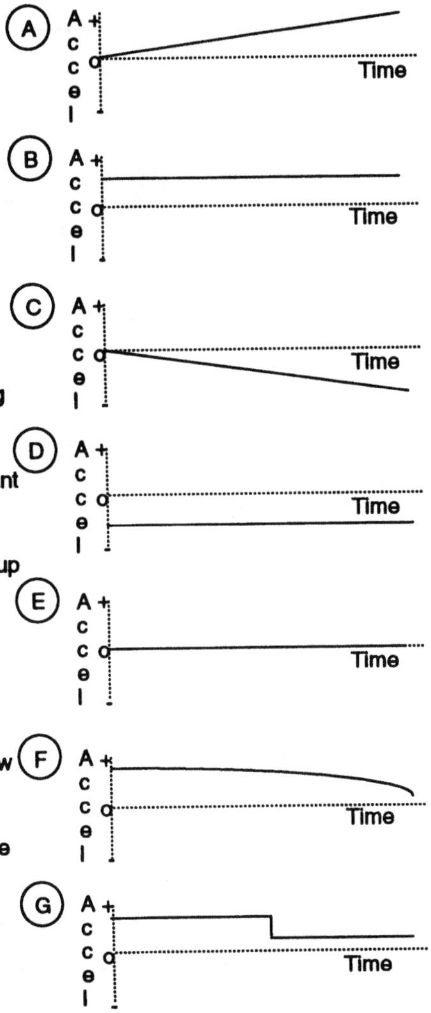

Fig.13.4. Acceleration time graphs

Previous data show that lectures in kinematics have almost no effect on student understanding of these fundamental motion concepts at the high school level (figure 13.5). Similar results are found at the university level. The use of MBL tools and curricula in a laboratory setting with correlated homework and class discussion leads to the large changes in learning shown above.

Essentially all students understand distance and velocity concepts after this work. The acceleration questions are particularly difficult but the error rates drop from about 90% to 35%. Students in honours classes do even better (figure 13.3). The acceleration questions are the first five questions shown in figure 13.4.

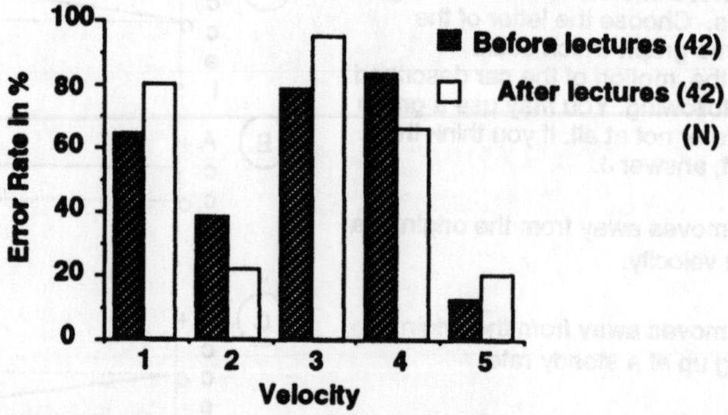

Fig.13.5. High School Before and After Motion Lectures.

A comparison of the of the high school results with those of students taking a non-calculus physics course at Tufts University show that the high school students who have used MBL understand the concepts better than college students after lectures (figures 13.6, Pre-MBL data) and almost as well as non-calculus physics college students after MBL and lectures.

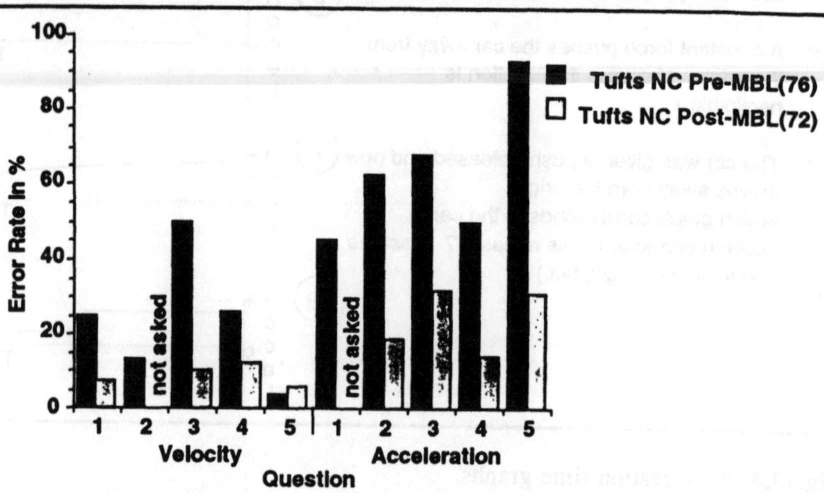

Fig.13.6. Tufts Kinematics 88 Non-Calculus - Error Rate Before and After MBL

In conclusion, MBL tools used in the context of a carefully developed constructivist curriculum can help students develop a solid conceptual understanding of kinematics. Data show substantial and persistent learning of basic physical concepts not often learned in lectures. Similarly positive results have been observed for heat and temperature concepts.

5. Modelling

Although a major reason for developing computers was to solve differential equations numerically, it has only recently occurred to educators that this power could be used by students prior to mastering the full formalism of calculus, differential equations, and numerical techniques.

Modelling not Models

One of the great challenges of science education is to find ways that enhance students' theory-building abilities. Information technologies should have a role in this; for the same reasons that MBL fosters the experimental side of science, the appropriate tools should be able to foster the theoretical side. The ability of computers to generate numerical solutions of complex systems should be an important part of this.

Models and simulations are commonly used in science education. Most software in these categories is based on the idea that the developer puts a model into the software then students learn about the model by varying one or more parameters. This can be a useful experimental exercise but it rarely helps students understand the internal model theoretically. A more valuable computer application comes from engaging the student directly in constructing models and exploring the consequences of different models. We have named this much more challenging approach *modelling*.

A large class of physical models are dynamic systems, requiring the solution of coupled, non-linear equations of the single independent variable time. Dynamic systems crop up in all the natural and social sciences in many cases where a model is needed to predict the future Behavior of a system, whether the system is a simple projectile or the world economy.

Research at TERC [28] has developed strategies to make this class of problems accessible to students as early as ninth grade. In one approach, students can specify the problem using STELLA, a software package that uses graphical metaphors that capture the essential mathematical ideas without the overhead of the formalism. This approach is an outgrowth of techniques developed at the Systems Dynamics group at M.I.T., educational pioneers who for years have used an hydraulic metaphor to represent systems of non-linear differential equations. They have used this metaphor to help business students who lack an understanding of the mathematical formalism, explain and understand complex dynamical systems. The key symbols in this system are the valve and tank which incorporate the intuitive ideas of calculus. The tank acts to accumulate or integrate the quantity that flows in the pipe and the pipe flow represents the rate of change or derivative of the quantity in the tank.

From an educational perspective, we believe that same thing happens for calculus that we have seen for graphing skills there is a decoupling between students' formal learning and their understanding. Most introductory physics teachers report students with a formal background in calculus cannot really use calculus because they fail to understand it. The converse seems to be possible with suitable software: students can understand calculus intuitively before mastering its formalism.

While STELLA gives a glimpse of what future software might be able to do, modern spreadsheets are almost as easily used to solve comparable problems. Spreadsheets that can be linked to graphical output provide an extremely powerful environment for exploring numerical solutions to differential equations. Spreadsheets explicitly show the calculations, are easily set up and modified, and provide quick, dynamic graphs that make it easy to explore the effect of parameters on a model.

We have also had young students use spreadsheets to solve dynamics problems. Students like spreadsheets, probably because they show all the calculations and thus seem less magical than the corresponding STELLA model. Spreadsheets may be easier for many students who are not comfortable with the highly linear thinking required by programming languages.

The solution of dynamic systems with software like STELLA and spreadsheets gives a broad range of students the tools with which they can understand complex systems. While not completely general, these tools do allow students to participate in the theoretical side of science in a way that nicely complements MBL's ability to allow students to participate in experimental science. The ease of understanding this important class of dynamical problems makes it more likely that students can gain theoretical insights from their own investigations.

A very wide range of problems from all the scientific disciplines can be solved using this approach. Furthermore, the problems can be complex, realistic, and interesting, not just limited to ideal and unobtainable situations. The results are available quickly, and the structure of the model is easily modified, so there is little penalty for constructing different modelling ideas. This gives students easy control over their models and enhances their understanding.

System dynamics does not represent a universal approach to modelling and theory-building. It can provide a powerful and instructive starting point for young theorists since important dynamical problems can be found in all fields. However other, more general tools are conceivable. Spreadsheets are very well adapted for creating and solving a broader range of models, and programming is the ultimate tool, capable of expressing any model. Highly graphical and interactive programming languages like Boxer [1] might be able to combine the features of all these computational environments.

Approaches such as these challenge the traditional math and science curriculum. If ninth grade students starting with an algebra background can understand and generate numerical solutions for complex problems, then we must question the validity of the five-year sequence of further algebra, pre-calculus, calculus, differential equations and, finally, numerical methods. Further, we must re-think science course content, much of which has been simplified because students are presumed to lack the mathematical skills to solve realistic, complex problems. In fact, we must question the implicit assumption that students must be protected from interesting, complex scientific problems. Students need to learn how to tackle complexity, how to find out what they need to know and to learn it.

6. Collaborative Science

Telecommunications can bring students, mentors and scientists together to cooperate internationally to conduct projects that are much more complex and sophisticated than any one student could handle alone.

The Evolution of Collaborative Science

The first large-scale curriculum based on collaborative student investigations is the NGS Kids Network developed by TERC and published by the National Geographic Society. Designed initially for grades 4-6, the project features six-week units each of which engages students in measurements resulting in data that can be meaningfully shared. Probably the most important feature of these units is that the results are not known in advance and there is a scientist participating in the experiment who is interested in the results and can communicate this interest to students.

The TERC LabNet and Star Schools project will be the next step in creating sophisticated collaborative science projects that combine the telecommunications of the Kids Network, the experimental power of MBL, the theoretical power of theory-building tools and the power of programming to give high school students an opportunity to participate fully in science exploration and discovery. Focused on a project lab and linked through a telecommunications network, students will be guided into undertaking their own projects by first having them participate in on-going monitoring networks.

An Example: Seismology Projects

An example will help clarify how these technologies could foster individual work on collaborative projects. One of the bulletin boards available on the network might contain ideas about possible projects. One of the proposed projects on the bulletin board might be the establishment of a network of seismic stations. When a moderator notices a sufficient level of interest in that idea, a separate bulletin board could be set up on seismology. A group of experts and mentors would be located to join the bulletin board. Designs for a simple, low-cost seismograph which students could easily build would be solicited from participating students and scientists. One can imagine a design using an MBL interface to scan real-time data for significant events. The computer could record interesting events and send these into the network. If there were any major events during the operating time, students could use their data to locate epicenters and to estimate the magnitudes of the events.

If students did no more than successfully construct, calibrate and maintain a seismic station designed by someone else and observe data from the network of which they were a part, they would have a realistic and rewarding introduction to research. But this experience could easily be the opening to a much richer experience. It would be natural for students to want to improve their station. Through the network, a group of students might begin identifying various problems in the seismic station design and agree to divide the attack on these problems. For instance, one subgroup might investigate alternative seismic detectors and experiment with their construction and placement; another group might look at the problem of synchronizing stations. Another subgroup might look at the software required and see whether any existing software could be adapted, or whether new programs have to be made. In either case, good programmers would have to be identified and asked to create the required software. Along the way technical help might be sought through the moderator of the subgroup who might find a consultant who had previously volunteered and been listed in the network. Once the techniques were decided upon, each of the participating experimenters would set up one of the basic stations and evaluate it. They could prepare a report on their progress and make suggestions on future improvements. The report could be submitted to another bulletin board responsible for publishing, and be peer-reviewed by other students participating in the network. The very best articles might be published.

As with so many projects, the more students work on them, the more they are led into interesting science from a broad range of fields. City students might record trucks and develop projects around road wear from heavy loads. No analysis of earthquakes is complete without understanding the difference between compressional and shear waves, ideas that are important in all kinds of wave propagation studies. Dispersion, the nature of the earth's core, the effect of pressure on wave speed, reflection, refraction, and attenuation are all concepts that might interest a student trying to understand data collected. Other students might want to continue improving the apparatus, and might study improved electronic or even optical methods for measuring small displacements. The curious student might stumble across contemporary research on gravitational wave detectors or interferometry. Other, more empirically oriented students might try for increased electronic gain, only to discover problems with noise and drift, which might stimulate an investigation of the nature and origin of noise. Students trying to improve the mechanical construction of the seismograph might raise questions of natural frequency and period, elasticity and ringing. Finally, students would be naturally lead into considering the social implications of their capacity. Can they record underground nuclear tests? What is the relation of seismic monitoring to the nuclear test ban treaty? As is often the case with projects, even the most narrowly conceived project leads naturally to a very wide slice of science; in this case, mechanics, heat, sound, electronics, planetary science and disarmament.

Collaboration is itself important educationally. Most contemporary science and engineering advances require wide-scale collaboration, increasingly facilitated with telecommunications. The model of the isolated researcher making a solo breakthrough fostered by awards and biographical sketches was probably never accurate, but is now completely misleading. It is important to teach students skills required for collaboration and to convey the message that technical fields are collaborative. This may have profound career implications for minorities and women and could be important in policy decisions in which any student might participate in as a citizen.

Technology Makes it Possible

As the seismology example shows, collaborative projects have a number of advantages over individual projects. Students and teachers who lack the necessary skills to complete all aspects of a project can still contribute to original work. Thus, telecommunications technology fosters collaboration and reduces the demand on each student. Students are engaged in all aspects of scientific research, including experiment design, background research, analysis, and communicating their results. The latter is a particularly important and often neglected part of teaching about science; practising scientists must not only make original contributions, but also convince others of their value. Most important, the collaboration allows students to contribute to contemporary problems and to contemplate their social implications. The collaborative project gives students a unique and accurate glimpse of contemporary engineering and scientific research.

It might seem that seismology was a particularly fortunate example. However, there are a large number of exciting projects in ecology, astronomy, atmospheric science, and the social sciences, where a geographically dispersed network of participating student scientists would provide equally exciting projects. Students could monitor the pH of rain, atmospheric or water pollutants, the spread of animal pests, radioactive fallout, atmospheric ozone concentrations, epidemics, the use of agricultural fertilizers. They might study a regional problem such as water pollution in Boston Bay. In addition, there are a large number of potential collaborative projects that do not use location as an important variable, but take advantage of the large number of experiments that can be performed jointly. Examples include examining plant physiology under carefully controlled conditions (perhaps using the computer to monitor and maintain fixed levels of variables such as temperature, light, and humidity) or performing experiments on learning or cognition which require a large N. Finally, there is a large class of experiments that are just plain difficult, where the collaboration effected through the network would put students with similar interests in contact with one another to work on the same problem together.

Another interesting possibility for collaboration enabled by telecommunications involves student access to research data, experiments and even instruments. As examples: There are vast quantities of ocean surface temperature data available that students might be able to access and use as the basis of original analysis. Long-distance student participation in underwater exploration using a remote submersible has been proposed. An explorer in the Mediterranean would transmit pictures and control the submersible with audio input from students. Telescopes can be controlled remotely and their images transmitted using telecommunications. This creates the possibility of student-run observations. With patience and good software, students could discover supernova and other time-varying events.

7. Conclusions

The three technologies—telecommunications, MBL, and modelling tools—all contribute to make collaborative student projects much more feasible and manageable. Telecommunications permit meaningful collaboration that reduces the demands on individual students and the responsibilities of the classroom teacher. MBL greatly expands the range of potential experiments by providing powerful, general instrumentation and contributes to student understanding by displaying data in ways that can be understood and discussed. Modelling and analytical tools expand the range of problems that students can realistically understand.

While advances in each of these technologies are desirable and expected, they are already sufficiently powerful to make large-scale student collaboration feasible. The chief impediments are, as usual, not technological. Schools are not aware of this exciting possibility or, if they are, they are not convinced that a constructivist alternative to traditional instruction is justified. Also, the collaboration will not happen automatically, it must be organized. Significant funding is needed to convince schools of the value of collaborative science and to launch initial collaborations. Once started, these networks could probably be self-sustaining and grow to make project work a regular part of the curriculum for all students.

The tools and approaches discussed here can support a transformation of science education. But it is one that will require major changes in evaluation, curricula and scheduling. These changes in turn depend upon even more fundamental changes in values and philosophy. Early results of using a constructivist approach to student science learning, enhanced and in some cases made practical by the educational technologies described in this chapter, are positive enough to undertake the long and difficult task of changing science education.

References

1. Boxer [a programming language]. See Plager, D. and diSessa, A., *Boxer research: An annotated bibliography,* The Boxer Group, Graduate School of Education, University of California at Berkeley, 1987.
2. Brasell, H.M., *Effectiveness of the microcomputer-based laboratory in learning distance and velocity graphs,* doctoral dissertation, University of Florida, 1986.
3. Bringuier, J. C., *Conversations with Piaget,* University of Chicago Press, Chicago, 1980.
4. Clement, J. & Lochhead, J., *On hobgoblins and physics,* University of Massachusetts, Amherst, 1979.
5. Excel [a graphing spreadsheet program], MicroSoft.
6. Grant Foundation., *The forgotten half: non-college youth in America,* Washington D.C. 1988.
7. Greenfield, L.B., Engineering student problem solving. In J. Lochhead and J. Clement, Eds., *Cognitive Process Instruction,* The Franklin Institute, Philadelphia, p. 229-238, 1979.
8. Halloun, I. A. & Hestenes, D., Common sense of college physics students. *American Journal of Physics,* 53(11), 1043-1055, 1985.
9. Hurd, P.D., State of pre-college education in mathematics and science. *Science Education,* 67(1), 57-67, 1983.
10. Laws, P., Workshop physics: replacing lectures with real experience. *Proceedings of the Conference on Computers in Physics Instruction,* North Carolina State University, 1988.
11. Lochhead, J., *The heuristics laboratory dialogue groups,* University of Massachusetts, Amherst, 1976.
12. McCloskey, M., Caramazza, A., & Green, B., Curvilinear motion in the absence of external forces: Naive beliefs about the motion of objects *Science,* 210, (December 5), 1139-1141, 1980.
13. Motion Unit [software & hardware], Queue, 562 Boston Ave., Bridgeport, CT 06610.
14. National Commission on Excellence in Education, *A nation at risk,* 1983.
15. *Northwest Regional Educational Laboratory,* Computer lab tools for science. Portland, OR.
16. Papert, S. & Tinker, R., *The MIT Educational Technology Center.* Proposal, MIT, June., 1988.
17. Papert, S., *A critique of technocentrism in thinking about the school of the future.* MIT, 1987.
18. Second International Mathematics Study, *The underachieving curriculum,* Champaign, IL: Stipes Publishing Company, 1987.
19. Second International Science Study, *Science achievement in seventeen countries,* New York: Pergamon Press, 1988.
20. Stella [modelling software], Lyme, NH: High Performance Systems.
21. Thornton, R. K., *Tools for scientific thinking,* Proposal to FIPSE, U.S. Department of Education, 1985.
22. Thornton, R. K., Access to college science: microcomputer-based laboratories for the naive science learner. *Collegiate Microcomputer,* V (1), 1987a.
23. Thornton, R. K., Tools for scientific thinking: microcomputer-based laboratories for physics teaching. *Physics Education,* 22, p. 230, 1987b.

24. Thornton, R. K., Tools for scientific thinking: learning physical concepts with real-time laboratory measurement tools. *Proceedings of the Conference on Computers in Physics Instruction,* North Carolina State University, 1988.
25. Tinker R. and Barclay W., *Development of microcomputer-based laboratory instructional materials.* Cambridge: Technical Education Research Centers, 1983.
26. Trowbridge, D.E. and McDermott, L.C., Investigation of student understanding of the concept of velocity in one dimension *American Journal of Physics, 48,* (12), 1020-1030, 1980
27. Zuman, J. with Kim, H., T*he successful use of MBL in large urban classrooms.* (in press).
28. Zuman, J. with Weaver S., Tools for teaching problem solving: an evaluation of a modelling and systems thinking approach *Presented at NARST* in April, 1988.

14

Technology for All Pupils: An English School System Context

Antony T. Gordon and Giles Job
Education Office,
Tipping Street,
Stafford,
Staffordshire, ST16 2DH

Abstract: This paper describes an initiative in the Staffordshire Education Authority in England to develop a technological component of the curriculum for all pupils in the Authority's schools throughout their compulsory schooling. The description is set in the context of the contemporary debate in England upon the structure and control of the school curriculum, and the role of technology within it.

Keywords: creativity, expert technology, National Curriculum, technological awareness, technology education, technology for all

1. The Curriculum Context

Since the early years of this century, the detailed curriculum of the English state (publicly funded) schools has been seen as largely the responsibility of professional educators, operating at school and local Levels. The role of central and local government has been to recommend, not to prescribe. (The only curriculum feature required of all schools by the seminal Education Act of 1944 is religious education; and even that requirement has been widely flouted.) This curriculum freedom has great potential both for radical innovation and for incoherence; but in practice this diversity has been kept in check by an elaborate system of externally-set academic examinations, taken at the end of compulsory schooling at age 16, which have carried high national status [1]. The traumatic shift currently in progress from this tradition to a prescribed National Curriculum is discussed later in this paper.

2. Technology Within the English School Curriculum Tradition

It is only within the last 20 years that there has been any significant consideration of "technology" in its own right [7] as a component of the English school curriculum. There has been a protracted and largely inconclusive debate about an effective operational definition for "technology" in this context [4]. Despite this there have been a number of significant advances in providing children with technological experiences that extend beyond the acquisition of craft and technical skills into project-based activity that requires the deployment of a range of appropriate skills and knowledge-bases in the problem-solving strategies directed to real and relevant goals [2]. The problem solving process adopted to describe much of the early work in this field is illustrated below.

Additionally, many of these initiatives stress the development of "technological awareness" [11]. Part of the national confusion about operational definitions of technology no doubt stems from the all-encompassing view of technology implicit in much of the current English debate [10].

Another perspective on this issue suggests that the confusion and ambivalence about the role and status of technology in the school curriculum reflects a general ambivalence in the English curriculum debate about the relative status of academic, practical and vocational values. The academic tradition, with its emphasis on the analytical and the literary, so highly prized in the English system, has social and linguistic roots in the "public" (i.e. private!) school system of the governing classes of the 19th century. By contrast, much that is valued in technological education has its roots in the tradition of practical knowledge, of making, fixing and fettling, that fuelled the Industrial Revolution but has never become fully incorporated into the "establishment" view of the appropriate ideals for school education for all [6].

In practice, much of the recent growth in technological activity in English schools has developed through the practical areas of the curriculum, largely through teachers with a background in craft and design, although there has been significant involvement of science teachers in some initiatives. Because of the power of the terminal academic examination system in England, efforts to award these technological developments with academic status have tended to stress the scientific dimensions of technology and thus to give it rather an "engineering" flavour [8].

3. Technology Education: A Local Initiative

Although debate continues, the focus has shifted from whether Technology should feature throughout the school curriculum, to how it is implemented. The Staffordshire Technology Education Programme is a local initiative to translate a broad view of technology and its role in education into a curriculum reality for all students in Staffordshire schools.

Staffordshire is a large rural county in central England, one of some 104 such authorities discharging all civic duties including police, fire, social services, housing, highways, consumer services, libraries and, last but not least, the education service. The Education department caters for the needs of some 187,000 pupils and students and employs 9,700 teachers and lecturers, located in some 450 primary (elementary - ages 5 to 11) and 100 secondary (high - ages 11 to 18) schools, 9 vocational colleges (age 16+) and 1 polytechnic (age 18+).

The Programme aims to establish a technological component in each child's curriculum throughout compulsory schooling from ages 5 to 16. This will be undertaken by the introduction of a phased programme (over 7 years) of curriculum development, staff training and resource provision for all schools, all pupils and many teachers.

The Programme has a budget of $7 million, and will be implemented by a central team of a director, 15 support teachers, and administrative and technical support staff. The team will be based in a purpose built Technology Centre, equipped at a cost of $250,000. Two mobile resource units (converted buses) are also used to provide local support for general and advanced developments.

It must be stressed that the programme would not be so comprehensive in its aims or impact, or so well resourced if it were not for the initiative and support of the local elected politicians, responsible for control of the education service and its budget. The politicians set the two schools Inspectors responsible for Science and for Design and Technology, the task of producing a plan for the implementation of the Technology Education Programme in Staffordshire, and undertook to provide the necessary finance and support.

4. Curriculum

The programme aims to develop the full range of technological experience for students from awareness through capability, and extending into technological creativity and criticism [10]. To give substance to such aims, the programme has been structured in such a way that two distinct strands were established: "Technology for All" , aimed at enhancing and informing all areas of the curriculum so that a technological component could be established, through to the second element, "Expert Technology", which is intended to give technological capability to the majority rather than all students.

In the "Technology for All" element, all phases of education (primary and secondary) will be involved in the development of a technological dimension of the existing curriculum. In the elementary schools, thematic approaches involving project work are used to develop technological awareness. In the high schools, subjects such as History, Geography, English and Music are developing project centred activities based upon technology, as an extension to, or a means of making more relevant, the current curriculum.

"Expert Technology" is centred upon the secondary sector, and aims to develop high-level skills in the enabling technologies such as micro-electronics, pneumatics, opto-technology, bio-technology, chemo-technology and communication technology. It should be noted that the use, or the study, of computers is not seen as a "Technology" in the sense of this initiative; any emphasis given to computers centres upon their use in extending existing or emerging technologies.

Each area of activity in the "Expert Technology" domain is supported by a County development group. Such groups provide a focus for good practice and innovation within schools, and a means of developing and disseminating curriculum development materials. The members of such groups are often involved in national, and occasionally international, developments.

5. Implementation

The concept of County-supported negotiated school-based development of the technological curriculum is central to the Staffordshire Programme.

In the elementary schools, it is intended that a whole school staff and the central team should become involved in the debate and the development of the technological curriculum. Groups of nearby elementary schools and the local high school, are encouraged to collaborate to foster community-based developments.

In the high schools, although it is not possible to involve every teacher in the associated curriculum development and the debate, it is possible to include a broad range of experience and subject areas, so that every high school arrives at a negotiated curriculum, in conjunction with the central team, which contains many strands of technological experience in the "Technology for All" element. Such negotiations will also influence considerably the form of the "Expert Technology" curriculum, although it is recognised that the curriculum areas usually associated with "technology" are likely, at least in the early days, to lead developments in the area of "Expert Technology."

At the conclusion of the negotiation phase, each school, in conjunction with neighbouring schools, will have proposed an implementation plan identifying the nature of the technological curriculum and showing the curriculum organisation, delivery methods, and specifying student competencies at ages 7, 11, 14 and 16. The plan will form the basis for the production of detailed teaching programmes, as well as a guide for the central team in providing external support activity such as staff training, resource allocation and curriculum development assistance.

6. Teacher Training

Appropriate and adequate training of the staff involved in the teaching of technology is vital to the success of the programme.

Every school involved in negotiating and implementing a technology programme needs to identify staff training needs. The needs are scheduled in short, medium and long term. The "short-term" training will largely be undertaken in the institution, by specially trained and recruited teacher trainers. This would appear an expensive use of a limited resource but evidence indicates that school-based training and development is often more appropriate to needs of the institution and its teachers and, consequently, more effective than conventional external courses. The medium term needs of the schools, usually associated with raising levels of expertise, would tend to be dealt with by attendance of County and national courses. The long term needs, usually those associated with planning and sustaining a major initiative, are dealt with on a school-by-school basis.

7. Resources

Once the curriculum plans and the teaching programmes are agreed by the Authority, the provision of resources and facilities can commence. The Authority purchases and distributes to every school the "core" resources to establish a viable technological curriculum. The exact specification of the final package, however, will depend upon the individual school's interests and expertise. Existing provision is also taken into account.

In the elementary schools, the resources are based upon "resource" trolleys. It is not necessary or wise to alter the elementary learning environment, so the trolleys are a flexible answer to a resource need. Being mobile they can be used and deployed in a number of ways to suit the school. The cost of the trolley plus equipment is in the order of $2,000 per school.

In the high schools, it is intended to provide a purpose built Technology Studio in which mechanical, electrical, pneumatic and gas services, and a design and manufacturing capability are installed. The cost of a fairly well equipped Studio is typically $50,000. The key to the use of the Studios is the flexibility and the ease with which many subject areas can gain access to designing, investigating, making and testing facilities. The most extensive use will be, however, in supporting courses aimed at equipping pupils with technological capability.

It is intended that the school staff should be involved in the debate regarding the final make-up of the resources provided for the school. From such negotiation one can foster emerging technologies such as bio-tech or chemo-tech in those institutions where expertise resides and could profitably develop.

With such curriculum support, training and resources, provided as part of the phased development of Technology Education in Staffordshire over a period of seven years, every school should be in a position to face a future, in which Technology Education figures, whether locally determined or nationally imposed.

8. Technology in the National Curriculum

A large and complex Education Reform Act has recently passed through the British Parliament. Various aspects of the Act dealing with the curriculum will assume the status of a legal imperative in the near future.

This legislation marks the culmination of a decade or more of acrimonious national debate about control of the curriculum, coloured by among other things, concern over the long-standing decline in the British industrial economy [8], and by tensions between local and national government. The current Government is placing major emphasis on the concepts of competition and enterprise, and has promoted a number of initiatives to give these impact within school education, and to give the curriculum closer orientation towards the needs of industry [12].

This radical legislation included proposals for the establishment of a national curriculum. Requiring all publicly funded schools, elementary and high, to follow a curriculum incorporating the "core subjects" of English, Mathematics and Science, and a number of "foundation subjects," each with nationally determined age-related attainment targets and programmes of study, and a national programme of assessment and testing at ages 7, 11, 14 and 16. In this context, it is perhaps not surprising to find "technology" listed as a "foundation subject" in the National Curriculum proposals [5]. The nature of this "technology" is as yet undefined, although the proposals imply that, in the elementary years, science and technology are so closely related in curriculum terms as to make difficult to distinguish between them.

The development of this curriculum framework into practical proposals is being entrusted to a number of national working groups, although the Secretary of State for Education through the recently established National Curriculum Council holds major powers to accept, reject or amend their recommendations. These working groups are composed largely of professional educators.

The formation of the working group for "Design and Technology" was announced after a considerable delay. The group has a very broad ranging brief including aspects of design and information technology as well as technology. This unexpected change of emphasis is clearly illustrated by the changing of the name of the group from technology to design and technology. Confirming graphically the difficulties faced by the Department of Education and Science in formulating guidelines for this area of the curriculum, and the impact of intense lobbying by groups representing the computing, home economics and design interests who are threatened by aspects of the National Curriculum proposals.

9. In Conclusion

This is a crucial period for technology education in England. Can the ambitious goal of a broad-based technological education for all school students that embraces awareness and competence, be translated into a national reality? Or will a need for a politically acceptable and expedient solution cause a reversion to a more limited craft-based interpretation? Much now depends on the ability of those committed to technology education not only to demonstrate the values of such local initiatives as that in Staffordshire, but also to operate effectively in a novel political arena.

The peculiarities of the English system have allowed professional educators to operate for decades with enviable freedom and flair in the "secret garden of the curriculum." The garden gate is now being thrown open. It remains to be seen whether we have bred plants sturdy enough to stand the trauma of cold wind and transplantation.

References

1. Broadfoot, P. *Assessment, Schools and Society*. London, Methuen 1980.
2. Black, P., Harrison, G. *In place of Confusion*. Nottingham, NCST. 1985.
3. Callaghan, J. Ruskin College Address. London, *Times Newspapers*. 1976.
4. Cross, A., McCormick, B. *Technology in Schools*. Milton Keynes, Open University Press 1986.
5. Dept of Education & Science *The National Curriculum*. London, HMSO. 1987.
6. Hargreaves, D.H. *The Challenge for the Comprehensive*. London, Routledge & Kegan Paul. 1982
7. McCullock, G.M., Jenkins, E., Layton, D. *Technological Revolution?* Brighton, Falmer. 1984 .
8. Penfold, J. From Handicraft to Craft Design and Technology Studies in Design Education, *Craft and Technology*, Vol. 20/1, pages 34-37. Stoke on Trent, Tretham Books. 1988.
9. Science Working Group. *Interim Report*. London, Dept of Education and Science. 1988.
10. Todd, R.D. Technological Literacy, an International Perspective *Proceedings, Technology Education Symposium* Blacksburg, VPI. 1986.
11. TVEI Unit. Technology for TVEI London, Manpower Services Commission. 1988.
12. Young, D. *Education Committee Minutes, House of Commons*, 20th December, 1982, page 16 London, HMSO. 1982.

15

Research in Advanced Educational Technology: Two Methods

Martial Vivet
Laboratoire informatique
Université du Maine BP 535
F 72017 LE MANS cedex
FRANCE

Abstract: We describe two ways of working which use advanced technology for educational purposes. The first part of the text is devoted to the description of an ITS (Intelligent Tutoring System) for algebraic manipulation. The focus is on the possibilities offered to solve problems, to deliver rich explanations and to encode declarative pedagogical knowledge.

The second part is devoted to the extension of the turtle microworld we have developed. We describe our micro-robotics approach and the pedagogical use of driving micro-robots. The focus is on the need for a good definition of pedagogical goals before use of devices. The tools we have designed are presented according to precise goals.

The conclusion shows that we need work in two complementary ways: ITS can be useful to support the learning of procedures, micro-worlds for learning basic concepts. More, we have not to conform to fashion and claim ITS as the only way for advanced educational technology (even if we think this way as a very interesting one!). Deeper work on advanced physical learning environments (micro-worlds in the sense of the floor turtle by Papert) is useful because a lot of things cannot be taught otherwise.

Keywords: AI, algebraic manipulations, expert system, Fischer technics, intelligent tutoring systems, ITS, LOGO, meta-knowledge, micro-robots, micro-worlds, microworld, motivation, student model, turtle, tutorial strategies

1. Introduction

The goal is to have learners learning! But the debate is not yet ready to be closed on how to make this possible. Do we have to teach or do we have to build learning environments where the students learn with problem solving activity allowing personal discoveries? Our answer is that we have to do both. This leads us to envisage uses of new technologies for information (NTI) in two separate but complementary ways: design of intelligent tutoring systems (ITS) and design of new micro-worlds in Papert's meaning.

Teaching consists generally of the transmission of knowledge with feedback based on exercises or questions allowing the verification of abilities gained with new pieces of knowledge. The second way consists in offering to the learner an environment helping him (or her) to discover and experiment new contents about a given matter.

This chapter is organised in two parts in order to illustrate the two ways we are working in our research. The first one concerns the ITS "AMALIA" devoted to the training of students in algebraic manipulation. The second one concerns the environments based on driving of micro-robots we are designing to make younger children learn about new technologies.

2. Different Aspects of AMALIA: A Knowledge Based Tutor for Mathematics

Intelligent Tutoring Systems (ITS) are generally built on knowledge based architectures. This allows the system to solve the problems submitted to or by the tutor during the student sessions and to reach good possibilities for explanations.

Some aspects of Intelligent Tutors

Three characteristics appear as fundamental to justify the use of knowledge based architecture to write so-called ITS :

i) an expert-system appears as a problem solver and this makes it able to solve exercises submitted to the learner or by the learner. The expression "competent tutor" is sometimes used to underline this possibility. This allows better correction for proposed exercises and pedagogical strategies in which the learner proposes challenges to the system: exercises to be solved taking account of given constraints. Writing the solver makes explicit useful knowledge to reach a given objective and in itself is very important for teaching.

ii) an expert-system can "explain" the solution it gives to a problem. Nowadays, most expert-system based tutors are limited to an analysis of knowledge of a field, an implementation of it in a production rule form or a semantic net of structured objects. Explanations are more or less restricted to a trace of the items (rules) applied during the solving process by an inference engine. We need to reach more interesting pedagogical possibilities.

Firstly, we need to make the meaning of the word "explanations" clearer. It appears than we can distinguish the terms, *Trace, Comment, Explanation, Justifications.*

- *Trace* is restricted to the output of items used to solve a problem. We cannot speak of explanations as there is no understanding, no interpretation, no formulation or reformulation of what is said.
- *Comment* consists of revealing essential phases, the presentation of the logical articulations of inferences sequences. This can be done with a syntactical analysis of the trace of applied rules. For example Safar [18] has used the concept of "pertinent facts" to prune the inference tree.
- *Explanation* have to be reserved for COMMENTS in which reference to the contents, the semantics of the rules, are done.
- *Justifications* imposes explicitation on the user of how and why the choices of knowledge used to solve a problem were made, explicitation of how, why a given strategy has been chosen, why not another one.

Secondly, to obtain interesting tutors, we need to reach the *Explanation* and the *Justification* levels. The *explanation* level supposes an access by the engine to the content of the rules and reasoning on this content. A first way to do this is to link rules with "soft texts" (messages with variables being filled up according to a context and printed by procedures deciding whether parts be written or not). We have explained in earlier papers [24] that the *Justification* level can only be reached if we use Knowledge on knowledge. The formalisation of this upper level knowledge leads to a so-called meta-knowledge which in some sense represents necessary tools to transform knowledge given in a declarative way into a procedural form for the learner.

The meta-knowledge, useful to perform the control of choices while building a solution, must be given under a declarative form like meta-rules. It is necessary to implement effectively declarative meta-knowledge. So tracing, commenting, explaining, ... meta-rule use is a way to work towards very powerful tutors. It deals with transmission of strategies to solve problems in the domain. This supposes that it's possible to explain how to use the transmitted knowledge to make it efficient;

iii) the tutorial component itself can also have an expert system architecture. This implies it is possible to write pedagogical rules to fill up the corresponding knowledge base. This also implies it is possible to write the meta-knowledge relevant when choices dealing with the control of the session have to be made.

From CAMELIA to AMALIA...

We are writing the AMALIA system, devoted to teaching algebraic manipulations, to train students solving problems like integration of numerical functions. The retained architecture is based on the cooperation of two expert-systems able to act as separate agents: our CAMELIA [23] system is used as the problem solver component and its shell (KEPLER) is also used in the tutorial component to conduct the session with appropriate pedagogical rules.

The retained architecture can be extended to reach more general tutors based on a pedagogical agent interacting with a solver agent under the control of a communication agent; later extensions will be examined to interpret also the student model as a cooperating agent.

The CAMELIA system is a knowledge based system to solve problems on algebraic manipulations, able to prove properties upon the calculations which are done. The system can manage mathematical knowledge and the mathematician's knowledge; it's able to use heuristic knowledge to decide to run algorithms. Rules encode such knowledge in a declarative form and the main characteristic is in the implementation under a declarative form (meta-rules) of the meta-knowledge useful to make choices. The system works with non-trivial mathematics (computation of integrals, limits of functions, evaluation of finite sums) and is able to reach so called "pedagogical solutions", by [12].

KEPLER

The design of the AMALIA system leads us to the definition of the KEPLER shell, which can be useful to write expert-systems, specially intelligent tutoring systems. Figure 15.1 gives its general organisation.

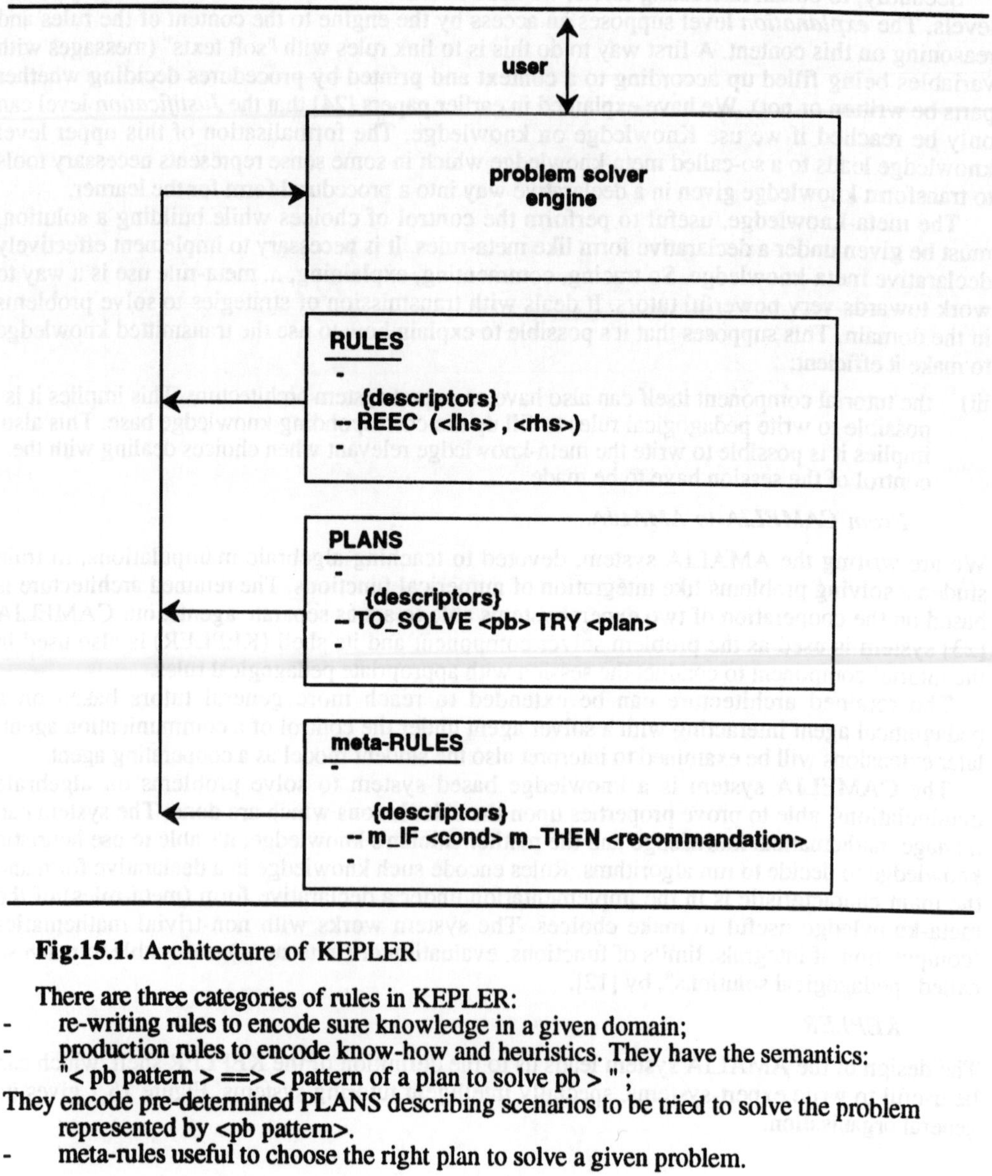

Fig.15.1. Architecture of KEPLER

There are three categories of rules in KEPLER:

- re-writing rules to encode sure knowledge in a given domain;
- production rules to encode know-how and heuristics. They have the semantics: "< pb pattern > ==> < pattern of a plan to solve pb > " ;

They encode pre-determined PLANS describing scenarios to be tried to solve the problem represented by <pb pattern>.

- meta-rules useful to choose the right plan to solve a given problem.

IV - AMALIA

Figure 15.2 gives the general organisation and the architecture of AMALIA, a system under development to train people on algebraic manipulation problems.

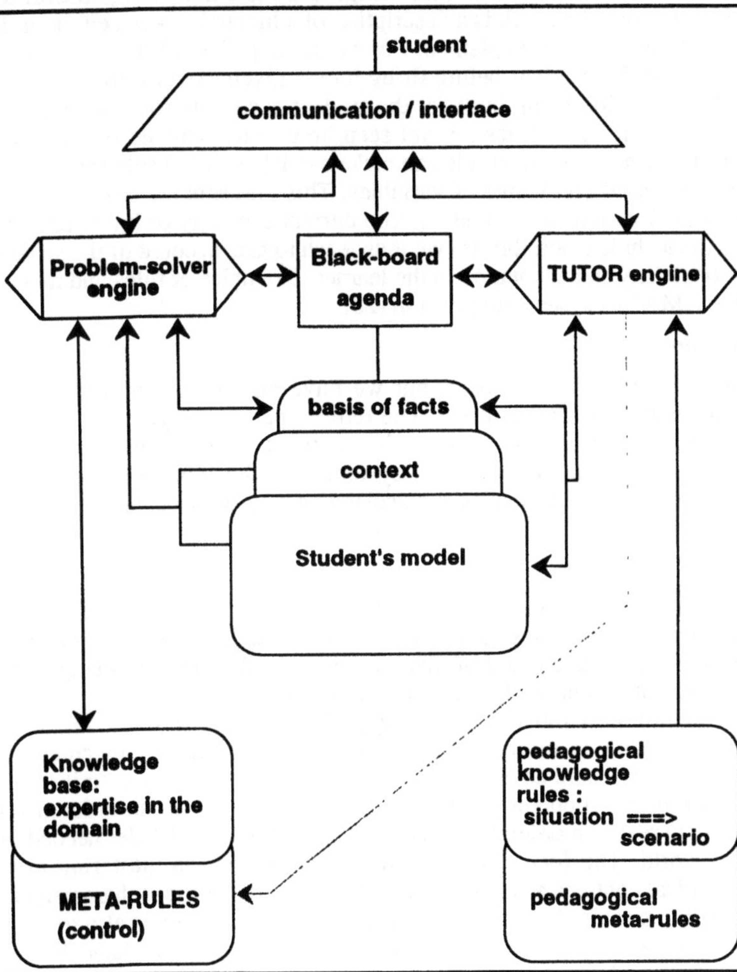

Fig.15.2. Architecture for AMALIA

The work focuses mainly on two fundamental aspects:

i) the problem of explanations ; The main advantage we get when a solver managing declarative meta-rules is available is in the possibility it offers to reach explanations dealing with the *Justification* level. For example, when calculating the integral $\int f(x)\,dx$, if we choose to integrate by parts, we are able not only to *explain how* to integrate f(x) by parts, but to *justify why* integration by parts has been chosen.

ii) the problem of pedagogical expertise. We re-use here rules coding pedagogical knowledge under a form of plans. This allows the description of possible scenarios to solve typical pedagogical problems. The strategies to choose the right scenario in a given context are given with pedagogical meta-rules. So, the KEPLER shell is used to implement the tutor part of AMALIA.

Hierarchy of Knowledge

Several kinds of knowledge items must be managed in such systems. Work we have done separates clearly the several types of knowledge and meta-knowledge useful to implement a knowledge based tutor. The result is a description of a hierarchy between them. Basic relations between theses types are now explained. For example, pedagogical rules can work on meta-rules useful to control the solver before firing it on a given exercise to be solved. This allows adaptation of the solution being built for the student according to an available model for the learner. So, if a given student has not yet seen how to use change of variables to integrate numerical functions, a pedagogical rule can make available for the solver a meta-rule excluding temporarily rules based on change of variables. This prevents the solver from presenting an incomprehensible solution to the student. The current typology of knowledge is presented in [27] showing the technical possibilities we thus reach to take account of the student model. This allows more flexibility and adaptation to the learner. Examples of rules and meta-rules we have written for the AMALIA system are given in [28].

Conclusion

AMALIA is still under development, but we have now really interesting possibilities of delivering explanations with the solver. The tutorial part is not yet sufficiently developed to imagine the kind of balance, atmosphere, interactions, possibilities of changes in styles of interactions, we will reach with such a system. But the tools are ready and the needed possibility of coding tutorial strategies in a declarative way is now clear.

3. Using Micro-worlds to Learn Technology

Some attempts are made to build micro-worlds in Papert's [37] meaning to train the learners to use inductive modes of reasoning. Some of them deal with learning experimental sciences [35] or can have an approach like that described in [39] or under the title "using technology in the construction of scientific knowledge" by Thornton in this book.

We are designing new tools to train young children (11-14 years old) with concepts in technology. This work is more concerned with an approach of mechanics, electronics, programming. We have here an approach very convergent with that described in this book by Gordon. We use micro-robots as central tools, aiming to design an ordered set of physical devices in order to reach an ordered set of concepts, abilities or attitudes needed in the physical and technical world. The focus for learning can be driven via mastering problem solving abilities or technical contents acquisition or tools involved. A proper characteristic of a robot is to fit, correctly, the purpose for which it has been built. This remark is also true for pedagogical robots. So we have analysed what can be learned with a robot and we have derived from this, a selection of different robots useful to approach different pedagogical problems. Experiments are going on and the children involved are well motivated. Similar work is also under development by R. Pelchat in Montreal [38].

In [48] we have discussed fundamental pedagogical questions such as "which robot for which audience?", "which thought process with which robot?", "which pedagogical process with which robot?" and "which goals with such tools?"

Our first conclusion is that for such work, we have to design devices from well defined pedagogical needs. This is in contrast to work sometimes observed starting from commercially available devices. Our second conclusion is that when this effort is done we can reach very rich pedagogical situations.

Micro-Robots

CARISTO: a first robot to reach the third dimension

Fig.15.3. Caristo

CARISTO is the name we have given to a first robot derived from the floor turtle by Papert. The shell has only been changed by the coachbuilding of a fork-lift truck, the pencil replaced by a fork. These changes, as shown in figure 15.3 allow a less childish feel and can be helpful to work with adults. We have used them with workers from factories. This tool allows also a first extension of the space available with the turtle: we have to manage the level of the fork. Projects like building stacks with boxes, carrying stacks are thus possible. It is possible to design algorithms to put stacks side by side according to the sizes of the boxes. The learner can also manage the weight or the sizes of the boxes and reach ways of driving the truck with local constraints (e.g., bridges allowing only passage with the truck empty or roof not too high). With exactly the same approach as the work being done with the turtle we reach a more open problem space and we have the opportunity to leave plane geometry.

CRANES: robots to solve problems in the third dimension

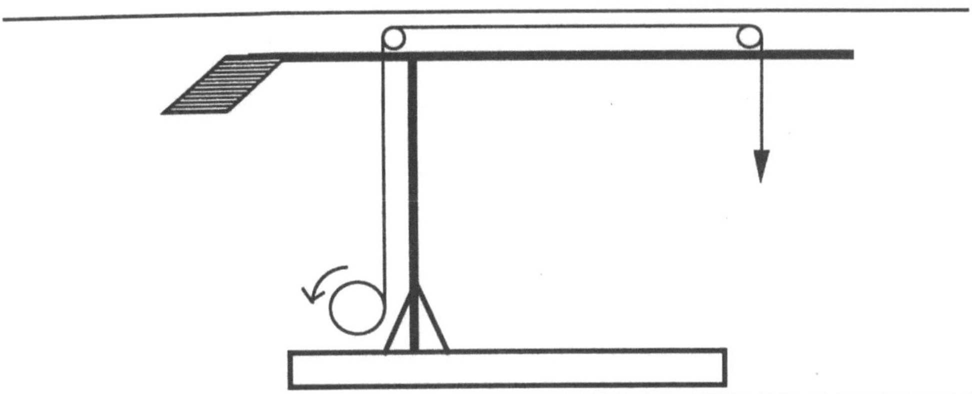

Fig.15.4. The Crane

We have built interfaces and designed LOGO primitive commands to drive jib cranes like that shown in figure 15.4 (generally sold as toys). The language used here looks like ROTATE-LEFT, ROTATE-RIGHT, PUSH-TRUCK, PULL-TRUCK, HOOK-UP, HOOK-DOWN. Thus we reach a new space with three dimensions, with polar geometry aspects. The main interest here is to reach a robot with a cylindrical geometry fitting well with the geometry of the human body. So, the possibility of mental body projection available for the turtle still works and is very useful to help solving problems. This micro-world allows problems like carrying boxes, stack of boxes from a given point to a target point with possible obstacles. Space modelling can be useful here and rich problems can be found making two or more cranes cooperating.

A simple and realistic approach of mathematical concepts can be available with these kind of tools as shown in the following two examples:

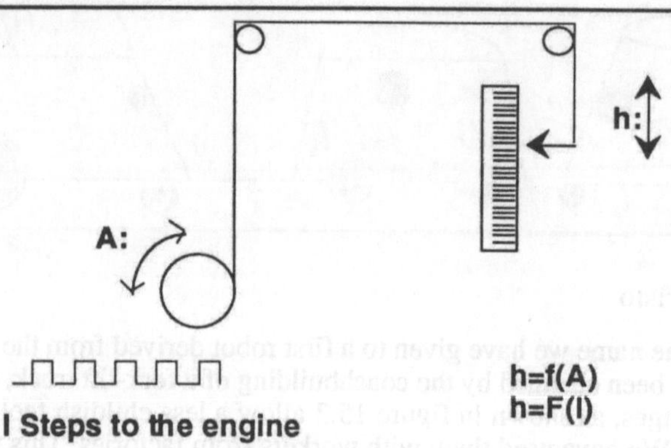

Fig.15.5. Study of a function

First example: the concept of function can be studied from the study of the level reached by the hook according to the number of steps given to the engine and the radius of a winding drum. For a given radius, we can as shown in figure 15.5 experimentally verify the linearity of the function l(s) (level reached according to the number of steps sent to the engine).

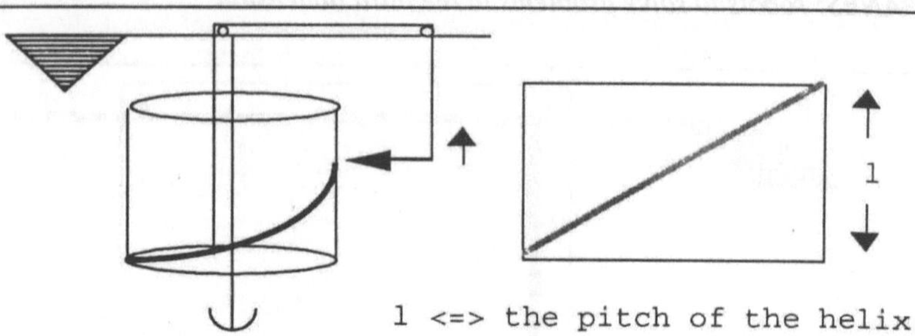


```
TO HELIX :ANG :H
REPEAT 360 / :ANG
       [ TURNBASE :ANG UP :H]
END
```

Fig.15.6. From the crane to the helix...

Second example: with the crane, we can experiment and study some aspects of the geometry of the helix: the concept of "pitch of an helix" being seen as the level reached by the hook when the arrow of the crane rotates exactly 360°, the hook moving up with a constant speed (cf. figure 15.6). This can be a good approach for the study of screwed rods, useful for later used robots. Such rods are available to transform the rotation of the rod into the translation of a Screw and can be studied as a primitive mechanical function.

We have described such work with more details in [48]

ARMS: robots to be built by the learners

When using technical objects with children, we have to be very attentive about the transparency of the tools we use. It appears that the floor turtle is not transparent enough in the following sense: we can never explain to the pupil how it is possible for the turtle to walk 10 units when we hit on the keyboard the string "FD 100" To make possible some understanding of basic questions in robotics like "how is it possible to move a bar or to turn a wheel with a computer?" we use Fischer Technics toys. The main interest is in the possibility of making the pupil build, with his (her) own hands, the mechanics needed. Its a way to approach primitive mechanical functions offered by tools like gear wheels, screwed rods, crank arms, etc. Making an engine turn can also be studied. We have designed LOGO primitive commands for the toys available and this appears as very interesting. Children are very happy when driving something they have built by themselves. Two approaches are possible here:

- first approach: we describe to the children, a task to be done and they have to imagine a physical device able to reach the goal when programming it. This way is used by [38] or Gordon in this book. We work here specially at the level of induction process, creativity, imagination, discipline in debugging a system, etc.
- second approach: we give a model and a plan of a toy to be built. The children must read carefully a plan, follow very precisely a check list to reach success. This can train him (or her) during the work and is a good complementary approach, relevant for other important aspects of education.

With the robot sold by Fischer Technik, a geometrical approach ("working geometry") is possible. It's possible to model precisely as shown in figure 15.6 the device and show in a fine way the role of modelling devoted to geometry, the difference between a real world and a model. The properties of the parallelogram can be studied while observing its role and the change of its shape when moving an arm (cf. figure 15.6).

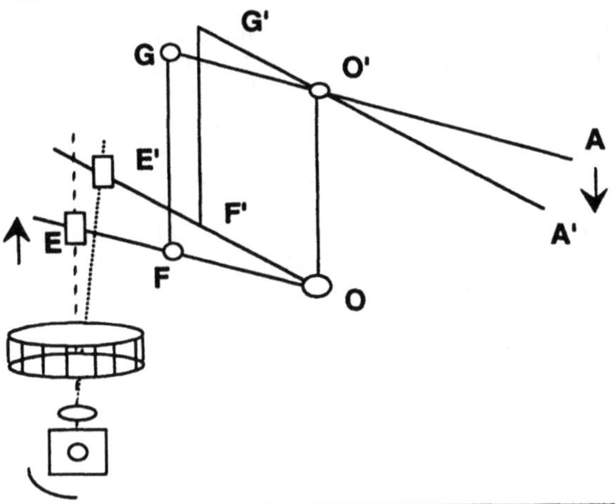

Fig.15.7. Working parallelograms

The study and a real use of Thales' theorem is also possible. In fact, we have observed how it's very important to have on the same desk, the model and the real world when approaching modelling activities. The text proposed in London in 1986 [49] gives more details and the figures shown in figure 15.7 reveal the relevant geometrical aspects.

SPA: A tool to learn flexibility concepts in production.

We have designed an environment to make older students (18-20 years old) learn the notion of flexibility as a basic concept in the production process in factories. The goal here is not to train a student on a specific machine or with specific ways to describe an automatic process of production. The goal is to train people to drive the production from an order form to a delivery for a customer.

Several production tools are available:

i) production machines,
ii) storages for tools , matter, produced pieces
iii) software for production control
iv) micro-computers network and automats network

The work we have done shows the type of interesting learning environments we can build with these ideas. We are sure that not enough work is being done in this way. The problem of teacher training still remains with these kind of open tools. The very impressive motivation shown by the pupils when working with these tools is an encouragement to do more.

5. Main Conclusion

We have worked on two completely different approaches of the use of computers in education. Our conviction now is that we need deeper work in the two ways. But it is possible now to consider the role of each approach in education. As claimed by S. Ohlsson in his chapter in this book, education of pupils imposes acquisition of "concepts" and "procedures". Our feeling is that ITS fit better for teach procedures and micro-worlds are more suitable for learning concepts. So the two approaches must be used in a complementary way and it is a good cooperation between them which can allow the best success.

As additional comments, it appears that:

- ITS are important as an experimental ground for educational theories, cognitive sciences. Here is a very rich field to obtain operational knowledge in the domain
- ITS are important to make links with the work done in AI. People working in AI have designed approaches, tools and methodologies relevant for educationalists. But, we can add that the attitude of educationalists can make the AI community doing some progress.
- ITS are important to be more operational in teachers training. The feedback from the work done on ITS for teacher training is not yet strong enough
- ITS underline the need for a better definition of the role of the teacher in relation to ITS. As the time for a replacement of the teacher by an ITS is yet very far off, teachers will have to cooperate with ITS. So the study of their role is important and can be helpful in the design of ITS.

Robot based micro-worlds are:

- important for basic concept acquisition
- important to keep contact with the reality and the approach of basic problems like modelling
- important to train student with inductive approaches, to make them imaginative

References

On ITS

1. Baron M., Vivet M. Systèmes experts et tuteurs intelligents, Congrès AFCET - *Reconnaissances des formes et intelligence artificielle,* ANTIBES, 16-20 nov 1988.
2. Bierman D. Intelligent simulation environments in education, *European Conference on AI* (ECAI) Brighton 1986, p.84-89. 1986.

3. Bonnet A., Cordier M.O., Kayser D., An ICAI system for teaching derivatives in mathematics, *In Computers in Education*, R. LEWIS and D. TAGG (eds), North-Holland 1981.
4. Clancey W.J. The epistemology of a rule based Expert system - a framework for explanations, *Artificial Intelligence*, 20, p. 215-251. 1983.
5. Ferret E., Jimenez C. A la découverte des méthodes algébriques. *Congrès Francophone sur l'enseignement assisté par ordinateurs - EAO87,* Cap d'Agde, ADI, mars 1987, p. 389-398. 1987.
6. Genesereth,M. The role of plans in intelligent teaching systems. In *Intelligent tutoring systems,* Academic Press, D. Sleeman and J.S. Brown (eds.) p.134-155. 1987.
7. Kassel G. Expliquer, c'est raisonner sur le raisonnement: le système CQFE, *VI ièmes Journées Internationales Systèmes Experts et Applications,* Avignon 1986, Vol. 2, p. 973-990. 1986.
8. Kassel G., Parchemal Y., Pitrat J., Safar B.: Pourquoi utiliser des métaconnaissances? . *Journées nationales sur l'intelligence artificielle,* PRC-IA, GRECO-CNRS, Aix-les-bains, 20/21 nov 1986, Cepadues éditions, p. 79-88. 1986.
9. Kodratoff Y. Is AI a sub-field of computer science? or is AI the science of explanations?, *Rapport de recherche* 312, LRI, ORSAY. 1986.
10. Mandl H., Lesgold A.M. (eds) *Learning issues for intelligent tutoring systems*, Springer Verlag, New-York. 1988.
11. Nicaud J.F., APLUSIX,*Congrès Francophone sur l'enseignement assisté par ordinateurs - *EAO87*, Cap d'Agde, ADI, mars 1987, p. 399-416. 1987.
12. Nicaud J.F., Vivet M. Les tuteurs intelligents: réalisations et tendances de recherche, synthèse sur les tuteurs intelligents. *Revue Techniques et Science Informatiques* -TSI, vol 7, n° 1, jan. 1988.
13. Nicolson R.I., The SUMIT intelligent arithmetic tutor, *The Fifth International Conference on Technology and Education*, Edinburgh, March 1988, p. 348-351. 1988.
14. O'Shea T., Bornat R., Du Boulay B., Eisenstadt M., Page I. Tools for creating intelligent computer tutors . In *Human and Artificial Intelligence*, Elithorn & Banerjii (eds), North Holland. 1984.
15. Ohlsson S. Some principles of intelligent tutoring. In *Instructional Science* 14, Elsevier, Amsterdam, p.293-326. 1986.
16. Pitrat J. Connaissances et métaconnaissances. In *Intelligence des mécanismes et mécanismes de l'intelligence.* Fondation DIDEROT. FAYARD (ed.: J.L. Lemoigne), p. 75-113. 1986.
17. Ross P. Plan recognition for intelligent tutoring systems, *Workshop IFIP-TC3,* Frascati, mai 1987, on Artificial Intelligence Tools in Education, Eds. North Holland. 1988.
18. Safar B. Explications dans les systèmes experts, *Journées Systèmes Experts,* Avignon 1985.
19. Self J. Artificial intelligence, its potential in education and training, *Jième Symposium Canadien sur la Technologie Pédagogique*, OTTAWA, 5-7 mai 1986, p. 69-77. 1986.
20. Self J. Student Models: what use are they?, *Workshop IFIP-TC3*, Frascati, mai 1987, on Artificial Intelligence Tools in Education. 1988.
21. Sleeman D. and Brown J.S. *Intelligent tutoring systems*, Academic Press, London. 1982.
22. Vivet M. CAMELIA: a knowledge based mathematical system, *European Conference on Artificial Intelligence* - ECAI, Sept. 1984, Pisa, p.603-612. 1984a.
23. Vivet M. *Expertise mathématique et informatique,* CAMELIA: un logiciel pour raisonner et calculer, thèse état, université Paris VI, 25 juin 1984. 1984b.
24. Vivet M. Systèmes experts pour enseigner : méta-connaissances et explications, *Congrès CESTA* : MARI-COGNITIVA 87, PARIS, 18/22 mai 1987. 1987a.
25. Vivet M. Hierarchy of knowledges in an intelligent tutoring systems; how to take account of the student, note interne CRIC, Presented during the *European Seminar on Intelligent Tutoring Systems*, TUBINGEN, 1987 October 25-31. 1987b.

26. Vivet M. Reasoned explanations need reasoning on reasoning and reasoning on the student, *Workshop IFIP-TC3,* Frascati, mai 1987, on Artificial Intelligence Tools in Education. 1988a.
27. Vivet M., Futtersack M., Labat M. Métaconnaissances dans les tuteurs intelligents, *International Conference Intelligents Tutoring Systems,* Montréal, June 1-3, 1988. 1988b.
28. Vivet M. Knowledge Based Tutors: Towards the design of a shell. *International Journal for Educational Research and Instruction* (IJERI), 1988, Numero special dirigé par H.Mandl. 1988c.
29. Vivet M. La prise en compte du contexte avec les tuteurs intelligents, *Premier congrès européan intelligence artificielle et formation,* APPLICA88, Lille 3-5 octobre 1988. 1988d.
30. Vivet M., Carrière E., Delozanne E. Presentation of different aspects of AMALIA : a knowledge based system for mathematics, *European summer university on intelligent tutoring systems,* le mans, 1988, october 26th- november 2nd. 1988e.
31. Wenger E. *Artificial Intelligence and tutoring systems* Morgan Kaufmann Los Altos. 1987.
32. Winans R.T., Whitaker E.T., Bonnel R.D. Theories of learning in computer-aided Instruction, *The Fifth International Conference on Technology and Education,* Edinburgh, March 1988, p. 86-89. 1988.
33. Yazdani (1986) Intelligent tutoring systems survey, *AI review* 1, p. 43-52.

On Learning Environments

34. Nonnon P. La robotique pédagogique, revue BUS, *AQUOPS Montréal,* Mai 1987, p.16-19. 1987.
35. Nonnon P., Laurencelle L., L'appariteur robot et la pédagogie des disciplines expérimentales, *SPECTRE,* P.34-36. 1984.
36. Nonnon P., Laboratoire d'initiation aux sciences assisté par ordinateur, Publication du *Vice-décanat à la recherhce,* faculté des sciences de l'éducation, Université de Montréal. 1986.
37. Papert S. *Mindstorms; children, computers and powerful ideas,* Basic Books, inc., Publishers, New-York. 1980.
38. Pelchat R. *Le robot enfouisseur de déchets nucléaires,* Guide d'activités, CARES, 10450 rue Meunier, Montréal, H3L 2Z4, Québec. 1987.
39. Rellier C. Ordinateur instrument de mesure et de représentation, *5th annual conference on computers in education,* Montreal, 18-20 nov 1987. groupe EVARISTE-CNAM, PARIS, France. 1987.
40. Robert F. Un exemple d'environnement programmable destiné à des débutants, Doc. interne, *INRP-DP5, Informatique et enseignement,* 191 rue Gabriel Péri, F92120 MONTROUGE, france. 1985.
41. Tanguy R. *Un réseau de mobiles autonomes pour l'apprentissage de la communication,* thèse Université, PARIS VI. 1987.
42. Vivet M. Apprentissage autonome, sur un usage de la technologie informatique dans l'éducation" Annexe du rapport *SIMON, "l'Education et l'Informatisation de la Société"* La documentation française. p.201-210. 1981a.
43. Vivet M. On the way data processing technology can be used in giving a basic general education" - IFIP - *WCCE* - Lausanne - Juillet 81. 1981b.
44. Vivet M. *LOGO : un environnement informatique pour la formation d'adultes,* Colloque National LOGO - Clermont-Ferrand - Déc.82. 1982.
45. Vivet M. LOGO : un outil pour une formation de base à la robotique. *Colloque National "LOGO et les enseignements technologiques"* - Le Mans - nov.83 , compte-rendu revue ETI-LISH/CNRS, n° 3, p.5-19. 1983.
46. Vivet M. Suggestions pour aborder la formation technologique avec *LOGO Colloque international ANTEM II* , PARIS, CESTA, 27/29 mars 84. 1984.
47. Vivet M., Delgoulet J., Guillot J.L., Froger M. ECLECT : un logiciel pour faciliter l'acquisition de l'écriture manuelle et de la lecture, *Congrès National EAO 84,* Lyon. 1984.

48. Vivet M. Pilotage de Micro-robots sous LOGO, un outil pour sensibiliser les personnels de l'industrie à la robotique" - 5e *Symposium Canadien sur la Technologie Pédagogique* - OTTAWA - 5/7 mai 1986. Paru dans le livre "A l'école des robots" , robothèque du CESTA, p. 195-210. 1986.
49. Vivet M. Driving Micro-robots under LOGO: a way to approach geometry. Proceedings of the *Second International Conference for LOGO and MATHS education.* Institute of education. University of London, 15/18 July 1986, P. 216-225. 1986.

16
Towards More Versatile Tutors for Programming

Benedict du Boulay
School of Cognitive and Conputing Science
University of Sussex,
U.K.

Abstract: This paper discusses intelligent tutoring systems and support environments for programming and describes current problems with these systems.

Keywords: critiquing, Diagrammatic traces, expert system, Intelligent Tutoring Systems, LISP, physics, programming, Prolog, PROUST, reflection, schemata

1. Introduction

Learning a "skill" (e.g. doing algebra, doing physics problem-solving or doing programming) typically involves mastering and coordinating a whole range of interacting sub-skills, concepts and principles. We argue that many Intelligent Tutoring Systems pay too little attention to *interactions* between sub-skills and to the way that expertise in a domain is often manifested by the expert's ability to solve problems in a number of *different* ways and see problems from a number of different *perspectives*.

This chapter is concerned largely with skills and sub-skills and has less to say about concepts and principles, important though these are. Ohlsson redresses this imbalance in his chapter on theoretical foundations. Also, we have focused on programming as a domain, but many of the observations (e.g. the taxonomy of problem-solving sub-skills below) apply more widely.

Intelligent tutors and support environments have been implemented to assist some parts of the programming process. Two current problems with these systems are their (i) *narrowness* of application within the programming process, and (ii) their *lack of flexibility* in the interactions with the student. We argue that some progress can be made in these issues and sketch some possible lines of development. The examples are taken mostly from programming in Prolog, but most of the issues are independent of the particular programming language chosen (and some of the issues are independent of programming as a domain).

2. Learning to Program

Programming consists of a variety of interrelated activities of which the following is a partial list. One of the difficulties for novices is the wide scope of these skills and the way that they interact both with each other (e.g. testing and debugging) and with other skills, knowledge and beliefs that the student might have (e.g. the belief that "programming is like instructing someone how to do a task"). Although the list below is expressed in "Top-Down" terms, neither novices nor experts necessarily follow (nor in principle *can* follow) the order of activities as given here when developing a program.

(i) Establishment of the Problem: students typically have highly specified programming problems given to them, but in project work they may well have to construct their own problem. It takes skill to see whether or not a real-world problem can be viewed broadly in computational terms and how complex it is likely to be.

(ii) Comprehension of the Problem: the student has to decide on what the main objects and procedures within the problem are and what might count as a solution. This decomposition into parts is largely expressed in problem domain terms, though the available computational tools will affect the division (e.g. consider the difference between a programmer decomposing a problem for eventual solution in Prolog compared to Fortran).

(iii) Specification of a Method: here the student re-orientates his view of the problem decomposition in terms of general classes of object and procedure made available in the programming language. At this point a mapping is made from problem domain terms to computational domain terms. Experts are said to have a stock of methods ("plans", "clichés") which they can employ as initial crude building blocks in this composition process. These building blocks are likely to be personal to the individual programmer and may conform to some standard method (e.g. Jackson's) or may be in some pseudo-language that has both English-like and programming-language-like features.

(iv) Coding and Compiling: the student translates the general objects and procedures from (iii) above into the programming language. The plans from (iii) are re-expressed according to the semantic and syntactic constraints of the particular programming language. Knowledge is also required of the editing/compiling environment.

(v) Interpreting Output and Debugging: typically programs do not behave as intended. First the student has to be aware of what behaviour he expected and how the output (or lack of it) can be interpreted in terms of the program both as a program (e.g. (iii) and (iv)) and as an expression of a problem (e.g. (ii) & (iii)). Unexpected behaviour can occur at various levels (e.g. from compiler error messages through to run-time surprises) and these can be due to errors/oversights/lack of precision at any of the levels of representation above. Knowledge of the how to diagnose compiler or program behaviour in terms of underlying mechanisms will be required, as will knowledge of the compiling/debugging and tracing tools.

(vi) Testing: in some ways this is a sub-activity of (v) but here the focus is more on exploring the limits of the program behaviour in terms of the original problem. Knowledge of the kinds of errors that can occur is needed in order that the student can satisfy himself that the program is reliable.

(vii) Documenting: in this part of the process the student learns how to describe the original problem and its decomposition, what method has been used to compute a solution, how the particular program embodies that method, how individual parts of the code work and so on.

(viii) Maintaining and Extending: it is common for professional programmers, and occasionally students, to be given someone else's (possibly partial) program to comprehend, debug or extend in some way. The program may be well or badly commented, well or badly structured and come with or without supporting documentation.

We should add to the above taxonomy of sub-skills the many concepts and principles also involved: the ontology of language dependent objects and procedures, the repertoire of plans and clichés, the rules of the language syntax and so on.

Mature Reflection

All the above apply both to novice and expert programmers. However there are some special issues that apply particularly to novices. These can be bundled under the collective heading of *mature reflection* and refer to a post-hoc analysis of both the *process* by which the program has come to be written as well as the *product*, i.e. the program's final structure. One may view the whole process of producing a program as a type of problem-solving, with its own distinctive features, which the student can learn to recognise and improve his understanding of. For example, he can learn how certain characteristic unexpected outputs suggest characteristic errors. In one implementation of Pascal, array elements that are unassigned in the program are given default values of some very large negative number. The appearance of such numbers anywhere in the output is an excellent clue to the general area of the error.

The student can also examine the structure of the problem, the specification or the program and its parts to see how these can be generalised. Is the current problem similar in surface or deep ways to others that have been solved? Can the methods that have been used be generalised in some way? Are there "plans" within the program-structure which look as if they may be useful again? Can the same problem be solved using other methods? What are the advantages and disadvantages of these methods? Can the method be implemented in other ways? What are the advantages of these other ways? What would the solution look like in a different language? What would happen if one extended the range of inputs?.

In du Boulay & Sothcott [8] we surveyed systems for assisting novices and divided them into three broad overlapping classes. There are "tutors" which choose problems, monitor solutions and provide advice; there are "bug finders" which compare a student's solution with some ideal and provide feedback about discrepancies; and finally there are "environments," tailored for novices, that support the process of program construction through the provision of various kinds of tool, e.g. for designing, editing, tracing and debugging.

There has been some progress since the above survey was written but the main drawbacks of lack of flexibility, limited perspective and narrow focus remain largely the same. Thus consider Prolog as an example of a target language for novices. In the area of support tools, for example, Eisenstadt and Brayshaw [11] have implemented a powerful graphic tracer that can provide very detailed pictorial and textual views of the actions underlying the execution of a

Prolog program. Different amounts of detail can be displayed and the user can zoom in on an event to see exactly what happened if need be. This provides ways of understanding the relationship between the code and the behaviour of the underlying Prolog machine in arbitrary detail. They are now working on the issue of how to present and trace more abstracted views of the code that take its higher level organisation into account, for example, tracing the execution of rules of an expert system implemented in Prolog in terms of the rules themselves rather than the code that implements those rules.

In the area of debuggers, Looi [18] has implemented a system that can spot and comment on errors in students' attempts to write simple Prolog programs (typically to sort lists using various standard methods). This system can judge which of several algorithms best fits the student's attempt at a solution but it cannot enter into much of a hypothetical dialogue about what his or her buggy code would do under various circumstances. Fung [13] is designing a system that will be able to diagnose certain standard novice misconceptions about Prolog flow of control, e.g. about backtracking, but it is unlikely to know what to do with its insights in terms of providing remediation. All these systems are impressive in their different ways but each embodies only limited amounts of the knowledge and skill that an expert teacher of programming might deploy.

3. Breadth of Application

Systems so far implemented tend to concentrate on particular parts of the programming process. Most systems have tended to cluster around the coding and debugging phases. The earlier phases of building a program, namely comprehension of problems and specification of methods, have received relatively little attention (because they are hard!). A start has been made by Bonar & Cunningham [3] with their Bridge system and de Castro et al. [7] with their system. In each case the student is invited to construct a description of the problem in a representation intermediate between the original problem expressed in natural language and the eventual solution expressed as a program. More work could be done here to explore the possibility of *critiquing* these intermediate representations. There may also be some scope for linking an ITS in this topic to current work in the development of Intelligent Project Support Environments see e.g. [4].

The area that seems to have received the least attention concerns Reflection. Tutors (both human and machine) are usually satisfied that the student can produce a single working solution to a given problem and although they may accept a range of answers do not ask the student to try to produce that range. It ought to be a straightforward extension of existing work to produce a system that expressly tackled the issue (perhaps in a manner similar to that developed in Abelson, Sussman & Sussman [1]) and making use of some kind of "genetic graph" from Goldstein [14] to represent possible development paths.

Students are not usually invited to examine the process by which they produced their solution to note points where they became stuck (and why), periods where they were "floundering," times when they were fixated on the wrong part of the program during debugging and so on. It ought to be possible to produce a collapsed and partially annotated transcript of a programming session either for the student to simply read or to be the subject of further tutoring. Some work e.g. [17,10] has been undertaken which shows possible ways forward.

4. Flexibility of Response

Anderson and Reiser [2] make a case that the rather inflexible (and authoritarian) teaching style of their system has special advantages for teaching the coding phase (i.e. that students do not learn their mistakes and that the system can tutor the student when the potential error is fresh in his mind and not later when he may have forgotten the context). However it is clear that students also need practice (and help) in learning how to extract themselves from situations which they are likely to get into in future and from which Anderson's system guards them.

Moves towards greater flexibility are described by Reiser in his chapter on Problem Solving and Explanation elsewhere in this volume. His GIL system deals with a limited subset of list-manipulation problems in LISP but allows the student to build the solution program (notated as a network of nodes and arcs) either from the input "towards" the output or in the other direction. That is, the student is given much more freedom to choose which of the coding sub-problems to work on, rather than being constrained to work in a particular order as in Anderson & Reiser [2].

Miller's [19] SPADE systems were interesting in that they conducted a dialogue with the student both at the level of code and at the level of program evolution, though the early versions had rather a fixed expectation about the way that a program should be developed which was at odds with what was psychologically plausible for beginners.

In a partially implemented system, Elsom-Cook [12] explored the idea of flexibly modelling what the student ought to be able to learn about LISP from his or her interaction with a LISP interpreter. It used this inference to suggest problems that the student might tackle (when he or she was not busy inventing problems for himself or herself). In a recent paper Self [21] has argued in a similar vein for systems to model the *beliefs* of learners (as opposed to *knowledge*) and sketched some of the consequent problems of the requisite underlying belief-maintenance system.

Elsom-Cook's work raises the further issue of how the system should model and conduct a coherent dialogue as well as maintain a sensible balance between telling students the answer or telling them what to do and giving them the chance to discover answers and methods for themselves.

Explanations

Tutors for programming (as for other topics) typically can explain a topic in only one way, but with increasing amounts of detail. They have no mechanism for adopting different kinds of global viewpoint or for offering explanations that are different in kind (e.g. causal as opposed to functional, see e.g. Cox, Jenkins & Pollitzer [6]). Tracing tools present one particular kind of description of underlying mechanisms (particular events and particular details may be included or not, but a different "story" [5] cannot usually be told). One of the hallmarks of a skilled teacher is that s/he can generate different kinds of explanation of some process or concept according to the needs of the student. Such explanations may differ along many dimensions such as diagrammatic/pictorial, sketchy/detailed, theoretical/applied etc. The need for different kinds of explanation is particularly important since the student is expected to master so many new skills that include identifying how a program makes the underlying notional machine work, identifying how standard program clichés or schemata fit and work together in the particular program, relating the program back to the requirements of the problem and so on.

Learning Prolog poses special difficulties for the novice in that it has a uniform and "un-highlighted" syntax [20], its standard plans or clichés are not well developed in textbooks, it admits both pictorial and textual descriptions and (perhaps most of all) a program can be described at a number of complementary and interacting levels that are more easily confused in Prolog than in other languages. Thus a Prolog program to solve some problem can be described: (a) in highly specific problem-related terms (i.e. as English statements about the domain entities, relationships and processes), or (b) as stylised logical statements containing symbols denoting domain entities and relationships, and logical inferences denoting domain processes, or (c) as stylised procedural statements about the sequential manipulation of data-structures together with incidental input/output behaviour.

The Prolog learner has to master these different perspectives on programs that s/he writes or that are provided by the teacher and has to master the mappings between these different kinds of explanation of "what is really going on."

We could imagine a system that took the following elements

(a) a problem description,

(b) a program,
(c) a mapping from program to problem,
(d) a mapping from program to the program schemata that it uses and
(e) a student model,

in order to provide as output a range of explanations that described the program or its behaviour in different ways. The choice of which kind of explanation was output would depend on the mutual goals of the user and the system.

Diagrammatic traces of Prolog execution are already available in various implementations of Prolog, as are program trace analysers and these would need to be adapted to fit into the comprehensive explanation system proposed. Exhaustive logical or procedural descriptive output can be achieved by implementing a meta-interpreter that produces an examinable trace of program execution. This trace can be traversed, following the trail of the program that generated it or in other ways, to emit comments about program execution or structure. Where the explanation deals only with salient issues, the user may interrupt it to request more detail if needed.

More difficult and interesting would be the development of the explanation pruning and focusing rules that enable attention to be concentrated on salient issues and thus invoke such phrases as "... and so on" or "the same process repeats for the other members of the list until..."

Development of such pruning rules would require empirical work recording and analysing skilled tutors' explanations to students. This would also have to examine the extent to which explanations interweave different kinds and styles of explanation e.g. logical, procedural and problem-domain.

One could imagine the further possibility (though this is much harder) of critiquing a student's own explanation of behaviour of a program, possibly using methods adapted from critiquing-style expert-systems. Other areas that could be explored include the development of explanations derived from incorrect programs as in the manner of PROUST [16] but based on reasoning about the code rather than simply through pattern matching onto pre-stored buggy plans.

Another possibility is a tutor similar to Quest [22] for electricity that engages the student in work on programming at increasing levels of sophistication (see also the chapters by White, and by Frederiksen & White elsewhere in this volume). This does not mean merely extending the range of programming constructs or plans but implies addressing the issue of what happens when a program runs in increasingly accurate (rather than detailed) terms. At each level of sophistication the system would need to have a library of standard buggy views available in order to be able to deal with students' misconceptions.

5. Conclusions

There is an inherent danger in the provision of more flexibility, more power and more features in tutors and environments for novices. This is that the load on the student for learning about the system itself is out of proportion compared to the learning load associated with the target programming skills. As windows proliferate and mouse sensitive icons litter the screen the student can become overwhelmed. Of course this is no worse than the bad old days of the student being mystified by the terseness of a single waiting prompt.

In [9] we sketched the problem of supporting a student in the process of choosing, developing, and implementing a program for a topic that related to his own interest and showed how it was likely to stay beyond the state of the art in AI (Artificial Intelligence) for some little while. Despite this caution, it appears that useful gains in breadth and flexibility can be made in the next few years by pulling together and developing themes that have already made some progress.

References

1. Abelson, H., Sussman, G.J. & Sussman, J. *Structure and Interpretation of Computer Programs*, MIT Press, 1985.
2. Anderson, J. R. & Reiser, B. J, The LISP Tutor *BYTE*, 10, 4, 1935.
3. Bonar, J. & Cunningham, R. Bridge: an intelligent tutor for thinking about programming, in *Artificial Intelligence and Human Learning*, Self, J. (ed.), Chapman and Hall, 1988.
4. Broughton, D. IPSEs for Commercial Application Systems, *Proceedings of workshop on Project Support Environments*, London, 1985.
5. Bundy, A., Pain, H., and Lynch, L. A proposed Prolog Story, Research Paper 283, *Department of Artificial Intelligence*, University of Edinburgh, 1986.
6. Cox, B.M., Jenkins, J., & Pollitzer, E. Understanding and Concept Acquisition in Adaptive Intelligent Tutoring Systems, *Proceedings of the Fifth International Conference on Technology and Education*, Edinburgh, 1988.
7. de Castro, M.I., Sanchez, A.D. & Maillo, M.F.V, Building a Programming Tutor by Dynamic Planning: case studies and a proposal, *Proceedings of the International Conference on Intelligent Teaching Systems*, Montreal, 1988.
8. du Boulay, J.B.H., & Sothcott, C. *Computers Teaching Programming*, in *Artificial Intelligence and Education* (Volume 1), Lawler, R.W. & Yazdani, M. (eds.), Ablex Publishing, 1987.
9. du Boulay, J.B.H. & Sloman, A., Bread Today, Jam Tomorrow: the impact of AI on education, *Proceedings of Fifth International Conference on Technology and Education*, Collins, J.H., Estes, N. & Walker, D. (eds) Edinburgh, 1988.
10. Eisenstadt, M. A Powerful PROLOG Trace Package, *ECAI-84: Advances in Artificial Intelligence*, T. O'Shea (ed.) Elsevier Science Publishers, 1984.
11. Eisenstadt, M., Brayshaw, M. *The Transparent Prolog Machine TPM: An Execution Model and Graphical Debugger for Logic Programming*, Technical Report 21, Human Cognition Research Laboratory, The Open University, 1986.
12. Elsom-Cook, M. T. *Design Considerations of an Intelligent Tutoring System for Programming languages*, University of Warwick, Department of Psychology, 1985.
13. Fung, P. Novice's Predictions of Prolog's Control Flow, *Centre for Information Technology in Education Report No. 35*, Institute of Educational Technology, Open University, 1987.
14. Goldstein, I.P. *The Genetic Graph: a representation for the evolution of procedural knowledge*, in *Intelligent Tutoring Systems* Sleeman, D. & Brown J.S. (eds.), Academic Press, 1982.
15. Jackson, M. *Principles of program design*, Academic Press, London 1975.
16. Johnson, W. L. *Intention-based diagnosis of errors in novice programs*, Computer Science Dept, Research Report No. 395 Yale University, New Haven, Connecticut, 1985.
17. Jones, J., Millington, M. & Ross, P. Understanding User Behaviour in Command-Driven Systems, in *Artificial Intelligence and Human Learning*, Self, J. (ed.), Chapman and Hall, 1988.
18. Looi, C.K. *Automatic Program Analysis in a Prolog Intelligent Teaching System*, unpublished Ph.D. thesis, Department of Artificial Intelligence, University of Edinburgh, 1988.
19. Miller, M.L. A structured planning and debugging environment for elementary programming, *International Journal Man-Machine Studies*, 11, 79-95, 1978.
20. Ross, P. Teaching PROLOG to Undergraduates, *Artificial Intelligence and Simulation of Behaviour Quarterly*, Autumn 1982.
21. Self, J., *Knowledge, Belief and User Modelling, in Artificial Intelligence III: methodology, systems, applications*, O'Shea, T. & Sgurev, V. (eds.), North-Holland, 1988.

22. White, B.Y. & Frederiksen, J.R., Qualitative Models and Intelligent Learning Environments, in *Artificial Intelligence and Education*, Volume 1, Lawler, R.W. & Yazdani, M. (eds.), Ablex, 1987.

17

Problem Solving and Explanation in Intelligent Tutoring Systems: Issues for Future Research

Brian J. Reiser
Cognitive Science Laboratory
Princeton University
Princeton, NJ 08542
U.S.A.

Abstract: The key to building effective intelligent tutoring systems is the representation of knowledge in the tutor's problem solver. The problem solving knowledge determines the reasoning of students that the system can understand and the type of feedback the system can provide. We discuss the form of problem solving knowledge in intelligent tutors and the use of problem solving knowledge to provide guidance and feedback. We argue that model tracing tutors can be extended by building more underlying knowledge into their rule bases, and briefly describe GIL, a programming tutor built upon this elaborated model. We describe some of the current issues facing intelligent tutoring research, including the integration of rule-based and qualitative reasoning, timing and content of feedback, pedagogical strategies, and human-computer interface issues.

Keywords: ACT*, addition, analogical retrieval, Artificial Intelligence, diagnosing, domain knowledge, error feedback, GIL, Graphical Instruction in LISP, immediate feedback, intelligent tutoring systems, interface, knowledge representation, learning complex skills, mental models, methodology, model tracing, multiple views, reasoning rules, rule-based reasoning, simulation, student model, task analysis, tutoring dialogues

1. Introduction

A central issue in current intelligent tutoring systems research is the nature of the knowledge represented in the system. In problem solving domains such as mathematics, computer programming, and the physical sciences, a tutor needs to be able to solve the problems presented to students, step by step, following any reasonable path to a solution. To be most effective, the system must trace the student's reasoning so that it can offer suggestions or criticisms on individual steps, rather than being limited to advice on a complete solution attempt. The problem solving knowledge is crucial for understanding the student's behaviour and for providing specific feedback. This paper presents a brief overview of some current research issues concerning the form of problem solving knowledge and its use in intelligent tutoring systems to provide feedback to students. We begin with a brief discussion of the model tracing methodology for building tutors using rule-based problem solving models, and argue that such models can be extended by augmenting problem solving rules with knowledge about the justification and consequences of each step in a solution. We discuss the GIL programming tutor which is an initial experiment using such an elaborated model. Considerations of problem solving knowledge and explanation raise a number of important research questions. These include the nature of problem solving knowledge, its use in the construction of explanations, the timing and content of feedback, pedagogical strategies for explanation, and the design of human-computer interfaces. Addressing these issues requires empirical studies of the effectiveness of computer and human tutors.

2. Constructing Explanations from Problem Solving Knowledge

Domain knowledge is often represented in tutors as a set of problem solving rules [2,17] or a network of plans and subplans [7,31,32]. Each rule contains a description of a particular problem situation and a step to take in that situation. Plan representations specify how to achieve a goal by decomposing it into subgoals or by executing a sequence of actions. A tutor based on such representations can track a student's solution by matching each student step against the actions of the rules or the plan decomposition in its problem solving model. Rule and plan-based problem solvers have been used as the basis for tutors for mathematics [3,11,52), computer programming [2,7,22,31,32,40], and medical reasoning [15,17].

Anderson and his colleagues, based on pedagogical implications of Anderson's (1983) ACT* learning theory, have developed the *model tracing* methodology for intelligent tutoring systems [1,2]. A model tracing tutor provides instruction in the context of problem solving by monitoring a student's solution and providing feedback when the student requests guidance or demonstrates a misconception. The tutor analyzes each step as it is taken to determine whether it is on the path toward a solution or indicates a misconception. The student's step is analyzed by comparing it with the rules currently considered by the tutor's problem solving model, called the ideal student model. If the student's action is one that would be produced by executing one of the rules considered by the ideal student model at that point in the problem, the model applies that rule, thus following the student's path through the problem. Following such a correct step, the tutor is silent and permits the student to continue. Alternatively, if the student's action does not correspond to a correct step, the tutor considers its Catalog of buggy rules, which represent general patterns of errors. Errors are diagnosed when the student's step matches the action of a buggy rule, whereupon the tutor interrupts with the advice associated with the rule. In this way the tutor understands each step the student takes and stays in the background when the student is following a path leading to a correct solution, but upon request or an erroneous step, it provides a hint or the next step in the solution, enabling the student to continue. For example, the CMU LISP Intelligent Tutoring System helps students learn to write LISP programs by providing feedback as students compose a program to solve a problem [5,22,40]. The system monitors each word a student enters in a function definition, matching the step taken by the student against the possible next steps suggested by the tutor's problem solver, providing immediate feedback when an error is diagnosed as well as hints concerning overall strategies and possible next steps when requested.

The model tracing methodology is quite effective in providing online feedback for students as they solve problems. One way to extend the capabilities of model tracing tutors would be for a tutor to construct explanations directly from its problem solving knowledge, rather than relying on canned text associated with the rules. However, a limitation in the form of many current tutors is that their explanations rely on knowledge that is not contained in the rules used by the tutor to solve problems (cf., [16]). For example, the ideal model rules in the CMU LISP Tutor are essentially *action-oriented,* in that they associate an action to take with a particular problem situation but do not encode the underlying causal knowledge explaining why that particular action would be effective. Model tracing tutors are presumably successful because they provide appropriate feedback and guidance. To the extent that the task analysis in the problem solving model is a good representation of students' reasoning, an explanation associated with a rule can be provided in the particular context in which it is relevant. Thus, by matching each student step against its correct and buggy rules, the model tracing tutor is very successful in tracking a student's reasoning, discovering when the student diverges from a correct solution path, and categorizing the type of misconception that most likely underlies the error. Explanations associated with correct rules selected by the ideal model can be provided as hints to suggest a strategy or step to take next, and explanations associated with buggy rules can be provided in response to errors to point out why a student step is wrong. However, these explanations are constructed from "canned" templates that draw on knowledge *not* represented in the problem solving rules. The tutor relies on the problem solving model to determine when an explanation is needed and which subskill in the domain needs instruction, but the instruction then conveys knowledge that is not contained in its domain model and was instead hand-crafted for each situation.

A more complete simulation of the student's reasoning makes possible an alternative approach in which explanations can be constructed directly from the content of the rules themselves. In such a system, whatever information was required to solve the problem could in principle be conveyed to the student. The knowledge used to explain an action would be the same knowledge used to reason about it, providing a more robust pedagogical tool than one in which explanations were individually prepared for each situation. More effective explanations could be constructed to help students reason about the conditions that enable an operator or plan to be used, the effects of executing the operator, and the way in which an operator achieves or brings the student closer to a goal. A problem solver with this type of knowledge would be able not only to construct a program but would be able to reason about its execution. This type of reasoning has begun to be explored by systems involving qualitative or mental models e.g., [56]. In order to build model tracing tutors that can explain their reasoning, it will be necessary to build problem solvers that combine rule-based behaviour with such qualitative reasoning.

Constructing a tutor with the ability to explain its reasoning has additional advantages. Explanations could be dynamically constructed in response to errors rather than relying on a bug catalog that contains specific recognizers for each error situation. Instead, the tutor can compare the student's step with the steps considered in the ideal model and describe the way in which the student's step results in less desirable consequences. In addition, explanations can be tailored to the particular student's current knowledge state. More or less detail could be given, contingent upon information in the student model.

We have constructed an intelligent programming tutor called GIL, *Graphical Instruction in LISP*, that begins to address these knowledge representation issues [41-43]. GIL follows the model tracing method used in the CMU LISP Tutor, but it contains a different type of problem solving model, designed to make explicit the causal knowledge about programming operations, and an explanation component that constructs hints and error feedback directly from the content of its problem solving knowledge. If an error in a student step is found, GIL's explainer analyzes the discrepancies between the student's step and the closest matching correct rule and offers suggestions to the student about how to improve the step. Explanations may draw upon the problem solving rule, general knowledge about the operator being used, and the higher-level plan of which the step is a part.

The GIL problem solver consists of a set of reasoning rules and high-level plans. Each rule contains a description of the properties of the intermediate products in the solution that the step creates. The tutor needs to understand how LISP transforms the data at each step so that it can guide the student in reasoning through a new plan. For example, it is not sufficient for the rules to encode the knowledge that taking the *first* of a reversed list will return the last element; the rules must also represent the reasoning in the algorithm, i.e., reversing the list results in the last element being moved into the first position, enabling the use of *first* to extract that element. To represent this knowledge, each rule describes the properties that are true of the input and output data for that step. Thus, the problem solver not only knows what step to take, but also knows how each step changes the data, and therefore why the step is effective. When the rule is executed, these properties are added to the current problem state as new inferences about the problem. These properties are then used to select further steps involving the object, and can be used to explain why a step is strategic or to explain why a student's step is in error. GIL contains a graphical programming interface that is structured to take advantage of this additional knowledge. Students build a program by connecting together objects representing program constructs into a graph, rather than by defining LISP functions in their traditional text form. Students take a step in GIL by selecting a LISP function and specifying its input and output data. Hence all intermediate products are explicit in the program graph. Rather than specifying only the sequence of operations, such as "take the first of the *rest* of (a *b c d),"* the student must indicate the input and output for each operation, e.g., "extract the element, *b,* by taking the *first* of *(b c d);* get *(b c d)* by taking the *rest* of (a *b c d)."* The use of intermediate products makes the process of combining steps more explicit and enables tutoring on individual steps in the solution. The interaction allows the tutor to monitor students more closely and provide more useful assistance as they learn programming plans than one in which students specify only the final surface form of the solution.

GIL constructs explanations in response to requests for a hint and in response to a legal or strategic error to point out the part of the step that is in error. The GIL explainer draws upon the same knowledge base that the problem solver uses to construct solutions: problem solving rules, plans, and general knowledge about the operators. If a hint is requested, the explainer selects a rule that best continues the problem solving exhibited by the student so far, and uses the information in the rule to construct a hint. The explainer uses a small number of general frames that guide the construction for each type of step, namely goal decomposition, forward reasoning, or goal achievement. These explanation frames indicate the parts of the goal and the rule that should be described and some general English to tie them together.

In the case of student errors, GIL finds the most similar matching rule and uses it to explain how the student's step is in error. Because the rules contain a description of the input and output, the student's step can be compared with the properties of the objects in the rule, and any discrepancies can be described. GIL handles legal errors, in which the step in the program does not correctly manipulate the selected data, and strategic errors, in which the chosen step is a legal LISP operation but is not strategically useful. GIL first describes what is good about the student's step and then points out the ways in which the step is in error or could be improved by explaining how the student's input, output, or function deviates from the properties in the correct rule. In this way, GIL responds to student errors without any bug catalog. Instead, explanations are dynamically constructed by comparing the student's step to the relevant problem solving rules.

3. The Content of Explanations

Our initial work on GIL demonstrates the potential for driving the explanation process directly from problem solving rules. In addition to resulting in a more complete psychological model of expertise, such a tutor is more flexible in that it can generate feedback dynamically to new situations, rather than being prepared with extensive bug catalogs and a catalog of English explanations associated with correct and buggy rules. This work raises several important questions. Our initial attempts at representing causal or underlying knowledge have been very simple, but seem to be effective in encoding the changes a particular step makes in the problem state. However, this scheme does not capture higher level organizations such as plans. It is often important in explanations to explain the role of a step in the overall strategy. We are currently working on using larger plan structures in the explainer, so that GIL can explain a single step in a solution within the context of its role in the solution plan. One difficulty is that it would be ineffective to explain a step in a solution by generating the entire chain of reasoning of which the step is a part. More complex explanation schemes are needed to generate an explanation for an entire plan. Although in principle the simple scheme of describing the properties of the input and output data for a step could be extended to generate an explanation of the entire chain of reasoning representing a plan, in most cases this would be too much detail. An important research question concerns how to integrate feedback on individual problem solving steps with more global explanations of strategy. We need to explore how to combine rule-based reasoning with the type of qualitative reasoning that can explain how the various components of a device or program interact.

A related explanation issue involved in integrating rules with larger plan structures concerns the problem of diagnosing the amount and level of information to provide in an explanation. As the material incorporated into an explanation becomes more complex, it becomes crucial to construct explanations focusing on the differential between the inferred knowledge of the student and that of the problem solver. Thus, the use of student models in focusing the content of explanations is an important area of research to pursue.

Another important research topic concerns the particular focus of explanations. Even when explanations are constructed and are therefore constrained to refer to the knowledge used by the problem solver, there are many choices in the type of information to include in error feedback. For example, the explanation could focus on the problem solving goal, the part of the student step that is correct, the location of the error, the reason why the step will not work, a description of the type of step that would be better, or the precise nature of the fix to the current step. Empirical work is necessary to investigate the type of information effective for error feedback, and the contingencies governing the selection of this information.

4. The Control and Timing of Feedback

The student's control of the tutoring interaction is another issue to be investigated. One possible answer to the problem in selecting the right information to provide to the student is to leave the selection of information up to the student. For example, a system might point out to the student that a step is in error, and leave to the student selection of information about the location of the error, explanations about why the step will not work, characteristics of a correct step, possible fixes, etc. Although letting the student control the explanation process fits well with some pedagogical philosophies, it remains an empirical question as to whether students will take advantage of the help provided, and will be able to select the information that would be most useful to them. In many situations, students may be reluctant to request assistance from a tutor, preferring instead to try to solve the problem themselves. Experiments on the content of feedback and issues of student control are needed to explore these issues.

One of the more controversial issues in the area of feedback concerns the timing of feedback. Anderson, Boyle, and Reiser [2] argued that a tutor should respond with "immediate feedback". Anderson et al. argued that there are clear advantages for providing immediate feedback upon errors because the learning mechanism for adjusting a faulty rule or forming a new correct rule relies upon the problem situation being active in memory. Empirical evaluations of the effectiveness of feedback in procedural learning indicate that students learn procedures more quickly when provided with this feedback. Students can more easily utilize feedback and explanations when the reasoning that led to the error is still accessible.

Furthermore, immediate feedback can prevent long episodes of counter-productive floundering. Consistent with this view, Carroll's experiments with "training wheel" interfaces demonstrate a large advantage in learning from environments that prevent typical error states [12,13]. Students learned computer skills more quickly because they committed less time recovering from error states the training interface prevented. The extra time spent by control subjects did not appear to be useful, indeed they scored lower on performance tests than the training wheel subjects. On the other hand, many educators argue that learning is more effective when students are given the opportunity to experiment and thereby "discover" and correct their own errors e.g., [10,49]. Guided discovery systems and learning environments are designed to enable students to learn through exploration e.g., [27,45,52,54]. One might argue, based on this view, that the immediate feedback provided by model tracing tutors circumvents the possible benefits from exploration. An important consideration in evaluating these arguments is precisely what is meant by the term "immediate feedback". In order for a discovery environment to be effective, the student must be able to directly elicit feedback from the environment. This is an important characteristic of reactive learning environments for science and mathematics e.g.,[27,45,52,54,56]. These environments in fact do supply a form of immediate feedback. Although the student is not given explicit feedback that a particular step is correct or incorrect, the environment gives them feedback about the *results* of a step, so that students can evaluate for themselves whether a particular experiment has been successful or not. Indeed, the psychological benefits of immediate feedback discussed by Anderson et al. apply very well to students trying to learn through exploration. These environments would not be very effective if this feedback were delayed. Students would not be able to keep track of their hypotheses and adjust their reasoning without being able to see the immediate results of each test. Immediate feedback of this sort appears to be an essential element of discovery environments.

It is also important to consider the behaviour of human tutors in providing feedback. The analyses of tutoring dialogues by Fox [25] demonstrate that tutors are very quick in the feedback they provide. Fox argues that tutors usually provide students an opportunity to correct their own errors by slightly delaying their feedback when the student makes an error. However, these delays are very short (*1-2* seconds) and typically feedback in the examples presented by Fox is always provided within the next sentence or two following the error. Furthermore, students become very attuned to the constant confirmatory feedback provided by the tutors. In most cases, the lack of immediate reassurance following a step is taken by students to indicate that they have made an error. Thus, human tutors appear to provide at least minimal feedback quickly following each student step.

It is important to stress, however, that this feedback may not correspond to the type of feedback typically provided by intelligent tutors. Lepper and Chabay [34] argued that tutors do not perform error diagnosis. They argued that human tutors do not offer students their own hypotheses about the faulty reasoning that led to a particular error. Instead, they direct the students attention to the part of their work that is in error, in an attempt to get the student to "discover" the error. Often the tutors will ask leading questions to focus the student on the part of the step that was in error. In many cases, the tutor's feedback is sufficient for the student to rethink the step and correct the mistake without further hints from the tutor. There is an important distinction to be made here. It is clear that the tutors in Lepper and Chabay's examples do not offer diagnosis and descriptions of the buggy reasoning that would account for a student error. On the other hand, through leading questions these tutors do focus students' attention on the parts of a step that need to be fixed. Their leading questions may even refer to the surface characteristics of the error, as in the following leading question from a tutor of a student learning addition "Now look at that again. Can you put two numbers down in one column here?" (data from Putnam cited by Lepper and Chabay, [34] p. 246).

These analyses of human tutors suggest that they exhibit certain aspects of the error diagnosis exhibited by some more aggressive computer tutors. Feedback from the human tutors is quickly used by students to realize they have made an error, and very focused questions from tutors may help students isolate the particular part of their step that is in error. However, tutors will not convey any detailed hypotheses about the particular buggy rule that would lead to the exhibited error, and do not seem to engage in questioning the student in order to further elucidate the nature of their misconception [39]. Furthermore, human tutors are able to provide feedback in a somewhat less intrusive manner than the typical verbal explanations provided by computer tutors, when simply by delaying simple confirmation (such as "ok" or "right") the student realizes that the step needs to be reconsidered. It is important also to consider the grain size of the interaction in these various cases. The human tutors in these studies respond approximately to a sentence or two of information from the student. This may correspond to a larger chunk of information than the immediate feedback in some model tracing tutors, such as the CMU LISP Tutor (which responds after each word is typed). It is necessary to explore issues in the grain size of interaction.

The import of the work so far indicates both pedagogical advantages and dangers associated with immediate feedback. Investigation of the tradeoffs involved in the delayed feedback in discovery learning and the immediate feedback of some tutoring systems is an important area for future research. It is necessary to examine not only on the timing of feedback, but also the particular content and degree of the feedback provided. To date, there has been little empirical work examining the role of feedback in learning complex skills, but this is clearly one of the areas in which intelligent tutors can be excellent experimental tools. Intelligent tutors can be used to run more fine-grained studies of feedback and learning e.g., [22] than have been previous undertaken in educational research.

5. Knowledge Representation: Cases and General Principles

Instruction in problem solving domains is typically based on a combination of text describing principles and examples demonstrating use of the principles. Students tend to rely heavily on these examples, using an example problem as a model to solve new problems, rather than attempting to translate abstract instruction into procedures [4,14,38,58]. Indeed, if instructions and examples are in conflict, subjects rely on examples instead of abstract instructions [35].

The role of examples in the explanation process of intelligent tutoring systems has yet to be much explored. Although many tutoring systems interact with students while they work on problems, and may use a model of the student in order to select which problem to give the student next (e.g., [28]), there has been little attention given the use of examples in feedback. One method used by human tutors is to propose a particular case as an example of a principle or a counter example to encourage the student to reevaluate hypotheses [21,44]. It is typical for tutoring systems to incorporate general information and examples when providing feedback or hints to students. For example, feedback in GIL combines these two types of information, explaining the general properties of the data (drawn from the rule) but instantiating them in the context of the specific example used to construct an algorithm for the program. In GIL, students design a program using a specific example of the input and output data, so discussing a strategy in terms of an example is quite feasible. However, if we were to apply the explanation construction techniques used in GIL to domains other than programming, constructing an example to use in an explanation becomes a more difficult issue. An example must be selected to illustrate a point that is connected with the current problem so that its relevance will be clear, yet simple enough to understand so that processing the example does not detract from the problem on which the student is currently working. Some initial heuristics for selecting or constructing examples have been discussed for declarative domains [21] and argumentation in law [44] but further research on systems that generate examples is required to develop general principles of teaching through examples. In addition, empirical studies are needed to explore the feedback situations in which examples aid explanations, and the most effective techniques for combining general information with specific examples.

Another form in which examples can be used is by reminding students of their own past work. The types and amount of similarities between new problems and previous examples affects whether relevant examples are retrieved and how easily they can be used [24,47,48].

Some research has suggested that retrieval of previous cases is strongly influenced by superficial similarities between situations (e.g., [26]), but in a problem solving context, students can retrieve structurally similar problems despite very different surface structures [24]. Remembering and adapting previous cases has been argued to be an important learning method (e.g., [29,33]). It may turn out to be a useful pedagogical strategy to exploit the utility of remindings, and to remind a student who asks for a hint of particular problems he or she has solved that might be relevant to the current problem.

There are many forms that tutors' reminding might take. Students making an error might be reminded of a previous problem in which such an error arose and was successfully corrected. Students asking for guidance could be given hints by reminding them of past problems they had solved using a strategy that would also be effective in the current problem. There are also potential dangers in reminding students of past solutions, however. In some cases, students make errors on current problems by misapplying techniques from previous problems, because they attempt to map solutions from problems whose superficial similarities are misleading, or interpret the technique in the previous problem in an overly specialized manner, and hence fail to map the solution at the appropriate level of generality [38,23]. Research on analogical retrieval is required to explore methods for organizing previous solutions in memory and recognizing relevant similarities so that this pedagogical strategy can be effectively incorporated in intelligent tutors. In addition, empirical work is needed to explore when remindings are effective, when students can correctly map strategies from previous solutions, and how to assist the student in forming the generalizations from similar examples at an optimal level of generality.

6. Problem Solving Representations and Interfaces

Students communicate with a tutoring system through an interface. These interfaces, given current hardware and software technology, cannot achieve anything approaching the bandwidth of person to person communication. Human tutors interacting with students communicate verbally, by drawing diagrams, pointing, and so on, all in a highly interactive fashion in which the tutor constantly corrects and interrupts his or her own behaviour based on an assessment of the student's reactions, drawing on visual data (the student's face), explicit verbal data, and inferred audio data (e.g., tone of voice). Nevertheless, a computer-human interface can be effectively used to provide students with a manner of better viewing the problem solving task. One goal is to structure the interface to get the students to be more explicit about the processes they are using to solve the problem, i.e., to have the structure of the interface reflect the students' own thinking [19,20]. For example, in Anderson, Boyle, and Yost's [3] Geometry Tutor the student generates a proof by constructing a tree connecting the givens with the goal statement, labelling each inference with the theorem that justifies it. Similarly in our GIL programming tutor a graphical interface is used to better represent the planning required to construct an algorithm. These systems effectively represent planning as a combination of forward and backward search. Although tutors employing these types of interfaces appear to be effective, it is important to disentangle the various benefits these systems provide. Direct evidence for the benefits of representing the structure of the problem space has not yet been provided. Furthermore, the process of designing a visual representation to provide insight into the structure of a problem solving system is still very much an art. The principles for effective visual representations remain to be elucidated (see [51,36] for initial discussions of some of these visual representation issues).

Another important property of intelligent tutors is the capacity to provide multiple views on a problem. Several researchers studying expert reasoning have proposed that expertise involves an ability to coordinate reasoning using multiple mental models (e.g., [46,54,57]). These views may involve reasoning about an object's behaviour in the real world, the underlying qualitative physical model, and quantitative analyses. A strategy being explored in several learning environments is that multiple perspectives will enable students to map from a better understood view to a more abstract view. This is a technique being exploited in Arithmekit [9] in which arithmetic problems can be displayed in a concrete domain (Dienes Blocks) and the symbolic domain (two column subtraction), in ThinkerTools described by White in her chapter in this book, in which the system provides various realistic and abstract representations of an object in motion, and Steamer, which enables the student to examine varying perspectives on the operating components of a steam plant [30].

Experiments are needed to address the effectiveness of multiple views during problem solving. Under what conditions does an additional view aid problem solving? How can we determine what types of views will be helpful? We need to develop a learning model that accounts for learning by mapping from one representation to another. Although the target skill (e.g., two column subtraction) may be well represented by rules, it is not clear whether rule-based models are the best representation for the knowledge in the base domain, manipulations of concrete blocks, nor might they explain why subtraction problems are first easier with blocks than with symbols.

7. Human Tutoring Strategies and Computer Implementations

Intelligent tutoring systems have been effective in encorporating some of the pedagogical advantages of human tutoring and cognitive apprenticeship [20]. Individualized tutoring is generally considered the most effective form of instruction [6,18]. In problem solving domains, human tutors moderate their control of the interaction to provide sufficient assistance for the student to solve the problem, while being careful to avoid leading the student too much. In particular, tutors provide enough hints to help students plan and effect a solution, and use error feedback and hints to prevent students from reaching situations from which it would be too difficult to recover.

More research is needed to characterize the strategies of human tutors and evaluate why they are effective. Furthermore, it does not follow that intelligent tutoring systems will be most effective when constructed as simulations of human tutors. The following issues are important to pursue in evaluating the relation of human tutoring strategies and computerized tutors.

First, it is important to consider how much of the effectiveness of a tutor depends on expertise in the problem domain. Much of the benefit of a human tutor may be due to encouraging the student to make the reasoning in a solution explicit rather than in the specific explanations and feedback provided by the tutor. Palincsar and Brown's [37] reciprocal teaching method and several programs for teaching "thinking skills" have stressed students' articulation of their problem solving processes as a method for building and debugging problem solving skills (see [8] for a discussion of such programs). If a large part of the benefit of interacting with a tutor is the articulation of one's own reasoning, then it may not always be necessary to provide expert tutors for students. Students may also benefit by being paired in a collaborative problem solving situation with the program. In this way, the program may be effective in forcing the student to articulate his or her reasoning and helping organize the work done so far, even if the tutor does not contain a powerful problem solver capable of solving the problem for itself.

Second, it is important to carefully examine whether computer tutors should implement all and only those strategies shown to be effective for human tutors. Human tutors have capabilities difficult to achieve currently within computer tutors, e.g., natural language, visual observation and analyses of subtle non-verbal cues from the student, etc. Similarly, computer tutors may have capabilities difficult for humans to emulate, such as automatic screen display of the current problem situation, graphical representations, and retrieval of past work. Thus, optimal strategies for computer tutoring may diverge from those used by human tutors. Further research is needed to describe the strategies used by effective human tutors and the contingencies governing their selection of strategies for particular problem situations and to explore which of these strategies can profitably be incorporated into computerized tutors.

8. Research Strategies

For all of these issues, both Artificial Intelligence research and psychological experimentation are required. We need to find out more about how experts reason, using both rules and mental models. This will involve empirical studies of human experts. Such work must be combined with AI research on how to simulate this reasoning. In order to study the pedagogical effectiveness of various methods for communicating this reasoning, it is necessary to build intelligent tutors and study how students learn by interacting with these programs. It is important to stress that these studies will require more than a simple comparison of a group of students learning with a computer tutor and a control group that learns the material without a tutor. Intelligent tutors can most profitably be used in experiments in which pedagogical variables of interest, such as the nature of an interface, the timing of feedback, student control of feedback, curriculum design, etc., are explored by implementing manipulations of these variables in the tutoring system. In addition to leading to more effective educational technology, such research on intelligent tutors will be invaluable in illuminating how students acquire cognitive skills.

References

1. Anderson, J. R., Boyle, C. F., Farrell, R. G., & Reiser, B. J. Cognitive principles in the design of computer tutors. In P. Morris (Ed.), *Modelling cognition,* New York, NY: Wiley. 1987.
2. Anderson, J. R., Boyle, C. F., & Reiser, B. J. Intelligent tutoring systems. *Science,* 228, 456-462. 1985.
3. Anderson, J. R., Boyle, C. F., & Yost, G. The geometry tutor. *Proceedings of the Ninth International Joint Conference on Artificial Intelligence,* Los Angeles, CA. 1985.
4. Anderson, J. R., Farrell, R., & Sauers, R. (1985). Learning to program in LISP. *Cognitive Science,* 8, 87-129.
5. Anderson, J. R., & Reiser, B. J. The LISP tutor. *Byte,* 10,159-175. 1985.
6. Bloom, B. S. The 2 sigma problem: The search for methods of group instruction as effective as one-to-one tutoring. *Educational Researcher,* 13, 4-16. 1984.
7. Bonar, J. G., & Cunningham, R. Bridge: Tutoring the programming process. In J. Psotka, L. D. Massey, & S. A. Mutter, Eds. *Intelligent tutoring systems: Lessons learned.* Erlbaum. 1988.
8. Bransford, J. D., Stein, B. S., Arbitman-Smith, R., & Vye, N. J. Improving thinking and learning skills: An analysis of three approaches. In Segal, J. W., Chipman, S. F., & Glaser R., Eds. *Thinking and learning skills, Volume 1: Relating instruction to research.* Erlbaum. 1985.
9. Brown, J. S. Learning by doing revisited for electronic learning environments. In M. A. White (Ed.), *The future of electronic learning,* Hillsdale, NJ: Erlbaum. 1983.
10. Bruner, J. S. The act of discovery. *Harvard Educational Review,* 31, 21-32. 1961.
11. Burton R.B. Diagnosing bugs in a simple procedural skill. In D.H. Sleeman & J.S. Brown (eds) *Intelligent Tutoring Systems* New York Academic, 157-183. 1982.
12. Carroll, J. M., & Carrithers, C. Blocking learner error states in a training wheels system. *Human Factors,* 26, 377-389. 1984.
13. Catrambone, R., & Carroll, J. M. Learning a word processing system with training wheels and guided exploration. *Proceedings of CHI+GI '87 Human Factors in Computing Systems.* New York: ACM, 169-174. 1987.
14. Chi, M. T. H., Bassok, M., Lewis, M. W., Reimann, P., & Glaser, R. Self explanations: How students study and use examples in learning to solve problems. *Cognitive Science,* 13,145-182.. 1991.
15. Clancey, W. J. Tutoring rules for guiding a case method dialogue. In D. H. Sleeman & J. S. Brown (Eds.), *Intelligent tutoring systems.* London: Academic Press. 1982.
16. Clancey, W. J. The epistemology of a rule-based expert system -- A framework for explanation. *Artificial Intelligence,* 20, 215-251. 1983.
17. Clancey, W. J. *Knowledge-based tutoring: The Guidon program.* Cambridge, MA: MIT Press. 1987.

18. Cohen, P. A., Kulik, J. A., & Kulik, C.-L. C. Educational outcomes of tutoring: A meta-analysis of findings. *American Educational Research Journal, 19*, 237-248. 1982.
19. Collins, A., & Brown, J. S. The computer as a tool for learning through reflection. In H. Mandl & A. Lesgold (Eds.), *Learning issues for intelligent tutoring systems*. New York: Springer-Verlag. 1988.
20. Collins, A., Brown, J. S., & Newman, S. E. Cognitive apprenticeship: Teaching the craft of reading, writing, and mathematics. To appear in L. B. Resnick (Ed.), *Cognition and instruction: Issues and agendas*. Hillsdale, NJ: Erlbaum. (in press).
21. Collins, A., & Stevens, A. L. Goals and strategies of inquiry teachers. In R. Glaser (Ed.), *Advances in Instructional Psychology, Volume 2*. Hillsdale, NJ: Erlbaum. 1982.
22. Corbett, A. T., Anderson, J. R., & Patterson, E. J. Problem compilation and tutoring flexibility in the LISP Tutor. *Proceedings of ITS-88: The International Conference on Intelligent Tutoring Systems*, Montreal, pp. 423-429. 1988.
23. Escott, J. A., & McCalla, G. I. Problem solving by analogy: A source of errors in novice LISP programming. *Proceedings of ITS-88: The International Conference on Intelligent Tutoring Systems*, Montreal, pp. 312-319. 1988.
24. Faries, J. M., & Reiser, B. J. Access and use of previous solutions in a problem solving situation. *Proceedings of the Tenth Annual Conference of the Cognitive Science Society*, Montreal. 1988.
25. Fox, B. A. *Cognitive and interactional aspects of correction in tutoring*. Technical Report #88-2. Institute of Cognitive Science, University of Colorado, Boulder, Colorado. 1988.
26. Gentner, D. Analogical inference and analogical access. In A. Prieditis (Ed.), *Analogica*, Los Altos, CA: Morgan Kaufman. 1988.
27. Glaser, R., Raghavan, K., & Schauble, L. Voltaville, a discovery environment to explore the laws of DC circuits. *Proceedings of ITS-88: The International Conference on Intelligent Tutoring Systems*, Montreal, pp. 61-66. 1988.
28. Goldstein, I. P. The genetic graph: A representation for the evolution of procedural knowledge. In D. H. Sleeman & J. S. Brown (Eds.), *Intelligent tutoring systems*. London: Academic Press. 1982.
29. Hammond, K. The use of remindings in planning. *Proceedings of the Eighth Annual Conference of the Cognitive Science Society*, Amherst, MA. 1986.
30. Hollan, J. D., Hutchins, E. L., & Weitzman, L. Steamer: An interactive inspectable simulation-based training system. *AI Magazine, 5*,15-28. 1984.
31. Johnson, W. L. *Intention-based diagnosis of errors in novice programs*. Palo Alto, CA: Morgan Kaufman. . 1986.
32. Johnson, W. L., & Soloway, E. PROUST: An automatic debugger for Pascal programs. In G. Kearsley (Ed.), *Artificial intelligence and instruction: Applications and methods*. Reading, MA: Addison-Wesley. 1987.
33. Kolodner, J. L. Extending problem solver capabilities through case-based inference. *Proceedings of the Fourth International Conference on Machine Learning*, Irvine, CA, Morgan Kaufman, 167-178. 1987.
34. Lepper, M. R., & Chabay, R. W. Socializing the intelligent tutor: Bringing empathy to computer tutors. In H. Mandl & A. Lesgold (Eds.), *Learning issues for intelligent tutoring systems*. New York: Springer-Verlag. 1988.
35. LeFevre, J. & Dixon, P. Do written instructions need examples? *Cognition and Instruction*, 3, 1-30. 1986.
36. Miller, J. R. The role of human-computer interaction in intelligent tutoring systems. In M. C. Polson, & J. J. Richardson (Eds.), *Foundations of intelligent tutoring systems*. Hillsdale, NJ: Erlbaum. 1988.
37. Palincsar, A. S., & Brown, A. L. Reciprocal teaching of comprehension-fostering and comprehension-monitoring activities. *Cognition and Instruction*, 1,117-175. 1984.
38. Pirolli, P. L., & Anderson, J. R. The role of learning from examples in the acquisition of recursive programming skills. *Canadian Journal of Psychology, 39*, 240-272. 1985.
39. Putnam, R. T. Structuring and adjusting content for students: A study of live and simulated tutoring of addition. *American Educational Research Journal*, 24,13-48. 1987.
40. Reiser, B. J., Anderson, J. R., & Farrell, R. G. Dynamic student modelling in an intelligent tutor for LISP programming. *Proceedings of the Ninth International Joint Conference on Artificial Intelligence*, Los Angeles, CA. 1985.

41. Reiser, B. J., Friedmann, P., Gevins, J., Kimberg, D., Ranney, M., & Romero, A. A graphical programming language interface for an intelligent LISP tutor. *Proceedings of CHI'88, Conference on Human Factors in Computing Systems,* ACM, New York, pp. 3944. 1988.
42. Reiser, B. J., Friedmann, P., Kimberg, D., & Ranney, M. Constructing explanations from problem solving rules to guide the planning of programs. *Proceedings of ITS-88: The International Conference on Intelligent Tutoring Systems,* Montreal, pp. 222-229.
43. Reiser, B. J., Kimberg, D. Y., Lovett, M. C., & Ranney, M. Knowledge representation and explanation in GIL, an intelligent tutor for programming. To appear in J. Larkin, R. Chabay, & C. Scheftic (Eds.), *Computer-assisted instruction and intelligent tutoring systems: Establishing communication and collaboration,* Erlbaum. (in press).
44. Rissland, E. L., & Ashley, K. D. Hypotheticals as heuristic device. *Proceedings of AAA1-86, Fifth National Conference on Artificial Intelligence,* Phila, PA, pp. 289-297. 1986.
45. Roschelle, J. *The Envisioning Machine: Facilitating students' reconceptualization of motion.* Paper presented at the Third International Conference on Artificial Intelligence and Education, Pittsburgh, PA. 1987.
46. Roschelle, J., & Greeno, J. G. *Mental models in expert physics reasoning.* Technical report #GK-2, School of Education, University of California, Berkeley. 1987.
47. Ross, B. H. Remindings and their effect in learning a cognitive skill. *Cognitive Psychology, 16, 371-416.* 1984.
48. Ross, B. H. This is like that: The use of earlier problems and the separation of similarity effects. *Journal of Experimental Psychology: Learning, Memory, and Cognition,* 13, 629639. 1987.
49. Schank, R. C., & Farrell, R. Creativity in education: A standard for computer-based teaching. *Machine-Mediated Learning.* 1987.
50. Segal, J. W., Chipman, S. F., & Glaser R., Eds. *Thinking and learning skills, Volume 1: Relating instruction to research.* Erlbaum. 1985.
51. Shneiderman, B. Direct manipulation: A step beyond programming languages. *IEEE Computer,* 16, 57-69. 1983.
52. Shute, V., Glaser, R., & Raghavan, K. Inference and discovery in an exploratory laboratory. To appear in P. L. Ackerman, R. J. Sternberg, & R. Glaser (Eds.), *Learning and individual differences.* San Francisco, CA: Freeman. (in press).
53. Sleeman, D. Assessing aspects of competence in basic algebra. In D. H. Sleeman & J. S. Brown (Eds.), *Intelligent tutoring systems.* London: Academic Press. 1982.
54. White, B. Y. ThinkerTools: Causal models, conceptual change, and science education. To appear in *Cognition and Instruction.* (in press).
55. White, B. Y., & Frederiksen, J. R. Qualitative models and intelligent learning environments. In R. Lawler & M. Yazdani (Eds.), *Artificial intelligence and education, Volume 1.* Norwood, NJ: Ablex. 1987.
56. White, B. Y., & Frederiksen, J. R. Causal model progressions as a foundation for intelligent learning environments. To appear in *Artificial Intelligence.* (in press).
57. Williams, M. D., Hollan, J. D., & Stevens, A. L. Human reasoning about a simple physical system. In D. Gentner & A. L. Stevens (Eds.), *Mental models,* Hillsdale, NJ: Erlbaum. 1983.
58. Zhu, X., & Simon, H. A. Learning mathematics from examples and by doing. *Cognition and Instruction, 4,* 137-166. 1987.

18

Mental Models and Understanding: A Problem for Science Education[1]

John R. Frederiksen and Barbara Y. White
Bolt, Beranek and Newman, Inc, Boston, Ma, U.S.A.

Abstract: Science, particularly physics, is a difficult, and apparently inaccessible subject, to a majority of American students. According to a recent report of the Educational Testing Service referred to in Science [12], "only 7% of 17-year-olds are adequately prepared for college-level science courses," and "more than half have so little scientific understanding that they cannot hold down jobs that require technical skills, benefit from specialized on-the-job training, or make informed decisions as citizens." Even students who have been interested in science and technology -- who, for example, enjoy tinkering with mechanics or electronics -- are often "put off" by physics as it is currently taught. The high school physics course is regarded by many students as perhaps the most difficult one offered. We are interested in why this is the case.

Our thesis is that there is a severe mismatch between the way people come naturally to view and understand the world, and the forms of physical theories with which they are presented in textbooks and classrooms. We are interested in mismatches between students' ways of reasoning about the physical world and the types of reasoning embodied in the physics curriculum. We shall also argue that physical theories -- presented solely as abstract, mathematical models -- do not do justice to the multiple types and levels of conceptualization that expert users of physics have built over years of experience with the subject. So the question becomes: What are the mismatches in form and content between the conceptual models of "textbook physics" and those of naive students of physics? What clues to more profitable ways of modelling physical systems can be found in the reasoning of expert practitioners of physics/engineering? And finally, how can we assist students in the construction of mental models of physical systems that will support a deep understanding of physical mechanisms from both a qualitative and a quantitative standpoint?

This inquiry will proceed from several sources. We will begin by recounting some experiences of a young student of physics (Tania, age 14), when she first encountered formal

[1] This work was supported by the U. S. Army Research Institute, Contract No. MND-903-87-C-0545 and by the Office of Educational Research and improvement, Contract OEG 0087-C1001. This paper does not necessarily reflect the views of the agencies supporting the research.

physics in high school. Her reactions to conventional physics instruction, particularly that dealing with electricity, will illustrate some of the successes and failures of conventional approaches, and will give us some leads concerning possible mismatches between students' requirements for understanding and textbook or classroom explanations. In addition, we shall refer to a survey we carried out of over 40 textbooks, which has substantiated for us the generality of the problems exemplified by Tania's course. An additional source of information comes from studies of the reasoning used by experts in solving physics problems. Together, these lines of evidence lead us to a number of hypotheses concerning characteristics of mental models that capture the "sense of mechanism" that people, both novices and experts, appear to look for in seeking to understand physical systems. Finally, we shall illustrate the form of mental model we have in mind with a brief description of a model for electricity that we believe has many of the characteristics needed for building an understanding of science.

Keywords: acausal reasoning, case relations, causal accounts, causal event sequences, causal reasoning, constraint-based reasoning, current electricity, device model, dynamic physical model, dynamic processes, Educational Testing Service, electricity, electrostatics, envisioning, macroscopic models, naive physics, physics, prior knowledge, qualitative arguments, qualitative model, qualitative theory, transient processes

1. Learning About Electricity

The physical science course Tania took included two units on electricity, one dealing with electrostatics, and the other on "current electricity." In the unit on electrostatics, the students developed a qualitative understanding of electrical fields and Coulomb's Law. They performed experiments using charged bars, metal and plastic disks, and electroscopes, and learned to solve problems involving the effects of attractions/repulsions between dissimilarly/similarly charged bodies through induction and conduction. An example of the type of problem they dealt with is given in figure 18.1A.

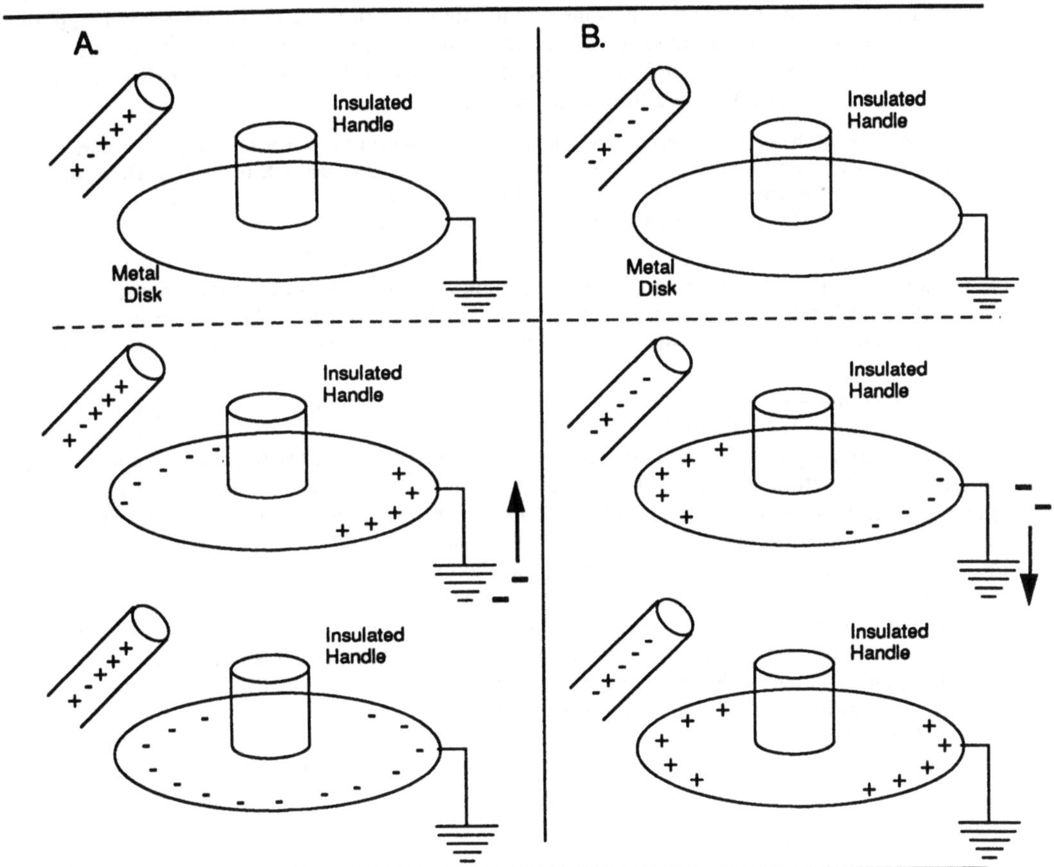

Fig.18.1. Examples of two problems taken from a high school course unit on electrostatics.

In this problem, a positively charged bar is brought near to a neutral metallic disk, which is connected to ground. The student's task is to show how charges on the bar/disk may change, and to explain why they do. We interviewed Tania 6 months after she completed her course on electricity. In solving Problem A, Tania created a qualitative, causal account of the experiment.

This is her explanation:

> "Because [the bar] is positive, it wants to be neutralized, so the electrons [in the disk] want to go into the bar to neutralize the bar. Also, electrons come out of the ground to the disk, because all the negatives are on the side of the disk next to the bar, and that leaves pluses next to the ground. So the disk has a positive charge there [next to the ground], even though it's grounded. The electrons in the ground want to neutralize the charge on that side of the disk. The positives over here [she points again to the grounded edge of the disk] attract negative electrons out of the ground."

Tania has constructed a series of qualitative steps to explain why there is a flow of electrons from ground to the metal plate. At first electrons on the disk were attracted to the bar and moved towards it, leaving an absence of electrons on the other side of the disk. In the second step, the positive charge created by an absence of electrons on the edge of the disk attracted electrons from the ground. Finally, this left an excess of electrons on the disk. Tania offers a similar explanation for the case (B) where the bar is negative:

> "This is sort of the opposite, because the bar is negative and the protons can't move (only electrons can move). Electrons are pushed away from the bar towards the grounded side of the disk. Then there are a bunch of electrons on the opposite side of the disk. They want to be neutralized, so then the electrons go into the ground, leaving the disk with a positive charge."

Judging from this student's reasoning in solving such problems, the course unit on electrostatics was quite successful in helping students to understand fundamental laws of electricity (Coulomb's Law) in *qualitative* terms, and how to apply those laws in reasoning about the effects of electrical forces within systems in which there is a movement of charge (such as the problems in figure 18.1). Students understand that there are attractions between unlike charged particles (or objects containing a net excess or absence of charged particles), and repulsions between like charged bodies. These forces are seen as strong over short distances, and weak over long distances. The movement of charged particles within an experimental situation is understood in terms of a series of *discrete events,* by quantizing both time and space. Solving problems thus involves an *envisioning* of how mobile charged particles (electrons) will move about after events occur that alter the distribution of charges. Thus, when the charged bar is brought near to the disk, mobile charges are seen to "flow" towards areas where they are lacking (i.e., positively charged areas). If a conductive path exists, the result is to establish an equilibrium of charge. We should note, finally, that the reasoning involved in solving such a problem is causal, and that the causal sequence of events is unique. Using such reasoning, an explanation has been generated for what causes an electric current, namely, an unequal distribution of charge across a conductor.

This form of reasoning differs strikingly from the form of reasoning developed in the course unit Tania was given on "current electricity." In this unit (as in all of the introductory textbooks on electricity and general physics that we examined), the core of a theory of electric circuits was a set of basic DC circuit laws. These include Ohm's law, the formulas for resistances in series and in parallel, and Kirchhoff's current law. (In more advanced courses, Kirchhoff's voltage law, and formulas for voltages in series circuits would also be included.) These laws are generally introduced (1) as basic principles (that is, a subset of them, such as Ohm's law and Kirchhoff's laws, are treated as axioms and the others are algebraically derived from them), (2) as empirical laws supported by laboratory measurements of voltages, currents, and resistances within circuits (which are often made by students in completing laboratory exercises), or (3) as analogous to observable properties of fluid systems. In Tania's course, approaches 2 and 3 were taken. The students carried out laboratory exercises which involved making measurements of voltages and currents for varying resistances. (The students also were taught the colour code for resistors!) For explanatory purposes, the water analogy was also developed. Here, the notion is to view voltage as a pressure (like that produced by a pump) which drives the electric current (defined as the rate of flow of fluid or electrically charged particles) through a resistance (such as is created by a narrow length of pipe).[2]

On the basis of these laws, students were taught in the course unit to reason algebraically, so as to solve for missing voltages (V), currents (I), or resistances (R) within a circuit for which a number of such values are given, as in the problem shown in figure 18.2. To solve such problems, the student must (1) recall one or more laws (circuit equations) that apply to the circuit, (2) substitute known values of V, I, and R into the equations, and (3) algebraically manipulate those equations (and perhaps recall additional equations) in order to solve for the unknown values. The solutions that students obtain are not unique. For example, Tania's solution is at the left of figure 18.2. She first recalls the equation for resistances in parallel, and then, when she finds that it has two unknowns in it (the unknown resistance R_4 and the total resistance), uses Ohm's law to solve for one of the unknowns, the total resistance R_T. She then substitutes that into her first equation, and solves algebraically for the required resistance R_4. The alternative solution at the right involves first solving for the current through each circuit branch (resistor) using Ohm's law, subtracting those from the total current (which is given) to get the current through R_4, and then using Ohm's law to solve for R_4.[3]

The first thing to note about this form of reasoning is that it is completely *acausal*: For instance, the circuit equations often incorporate multiple causal principles (for example, I=V/R expresses a direct proportionality between current and voltage, and an inverse proportionality between current and resistance). Moreover, the assignment of dependent and independent variables within the equations is arbitrary, dictated by algebraic convenience in solving the equations (for example, two forms of Ohm's law, I=V/R and R=V/I, were used in the alternative solution to the problem in figure 18.2). Also, the circuit equations are as a set redundant (for example, the formula for the resistance of parallel resistors can be derived from Ohm's Law and the idea of a constant current). Finally, as we have seen, the *algebraic derivations* involved in solving a problem *are not unique*, and so do not reflect the operation of any physical process. For students learning about electricity, this approach does not develop an understanding of any physical mechanism for electricity, such as was developed in the earlier unit of Tania's course dealing with electrostatics.

---

2 Use of the water analogy seems to be based upon the idea that students will be more familiar with phenomena of fluid flow than with electricity, which may not be the case. For instance, primitive concepts of resistance and pressure or force are more likely to be derived from a child's direct interaction with the world as a causal agent than from observation of flow within physical systems. Pressure and resistance can be felt, but to be observed within a system, they must be measured. The water analogy also leads to misconceptions about the propagation of forces within an electrical circuit. Within a fluid system, the incompressibility of water provides a mechanism for the transfer of force throughout the system, whereas the transport of electrons is due to electrical forces existing at each point within the circuit, and those forces are due to the differences in the distribution of charged particles within the circuit (see Haertel [9] for a more complete discussion).

3 This solution is directly derived from the concept of current dividing within a parallel circuit. It is interesting to note that Tania's solution has no simple interpretation in terms of an underlying model of current flow within the circuit.

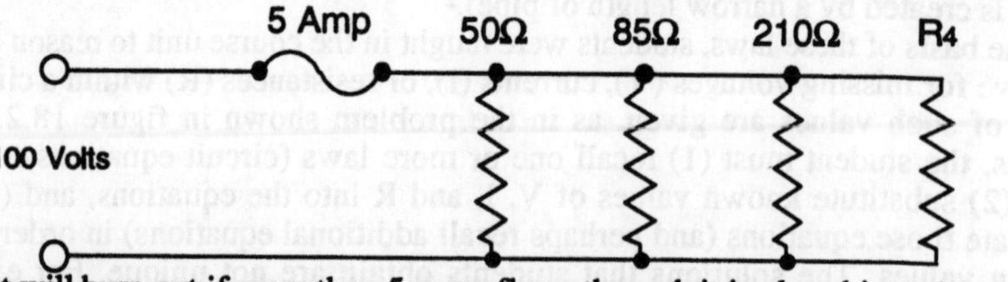

A fuse that will burn out if more than 5 amps flows through it is placed in a circuit that contains three appliances wired in parallel. The voltage is 100 volts. The resistances of these appliances are 50,85 and 210Ω. If a fourth appliance is hooked into the circuit, what is the least resistance it can have before the fuse burns out?

Students Solution:	**Alternative Solution:**
$\frac{1}{R_1}+\frac{1}{R_2}+\frac{1}{R_3}+\frac{1}{R_4}=\frac{1}{R_T}$	$I_1=\frac{V}{R_1}=\frac{100}{50}=2\text{ Amps}$
$\frac{1}{50}+\frac{1}{85}+\frac{1}{210}+x=\frac{1}{R_T}$	$I_2=\frac{V}{R_2}=\frac{100}{85}=1.176\text{ Amps}$
$R_T=\frac{V}{I_T}=\frac{100}{5}=20\Omega$	$I_3=\frac{V}{R_3}=\frac{100}{210}=.476\text{ Amps}$
$.0365+x=.05,\ x=.01348$	$I_T=I_1+I_2+I_3+I_4$
$R_4=\frac{1}{x}=74\Omega$	$I_4=I_T-I_1-I_2-I_3$
	$=5-2-1.176-.476=1.347$
	$R_4=\frac{V}{I_4}=\frac{100}{1.347}=74\Omega$

Fig.18.2. A typical circuit problem and two solutions for it.

In fact, this is true even for students who have been taught a qualitative model for understanding problems in electrostatics. For example, when we asked Tania if she saw any relationship between the electrostatic problems and the circuit problems, she said, "I have absolutely no concept of the relation between the two." When we pressed her by asking, "What is voltage?" she answered, "I don't know. They taught them as facts, formulas. I never knew what they were." We then asked her, "What is current?" She answered, "Don't know. We never learned that kind of thing." Thus, her algebraic reasoning about circuits (which is extremely competent) is completely divorced from her understanding of a physical mechanism for electricity.

In general, textbooks that include material on electrostatics *fail to integrate* the causal reasoning involved in electrostatic problems with the algebraic, constraint-based reasoning employed in circuit theory. "Current electricity" is often regarded, as in Tania's course, as a separate subject, and a student's knowledge of electric charges and their interaction does little to help them understand circuit theory. It is only in two advanced college textbooks [10,11] that we found derivations of such a basic circuit law as Ohm's Law from a consideration of the effect of electrical force on the motion of electrons within a resistive medium (i.e., from Coulomb's Law and Newton's Second Law -- F=mA; however, even in these derivations, a uniform electrical field is assumed to exist across a resistor, and no physical explanation for this assumption is offered the student). Moreover, while students may, in their study of electrostatics, learn how charges flow in order to establish an equilibrium, they are not led to regard this momentary flow of electricity as a current. They are not shown how the mechanism producing a displacement or flow of charge in an electrostatic problem (a gradient of charge density) is also responsible for producing currents in an electrical circuit. And the central idea that changes in charges will occur until a *steady state has been reached* is not extended to electrical circuits which contain a voltage source and in which the steady state is a dynamic, rather than a static one. Thus, while Newton's Second Law and Coulomb's Law describe how electrical forces will accelerate charged particles, this dynamic view of electricity is lost when the circuit context is introduced.

Students are not taught how to *envision* what happens to the distribution of electrons within a circuit when an action is taken which changes voltages or resistances within a circuit (for example, when a switch is closed or a resistance is changed). Transient redistributions of charge occur when a circuit is altered in these ways, and these changes continue until there is no net change in the density of charge at any point in the circuit. It is only then that a steady state is achieved. This steady state is describable in terms of circuit laws such as Kirchhoff's current law, which may not apply outside of the steady state. Viewed from this perspective, the circuit laws provide a set of propositions that are simultaneously true about the circuit in its steady state. Reasoning about the circuit using this set of propositions is therefore acausal and ahistoric. There is thus a basic epistemological distinction to be made between transient, dynamic theories of circuit behaviour and constraint-based descriptions of circuits in their steady state. This distinction is important if students are to be able to reconcile the constraint-based reasoning of algebraic circuit theory with a causal understanding of current flow within an electrical circuit.

While transient processes are for the most part ignored in presenting DC circuit theory most textbooks do introduce such ideas in developing AC circuit theory. Devices such as capacitors, inductors, and transistors are typically described using differential equations involving time, making them difficult to understand for students who are not well versed in the Calculus. In addition, many texts we have studied supplement such differential equations with physical models for these devices, which qualitatively portray the effects of changes in voltage or current on the device, and the resulting effects on the conductivity of the device and on voltages and currents within the circuit.

Summary

We can summarize the instructional issues raised in our review of science textbooks and in our analysis of Tania's course in terms of four problems:

1.1 The physical-mechanism problem.

While many texts supply physical mechanisms for "special" devices such as transistors and diodes, only two advanced college textbooks attempted to provide any physical mechanism for explaining circuit principles such as Ohm's Law, or how current is propagated within a circuit. Dynamic processes are generally introduced in mathematical form using differential equations, making them difficult to understand for students who are not well versed in the Calculus. Textbooks often rely on analogies, usually the water analogy, rather than on building a physical model of electricity.

1.2 The reasoning-from-constraints problem.

The quantitative forms of circuit laws and the algebraic, constraint-based reasoning involved in solving quantitative circuit problems are acausal. The algebraic steps taken in solving a problem are chosen opportunistically for meeting algebraic goals of simplifying expressions and eliminating unknowns, rather than for understanding of the physical mechanism that creates a flow of charge within a circuit. Consequently, students cannot relate circuit theory to any qualitative, causal model of what is going on, nor can they map circuit concepts to phenomenologically primitive notions such as forces (pushes and pulls) and resistance.

1.3 The quantitative-argument problem.

Some textbooks rely on mathematical arguments, without developing qualitative arguments to motivate them. Others provide incomplete, "spotty" qualitative arguments, motivating some mathematical statements but not others. The student is left with the notion that physical systems can only be understood through mathematical theories, and that these cannot be understood in terms of any underlying physical mechanism apart from the equations themselves.

1.4 The coherence problem.

A coherence problem therefore exists in most textbooks in the lack of integration of a physical model of electricity and the study of electrostatics with circuit theory. Circuit theory is often treated as a separate topic, requiring its own set of laws and modes of reasoning. Moreover, students are not acquainted with epistemological distinctions between types of explanation in physics in general, and between transient and steady-state representations of circuit behaviour in particular.

Faced with such textbooks and courses, it is not surprising that students find electricity to be a difficult, abstract subject. Beyond their study of electrostatics, there is little possibility for students to relate the abstract mathematics of circuit theory to their qualitative notions of force and motion, and their understanding of mechanisms in terms of causal event sequences.

2. How Do Novices Prefer to Reason?

In approaching this problem, emphasis has been placed in the science education literature on (1) students' misconceptions concerning physical phenomena within a domain (Collins, [2], for example, has listed a number of specific misconceptions students may have about electricity), (2) on the relation of the physical concepts and processes they seek to understand to their direct experiences [4] and (3) on students' tendency to view problems in terms of surface characteristics rather than the underlying physical principles involved [1]. These sources of difficulty are all concerned with students' prior knowledge (their naive physics) of the domain, and its effects on their approach to problem solving within the domain. While these are important factors, here we are seeking to draw attention to difficulties associated with the character of scientific reasoning and the epistemology of scientific explanations, each of which we believe constitutes a significant source of difficulty for students. We include here students' preconceptions about the nature of physical mechanisms and the forms of physical theories, and the form of reasoning employed in understanding such mechanisms.

Investigators have found that there are parallels between the psychological/social models and linguistic forms people have developed for understanding and describing events in the social world, and the models and language they use to understand and describe the physical world. Just as the social world is understood in terms of case relations associated with discrete events or interactions among people and objects (e.g., agent, object and instrument relations), the physical world appears to be explained from a similar perspective, which is both qualitative and causal [5,7]. For instance, in our example of a student's reasoning about electrostatics, we saw that the situation is viewed in terms of elementary interactions occurring between objects that are in proximity. The objects are such things as charged bars and disks, or mobile, charged particles, and the actions involve elementary forces such as pushes and pulls. Thus, when the charged bar (the agent) is near to the neutral disk, it attracts mobile electrons (the objects) to that side of the disk, due to electrical attraction between opposite charges (the instrument). Moreover, actions such as these are linked in causal chains. For instance, in Tania's model, the movement of electrons towards the bar causes a reduction in electrons on the grounded side of the disk (see figure 18.1A), which in turn cause electrons to flow from the ground to the disk, filling in for those that have been attracted to the bar.

In summary, students appear to reason about physical mechanisms in terms of *discrete events*, and their concept of an event frame involves a notion of *causality*: the case frame for an event includes notions of an agent and object, with the electrical force as an instrument. Interactions among objects are *local*, occurring only when objects are in proximity to one another. Their use of qualitative reasoning entails *quantizing space and time*, and dynamics are understood in terms of *event sequences*. They also appear to have a notion of *conservation*, in that charged particles are not created out of the blue, by must arise from some source (for example, in rubbing a bar with a silk cloth, electrons may be transferred from the rod to the cloth, resulting in a positive charge on the bar). They successfully develop a notion of *equilibrium* or balance: if two unlike charged objects are allowed to contact one another, the charges on the objects will be equalized by conduction. And finally, they use the notion of an electrical force (e.g., an attraction due to unlike charges) that causes a movement of charged particles (although students' understanding of accelerations is poorly developed [14].

In this way, students can model the electrostatic problems using qualitative, causal reasoning about discrete events and event sequences, in which objects interact locally. This is the framework within which we generally view the world and come to understand its physical mechanisms. This form of reasoning has its limitations, however: For example, it does not apply well to reasoning about systems in a steady state. We have seen that, in such systems, multiple (and redundant) constraint equations, or propositions about the world, are simultaneously true, and that they can be used to derive other propositions about the system. This constraint-based reasoning does not appear to be directly supported by elementary linguistic forms [13]. When students attempt to understand such situations in causal terms, they run into inconsistencies when they attempt to apply causal reasoning. We believe that the formal, constraint-based, algebraic reasoning that is required in physics courses is foreign to most beginning students of science. While it can be mastered by some students, this mastery still provides little understanding of the underlying physics. What is needed is for students to develop an understanding of how steady states of systems develop, in terms of an underlying dynamic process such as that of electrical forces acting on mobile particles within the system. They may then learn how one can characterize systems in their steady state in terms of circuit principles such as Ohm's law, and, lastly, how to apply to those principles to reason about how a circuit operates.

2.1 How Do Experts Reason?

It is interesting to inquire whether or not experts who design circuits or who troubleshoot electrical devices actually use the kind of constraint-based reasoning represented in most textbooks and which they have been taught in science courses. We will here draw on our studies of two experts, one an electrical engineer and university teacher, and the other a teacher in a technical high school and trouble-shooter of automotive electrical systems [16,17]. To each expert, we presented a number of electrical circuits and asked for an explanation of how they worked.

What we found was that, while experts are capable of quantitative, constraint-based reasoning such as that represented in most texts, they have evolved a qualitative, causal perspective on the operation of circuits that shares many of the characteristics of what we believe to be students' preferred mode of reasoning about physical systems. Experts come to view a circuit as composed of a set of *devices* having one or more qualitative *states* which together determine its function. For instance, a light bulb can be off or on, and a transistor can be unsaturated or saturated. For each device, they have what we call a "device model," which specifies what conditions cause the device to enter each state and the effects of the state on the device's conductivity. These device models are entirely local: voltages applied to a device's ports cause internal changes in the device. Thus, a voltage applied to a light bulb causes it to enter the "on" state, with no change in conductivity. A voltage applied to the base and emitter of a transistor (in the proper polarity) causes it to enter the "saturated" state, and the collector-emitter pathway of the transistor becomes conductive.

In reasoning about the effects of changes in devices' states (and thereby their conductivities) on the behaviour of other devices within the circuit -- in other words, in making causal propagations within an operating circuit, a number of different methods are used. In the simplest, voltages are regarded as having only two qualitative values: present or absent. Thus, voltages are viewed as either present or absent across any device within a circuit. Therefore, when a device changes its conductivity (e.g., a switch is closed or a transistor becomes saturated), the expert applies principles for ascertaining the distribution of voltages drops within the circuit given the present set of device conductivities. Once the voltage drops across devices within the circuit are known, the expert can determine the current state of all devices within the circuit by applying the device models. The overall model for reasoning about circuit behaviour thus involves a cycle, shown in figure 18.3: State changes cause voltage redistributions, which can cause changes in device states, which in turn can cause further voltage redistributions, and so on. A simple illustration of the application of this model is given in figure 18.4.

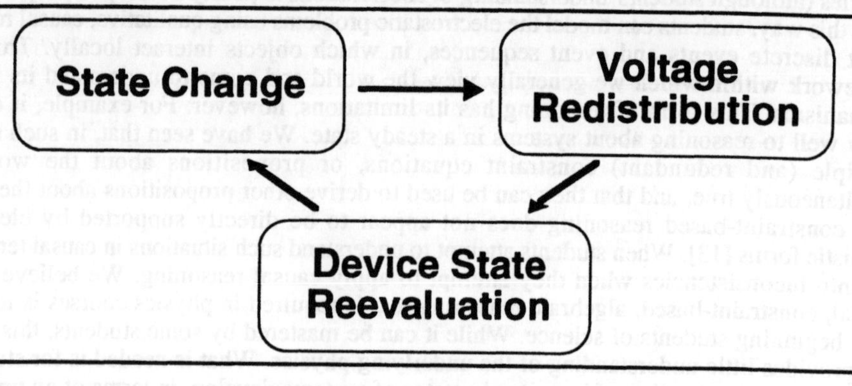

Fig.18.3. The cyclic control process of the qualitative model of circuit behaviour.

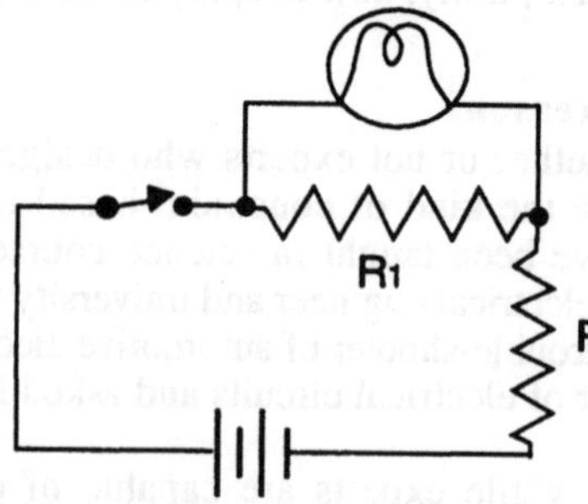

1. Closing the switch changes the conductivity of the switch
2. This causes a voltage reevaluation:
   - voltage drops occur across resistive devices within the series circuit made up of R2 and the parallel subcircuit(consisting of R1 and the lightbulb)
   - voltage drops occur across both elements of the parallel subcircuit (R1 and the lightbulb)
3. The change in voltage across the lightbulb causes it to revaluate its state; it goes from "off" to "on"
4. Since the conductivity of the lightbulb is unchanged, the circuit behavoir is now stabilized

Fig.18.4. A simple example of the sequence of steps in applying the qualitative circuit model.

Experts can also reason about how *increments* in voltages or resistances can cause changes in the size of voltages and currents within a circuit. This incremental qualitative model, which elsewhere we have called a "first order model" [17], has a similar structure to that outlined above for reasoning simply about the presence or absence of voltages within a circuit. Finally, experts can reason functionally about interactions among sub circuits, viewing circuit operation in terms of an exchange of information (signals) among functional units (sub circuits). For our present purposes, we want to point out that each of these models (1) reduces continuous processes to a series of discrete changes in resistance, voltage, and current, (2) incorporates qualitative device models, and (3) employs rules which allow a propagation of the effects of state changes on the basis of the topology of the circuit. These qualitative rules can generally be mapped onto the constraint equations of quantitative circuit theory. However, experts appear to prefer to construct causal accounts of circuit operation, by regarding changes in device conductivities as precipitating events, leading to changes in voltages or currents, which in turn cause further changes in devices' states.

2.2 An Instructional Model of Electricity

The qualitative model for circuit behaviour we have described, while it is causal at the level of device model interactions, still employs rules for ascertaining the effects of changes in conductivity on voltage distributions and currents within a circuit. These principles are qualitative equivalents of the steady-state circuit laws of quantitative circuit theory. A problem thus remains of creating a coherent qualitative theory of electricity that links these circuit laws to an underlying mechanism based upon attractions and repulsions among charged particles that can move within the circuit. In the remaining section of this paper we shall illustrate one such model we have created which attempts to link the kind of qualitative reasoning that students such as Tania evolve in their study of electrostatics to an understanding of the origin and nature of the circuit laws.

Our goal was to unpack the voltage redistribution process via a dynamic physical model. The model we sought would introduce a simple causal mechanism that would drive the process. The causal mechanism would be based on what diSessa [3] refers to as phenomenological primitives, i.e., things that you can experience with your own body, such as pushes and pulls and a sense of equilibrium. Furthermore, it would be based on more fundamental physical laws such as F=mA and Coulomb's law, rather than on the steady state circuit laws. The form of reasoning it would employ would be compatible with the qualitative, causal reasoning about sequences of discrete events that students prefer in conceptualizing the operation of physical mechanisms. Another important property of this model would be that by watching this physical model run, the steady state circuit laws would emerge. In other words, it would be a model based on Coulomb's Law and Newton's second law, and Ohm's and Kirchhoff's laws would be emergent properties of the physical process embedded in the model.

The fact that we didn't find such a physical model presented in any of the text books we reviewed suggests that, from the perspective of physicists, either it is unnecessary to develop such a model of transient phenomena within circuits, or such dynamic models are so complex as to confuse rather than enlighten. However, while such dynamic, physical models are not available for electricity, they are fairly common in the study of gas diffusion and heat flow (although they are generally presented in the form of differential equations). Moreover, while physicists may accept abstract, algebraic derivations of circuit laws without any necessary link to a transient, physical model, in the initial stages of learning most students find that mathematical abstractions and algebraic derivations make sense only after the domain is understood in causal terms. If a dynamic model is not supplied, they may attempt to build their own, or to interpret the circuit laws in terms of their prior conceptions of electricity.

We therefore focused on creating a model that would embody a simple mechanism which would help people to understand the origins of circuit behaviour such the voltage redistribution process. The model is based on a simplification of Coulomb's law in which we quantize distance by dividing resistors up into little slices. We also ignore surface charges and regard the resistor as essentially one dimensional. Within each slice of the resistor, we represent the charge of that slice. For example, the middle slice (with the holes filled with minuses) shown in figure 18.5 is neutral, the one on the right has a negative charge, and the one on the left has a positive charge. These circles and minuses are not meant to represent individual atoms and electrons. They are just a representation of the charge of that slice. If you prefer, you can think of them as being replaced with a number, so the middle slice has a charge of 0, the right is -5, and the left slice is +5. Now if you put two of these slices next to one another, and if there is a difference in their charge, then there will be an electrical force exerted on charged particles within the two adjacent slices. This can be thought of as due to the negative charges repelling one another and the positive charges attracting the negative charges. These forces will accelerate the mobile charges (the minuses), causing them to migrate (i.e., be redistributed) from the relatively more negatively charged slice to the more positively charged slice until both slices have the same charge.

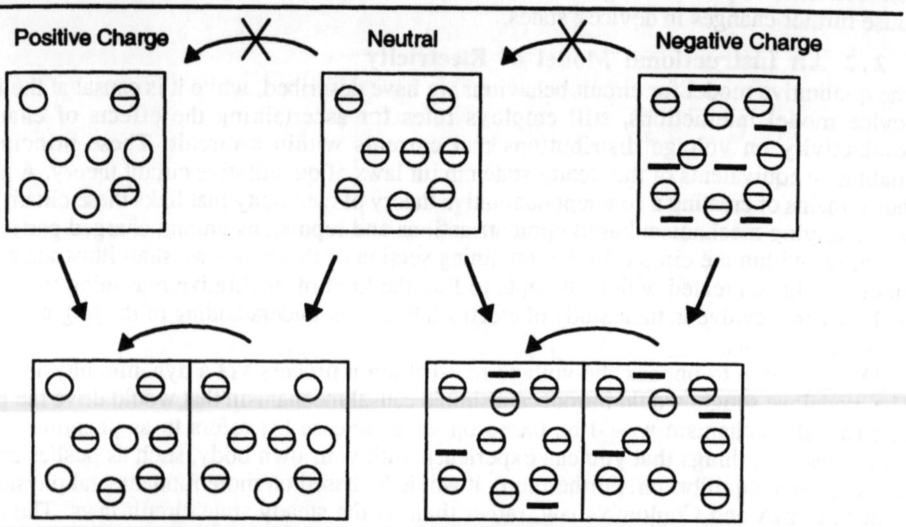

Fig.18.5. Representations of charge densities and charge redistributions through conduction.

We can increase the resistance of a resistor by putting more and more of these slices next to one another. We model a battery by simply saying that it is a device which maintains a constant difference between the positive charge on one of its terminals and the negative charge on the other of its terminals. Then, for example, if you attach the negative terminal of a battery to one end of a resistor as in figure 18.6 (you do not yet have a complete circuit), you can watch what happens over time. Within the model, time is also quantized. Within each time interval, a certain proportion of mobile charges will be redistributed, the actual number depending on the difference in charge between the two adjacent slices. As this model runs, one can see that on each time increment, adjacent slices go part way towards reaching equilibrium. In this way, one can watch the system settle down into a final, steady state. In this case, when equilibrium is reached, there will be no voltage drop across the resistor and the source voltage will be developed across the open segment of the circuit. Furthermore, if you put together a complete circuit, like the one shown in figure 18.7 and let the process run until it reaches a steady state, you see how you get Ohm's law and Kirchhoff's laws from a system that behaves in accordance with Coulomb's law. In this case, the equilibrium that is reached (unlike that in figure 18.6) is a *dynamic* equilibrium. The net charge on a slice of a resistor remains the same, not because there is no longer a current flowing, but because the current flow *into* any slice of a resistor is exactly equal that *leaving* the slice. (Thus, Kirchhoff's current law emerges from the behaviour of the simulation.) Moreover, this equality of charge flowing into and out of a slice is seen as directly due to the symmetry in the gradient of charge on either side of each resistor slice. (This is the mechanism producing a constant electrical field along the length of the resistor.) The only way for charges to stabilize across the resistor is for the gradient of charge to be constant. This is a nice example of how you can start with some very simple ideas about attraction, repulsion, and equilibrium such as those Tania developed, and show how a system that operates according to a mechanism based on these ideas will settle down into a steady state that itself has a number of clear cut, lawful properties.

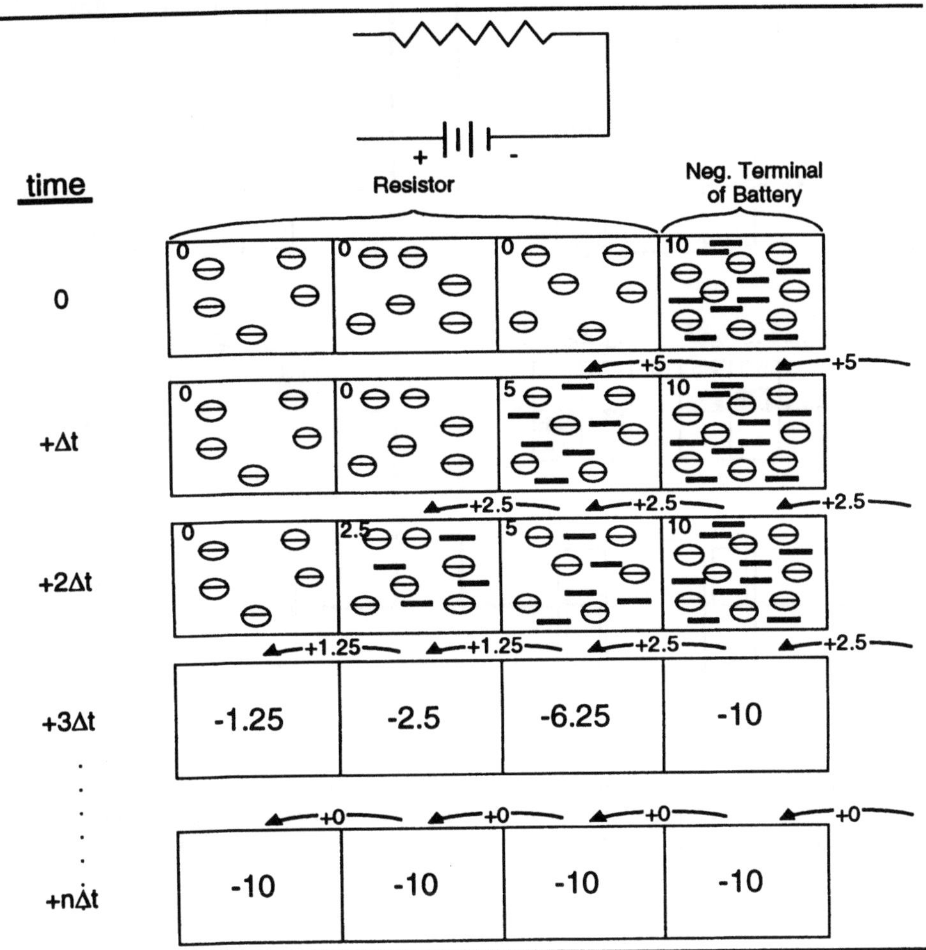

Fig.18.6. The sequence of charge redistributions that occur for a simple example where the final, steady state does not entail a current flow.

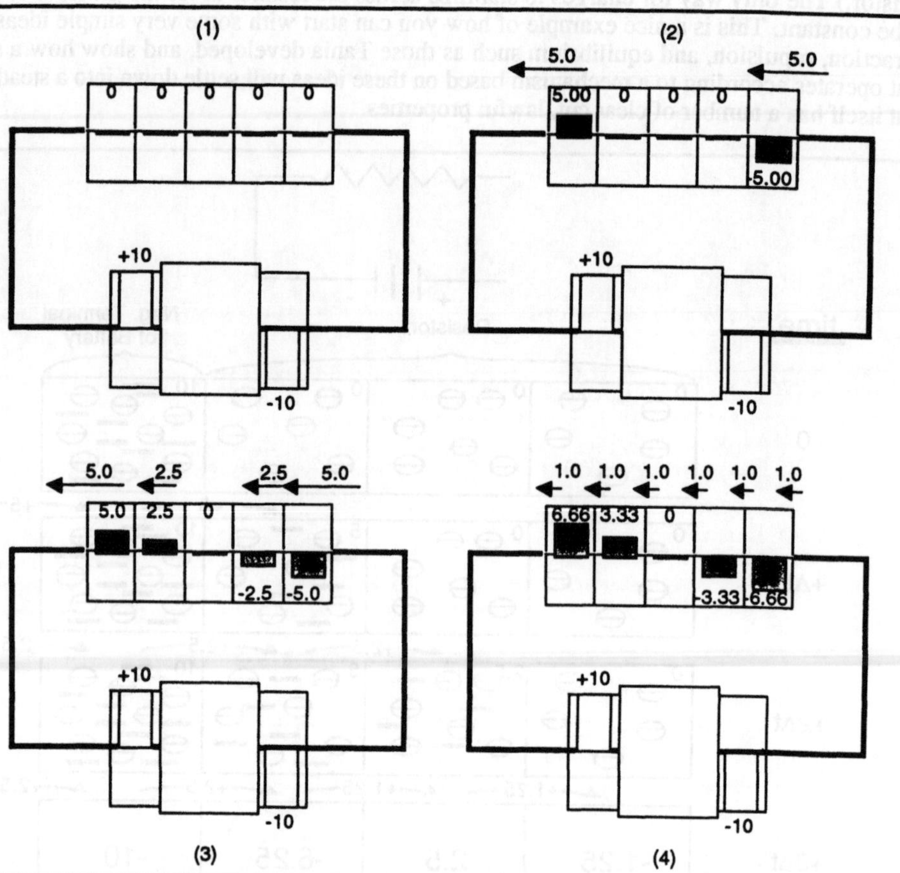

Fig.18.7. The sequence of charge redistributions that occur for a circuit where the final, steady state is dynamic and involves a current flow. The first three panels represent, respectively, the initial charges, and the first two charge redistributions as the model is run. The final panel shows the charges on the resistor after the circuit has stabilized.

By providing a bridge between elementary notions of electrical attraction and repulsion and the behaviour of electrical circuits, this model makes the equations of circuit theory "make sense". It provides a sense of mechanism, so that the macroscopic models of circuit behaviour that experts use, and the causal models of charge redistribution developed in solving electrostatics problems, are both understood within a single, unified conceptual framework. The model creates a sense of mechanism because it employs causal reasoning about sequences of discrete events that represent changes in the state of the electrical system under analysis. This model is, however, far from "complete" Firstly, there is no model provided to explain how electrical force gets produced by a battery. (To explain this, a chemical model of ion transport would need to be introduced.) Secondly, the holes and minuses are not meant to represent individual atoms and electrons. Instead they provide a representation of the charge of each slice of a resistor. And, unless you actually represent the individual electrons and animate them by showing them moving and bumping into atoms, you do not get a good sense of what resistance is. So, one could hypothesize that we may need is to unpack one more level, and show the behaviour of atoms and electrons. However, we argue that this is unnecessary. People already have good intuitions about resistance. The hard and key ideas are voltage drop and the process by which voltages get redistributed. This model represents that concept and process succinctly.

By interacting with such models, students can also come to appreciate some important distinctions among physical theories: The laws that are used to describe the steady state are usually redundant. They provide multiple constraints on the configuration of charges in the steady state. Given their redundancy, if several statements are given, one can derive the remaining ones (this is an example of constraint-based reasoning). In this way, students can be introduced to constraint-based reasoning in a qualitative form as a precursor to its algebraic forms. In general, students can come to appreciate epistemological distinctions among forms of physical theories and ways of reasoning, and learn how they can exist side by side as alternative ways of viewing the physical world.

Another interesting property of this process model emerged when describing it to physicists. We would say, "This is a diffusion model which represents a first approximation to what happens in electrical circuits. It is the kind of model that you might use, for example, to explain heat flow to someone." The physicist would say " Oh yes, you could use it to explain what happens in gases as well". These discussions implied that there are a small number of key processes, like this diffusion process. These key processes are understandable because they can be grounded in phenomenological primitives (i.e., can introduce a simple mechanism that relates to things you can do with your own body). They also have the property that they can be used to help students understand a wide range of physical domains. Thus they can play a key role in enabling students to learn science.

References

1. Chi, M. T. H., Feltovich, P. J., & Glaser, R. Categorization and representation of physics problems by experts and novices. *Cognitive Science*, 5, 117-123. 1981.
2. Collins, A. Component models of physical systems. In *Proceedings of the Seventh Annual Conference of the Cognitive Science Society*. 1985.
3. diSessa, A. Phenomenology and the evolution of intuition. In D. Gentner & A. Stevens (Editors), *Mental Models*. Hillsdale, NJ: Lawrence Erlbaum Associates. 1983.
4. diSessa, A. Toward an epistemological of physics. Berkeley, CA: Cognitive Science Report No. 48. 1987.
5. Fillmore, C. J. The case for case. In E. Bach & R. T. Harms Eds., *Universals of linguistic theory*. New York: Holt, Rinehart, & Winston, pp. 1-90. 1968.
6. Forbus, K.D. Qualitative process theory. In Bobrow, D.G. (Ed.). *Qualitative Reasoning about Physical Systems*. Cambridge, MA: MIT Press. 1985.
7. Frederiksen, C. H. Representing logical and semantic structure of knowledge acquired from discourse. *Cognitive Psychology*, 7, 371-458. 1975.
8. Frederiksen, J., & White, B. "Intelligent tutors as intelligent testers." To appear in N. Frederiksen, R. Glaser, A. Lesgold, & M. Shafto (Editors), *Diagnostic Monitoring of Skill and Knowledge Acquisition*. Hillsdale, New Jersey: Lawrence Erlbaum Associates. (in press).
9. Haertel, H. A qualitative approach to electricity. Palo Alto, CA: Institute for Research on Learning, Report No. IRL87-0001. 1988.
10. Pugh, E. M., & Pugh, E. W. *Principles of Electricity and Magnetism*. Reading, MA: Addison-Wesley. 1970.
11. Purcell, E. M. *Electricity and Magnetism*. New York: McGraw-Hill. 1985.
12. Science achievement in schools called "Distressingly low." *Science*, 241, 1751. 1988.
13. Talmy, L. Force dynamics in language and cognition. *Cognitive Science*, 12, 49-100. 1988.
14. White, B. Y. Sources of difficulty in understanding Newtonian dynamics. *Cognitive Science*, 7(1), 41-65. 1983.

15. White, B., & Frederiksen, J. Intelligent tutoring systems based upon qualitative model evolutions. In the *Proceedings of the Fifth National Conference on Artificial Intelligence*, Philadelphia, Pennsylvania. 1986.
16. White, B., & Frederiksen, J. Qualitative models and intelligent learning environments. In *AI and Education*. R. Lawler & M. Yazdani (Editors), Ablex Publishing Corporation. 1987a.
17. White, B., & Frederiksen, J. Causal Model Progressions as a Foundation for Intelligent Learning Environments. Report No. 6686, BBN Labs, Cambridge, MA. To appear in *Artificial Intelligence*. 1987b.

19
A Microworld-Based Approach to Science Education

Barbara Y. White
Bolt Beranek & Newman Inc, Boston, MA, U.S.A.

Abstract: Our objectives in this project[1] were to reconceptualize what it means to understand physics and to improve how it is taught. To achieve these objectives, we created an experimental curriculum in which students' learning centers around interacting with computer microworlds (i.e., interactive simulations), and where the focus is as much on learning about the form and evolution of scientific knowledge as it is on the subject matter (which is Newton's laws of motion). We conducted experimental trials of this curriculum with regular sixth grade students (i.e., 11 and 12 year olds) and regular sixth grade teachers. When we evaluated its effectiveness, we found that the sixth grade students taught with this approach did better on a set of classic force and motion problems than did a group of high school physics students taught using traditional methods.

Keywords: cognitive science, collaborative problem solving, design experiments, evolution phase, falsification, formalization phase, instructional cycle, joystick, mental model, microworlds, motivation, Newtonian mechanics, phenomenological problems, physics, scientific inquiry, scientific method, ThinkerTools, transfer phase, transfer test

---

1 The author's collaborator on this project was physicist Paul Horwitz. This research was sponsored by the National Science Foundation, under award number DPE-8400280 with the Directorate for Science and Engineering Education.

1. Introduction

Our goal in creating the "ThinkerTools" curriculum (see also, [24,13,27]) was to make physics accessible and interesting to everyone, not just high ability males over the age of 16. Why, one might ask, would anyone want to pursue such a goal, i.e., to inflict this abstract and difficult subject matter on the general population? Firstly, there is an urgent need in the U.S. to interest more students in taking physics courses and more teachers in teaching them. So, we wanted to make physics fun both to learn and to teach. Secondly, we wanted to create informed citizens who understand the form of scientific knowledge, the processes by which scientific knowledge evolves, and the issues that come up when one applies scientific knowledge to solving real world problems. Finally, we wanted students to understand some of the most fundamental concepts and principles of Newtonian mechanics, that is, how forces affect the motion of objects. Force and motion is an interesting topic from a cognitive science perspective since research indicates that students can pass high school and even college physics courses and yet maintain many of their misconceptions (e.g., [1,3,6,11,14,16,21,22,26]). We hypothesized that it might be easier for students to learn Newtonian mechanics at an early age, and thereby prevent or overcome their misconceptions.

In order to create a curriculum that achieves these goals, we designed a sequence of computer microworlds in which each microworld embodies an increasingly sophisticated model of how forces affect the motion of objects. This succession of microworlds is designed to help students build on their existing knowledge in gradual increments, and to introduce them to important laws and concepts such as force, velocity and acceleration. In addition, we created an instructional approach in which students' learning centers around problem solving and experimentation within the microworlds. In this approach, extensive use is made of group problem solving, and students address issues such as, "What is the best law to describe the Behavior of this microworld?" and "How do you apply this law to solve real world problems?" Thus, the instruction focuses on learning about the form of scientific laws, and on transferring laws learned in one context, i.e., the microworld, to new contexts.

The Representation of Force and Motion in the Microworlds

In order to provide a context for describing the instructional approach in more detail, we need to describe the first microworld. Microworld #1 is a simple one-dimensional world in which there is no friction or gravity. The students' task is to control the motion of an object, called "the dot", by applying impulses to it (impulses are forces that act for a short time, like a kick). In this microworld, one can only apply impulses to the right (-->) or to the left (<--). Whenever one applies an impulse, it is always the same size. Thus, this first microworld is an idealized, one-dimensional world of quantized impulses.

Within the microworld, there are a variety of representations of motion (see figure 19.1). Firstly, there is the motion of the dot itself. There are also what we call "wakes" which provide a history of the dot's speed by leaving little dots on the screen at fixed time intervals. There is also a speedometer, called a "datacross", which enables students to see, whenever they apply an impulse, how it affects the speed of the dot. These alternative, linked representations, as will be discussed later, are crucial for the evolution of the students' understanding of Newtonian mechanics.

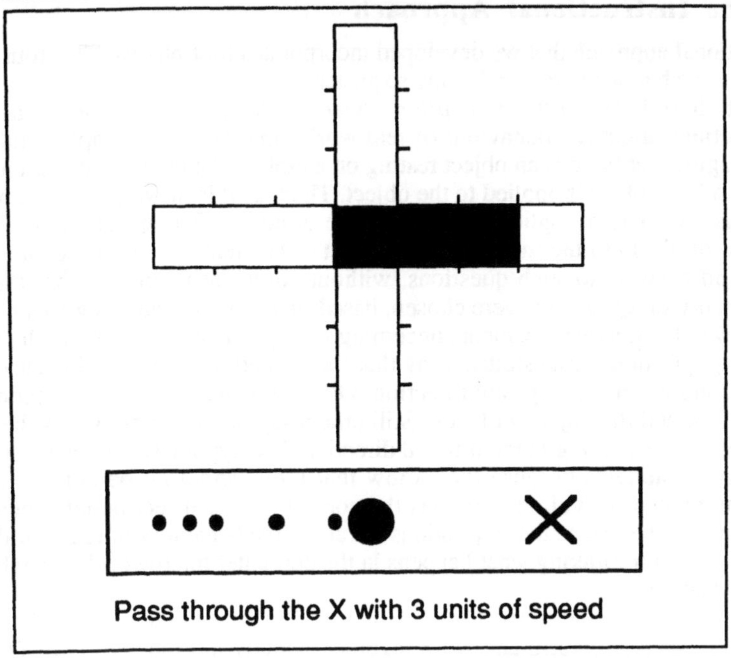

Fig.19.1. Goal: Make the dot hit the target at a specified speed.

2. The Instructional Approach

The instructional approach that we developed incorporates four phases. This four phase cycle is repeated with each new microworld in the sequence.

The first phase is called the *motivation phase*. In this phase, the teacher asks students to make predictions about the behaviour of real world objects. For example, students might be asked to imagine that there is an object resting on a table -- the table is very smooth, so there is no friction. A blast of air is applied to the object. Then, as it is moving along, a blast of air, the same size as the first, is applied in the opposite direction. The question is: "What will the second blast of air do to the motion of the object?" The teacher simply records the students' reasoning and answers to such questions, without commenting on whether the answers are correct or incorrect. Questions were chosen, based on extensive interviews with sixth graders, to be those which elicit disagreement concerning the right answer. For example, in response to the preceding question, some students say that the second blast of air will cause the object to turn around and go in the opposite direction. Other students say that the second blast of air cancels the first and the object will stop. Still others say that it simply slows the object down, but the object keeps moving in the original direction. We hypothesized that such disagreement would motivate students because they know that they cannot all be correct, and thus they should be motivated to find out who has the correct and incorrect beliefs about how forces affect motion. Further, since these questions are about the behaviour of real world objects, they create the potential for linking what happens in the computer microworld with what happens in real world situations.

The second phase of the instructional cycle is called the *evolution phase*. In this phase, the students go to the microworld and work together, usually in groups of two. They attempt to solve a series of game-like problem solving activities. These activities are designed to help students induce the laws of the microworld for themselves. For example, in the first game (see figure 19.1), students have to make the dot hit a target while it is travelling at a given speed (e.g., set VX=3). If the dot is travelling at the given speed, the target "catches" the dot. If not, the dot crashes into the end walls and explodes. In the next game in the sequence, the end walls are removed and the students have to navigate the dot off the screen in order to be able to achieve the given velocity (see figure 19.2). When the dot is off the screen, the only way that the students can see the effects of the impulses they are applying is to look at the datacross (i.e., the speedometer). By focussing on this representation, they should notice that whenever they apply an impulse, it adds or subtracts a unit of speed from the dot's velocity. Through sequences of activities such as these, that make use of the alternative representations of motion displayed in the microworld, students can potentially induce the laws of the microworld for themselves. However, we do not rely, at least initially, on sixth graders being able to derive well articulated laws. Thus, we go next to what is called the formalization phase of the instructional cycle.

In the *formalization phase*, the students work together at their computers, usually in small groups of three or four students. They are given a set of laws as possible laws to describe behaviour of the microworld. The task is to sort the laws into two piles: (1) those they think are correct, and (2) those they think are incorrect. For the laws they believe to be incorrect, they have to be prepared to show the rest of the class a case where that law does not hold. In other words, they have to falsify that particular law. For those they think are correct, they are asked to imagine that they can only have one of these laws in their head to use to make predictions about the behaviour of the dot in the microworld. The question they are asked is: "Which one of these laws would you pick and why?" After the class finishes debating in small groups, the whole class gets together and attempts to agree on the best law.

These sets of laws were carefully designed to elicit discussion about the properties of a good scientific law. For instance, some of the laws are too long and difficult to remember. Others are not precise. For example, "whenever you apply an impulse to the dot, you change its speed" --

That is correct, but it does not predict how the speed will change. Others are true but only apply in limited circumstances. For instance, "if the dot is moving to the right and you apply an impulse to the right, you will increase its speed" -- That is true, but it only applies when the dot is moving to the right. The law that we wanted students to select as being the "best" law always had the properties of being correct, simply stated, and generally applicable.

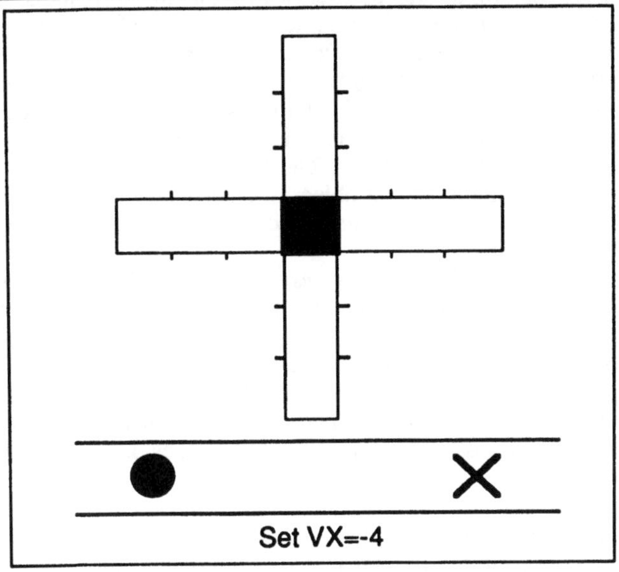

Fig.19.2. Goal: Make the dot hit the target at a specified speed. Note that this requires moving the dot off the screen and relying on the datacross.

The final phase of the instructional cycle is called the *transfer phase*. It focuses on applying the laws of the microworld to real world situations. The transfer phase has two subphases. Firstly, students are asked to recall the predictive questions that they were asked, usually about a week ago at this point. Their task is to determine how the law that the class voted on as being the best law would answer these predictive questions. The teacher then points out that they did not all give the same set of answers that the law predicts. S/he asks them why that might be -- are some of them just less intelligent than others, or might there be some other explanation. Usually, at this point, one of the students will say, "Well, you asked us to imagine no friction, but that is difficult to think about because it doesn't happen very often". The teacher then asks the students to go the microworld, and to experiment by putting in different values for friction, to see if they can get the microworld to behave according to some of their intuitions. In this way, students begin to see the relationship between the microworld and the behaviour of objects in the real world.

The second subphase of the transfer phase is concerned with getting students to relate laws, learned in the microworld context, to a variety of real world situations. For example, the students are given experiments to do -- such as controlling the motion of a bowling ball by hitting it with a rubber mallet, or experimenting with ping pong balls and blow guns. In these activities, the students are asked to think about the question: "Do the laws of the microworld help you to predict and control what happens in these real world contexts?"

These four phases of the instructional cycle are repeated with each new microworld in the curriculum. Notice that this four phase cycle corresponds to the classic conception of the scientific method: asking questions, doing experiments, formulating laws, and investigating how the laws generalize to different contexts. This correspondence will be discussed later in the section of the paper concerned with scientific inquiry.

3. The Progression of Microworlds

This section describes the progression of microworlds and the corresponding desired evolution in the students' understanding of how forces affect the motion of objects.

Microworld #1: Understanding One Dimensional Motion. In the first one-dimensional microworld, described previously, students are given tasks such as having to hit a target at a specified speed (see figures 20.1 & 20.2). Through such tasks, they can use the datacross representation (i.e., the speedometer) and their knowledge of scalar arithmetic (i.e., 1+1=2) to see that the effects of forces are additive. The law that they evolve in this microworld is: "Whenever you apply an impulse to an object, it changes its speed -- if applied in the same direction it is moving, it adds a unit to its speed, and if applied in the opposite direction, it subtracts a unit from its speed."

Microworld #2: Understanding Two Dimensional Motion. The second microworld is a two-dimensional world in which students can apply impulses up or down, as well as to the left or right. In this microworld, students are introduced to yet another representation for the motion of objects: Two arrows, one vertical and one horizontal, that remain constantly pointed at the dot. These arrows represent the horizontal velocity of the dot and the vertical velocity of the dot, i.e., its orthogonal velocity components. Thus, in this microworld, students are exposed to four alternative representations for motion: the dot, its wakes, its arrows, and its datacross (see figure 19.3). These representations correspond to ways that physicists use to think about motion: (1) the speed and direction of an object's motion, and (2) its orthogonal velocity components (i.e., its speed in the X dimension and its speed in the Y dimension). The speed and direction of the dot's motion is represented in a dynamic form by the motion of the dot itself, and in a more abstract form by the dot's wake (i.e., the little dots that it leaves on the screen at fixed time intervals). The dot's orthogonal velocity components are represented in a dynamic form by the horizontal and vertical arrows that remain constantly pointed at the dot, and in a more abstract form by the datacross (where the horizontal bar of the datacross shows the dot's speed in the horizontal dimension and the vertical bar of the datacross gives the dot's speed in the vertical dimension).

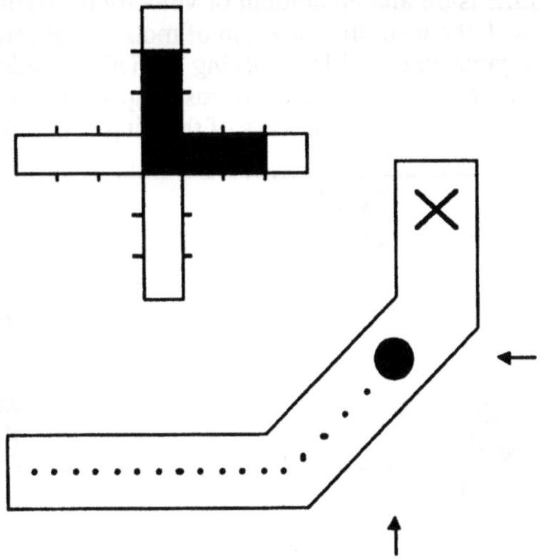

Fig.19.3. Linked alternative representations of motion employed within the microworlds

Initially, students are encouraged to think in terms of orthogonal velocity components. They are given tasks, such as the one illustrated in figure 19.4, where one student has to control the motion of the horizontal arrow and another student has to control the motion of the vertical arrow. By performing this task, students should induce two principles. The first is that the law induced in the first microworld, concerning the additivity of impulses, applies to this new vertical dimension of motion. The second is that impulses applied in the vertical dimension have no effect on the dot's horizontal velocity, and vice versa -- In other words, the dot's horizontal and vertical velocity components are independent of one another.

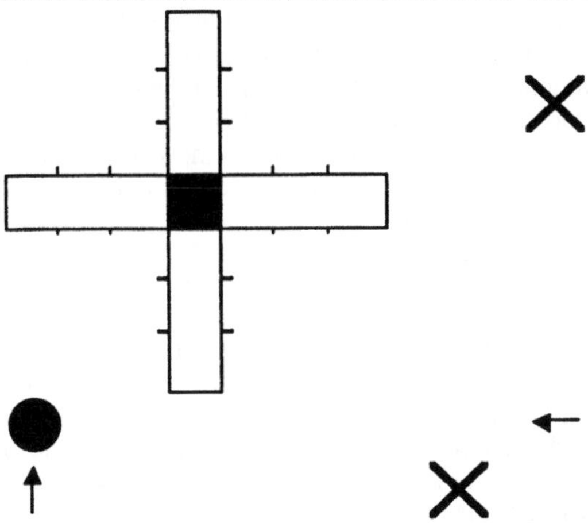

Fig.19.4. Goal: Stop the arrows on their respective targets

Later in the progression of tasks for microworld #2, students go on to thinking in terms of the speed and direction representation of motion, and to understanding how orthogonal velocity components combine to determine the speed and direction of the dot's motion. For example, in the task shown in figure 19.5, students have to set the datacross by giving it an amount of velocity in the vertical dimension and an amount of velocity in the horizontal dimension, such that when the dot is released, the resulting direction of motion will cause the dot to pass through the target. Through such game-like problem solving activities, students learn to think both in terms of orthogonal velocity components and in terms of speed and direction of motion, as well as to translate between these two alternative ways of thinking about motion.

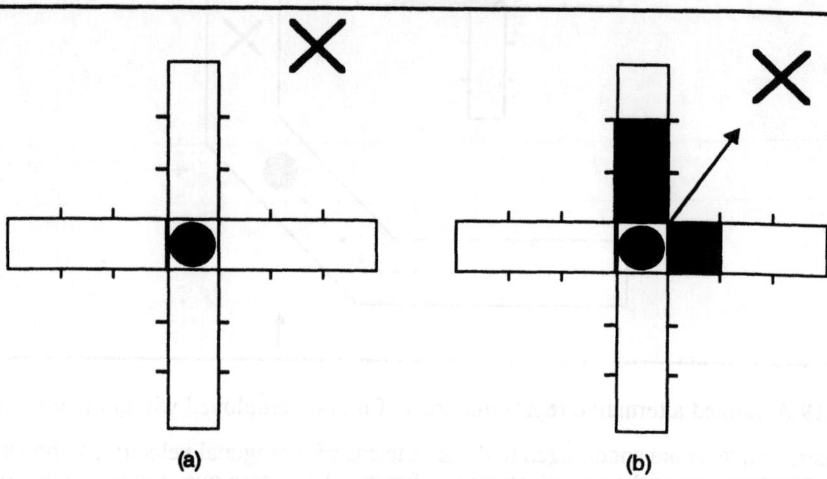

Fig.19.5. Goal: Set the datacross so that the dot will hit the target.

Microworld #3: Understanding Continuous Forces. The third microworld incorporates a model for reasoning about the effects of continuous forces. It is a one-dimensional microworld in which students can only apply impulses either upwards or downwards. The purpose is to enable students to model a continuous force, such as gravity, as a lot of little impulses closely spaced in time. In this way, they can use their law, concerning the additive effects of impulses, to predict the effect of a constant force. This model is introduced via a limit process. Students are allowed to change the rate at which impulses can be applied in the microworld. In the first two microworlds, if students hold down the fire button on the joystick (which is used to apply impulses), they get a series of impulses at the rate of one every three-quarters of a second. In microworld #3, students can press specified keys on the keyboard which change the frequency with which impulses are applied -- they can repeatedly double the rate at which impulses are applied, but every time they do this, the size of the impulse is halved, so they end up with effectively the same force being applied. This new feature of microworld #3 allows students to increase the rate at which impulses are applied and thereby enables students to approximate a continuous force by applying a lot of little impulses closely spaced in time. Since they previously learned that the effect of each impulse is additive, they can use this law the learned in the first microworld to reason about the additive effects of continuous forces. To foster the evolution of this model, students are given experiments to perform and analyze, such as: "Describe and explain what happens when you throw a ball up in the air -- What happens to the motion of the ball and why?" They reason, for example, that "the ball will start by going up and will gradually slow down because gravity keeps pulling and adding another impulse down, and there will be an instant when the ball is stopped in the air, and then it will start coming down and will gradually speed up because gravity keeps adding another impulse down".

Microworld #4: Analyzing trajectories. In the fourth and final microworld, students are required to utilize all of their knowledge, acquired in the prior microworlds, in order to analyze trajectory problems. This fourth microworld is a two-dimensional world in which gravity is acting in the vertical dimension. The students are asked to analyze problems such as: "If you have two balls sitting on the edge of a table, and you give one ball a large horizontal kick off the edge, and the other ball a soft horizontal kick off the edge, and both kicks are applied to both balls at the same time, which ball lands first?" The somewhat counter intuitive answer is that both balls land at the same time (see figure 19.6). By consolidating what they learned in the prior microworlds, students should have the knowledge needed to correctly analyze such situations.

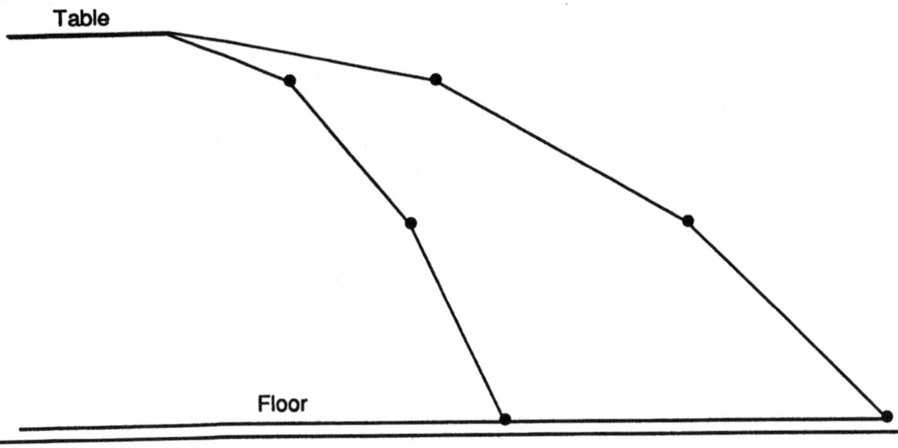

Fig.19.6. Trajectories of two balls launched from a table with different horizontal velocities.

The mental model students could evolve by interacting with this progression of microworlds and problem solving activities would enable them to predict and explain how forces affect motion. For instance, they would understand the additivity of impulses. They would know about the independence of X and Y motion. They could translate between alternative representations of motion, such as the component way of thinking about motion and the speed and direction way of thinking about motion. Finally, they could model a continuous forces as a lot of little impulses closely spaced in time. The consolidation of this knowledge embodies quite a sophisticated mental model (see [27] for more detail). It is the kind of reasoning that physicists themselves use when, for example, analyzing projectile motion. Thus, we argue that through this progression of microworlds and problem-solving activities, combined with this instructional approach, students could acquire a powerful mental model for reasoning about force and motion.

4. The Effectiveness of the Microworld-Based Approach

The ThinkerTools curriculum was implemented by a teacher who was responsible for five science classes in the sixth grade of a middle school located in a middle class Boston suburb. One of the five classes was used for a pilot trial of the first two modules of the curriculum. Of the remaining four classes, two were used as a peer control group (containing 37 students), and the other two were given the ThinkerTools curriculum (containing 42 students). The curriculum took two months to complete. During this period, the students had a science class every school day for 45 minutes, and the ThinkerTools curriculum occupied the entire class period. Students in the control classes received the standard curriculum which, at this point in the year, was devoted to a unit on inventions.

In addition to the peer control group of sixth grade students, two further control groups were employed, consisting of high school physics students drawn from the same school system as the sixth graders, and who had chosen to enrol in a physics course in the 11th or 12th grade.

The first group consisted of two classes (containing 41 students) who had just completed two and one half months studying Newtonian mechanics using the text book "Concepts in Physics" (Miller, Dillon, & Smith, 1980). The second group consisted of two classes (containing 45 students) who were at the very beginning of their physics course -- before they had studied Newtonian mechanics.

The results will be discussed with respect to a transfer test designed to measure students' understanding of Newtonian mechanics in real world problem solving contexts (additional results can be found in White, [27]). This test was administered to the experimental group and the three control groups. It is composed of questions used by other researchers in studying misconceptions among physics students [6,11,15,16,17,26]. All of the problems are non-computational and require an application of the basic principles of Newtonian mechanics. An example is the spiral problem, shown in figure 19.7, in which students are asked to predict the trajectory of a ball when it emerges from passing through a spiral tube. The questions are thus simple predictive questions to which high school and college physics students frequently give wrong answers.

In the first analysis of this transfer test, we compared all four groups. A two-way between-subjects analysis of variance was carried out with (1) treatment group and (2) gender as the two factors. There was a highly significant main effect of treatment ($F[3,156]=22.4$, $p<.0001$), and a highly significant main effect of gender ($F[1,156]=33.3$, $p<.0001$). However, the interaction was not significant ($F[3,156]=1.58$, $p=.2$). This analysis was used as the basis for a series of planned comparisons done first with respect to gender and then with respect to treatment. figure 19.8 summarizes these results.

With respect to gender effects, the performance of the naive sixth grade males on this test is marginally better than the naive six grade females ($t[156]=1.71$, $p=.09$). The performance of the naive high school females is no better than the naive sixth grade females ($t[156]=0.0$, $p=.99$). In contrast, the performance of the naive high school males is significantly better than the naive sixth grade males ($t[156]=2.13$, $p=.03$). Thus, the gender effect is larger for the naive high school students than for the naive sixth graders. It is difficult to interpret this result because the high school students differ from the sixth graders not only in terms of age but also in terms of selection -- at the sixth grade level, all students participated in this study, whereas at the high school level, only students who chose to take a physics course participated. Thus it might be, for example, that there is an improvement on this test with age for everyone, but that only females with poor physical intuition take physics courses -- although this seems to be an unlikely hypotheses. It is more reasonable to hypothesize that males improve with age on this task more than females (and this is a disturbing result).

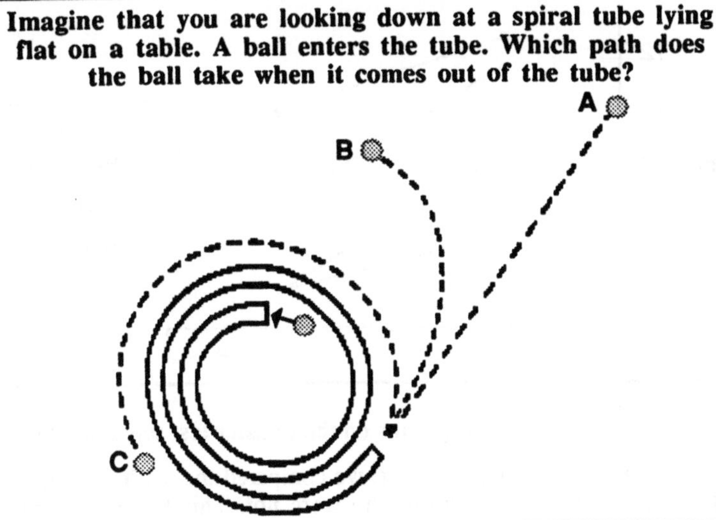

Fig.19.7. The spiral problem

The ThinkerTools students did significantly better on this transfer test than the high school physics students (t[156]=2.33, p=.02), who were on the average six years older and had been taught about force and motion using traditional methods. Further, while both the high school physics course and the ThinkerTools curriculum produced significant improvements in performance on this test over their respective controls, the ThinkerTools curriculum produced significantly greater improvement than the high school physics course (t[156]=2.76, p=.007). This result is somewhat surprising, since the high school students are older (which should make it easier to learn this material), and they are a self selected group (i.e., they chose to take physics). Both these factors should favour the high school students learning more from their physics course. However, since there are at least three systematic differences between the ThinkerTools students and the high school physics students (i.e., (1) age, (2) selection, and (3) treatment), one cannot conclude from this result alone that the ThinkerTools curriculum is more effective in developing an understanding of force and motion. For example, the result could be an age effect (older students learn less), or a selection effect (students who choose to take physics courses are poor learners), although these explanations are both counter intuitive. Fortunately, there is additional evidence supporting the conjecture that the superior improvement is due to the curriculum itself, not age or selection effects. When, in an earlier study, White (1981, 1984) tried similar microworld—based activities with high school physics students, the same dramatic improvements in performance were found on a similar test of force and motion problems.

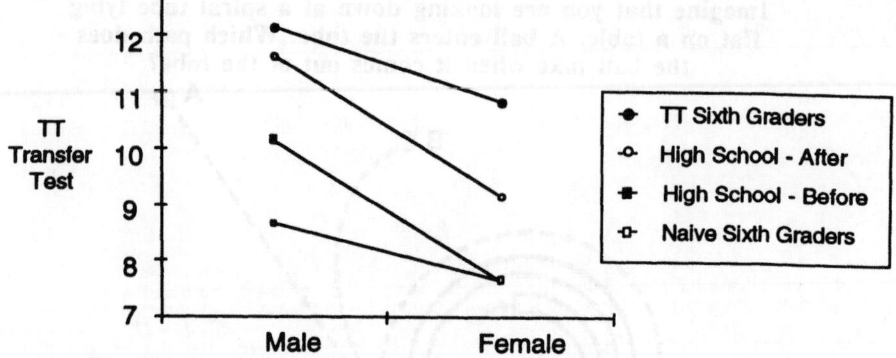

Fig.19.8. Performance of the four groups on the transfer test separated by gender.

In the second analysis of the transfer test, we compared the sixth graders who were given the ThinkerTools curriculum with those who were not. This three-way, between subjects analysis of variance included three factors: (1) treatment group (ThinkerTools versus control), (2) gender, and (3) ability (low, middle, and high, based upon California Achievement Test (CAT) total scores). This design allowed us to assess the effectiveness of the experimental curriculum for subjects of each gender and ability level. There was a highly significant main effect of instructional treatment ($F[1,62]=62.9$, $p<.0001$), and of gender ($F[1,62]=8.1$, $p=.006$), but not of ability ($F[2,62]=2.25$, $p=.11$). The average number correct for the experimental subjects was 11.2 (out of 17 questions), while the average for the control subjects was 7.6. In addition, there was no significant interaction of gender with treatment ($F[1,62]=.22$, $p=.64$), or of ability with treatment ($F[2,62]=.83$, $p=.44$). Thus, the ThinkerTools curriculum was equally effective for females and males, as well as for students of different ability levels as measured by the CAT.

A comparison of performance for the four groups of students on individual items on the transfer test revealed some interesting findings. This analysis (described further in White, [27]) indicates that the ThinkerTools students could apply the laws they learned not only in familiar contexts, but also in unfamiliar contexts. For example, one of the unfamiliar contexts for the ThinkerTools students is a problem, shown in figure 19.9, about two boats crossing two identical rivers -- the only difference between the two rivers is that one has a current flowing and the other does not. This is a problem that requires understanding the independence of X and Y motion for its correct solution. This principle is addressed in the ThinkerTools curriculum, but the ThinkerTools students had never been asked to think about this principle in the context of boats crossing rivers before. On this problem, the ThinkerTools students do as well as the high school physics students ($X^2{}_1 = .05$, $p = .83$), and the high school physics students do much better than the high school students who have not yet taken their physics course ($X^2{}_1= 9.29$, $p = .002$). This results indicates that many ThinkerTools students can transfer the independence of X and Y principle to this new context.

Some of the most interesting results of this item analysis relate to problems where the ThinkerTools students do dramatically better than the high school physics students. Such differences occurred primarily on very simple problems, such as the one shown in figure 19.10 where students are asked to predict the trajectory of a ball that is kicked off the edge of a cliff, or where they are asked to describe the speed of a ball as it falls to the ground. These are very simple phenomenological problems and it is not surprising that the ThinkerTools students give correct answers to such questions. What is surprising is that the high school physics students do not. It is as though the high school students can apply what they learn in physics class to formal problems, but cannot apply their physics knowledge to simple everyday situations. This result, although surprising, is supported by much research in the cognitive science and physics education literature (see McDermott's review, [16]).

Suppose that we have two identical rivers with two identical boats trying to cross those rivers. The only difference is that one river has a current flowing and the other does not. Both boats have the same motors and leave at the same time. Which boat gets to the other side first?

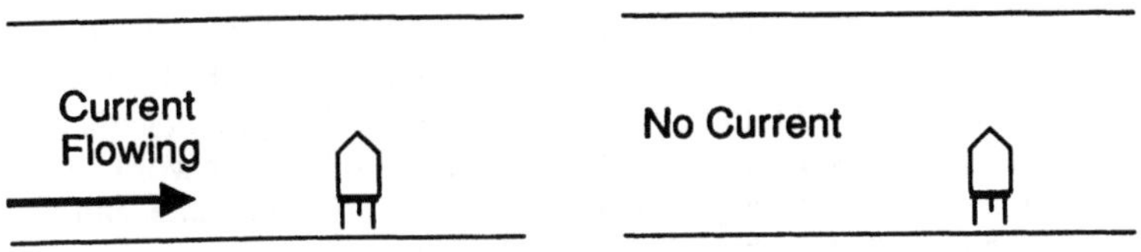

(a) The one crossing the river without a current flowing.

(b) The one crossing the river with a current flowing.

(c) Both boats get to the other side at the same time.

Fig.19.9. The river crossing problem

Imagine that you kick a ball sideways off a cliff. Which path does the ball take as it falls to the ground?

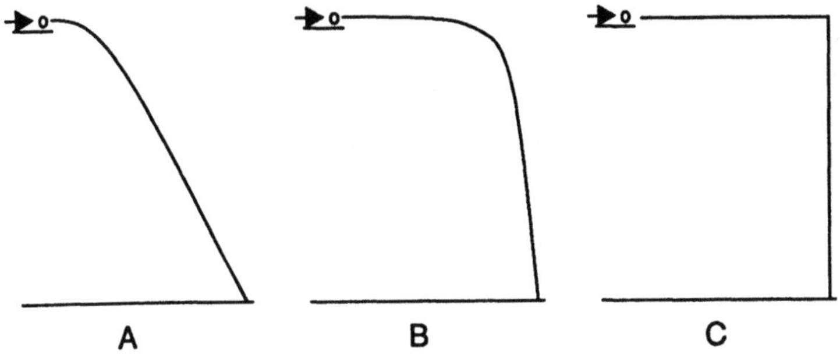

Fig.19.10. The trajectory problem

5. Why Was the Approach Successful?

The use of computer microworlds enabled us to create idealized simplifications of the real world, and to make abstractions, such as orthogonal velocity vectors, into concrete manipulable representations (i.e., the datacross). Thus, students confront their misconceptions in a world designed to make the phenomenon easy to see. In addition, the progression of microworlds enables students to gradually build on their prior knowledge, such as their knowledge of scalar arithmetic and their correct intuitions about force and motion (e.g., kicks change a ball's velocity). Further, the alternative representations of motion displayed in the microworlds enable students to see dynamic representations of physical phenomena (that relate to physical intuition) linked to more abstract representations (that are useful for problem solving). This potentially allows students to relate and apply their formal knowledge (e.g., orthogonal velocity vectors, i.e., the datacross representation, and vector addition) to everyday situations.

One reason why many of the ThinkerTools students are able to transfer what they know to novel contexts may be that whenever they think about the motion of an object, such as a bowling ball or a spaceship, they have learned to think in terms of abstract representations, such as its wake and its datacross. In other words, they have had practice at applying the same abstract representations to different contexts. The fact that they can apply such representations across different contexts may facilitate their understanding of the commonality of different force and motion situations.

Another reason why many ThinkerTools students are able to transfer what they have learned might be derived from the formalization phase of the instructional cycle. In this phase, students summarize what they have learned into a simple, easy to remember principle that allows them to make precise predictions across a range of different contexts. In other words, they summarize their knowledge into a form that is easy to remember, generally applicable, and powerful. Thus their knowledge is in a form that enables it to be applied across a range of different situations.

Finally, in the transfer phase of the instructional cycle, the students learned to apply their knowledge derived from one context, i.e., the microworld context, to a variety of different, real-world contexts. In other words, the fact that our primary instructional tool was a computer microworld, forced us to address the transfer issue head on. Students needed to be able to take principles learned in the microworld context and apply them to the real world. Our instructional cycle thus explicitly incorporated a phase where the students had practice at transfer. This practice may have played a role in enabling students to correctly solve novel problems on the transfer test.

6. Facilitating Scientific Inquiry

In addition to helping students understand Newtonian mechanics, we also had the goal of helping students learn about the processes of scientific inquiry. In our pilot studies, we found that there is an important sense in which children are not born scientists. For example, they do not know what is meant by a scientific law, and they do not know how to design experiments. Thus, students need to learn scientific inquiry skills, and this objective formed one of the major foci of our curriculum.

As was described earlier, there is a correspondence between the classic conception of the scientific method and the four phases of our instructional cycle: formulating questions, doing experiments, evolving laws, and investigating generalizations. Thus, there is a relationship between what the students do in the phases of the instructional cycle and the scientific method. However, in the beginning, the students were given the questions to think about, they were given the experiments to do, they were given alternative laws to evaluate, and they were given the contexts in which to investigate generalizations. They were thus not initially making these decisions for themselves, and were therefore not fully practising scientific inquiry. The approach we took was to start with this structure, and then to gradually remove it. So, in the beginning, the students were given experiments to do and alternative laws to evaluate, and then, later in the curriculum, they were just given the experiments and had to formulate their own laws. Similarly, they were initially given experiments to do, and later in the curriculum, once they had done these experiments and had formulated a law, they had to design an experiment that would help someone else to formulate the law. Thus, as the curriculum progressed, they had experience at formulating their own laws and at designing their own experiments.

When we examined what the students did in response to these challenges, the results were not entirely satisfactory. For example, although students were readily able to formulate laws for themselves, they did not spontaneously investigate the generality of their laws by, for example, seeing if their laws applied in real-world contexts. Similarly, when they were asked to design an experiment, they were not adept at creating good instructional experiments. However, if you analyze our approach to introducing scientific inquiry, these results should not, in retrospect, be too surprising. Neither the process of formulating laws nor the process of designing experiments was modelled for students. They were simply given examples of good and bad laws, and then asked to formulate their own. In the case of experiments, they only saw examples of good experiments, not bad, and they never had to discriminate between good and bad experimental design.

To improve this approach, we need to create a carefully worked out progression for introducing scientific inquiry, as we did with the subject matter knowledge. Students would start with a lot of structure by being given the experiments to do and the laws to evaluate. They would also be given examples of how one goes about formulating laws and designing experiments. This new approach would combine the technique of gradually removing structure [18] with the technique of modelling scientific inquiry processes. The difficulty with utilizing a modelling approach for middle school physics is that one cannot expect sixth grade teachers to model scientific inquiry since most have not even taken a physics course, let alone fully understood the processes of scientific inquiry. This fact creates a need for either an AI system that can model these processes, and/or for the creation of instructional materials that do not rely upon the teacher modelling scientific inquiry -- such as activities where students are asked to act out transcripts of someone designing experiments and formulating laws, and must critique the process.

If the students did not become adept at experimental design, what did they learn with respect to scientific inquiry? Based upon observations of classroom discussions, we infer that students' experience at selecting the "best" law helped them to appreciate that a good scientific law is one that is precise, concise, and generally applicable. They also had experience with falsification, that is, creating situations which show a given law is incorrect. They also saw how laws evolve in response to the increasing complexity of the sequence of microworlds. Finally, they had experience at generalizing the application of a law from the microworld context to a variety of real-world contexts.

What we do not know, based on this instructional experiment, is whether the students acquired a metaconceptual awareness of these features of scientific inquiry and knowledge, so that they could transfer this understanding to another domain. For example, we could have given them different microworlds, such as a series of electricity microworlds, and investigated whether they could formulate scientific laws that were precise, concise, and general in that context. Since we did not do such a transfer test with respect to scientific inquiry, we do know to what extent the students abstracted the general properties of scientific knowledge and the processes of scientific inquiry from their experience with the ThinkerTools curriculum.

7. Summary

In this project, we redefined the goals of science education to focus on acquiring causal models for a domain, and on understanding the processes of scientific inquiry. We also created an instructional approach that is based on getting students to construct an understanding of the subject matter for themselves, via collaborative problem solving and inquiry, while interacting with a series of computer microworlds. Finally, we demonstrated the effectiveness of this approach.

References

1. Caramazza, A., McCloskey, M., & Green B. Naive beliefs in "sophisticated" subjects: Misconceptions about trajectories of objects. *Cognition*, 9, 117-123. 1981.
2. Carey, S. Cognitive science and science education. *American Psychologist*, 41-10, 1123-1130. 1986.

3. Champagne, A., & Klopfer, L. Research in science education: The cognitive psychology perspective. In D. Holdzkom & P. Ludz (Eds.), *Research Within Reach: Science Education*. Washington, DC: National Science Teachers Association. 1984.
4. Chi, M., Feltovich, P., & Glaser, R. Categorization and representation of physics problems by experts and novices. *Cognitive Science*, 5, 121-152. 1981.
5. Clement, J. A conceptual model discussed by Galileo and used intuitively by physics students. In D. Gentner & A. Stevens (Eds.), *Mental Models*, Hillsdale, NJ: Lawrence Erlbaum. 1983.
6. Clement, J. Students' preconceptions in elementary mechanics. *American Journal of Physics*, 50, 66-71. 1982.
7. Collins, A. & Brown, J. The computer as a tool for learning through reflection. In H. Mandl & A. Lesgold (Eds.), *Learning Issues for Intelligent Tutoring Systems*. New York: Springer-Verlag. 1988.
8. Collins, A., Brown, J., & Newman, S. Cognitive apprenticeship: Teaching the craft of reading, writing, and mathematics. BBN Report No. 6459, Cambridge, MA. 1986.
9. diSessa, A. Toward an epistemology of physics. *Working paper, EMST* program, uc (Berkley) 1987.
10. diSessa, A. Phenomenology and the evolution of intuition. In D. Gentner & A. Stevens (Eds.), *Mental Models*, Hillsdale, NJ: Lawrence Erlbaum. 1983.
11. diSessa, A. Unlearning Aristotelian physics: a study of knowledge-based learning, *Cognitive Science*, 6(1), 37-75. 1982.
12. Gentner, D., & Stevens, A. L. *Mental Models*. Hillsdale, NJ: Lawrence Erlbaum Associates. 1983.
13. Horwitz, P. Interactive simulations and their implications for science teaching. *The 1988 AETS Yearbook*. 1988.
14. Larkin, J.H., McDermott, J., Simon, D.P., & Simon, H.A. Expert and novice performance in solving physics problems. *Science*, 208, 1335-1342. 1980.
15. McCloskey, M., Caramazza, A., & Green, B. Curvilinear motion in the absence of external forces: Naive beliefs about the motion of objects. *Science*, 210, 1139-1141. 1980.
16. McDermott, L.C. Research on conceptual understanding in mechanics. *Physics Today*, 37, 24-32. 1984.
17. Minstrell, J. Conceptual Development Research in the Natural Setting of the Classroom. In Budd Rowe, M. (Ed.). *Education in the 80's -- Science*. Washington, D.C.: National Education Association. 1982.
18. Palinscar, A. & Brown, A. Reciprocal teaching of comprehension fostering and monitoring activities. *Cognition and Instruction*, 1(2), 117-175. 1984.
19. Papert, S. *Mindstorms: Computers, Children, and Powerful Ideas*. New York: Basic Books. 1980.
20. Resnick, L. Mathematics and science learning: A new conception. *Science*, 220, 477-478. 1983.
21. Trowbridge, D.E., & McDermott, L.C. Investigation of student understanding of the concept of acceleration in one dimension. *American Journal of Physics*, 49, 242-253. 1981. 1981.
22. Viennot, L. Spontaneous reasoning in elementary dynamics. *European Journal of Science Education*, 1, 205-221. 1979.
23. White, B. & Frederiksen, J. Causal model progressions as a foundation for intelligent learning environments. BBN Report No. 6686. Cambridge, MA. (To appear in *Artificial Intelligence*.) 1987.
24. White, B., & Horwitz, P. Computer Microworlds and Conceptual Change: A New Approach to Science Education. In *Improving Learning: New Perspectives*. P. Ramsden (Ed.), Kogan Page, London. 1988.
25. White, B. Designing computer activities to help physics students understand Newton's laws of motion. In *Cognition and Instruction*, 1, 69-108. 1984.
26. White, B. Sources of difficulty in understanding Newtonian dynamics. In Cognitive Science, 7(1), 41-65. 1983.
27. White, B. ThinkerTools: Causal Models, Conceptual Change, and Science Education. Report No. 6873, BBN Laboratories, Cambridge, Massachusetts. To appear in *Cognition and Instruction*..

Biographies

Marlene Jones

Dr. Marlene Jones is a senior researcher in Artificial Intelligence in the Alberta Research Council's Department of Advanced Technologies and an adjunct professor in the Department of Computational Science at the University of Saskatchewan. Prior to joining the Alberta Research Council in January 1987, Dr. Jones was a tenured Associate Professor at the University of Waterloo. Her qualifications include a PhD (Computer Science) from the University of Toronto and an MEd (Education of Exceptional Children) from the University of Saskatchewan. Her research experience expands more than a decade, with the last 8 years focussed upon research in the area of AI and Education. Dr Jones' recent research projects include the development of expert systems for educational diagnosis, expert environments for curriculum and course development, and user modelling.

Allan Collins

Dr. Allan Collins has been a leader in developing the field of Cognitive Science and has served both as Editor of the journal Cognitive Science and as first chair of the Cognitive Science Society. He is best known for his experiments on human semantic memory with Ross Quillian. In collaboration with Jaime Carbonell Sr. he developed the Scholar system, which was the first example of an intelligent tutoring system. Subsequently he developed a computational theory of inquiry teaching derived from analyses of a variety of inquiry teaching dialogues, which was used in building the WHY intelligent tutoring system. Most recently he has been writing a book on "cognitive apprenticeship" methods of teaching with John Seely Brown, and conducting experiments on people's plausible reasoning and mental models of physical systems.

Kurt VanLehn

Kurt VanLehn is an Assistant Professor of Computer Science and Psychology at Carnegie Mellon University. He received his B.S. in mathematics from Stanford University in 1974, and his M.S. and Ph.D. in computer science from the Massachusetts Institute of Technology in 1978 and 1983, respectively. Prior to joining CMU, he was a Research Associate at the Xerox Palo Alto Research Center, Palo Alto, CA and at Bolt Beranek and Newman, Cambridge, MA.

Dr. VanLehn's research concerns learning, both machine learning (a branch of Artificial Intelligence) and human skill acquisition. His SIERRA system, for instance, is a machine learning system that acquires hierarchical problem solving knowledge by generalization of specific examples of problem solving, which are given to it by a human teacher. SIERRA is also a model of human skill acquisition for basic mathematical skills. When given an incomplete training sequence, it exhibits the same misconceptions that human students exhibit. Systems developed more recently, TETON and CASCADE, explore the acquisition of problem solving strategies while studying examples and working problems. The CIRRUS system applies the machine learning techniques of SIERRA to practical problems in protocol data analysis.

Dr. VanLehn was elected a Spencer Foundation Research Fellow in 1986. He serves as an editor for the journal, *Interactive Learning Environments.*

David L. Ferguson

David L. Ferguson is associate professor in the Department of Technology and Society in the College of Engineering and Applied Sciences at the State University of New York at Stony Brook. He has published papers in the areas of quantitative methods, the discovery of algorithms, and computer-based learning environments. He has held research grants in mathematics and computer science education from the National Science Foundation and U. S.

Department of Educations Fund for the Improvement of Postsecondary Education. He has served on several national panels, including the Advanced Technologies panel of the National Science Foundation. He was one of the developers of a national report, sponsored by the U. S. Department of Education, on Computers in Postsecondary Education.

Dr. Ferguson teaches an undergraduate course on quantitative methods to liberal arts students. He teaches graduate courses in educational computing. He has taught a wide range of students junior high through graduate school -- and enjoys helping students develop their mental capabilities.

Charles M. Reigeluth

Dr. Charles M. Reigeluth has a B.A. in Economics from Harvard University and a Ph.D. in Instructional Psychology from Brigham Young University. He taught science at the secondary level for three years and spent 10 years on the faculty of the Instructional Design program at Syracuse University, ending as chair of the program, before his current position as professor of Instructional Systems Technology at Indiana University. He has also served as an instructional consultant for corporate, health, public, and higher education institutions. Dr. Reigeluth's interests include improving the structure of public schools and designing high quality educational resources. He has published three books and over 25 articles and chapters on those subjects, and has produced several educational software programs. He is the major developer of the elaboration theory and simulation theory. Two of his books received an "outstanding book of the year" award from the Association for Educational Communications and Technology.

Denis Newman

Denis Newman is a senior scientist at BBN Systems and Technologies Corp. His research is concerned with the integration of technology in instructional contexts and social processes in cognitive change. He has a Ph.D. in Psychology from the City University of New York. He has held research positions at University of California, San Diego in the Laboratory for Comparative Human Cognition and at Bank Street College of Education (New York) before joining BBN in 1987. He is the author, with Michael Cole and Peg Griffin, of *The Construction Zone: Working for Cognitive Change in School* (Cambridge University Press).

Stellan Ohlsson

Dr. Ohlsson received his Ph. D. from the Department of Psychology, University of Stockholm in 1980. His thesis topic was computer simulation of common sense reasoning about spatial arrangements. He spent two years at the Computer Science Department at the University of Uppsala. During this time, he designed and implemented two simulation models of learning processes. In 1983, he joined Patrick Langley's research group at the Robotics Institute, Carnegie-Mellon University, with the purpose of implementing a system for automatic cognitive diagnosis. In January, 1985, Dr. Ohlsson accepted a position at the Learning Research and Development Center, where he is currently involved in research on intelligent tutoring systems for elementary mathematics and science.

Ernesto Costa

Ernesto Costa, is Associate Professor of computer science at the University of Coimbra where he is the head of the artificial intelligence group. He received his 3rd cycle thesis in theoretical computer science in 1981 at the University of Paris VI (France), and his Ph.D. in computer science in 1985 at the University of Coimbra (Portugal). His principle research interests include real time expert systems for fault diagnosis and machine learning applications to education. He is member of the board of directors of the Portuguese association for AI (APPIA) since the foundation in 1982 and the representative of that association in the European Coordinating Committee for Artificial Intelligence (ECCAI).

Gordon McCalla

Gordon McCalla is a Professor of Computational Science at the University of Saskatchewan and Director of the Laboratory for Advanced Research in Intelligent Educational Systems (ARIES). He completed his B.Sc. degree with Honours in Mathematical-Statistics in 1968 and his MSc degree in Computing Science in 1970 both at the University of Alberta. His PhD in Computer Science from the University of British Columbia was awarded in 1977. His research for both his MSc. and Ph.D. degrees investigated knowledge representation issues for natural language understanding. Subsequent to his doctoral studies, Dr. McCalla's research interests have expanded to encompass work in dynamic planning, and since 1980 to include a growing involvement in the area of artificial intelligence and education. He is an author or co-author of over 40 technical papers and co-editor of a book on knowledge representation. As well, he is co-editor of the international artificial intelligence journal **Computational Intelligence**, serves on the editorial board of the rapid publication journal **Applied Mathematics Letters**, has been on numerous Canadian and international conference program committees, and is a member of two National Research Council of Canada Associate Committees, on Artificial Intelligence, and Instructional Technology. He is a member of the American Association for Artificial Intelligence, the Association for Computational Linguistics, and the Canadian Society for Computational Studies of Intelligence, serving this society as its Newsletter Editor from 1980 to 1982, the General Chairman of its biennial conference in 1982, its Vice-President from 1982 to 1984, and its President from 1984 to 1986. He owns a golden retriever named Minimax.

David H. Jonassen

David H. Jonassen is professor and Chair of Instructional Technology at the University of Colorado at Denver where he teaches courses in instructional design, individual differences and computer applications. He has previously taught at the University of North Carolina. Syracuse University, and Temple University, where he earned his doctorate in educational technology and psychology. He has also taught in Public schools and worked in media design and production for consulting firms. He is the author of over 150 books, articles and professional papers on text design, task analysis, computer-based instruction, expert systems, and hypertext. His current research interests include externalizing knowledge representation for the design of knowledge based information systems, design of generative computing environments, and the integration of expert systems and hypertext.

Randall B. Smith

Randall B. Smith received his Ph.D. in theoretical physics at the University of California at San Diego and taught for two years before becoming involved in computer science with Atari Computer Corporate Research Group. He joined the Xerox Palo Alto Research Center a year later, where he completed the work described in his chapter. He is now at Sun Labs, Palo Alto. His interests include object-oriented programming languages and environments, educational uses of computers, and computer support for collaborative work.

Ronald K. Thornton

Ronald K. Thornton received an A.B. from Hamilton College and a PhD from Brown University. He is a former high energy physicist and professor of physics who now works primarily on developing effective methods of teaching science to students from the middle school through college. He is the Director of the Center for Science and Mathematics Teaching at Tufts University where he directs a number of national and international science curricula into schools and universities.

Robert Tinker

Robert Tinker directs the Technical Education Research Centers in Cambridge, MA a non-profit educational research and development center that has specialized in the application of technology to education. Bob earned his PhD in experimental low temperature physics from M.I.T. and has taught college physics for ten years. One of the pioneers in constructivist uses of educational technology, he is currently responsible for TERC's efforts on the MBL, Kidnet, LabNet and Star Schools projects.

Anthony Gordon

Born in 1948 in London, and educated at London University and Bowling Green State University, Ohio. After a period in industry trained as a teacher of design and technology, and science. Having taught in a number of schools in the South east of England, moved to a government research project examining the use of microelectronics in education.

For the last eight years, has been employed as a County Inspector for Design and Technology with Staffordshire County Council Education Department. This entails responsibility for both monitoring and inspecting the work of teachers and schools. In addition, also responsible for the development and support of design and Technology education in all county schools (approx. 400 elementary and 90 high schools as well as 8 colleges) in this large school district employing some 9,000 teachers, catering for the educational needs of some 150,000 school students.

Also involved in a number of major curriculum implementation development in the England and Wales, and in the States of Michigan and New York.

Martial Vivet

Vivet Martial is 43 and has a background of mathematician. He entered the French University DU MAINE in Le Mans (the town of the famous race cars) in 1971. He got a first thesis in artificial intelligence in 1973 with a work done under the control of J. PITRAT in the PARIS's university and devoted to automatic theorem proving (recurrent reasoning). He got a state thesis in 1984, still under the control of J. Pitrat, for the realisation of the CAMELIA system. This knowledge based mathematician system makes the useful links between algebraic manipulation and theorem proving allowing for example proof of mathematical properties on worked on expressions. Algorithmic and heuristic techniques can cooperate with a knowledge representation based on the concept of Plans. The system delivers solutions which can be explained and followed step by step by the user allowing so called "pedagogical solutions."

Martial Vivet had an early great interest for pedagogical problems. He trained teachers for mathematics and computer science. He worked to the introduction of LOGO in France around 1977 and has conducted with it a lot of experiments done by teachers in schools during the last ten years. In 1986, as scientific consultant in the French Ministry of education, he began a reflection on applications of AI to education and a work on intelligent tutoring systems. He has worked for CEE in Bruxelles as an expert for European programs like ESPRIT or DELTA.

Benedict du Boulay

Benedict du Boulay is a Professor in Artificial Intelligence in the School of Cognitive and Computing Sciences at the University of Sussex. Prior to this he worked in the departments of Artifical Intelligence Univeristy of Edinburgh and the department of Computing Science, University of Aberdeen and is past chair to the Society for the study of Artificial Intelligence and Simulation of Behaviour.

His main research interest lies in the application of A.I. techniques to education and particularly in understanding the learning of programming especially Prolog, and the development of systems to support such learning.

Brian J. Reiser

Assistant Professor of Psychology at Princeton University. He received his Ph.D. from the Yale University Cognitive Science Program in 1983. His research investigates who to support "guided learning by doing" with computer environments. His research group is constructing GIL, an intelligent tutor that facilitates learning with visual representations and explanatory feedback.

John R. Frederiksen

Director of the Educational Testing Service's Bay Area Cognitive Science Research Center, and Adjunct Professor of Education at the University of California, Berkeley. His research has included studies of students' learning of physics, particularly electricity, through the use of intelligent computer-based learning environments. In his recent research he has been developing new approaches to the assessment of cognitive skills and learning strategies in science that directly foster improvements in students' learning.

Barbara White

Barbara White received her Ph.D. in computer science from the Massachusetts Institute of Technology. Barbara has a broad ranging academic background encompassing computer science, education, psychology, and mathematics. She is presently an associate professor of education and computer science at the University of California at Berkeley. Barbara's interest is in making science and mathematics interesting and accessible to a wide range of students. Her research focuses on investigating the nature of scientific and mathematical expertise, and on developing new instructional approaches and technologies.

Subject Index

abstract knowledge 74, 77, 82, 83, 86, 89
abstract principle 77
acausal reasoning 215
ACM 28, 99
ACT* 9, 24, 87, 88, 200
addition 26, 29, 81, 125, 204
affective learning 55
algebraic manipulations 179
Alternate Reality Kit, (ARK) 110, 131
alternative conceptions 85
analogical retrieval 206
applications tools 35, 39
architecture 114
arithmetic algorithms 25
Artificial Intelligence, (AI) 1, 24, 55, 72, 85, 88, 98, 108, 186, 208
assignment of blame problem 72
belief systems 84, 105
boxer 110, 166
bug library 93
CASCADE 28
case relations 218
causal accounts 221
causal event sequences 218
causal reasoning 219, 224
CIRRUS 27
cognitive behaviour 25
cognitive change 63
cognitive conflict hypothesis 90
cognitive diagnosis 7, 74, 92, 244
cognitive overhead 125
cognitive processes 8, 43, 63, 90
cognitive science 24, 46, 63, 75, 83, 140, 228
cognitive skills 8, 44, 73
collaboration 167
collaborative learning 47, 69
collaborative problem solving 241
Collaborative Science 166
Component Display Theory 4
computer science formalisms 115
computer-based collaborative learning 132
computer-based learning 33, 41, 149
constraint-based reasoning 219
constructionism 155
constructivism 155
constructivist curriculum 164
constructivist educational strategies 157
creativity 42, 79, 155, 173
critiquing 194, 196
current electricity 213
databases 39, 65, 156
decision rule 82
declarative knowledge 52, 75
DEDU 87, 88
design environments 38
design experiments 17, 18, 46, 64, 240
design theory 2, 20
device model 219
diagnosing 93, 102, 203
diagrammatic traces 196
directed activities 34
discrimination trees 100
distributed software systems 136
domain knowledge 200
drill and practice 34
dynamic physical model 221
dynamic processes 217
dynamic text 124
educational assessment 46
educational objectives 47, 68
Educational Technology 46, 52, 61, 111, 118
Educational Testing Service 211
electricity 213
electronic mail system 64
electrostatics 213
envisioning 214
episodic knowledge 75
error feedback 203
evaluation 18, 43, 88, 117, 142
evolution phase 230
expert system 5, 58, 85, 105, 110, 116, 127, 179, 194
expert systems 113
Expert Technology 173
explanation-based generalization 88
Explanation-Based Learning, (EBL) 101
Exploratory environments 35
external validation 116
factual knowledge 75, 154
falsification 241
fine tuning 128
Fischer Technics 185
formalization phase 230
formative evaluation 53
formative experiments 64
free recall protocols 126
generalization hierarchy 26
generativity 78
Gestalt 79, 86
GIL 200

goal lattice 10
graphical browsers 126
graphical instruction in LISP 201
graphs 160
GUIDON 110
higher-order thinking 33, 42
HS model 88
Hypertext 124
Immediate feedback 25, 72, 111, 201, 203, 204
impasse 26, 79
induction hypothesis 89
inquiry teaching 7
instructional cycle 231, 240
Instructional design 2, 9, 72, 112
instructional management 57
instructional theory 3, 7, 52
integration of information 129
intelligent computer-assisted instruction 2
intelligent instructional systems 66
Intelligent Tutoring Systems, (ITS) 2, 36, 52, 72, 97, 98, 107, 118, 178, 192, 199, 205
interface 206
internal validation 115
interpretative productions 87
joystick 234
kinematics 40, 142, 149, 163
knowledge communicating system 105
knowledge compilation 87
knowledge elicitation techniques 6
knowledge representation 27, 101, 205, 245
laboratory curriculum 150
learner control 34
learning complex skills 205
learning hierarchies 10
learning models 87
learning outcome 4, 116
learning theories 23, 24, 72
LISP 81, 109, 195
LISP Tutor 110
Local Area Network 64, 132
logic-based knowledge representation 113
LOGO 38, 110, 183, 246
Machine learning 29, 93, 97, 98, 99
macroscopic models 224
MBL tools 159
mechanics 142
Media Space 134
mediational systems 56
mental model 235
mental models 206
meta-knowledge 179, 182
METADENDRAL 28
methodology 15, 17, 85, 99, 111, 200
micro (small) discovery activity 36
micro-robots 177
micro-worlds 186
Microcomputer-Based Laboratory 39, 139, 158
microcomputer-based labs 157
microworld 177
Microworlds 38, 156, 227, 232
model tracing 200
modelling 165
motivation 5, 41, 64, 132, 133, 186, 230
motivational strategies 55, 57
multiple innovations 17
multiple views 206
MYCIN 109
naive physics 218
National Curriculum 172, 175
naturalistic study 84
navigation 124
network interface system 65
newtonian mechanics 228, 236
object-oriented 135
one-one mapping 81
PEDAGOGUE 10
personal workspace 65
phenomenological problems 238
physical intuition 140
physics 25, 85, 116, 139, 140, 160, 192, 211, 227, 228, 241
PLANNER 109
prescriptive instructional theory 54
principle of cardinality 81
prior knowledge 218
probe 158
probes 141
procedural knowledge 52, 74, 77, 82, 85
programming 192
Programming Environments 39
Prolog 193
PROSPECTOR 109
protocol analysis 116
PROUST 110, 196
psychology 25, 29, 86, 115
qualitative arguments 218
qualitative model 216
qualitative theory 221
rational learning 87
real-time video links 132
reasoning 215
reasoning rules 202

Recovery Boiler Tutor 110
reflection 193, 194
restructuring 127
routines 7
rule revision 72
rule-based reasoning 203
SAPA 28
scaffolding 63
SCENT 114
schemata 87, 127, 195
schemata, 7
science education 156
science misconceptions 154
science teaching 160
scientific inquiry 240
scientific method 240
seismology 167
self improving instructional planner 114
semantic networks 127
sensor 158
sequencing 3, 56, 128
sequencing strategy 4
SharedARK 131
SIIP 114
simulation 35, 43, 52, 75, 128, 165, 201
skill acquisition 24, 74, 83
Smalltalk-80 135
snowball method 4
SOAR 24, 27
SOPHIE 110
Spreadsheets 166
STELLA 165
Structured Learning Theory 3
student model 69, 104, 179, 200
student module 98
students' reflection 69
subject matter analysis 7
subtraction 26, 72, 88, 99
success models 107, 109
symbolic computation 93
tacit knowledge 8
task analysis 4, 29, 67, 91, 201
technological awareness 172
technological innovations 19
Technology Education 172
Technology for All 173
technology innovation 19
telecommunications 168
TERC 165
TETRAD 28
textual programming 134
theory-based design of instruction 91
Theory-based instruction 72
think-aloud protocol 6, 92
ThinkerTools 228
transducers 159
transfer phase 231
transfer test 92, 236, 237
transient processes 217
turtle 183
TURTLETALK 38
tutorial strategies 103, 182
tutoring dialogues 204
types of learning 43, 54
universal theories of cognition 24
validation 112, 115
virtual reality 132, 137
visual programming 136
workbench 27
XCON 109
zone of proximal development 63

NATO ASI Series F

Including Special Programmes on Sensory Systems for Robotic Control (ROB) and on Advanced Educational Technology (AET)

Vol. 22: Software System Design Methods. The Challenge of Advanced Computing Technology. Edited by J. K. Skwirzynski. XIII, 747 pages. 1986.

Vol. 23: Designing Computer-Based Learning Materials. Edited by H. Weinstock and A. Bork. IX, 285 pages. 1986.

Vol. 24: Database Machines. Modern Trends and Applications. Edited by A. K. Sood and A. H. Qureshi. VIII, 570 pages. 1986.

Vol. 25: Pyramidal Systems for Computer Vision. Edited by V. Cantoni and S. Levialdi. VIII, 392 pages. 1986. *(ROB)*

Vol. 26: Modelling and Analysis in Arms Control. Edited by R. Avenhaus, R. K. Huber and J. D. Kettelle. VIII, 488 pages. 1986.

Vol. 27: Computer Aided Optimal Design: Structural and Mechanical Systems. Edited by C. A. Mota Soares. XIII, 1029 pages. 1987.

Vol. 28: Distributed Operating Systems. Theory und Practice. Edited by Y. Paker, J.-P. Banatre and M. Bozyiğit. X, 379 pages. 1987.

Vol. 29: Languages for Sensor-Based Control in Robotics. Edited by U. Rembold and K. Hörmann. IX, 625 pages. 1987. *(ROB)*

Vol. 30: Pattern Recognition Theory and Applications. Edited by P. A. Devijver and J. Kittler. XI, 543 pages. 1987.

Vol. 31: Decision Support Systems: Theory and Application. Edited bv C. W. Holsapple and A. B. Whinston. X, 500 pages. 1987.

Vol. 32: Information Systems: Failure Analysis. Edited by J. A. Wise and A. Debons. XV, 338 pages. 1987.

Vol. 33: Machine Intelligence and Knowledge Engineering for Robotic Applications. Edited by A. K. C. Wong and A. Pugh. XIV, 486 pages. 1987. *(ROB)*

Vol. 34: Modelling, Robustness and Sensitivity Reduction in Control Systems. Edited by R.F. Curtain. IX, 492 pages. 1987.

Vol. 35: Expert Judgment and Expert Systems. Edited by J. L. Mumpower, L. D. Phillips, O. Renn and V. R. R. Uppuluri. VIII, 361 pages. 1987.

Vol. 36: Logic of Programming and Calculi of Discrete Design. Edited by M. Broy. VII, 415 pages. 1987.

Vol. 37: Dynamics of Infinite Dimensional Systems. Edited by S.-N. Chow and J. K. Hale. IX. 514 pages. 1987.

Vol. 38: Flow Control of Congested Networks. Edited by A. R. Odoni, L. Bianco and G. Szegö. XII, 355 pages. 1987.

Vol. 39: Mathematics and Computer Science in Medical Imaging. Edited by M. A. Viergever and A. Todd-Pokropek. VIII, 546 pages. 1988.

Vol. 40: Theoretical Foundations of Computer Graphics and CAD. Edited by R. A. Earnshaw. XX, 1246 pages. 1988.

Vol. 41: Neural Computers. Edited by R. Eckmiller and Ch. v. d. Malsburg. XIII, 566 pages. 1988.

NATO ASI Series F

Including Special Programmes on Sensory Systems for Robotic Control (ROB) and on Advanced Educational Technology (AET)

Vol. 42: Real-Time Object Measurement and Classification. Edited by A. K. Jain. VIII, 407 pages. 1988. *(ROB)*

Vol. 43: Sensors and Sensory Systems for Advanced Robots. Edited by P. Dario. XI, 597 pages. 1988. *(ROB)*

Vol. 44: Signal Processing and Pattern Recognition in Nondestructive Evaluation of Materials. Edited by C. H. Chen. VIII, 344 pages. 1988. *(ROB)*

Vol. 45: Syntactic and Structural Pattern Recognition. Edited by G. Ferraté, T. Pavlidis, A. Sanfeliu and H. Bunke. XVI, 467 pages. 1988. *(ROB)*

Vol. 46: Recent Advances in Speech Understanding and Dialog Systems. Edited by H. Niemann, M. Lang and G. Sagerer. X, 521 pages. 1988.

Vol. 47: Advanced Computing Concepts and Techniques in Control Engineering. Edited by M. J. Denham and A. J. Laub. XI, 518 pages. 1988.

Vol. 48: Mathematical Models for Decision Support. Edited by G. Mitra. IX, 762 pages. 1988.

Vol. 49: Computer Integrated Manufacturing. Edited by I. B. Turksen. VIII, 568 pages. 1988.

Vol. 50: CAD Based Programming for Sensory Robots. Edited by B. Ravani. IX, 565 pages. 1988. *(ROB)*

Vol. 51: Algorithms and Model Formulations in Mathematical Programming. Edited by S. W. Wallace. IX, 190 pages. 1989.

Vol. 52: Sensor Devices and Systems for Robotics. Edited by A. Casals. IX, 362 pages. 1989. *(ROB)*

Vol. 53: Advanced Information Technologies for Industrial Material Flow Systems. Edited by S. Y. Nof and C. L. Moodie. IX, 710 pages. 1989.

Vol. 54: A Reappraisal of the Efficiency of Financial Markets. Edited by R. M. C. Guimarães, B. G. Kingsman and S. J. Taylor. X, 804 pages. 1989.

Vol. 55: Constructive Methods in Computing Science. Edited by M. Broy. VII, 478 pages. 1989.

Vol. 56: Multiple Criteria Decision Making and Risk Analysis Using Microcomputers. Edited by B. Karpak and S. Zionts. VII, 399 pages. 1989.

Vol. 57: Kinematics and Dynamic Issues in Sensor Based Control. Edited by G. E. Taylor. XI, 456 pages. 1990. *(ROB)*

Vol. 58: Highly Redundant Sensing in Robotic Systems. Edited by J. T. Tou and J. G. Balchen. X, 322 pages. 1990. *(ROB)*

Vol. 59: Superconducting Electronics. Edited by H. Weinstock and M. Nisenoff. X, 441 pages. 1989.

Vol. 60: 3D Imaging in Medicine. Algorithms, Systems, Applications. Edited by K. H. Höhne, H. Fuchs and S. M. Pizer. IX, 460 pages. 1990.

Vol. 61: Knowledge, Data and Computer-Assisted Decisions. Edited by M. Schader and W. Gaul. VIII, 421 pages. 1990.

Vol. 62: Supercomputing. Edited by J. S. Kowalik. X, 425 pages. 1990.

Vol. 63: Traditional and Non-Traditional Robotic Sensors. Edited by T. C. Henderson. VIII, 468 pages. 1990. *(ROB)*

NATO ASI Series F

Including Special Programmes on Sensory Systems for Robotic Control (ROB) and on Advanced Educational Technology (AET)

Vol. 64: Sensory Robotics for the Handling of Limp Materials. Edited by P. M. Taylor. IX, 343 pages. 1990. *(ROB)*

Vol. 65: Mapping and Spatial Modelling for Navigation. Edited by L. F. Pau. VIII, 357 pages. 1990. *(ROB)*

Vol. 66: Sensor-Based Robots: Algorithms and Architectures. Edited by C. S. G. Lee. X, 285 pages. 1991. *(ROB)*

Vol. 67: Designing Hypermedia for Learning. Edited by D. H. Jonassen and H. Mandl. XXV, 457 pages. 1990. *(AET)*

Vol. 68: Neurocomputing. Algorithms, Architectures and Applications. Edited by F. Fogelman Soulié and J. Hérault. XI, 455 pages. 1990.

Vol. 69: Real-Time Integration Methods for Mechanical System Simulation. Edited by E. J. Haug and R. C. Deyo. VIII, 352 pages. 1991.

Vol. 70: Numerical Linear Algebra, Digital Signal Processing and Parallel Algorithms. Edited by G. H. Golub and P. Van Dooren. XIII, 729 pages. 1991.

Vol. 71: Expert Systems and Robotics. Edited by T. Jordanides and B.Torby. XII, 744 pages. 1991.

Vol. 72: High-Capacity Local and Metropolitan Area Networks. Architecture and Performance Issues. Edited by G. Pujolle. X, 536 pages. 1991.

Vol. 73: Automation and Systems Issues in Air Traffic Control. Edited by J. A. Wise, V. D. Hopkin and M. L. Smith. XIX, 594 pages. 1991.

Vol. 74: Picture Archiving and Communication Systems (PACS) in Medicine. Edited by H. K. Huang, O. Ratib, A. R. Bakker and G. Witte. XI, 438 pages. 1991.

Vol. 75: Speech Recognition and Understanding. Recent Advances, Trends and Applications. Edited by P. Laface and Renato De Mori. XI, 559 pages. 1991.

Vol. 76: Multimedia Interface Design in Education. Edited by A. D. N. Edwards and S. Holland. XIV, 216 pages. 1992. *(AET)*

Vol. 77: Computer Algorithms for Solving Linear Algebraic Equations. The State of the Art. Edited by E. Spedicato. VIII, 352 pages. 1991.

Vol. 78: Integrating Advanced Technology into Technology Education. Edited by M. Hacker, A. Gordon and M. de Vries. VIII, 185 pages. 1991. *(AET)*

Vol. 79: Logic, Algebra, and Computation. Edited by F. L. Bauer. VII, 485 pages. 1991.

Vol. 80: Intelligent Tutoring Systems for Foreign Language Learning. Edited by M. L. Swartz and M. Yazdani. IX, 347 pages. 1992. *(AET)*

Vol. 81: Cognitive Tools for Learning. Edited by P. A. M. Kommers, D. H. Jonassen and J. T. Mayes. X, 278 pages. 1992. *(AET)*

Vol. 82: Combinatorial Optimization. New Frontiers in Theory and Practice. Edited by M. Akgül, H. W. Hamacher and S. Tüfekçi. XI, 334 pages. 1992.

Vol. 83: Active Perception and Robot Vision. Edited by A. K. Sood and H. Wechsler. IX, 756 pages. 1992.

NATO ASI Series F

Including Special Programmes on Sensory Systems for Robotic Control (ROB) and on Advanced Educational Technology (AET)

Vol. 84: Computer-Based Learning Environments and Problem Solving. Edited by E. De Corte, M. C. Linn, H. Mandl and L. Verschaffel. XVI, 488 pages. 1992. *(AET)*

Vol. 85: Adaptive Learning Environments. Foundations and Frontiers. Edited by M. Jones and P. H. Winne. VIII, 408 pages. 1992. *(AET)*

Vol. 86: Intelligent Learning Environments and Knowledge Acquisition in Physics. Edited by A. Tiberghien and H. Mandl. VIII, 285 pages. 1992. *(AET)*

Vol. 87: Cognitive Modelling and Interactive Environments. Edited by F. L. Engel, D. G. Bouwhuis, T. Bösser and G. d'Ydewalle. IX, 311 pages. 1992. *(AET)*

Vol. 88: Programming and Mathematical Method. Edited by M. Broy. VIII, 428 pages. 1992.

Vol. 89: Mathematical Problem Solving and New Information Technologies. Edited by J. P. Ponte, J. F. Matos, J. M. Matos and D. Fernandes. XV, 346 pages. 1992. *(AET)*

Vol. 90: Collaborative Learning Through Computer Conferencing. Edited by A. R. Kaye. X, 260 pages. 1992. *(AET)*

Vol. 91: New Directions for Intelligent Tutoring Systems. Edited by E. Costa. X, 294 pages. 1992. *(AET)*

Vol. 92: Hypermedia Courseware: Structures of Communication and Intelligent Help. Edited by A. Oliveira. XI, 297 pages. 1992 *(AET)*

Vol. 93: Interactive Multimedia Learning Environments. Human Factors and Technical Considerations on Design Issues. Edited by M. Giardina. VIII, 254 pages. 1992. *(AET)*

Vol. 96: New Directions in Educational Technology. Edited by E. Scanlon and T. O'Shea. VIII, 251 pages. 1992. *(AET)*

Vol. 97: Advanced Models of Cognition for Medical Training and Practice. Edited by D. A. Evans and V. L. Patel. XI, 372 pages. 1992. *(AET)*

Vol. 100: Communication from an Artificial Intelligence Perspective. Theoretical and Applied Issues. Edited by A. Ortony, J. Slack and O. Stock. XII, 260 pages. 1992.

FSC
www.fsc.org

MIX
Papier aus verantwortungsvollen Quellen
Paper from responsible sources
FSC® C105338

If you have any concerns about our products,
you can contact us on
ProductSafety@springernature.com

In case Publisher is established outside the EU,
the EU authorized representative is:
Springer Nature Customer Service Center GmbH
Europaplatz 3, 69115 Heidelberg, Germany

Printed by Libri Plureos GmbH
in Hamburg, Germany